Myanmar Media
in Transition

ISEAS YUSOF ISHAK INSTITUTE

The **ISEAS – Yusof Ishak Institute** (formerly Institute of Southeast Asian Studies) is an autonomous organization established in 1968. It is a regional centre dedicated to the study of socio-political, security, and economic trends and developments in Southeast Asia and its wider geostrategic and economic environment. The Institute's research programmes are grouped under Regional Economic Studies (RES), Regional Strategic and Political Studies (RSPS), and Regional Social and Cultural Studies (RSCS). The Institute is also home to the ASEAN Studies Centre (ASC), the Nalanda-Sriwijaya Centre (NSC), and the Singapore APEC Study Centre.

ISEAS Publishing, an established academic press, has issued more than 2,000 books and journals. It is the largest scholarly publisher of research about Southeast Asia from within the region. ISEAS Publishing works with many other academic and trade publishers and distributors to disseminate important research and analyses from and about Southeast Asia to the rest of the world.

Myanmar Media in Transition

Legacies, Challenges and Change

EDITED BY

LISA BROOTEN
JANE MADLYN McELHONE
GAYATHRY VENKITESWARAN

 YUSOF ISHAK INSTITUTE

First published in Singapore in 2019 by
ISEAS Publishing
30 Heng Mui Keng Terrace
Singapore 119614

Email: publish@iseas.edu.sg
Website: bookshop.iseas.edu.sg

All rights reserved. No part of this publication may be reproduced, stored in a retrieval system, or transmitted in any form or by any means, electronic, mechanical, photocopying, recording or otherwise, without the prior permission of the ISEAS – Yusof Ishak Institute.

© 2019 ISEAS – Yusof Ishak Institute, Singapore

The responsibility for facts and opinions in this publication rests exclusively with the authors and their interpretations do not necessarily reflect the views or the policy of the publisher or its supporters.

ISEAS Library Cataloguing-in-Publication Data

Myanmar Media in Transition : Legacies, Challenges and Change / edited by Lisa Brooten, Jane Madlyn McElhone and Gayathry Venkiteswaran.
  1. Mass media—Political aspects—Myanmar.
  2. Mass media—Social aspects—Myanmar.
  3. Government and the press—Myanmar.
  4. Journalism—Myanmar.
  5. Freedom of expression—Myanmar.
  6. Digital media—Myanmar.
  I. Brooten, Lisa, editor.
  II. McElhone, Jane Madlyn, editor.
  III. Venkiteswaran, Gayathry, editor.
P92 B9M99   2019

ISBN 978-981-4843-09-6 (soft cover)
ISBN 978-981-4843-40-9 (e-book, PDF)

Typeset by International Typesetters Pte Ltd
Printed in Singapore by Mainland Press Pte Ltd

The image on this book's cover is entitled "Twilight", and was created by *Myanmar Media in Transition* contributor Eaint Thiri Thu. As she explains, twilight is the period between daylight and night, before sunrise or sunset, transitioning us to the light or the dark. Myanmar's freedom of expression is at its twilight, between darkness and light, hope and despair. Is this twilight leading us to the sunset or the sunrise? To create this image, Eaint Thiri Thu asked Myanmar journalists, poets, writers, activists, photographers and filmmakers of diverse ages, genders, religions and ethnicities the following question: "What would you say if you had to describe the freedom of expression and media freedom situation during the current transition period in a word or a sentence?" The right side of the face is open, offering the answers to this question. The left side remains dark, and the eye closed to represent the things they were not able to share.

Contents

Contributors and Editors	ix
Burma or Myanmar? A Note on Terminology	xvii

1. Introduction: Myanmar Media Historically and the Challenges of Transition   1
   Lisa Brooten, Jane Madlyn McElhone and Gayathry Venkiteswaran

Part I Structural Constraints and Opportunities

2. Legal Changes for Media and Expression: New Reforms, Old Controls   59
   Gayathry Venkiteswaran, Yin Yadanar Thein and Myint Kyaw

3. Whispered Support: Two Decades of International Aid for Independent Journalism and Free Expression   95
   Jane Madlyn McElhone and Lisa Brooten

4. The Changing Face of Print Media: An Interview with News Veteran Thiha Saw   131
   Interviewed by Jane Madlyn McElhone and Gayathry Venkiteswaran

5. Privacy Risks in Myanmar's Emerging ICT Sector   137
   Kamran Emad and Erin McAuliffe

Part II Journalism in Transition

6. Silencing a Snakehead Fish: A Case Study in Local Media, Rural-Based Activism, and Defamation Litigation in Southern Myanmar
   Jennifer Leehey — 151

7. Precarity and Risk in Myanmar's Media: A Longitudinal Analysis of Natural Disaster Coverage by *The Irrawaddy*
   Susan Banki and Ja Seng Ing — 177

8. Educating a New Generation of Watchdogs: Interview with Ye Naing Moe, Director of the Yangon and Mandalay Journalism Schools
   Interviewed by Nai Nai and Jane Madlyn McElhone — 201

9. The Metamorphosis of Media in Myanmar's Ethnic States
   Jane Madlyn McElhone — 210

10. Covering Rakhine: Journalism, Conflict and Identity
    Eaint Thiri Thu — 229

11. Media in Myanmar: Laws, Military and the Public
    Lawi Weng — 239

12. Cracking The Glass Ceiling in Myanmar Media
    Thin Lei Win — 243

13. Media and the 2015 General Elections
    Carine Jaquet — 251

Part III Creative Expression

14. Myanmar's Pop Music Industry in Transition   265
    Heather MacLachlan

15. New Video Generation: The Myanmar Motion Picture Industry in 2017   287
    Jane M. Ferguson

16. Films for Dignity   307
    Mon Mon Myat

17. A "Fierce" Fear: Literature and Loathing after the Junta   315
    Ma Thida

Part IV Society and Media

18. The Tea Shop Meets the 8 O'clock News: Facebook, Convergence and Online Public Spaces   325
    Yan Naung Oak and Lisa Brooten

19. From Blogging to Digital Rights: Telecommunications Reform in Myanmar   366
    Htaike Htaike Aung and Wai Myo Htut

20. Counter-Narratives: Myanmar's Digital Media Activists   377
    Sarah Oh

    Epilogue: Media Studies in Myanmar – Where Do We Go from Here?   387
    Lisa Brooten, Jane Madlyn McElhone and Gayathry Venkiteswaran

Index   395

Contributors and Editors

Editors

Lisa Brooten has been researching and writing about Burmese media since the mid-1990s, and also conducts research in Thailand, the Philippines and the United States. She lived along the Thailand-Burma border from 1989 to 1992 and returns regularly to conduct research in Myanmar. She completed her PhD from Ohio University in 2003 with a dissertation focused on Burma's exiled media and the politics of communication. She is currently an Associate Professor at Southern Illinois University Carbondale, a Fulbright scholar and a member of the roster of Fulbright specialists for Myanmar, Thailand and the Philippines. She has published widely on media reform, media representations of marginalized groups, media and human rights, social movement media, and various forms of media activism. She has also been a consultant for Freedom House's *Freedom of the Press* report, PEN American Center, and Radio Free Asia Burmese Service.

Jane Madlyn McElhone is a Canadian-British consultant currently living in Myanmar. She has extensive experience supporting and building the capacity of media outlets and journalists in closed and transitional societies, and has collaborated on media projects around the world, including working in Myanmar, Afghanistan and Timor-Leste. Her areas of expertise include journalism, media development, philanthropy, human rights, migration, research in the fields of media and free expression, and strategic project development and evaluation.

Jane has documented the media and media development sector in Myanmar, including in the ethnic states, and has authored reports on free expression, media capture, ethnic media, media development, and media and peacebuilding. Previously she worked for the Open Society Foundations and for the Canadian Broadcasting Corporation. Jane has a Master of Science in Migration, Mobility and Development from SOAS and is a member of International Media Development Advisors (www.imdadvisers.com).

Gayathry Venkiteswaran worked on advocacy and capacity building related to media reforms and press freedom in Southeast Asia in her capacity as Executive Director of the Bangkok-based Southeast Asian Press Alliance (SEAPA) from 2010 to 2015, with Myanmar being a key focus for the organization since 2007. She is Assistant Professor at the University of Nottingham Malaysia Campus, where she is also a PhD candidate. Her academic research focuses on media reforms and the role of civil society in Indonesia and Myanmar. She has a wide network of contacts from the media and civil society inside and outside of Myanmar. She received her undergraduate degree in Mass Communication from the University of Science Malaysia and a Master of Arts (International Relations) from the Australian National University. She has published papers and reports on media freedom and reforms in Southeast Asia, freedom of expression and the internet in Asia, and gender and surveillance.

Contributors

Eaint Thiri Thu is a Fulbright scholar doing a Master of Human Rights degree at the Humphrey School of Public Affairs and the College of Liberal Arts, University of Minnesota (2017–19). She previously worked for six years as a researcher and media fixer in Myanmar, including numerous research trips to Rakhine State. In December 2016 she conducted fieldwork on the ways Rakhine Buddhists, Rohingya Muslims and Kaman Muslims access and share information, and the role information, social media and rumours play in creating and solving the conflict.

Susan Banki researches the political, institutional and legal contexts that explain the roots of and solutions to international human rights violations. In particular, she is interested in the ways that questions of sovereignty, citizenship/membership and humanitarian principles have shaped our understanding of and reactions to various transnational phenomena, such as the international human rights regime, international migration and the provision of international aid. Susan's focus is on the Asia-Pacific region, where she has conducted extensive field research in Thailand, Nepal, Bangladesh and Japan on refugee/migrant protection, statelessness and border control. Her current project, *Refugee Activism and Social Movements: The Transformation of Homeland Politics*, funded by the Australian Research Council, investigates the phenomenon of exiled dissidents and homeland activists in countries of the Global South.

Kamran Emad was based in Myanmar from 2013 to 2015, most recently focusing on the human rights impacts of ICT sector growth at the Myanmar Centre for Responsible Business in Yangon. During his time in Myanmar, mobile phone penetration increased from zero to over fifty per cent, while the cost of SIM cards fell from $150 to under $2. Kamran is currently an analyst at T-Mobile US, based in the Seattle area.

Jane M. Ferguson is a Senior Lecturer in Anthropology and Southeast Asian History in the School of Culture, History and Language at the Australian National University. She is currently Editor of the *Journal of Burma Studies*. She has conducted fieldwork in ethnic Shan communities as well as among Bamar in urban Myanmar. Her range of research and publications include work on ethno-nationalism, land laws, popular music, cinema and aviation.

Htaike Htaike Aung Htaike Htaike Aung is the co-founding Executive-Director of the Myanmar ICT for Development Organization (MIDO), the first ICT-focused NGO in Myanmar. MIDO works on ICTs for development, internet freedom, and internet policy advocacy. Its projects include the anti-hate speech campaign Panzagar, the election monitoring application Kyeet, the Myanmar Internet Freedom Forum,

Peace Tech Exchange, and Lighthouses (community information centres). Htaike Htaike is also a digital security and privacy trainer/consultant for human rights defenders. She was awarded the Jemseh TaTa Fellowship – ICT Champions.

Ja Seng Ing is an advocate for the rights of internally displaced people (IDPs), vulnerable migrants and victims of trafficking. She has significant experience with migration issues, having worked with the United Nations Action for Cooperation against Trafficking in Persons (UN-ACT), the International Organization for Migration (IOM), World Vision and the Kachin Baptist Convention (KBC). A trained medical doctor, Ja Seng studied Medicine at the University of Medicine in Yangon and received her Master of Human Rights degree from the University of Sydney, Australia. She is currently working as a National Legal Researcher at the International Commission of Jurists (ICJ), based in Yangon, researching human rights violations in Myanmar, with a focus on citizenship issues, freedom of religion and belief, and human trafficking.

Carine Jaquet is an Associate Researcher at the Research Institute on Contemporary Southeast Asia (IRASEC) in Bangkok, Thailand. She holds a Master of Political Science degree from the Sorbonne and a degree in Burmese Language from the Yangon University of Foreign Languages (YUFL). She collaborated extensively with the Union Election Commission of Myanmar from 2014 to 2016 in her capacity as Senior Technical Advisor for the Institute for Democracy and Electoral Assistance (IDEA).

Lawi Weng is a Mon journalist renowned for his conflict reporting. He has worked for *The Irrawaddy* for nine years, including five years in exile in Thailand, where he reported on rights abuses in the conflict-ridden ethnic areas. After he moved back home in 2013 he began covering anti-Muslim religious conflict and often travelled to Rakhine State to cover the plight of the Rohingya. In 2017 Lawi Weng and two of his colleagues were accused of unlawful association and were imprisoned for two months in northern Shan State. The charges against them were dropped in September of that year.

Jennifer Leehey is a sociocultural anthropologist affiliated with the Regional Center for Social Science and Sustainable Development (RCSD) at Chiang Mai University (Thailand) and a freelance research consultant for local and international NGOs in the region. Engaged with Myanmar since the mid-1990s, she has published academically on topics related to culture and censorship. She earned her doctorate from the University of Washington in 2010. Her dissertation, *Open Secrets, Hidden Meanings: Censorship, Esoteric Power and Contested Authority in Urban Burma in the 1990s*, explores the production of public meaning in Myanmar under military rule, focusing on literary and popular religious domains.

Heather MacLachlan earned a doctorate in ethnomusicology from Cornell University in 2009. She is Associate Professor in the Department of Music at the University of Dayton in Dayton, Ohio and served as Visiting Professor of the Humanities at Parami Institute in Yangon, Myanmar in 2018. She is the author of *Burma's Pop Music Industry: Creators, Distributors, Censors* (2011) and has written scholarly articles on music making among Burmese refugees in the United States. Dr MacLachlan has also published articles on other topics, including American country music, music pedagogy, and identity formation. She speaks English, French and Burmese and has taught in each of these languages at various times.

Ma Thida is an award-winning writer and free expression advocate. She was the founding president of the PEN Myanmar Centre (2013–16) and is currently the coordinator of its Writers in Prison programme. She lectures globally on democracy and human rights and is a member of the PEN International board. Sentenced to twenty years in prison in 1993 for her pro-democracy writing, Ma Thida was released in 1999 due to political pressure. She was awarded the PEN/Barbara Goldsmith Freedom to Write Award in 1995 and has published several books, including *Prisoner of Conscience – My Steps through Insein*.

Erin McAuliffe was an MA student at the University of Washington's Jackson School of International Studies at the time of writing. She was also a Cybersecurity Policy Fellow in the Jackson School's International

Policy Institute and involved in designing a curriculum for data literacy and transparency in transitioning societies as part of a collaborative project between organizations in Myanmar, the University of Washington, and major U.S. donors. She is currently a PhD student in Sociology at the University of Michigan.

Mon Mon Myat is an independent writer, journalist and producer and the founder and former Executive-Director of the Myanmar Human Rights, Human Dignity International Film Festival. Her documentary film *The Floating Tomatoes* won second prize in the reportage category at the 2010 ASEAN Festival of Photos in Vietnam. Her later films include *Transparency or Accountability in Practice* and *An Old Man's Homesickness*. Mon Mon Myat is currently doing her PhD in Peacebuilding Studies at Payap University in Chiang Mai, Thailand.

Myint Kyaw joined the *Myanma Dana* business magazine as a reporter in 2003. He covered business, social and other stories. Myint Kyaw founded Myitmakha Media Group with May Thingyan Hein in 2008. Two years later, he established another news group, Yangon Press International (YPI), with other journalist colleagues. Taking advantage of the government's media relaxation policy, YPI was the first uncensored online news agency in Myanmar. He is a secretary of the Myanmar Journalist Network and Myanmar Press Council. He works as a journalism advisor at Internews, Myanmar and as a media trainer and consultant.

Nai Nai was born and raised in Yangon, Myanmar. She is currently a Regional Coordinator with the Sweden-based Fojo Media Institute, primarily responsible for the Southeast Asian Media Training Network (SEAMTN), which conducts capacity building with six media training institutes in Cambodia, Laos, Myanmar and Vietnam. Prior to joining Fojo she worked with the Bangkok-based Southeast Asian Press Alliance (SEAPA), which advocates for greater media freedom in the region. She spent eleven years as the SEAPA fellowship coordinator. Before joining SEAPA, she worked as a TV and radio journalist. She earned her master's degree in education from Assumption University in Bangkok. Her passion is to learn, share and empower people on issues related to gender, leadership and ethnic diversity.

Sarah Oh is a researcher based in Silicon Valley. She has worked at the intersection of digital media, development, social change and tech for more than ten years. From 2014 to 2016 she lived in Myanmar, where she worked with entrepreneurs, civic leaders and international tech companies during the country's political transition. Sarah earned her bachelor's degree in political science with honours from Northwestern University and has been a Visiting Scholar at The Center for Information Technology Research in the Interest of Society and the Banatao Institute at the University of California.

Thin Lei Win was born and raised in Yangon, Myanmar's former capital, before leaving the country for further education. Bouts of closures of schools and universities by the junta forced many young students out of Myanmar in the late 1980s and 1990s. Thin studied in Singapore and the United Kingdom, and caught the journalism bug early on, much to the initial consternation of her parents and relatives, who were aware of the Myanmar junta's hostility towards journalists. She now has more than fifteen years' experience as a journalist, including as a correspondent with the Thomson Reuters Foundation (TRF), the non-profit arm of Thomson Reuters, the world's biggest news and information provider, where she has worked since 2008. In 2015 she returned home to establish and lead Myanmar Now, an award-winning bilingual news agency supported by TRF. She is also the co-founder of The Kite Tales, a website dedicated to chronicling the lives, histories and memories of ordinary people across Myanmar. She currently works as a food security correspondent for TRF.

Wai Myo Htut is a Project Coordinator at Myanmar ICT for Development Organization (MIDO). He heads the "Light House Telecenters by Telenor" project, which provides internet connection and access to information in rural areas. His areas of interest are ICT policy and public administration and he also holds a Master of Public Administration degree.

Yan Naung Oak is a Senior Advisor at Phandeeyar: Myanmar Innovation Lab, a community technology hub that promotes civic tech and tech entrepreneurship. Since 2014 he has worked to bring Myanmar's tech community together with its civil society and independent media to collaborate on building technology tools and initiatives for the country's development. These initiatives include building Myanmar's first makerspace, founding Open Development Myanmar (the Myanmar chapter of an open data portal for the Mekong region) and organizing community events such as hackathons to promote tech entrepreneurship. Prior to that he worked as an educator and a researcher in economics. He holds a Master of Economics degree from the National University of Singapore and a Bachelor of Physics and Economics from Middlebury College, USA.

Yin Yadanar Thein is the co-founder and Director of the national human rights organization, Free Expression Myanmar (FEM). Prior to co-founding FEM, Yin was the country manager for the free expression INGO Article 19, and before that a women's rights activist. Yin has worked in Myanmar, London, Geneva and within ASEAN on a range of human rights issues, especially on media law reform, the right to information, protest, hate speech, gender rights, and digital rights. Yin specializes in gender-based censorship in all its forms, and has since 2012 advocated with the Myanmar government and national and international stakeholders on the importance of adopting international standards for the country's news media laws, Assembly Law, Telecommunications Law, bills on public service media, right to information, and hate speech. Yin has spent time working in Myanmar's IDP camps in Rakhine State and working with the UN special mechanisms in Geneva. Yin previously worked as a magazine editor at a time when pre-publication censorship was still in place.

Burma or Myanmar? A Note on Terminology

In editing a collection such as this one, we are faced with the issue of what to call the country: Burma or Myanmar, or both? Using which criteria? This issue has long been contentious, and any discussion of the transition period must in some way address the concerns that continue to be raised about the country's name and how it should be historically referenced.

The country became the Union of Burma upon its independence from the British in 1948. Shortly following the massive and violently suppressed uprisings of 1988, the military regime, the State Law and Order Restoration Council (SLORC), enacted the 1989 Adaptation of Expressions Law, changing the name of the country to the Union of Myanmar and many place names to reflect their Burmese-language pronunciation rather than the anglicized spellings prescribed by British colonial authorities. Rangoon, for example, became Yangon. Although the SLORC argued that the switch to Myanmar was more inclusive of ethnic minority groups, the name change was met with stiff resistance by opposition activists pushing for democratic change, who argued that it was made by an illegitimate, unelected regime without the people's approval through a national referendum. Many of those who sympathized with the opposition felt the name Burma was more inclusive than Myanmar. As a result, the use of one name over the other was, and remains for some, an indication of one's political position with respect to the military regime (Rogers 2012). The reaction of ethnic minority groups in the country has been mixed, but many feel that both names lack a sense of inclusion because they refer to the country's dominant ethnic group (Dittmer 2014).

International news outlets and governments around the world have taken different positions on this issue. The name change was recognized during military rule by the United Nations and by the governments of Japan and France, for example, but was not recognized by the United States, United Kingdom, Australia or Canada, which continued to refer to the country as Burma. The British Broadcasting Corporation (BBC) also referred to the country as Burma during the period of military rule, which they argued was due to the familiarity of the name rather than politically motivated (BBC 2007). The policy of the U.S. National Public Radio (NPR) network was to use Myanmar but to then reference the fact that the country was once called Burma (Memmott 2011). Even guidebooks have taken different positions. The Lonely Planet guidebook used the name Myanmar during military rule, while Rough Guides did not publish a guidebook out of support for the opposition movement's call for a tourism boycott (BBC 2007).

Academics and advocates have taken differing stances. Some authors use the two names interchangeably, some use Burma, some use Myanmar, and some choose to follow "the European Union's catch-all solution: 'Myanmar/Burma'" (Dittmer 2014, p. 2). Others have chosen to use Myanmar — as well as other changed place names — from 1989 onwards, while using Burma for the period when the country was called by that name (Cheesman, Skidmore and Wilson 2012). International human rights groups — like Human Rights Watch, the Burma Campaign UK and Altsean-Burma — continue to use Burma. The participatory rights-based policy research and advocacy organization Progressive Voice notes that it generally uses Myanmar in acknowledgement of the fact that most people in the country use this term. It adds, however, that "the deception of inclusiveness and the historical process of coercion by the former State Peace and Development Council military regime into usage of 'Myanmar' rather than 'Burma' without the consent of the people is recognized and not forgotten. Thus, under certain circumstances, 'Burma' is used" (Progressive Voice 2018).

Inside the country, both terms are widely used, and several sources note that Myanmar is the more formal, literary term, while Burma is the term used more often in informal, everyday speech (BBC 2007). During the transition period starting in 2010, the name Myanmar has become much more common among those who may in the past have been unwilling or unsure which to use, and debate on this issue has cooled. Several non-governmental organizations and media outlets that were in exile or worked along the borders with Thailand and that used Burma in their titles have either changed their names in order to operate in the country or have registered themselves using their popular acronyms to get around the official requirement to use the name Myanmar. The names of cities, states and regions have also changed in many cases, both in casual conversations and written form; their names and their spelling can thus be inconsistent.

In *Myanmar Media in Transition*, we have chosen to use Myanmar for the period following the elections in 2010, and Burma for the period prior to this, except when replicating the usage in direct quotations or summaries of work by others. In these latter cases, we will remain consistent with the terminology used in the original work.

References

BBC. 2007. "Should it be Burma or Myanmar?" 2007. *BBC News Magazine*, 26 September 2007. http://news.bbc.co.uk/2/hi/7013943.stm.

Cheesman, N., M. Skidmore, and T. Wilson, eds. 2012 *Myanmar's Transition: Openings, Obstacles and Opportunities*. Singapore: Institute of Southeast Asian Studies.

Dittmer, L., ed. 2014. *Burma or Myanmar? The Struggle for National Identity*. New Jersey: World Scientific.

Memmott, M. 2011. "Why Burma? Why Myanmar? Why Both?" National Public Radio, 2 December 2011. http://www.npr.org/sections/thetwo-way/2011/12/02/143049567/why-burma-why-myanmar-why-both.

Progressive Voice. 2018. "Repression by Any Means Necessary". https://progressivevoicemyanmar.org/2018/09/19/repression-by-any-means-necessary/.

Rogers, B. 2012. *Burma: A Nation at the Crossroads*. Rider Books.

1

Introduction: Myanmar Media Historically and the Challenges of Transition

Lisa Brooten, Jane Madlyn McElhone and Gayathry Venkiteswaran

At the end of August 2018, as this book was about to go to press, the United Nations Human Rights Council (UNHRC) released its report summarizing the main findings and recommendations of its Independent International Fact-Finding Mission on Myanmar. The report outlines serious human rights violations and abuses in Kachin, Shan and Rakhine States. It recommends that six senior military figures be investigated for genocide against the Rohingya, including Myanmar's armed forces commander-in-chief Senior General Min Aung Hlaing, and that the case be taken up by the International Criminal Court (ICC), or alternatively that an ad hoc international criminal tribunal be created (Human Rights Council 2018).[1] The report notes that "The role of social media is significant. Facebook has been a useful instrument for those seeking to spread hate, in a context where for most users Facebook *is* the internet. Although improved in recent months, Facebook's response has been slow and ineffective"

(p. 74). Facebook quickly responded to the report's release by removing the accounts of eighteen high-profile army figures in Myanmar, including Senior General Min Aung Hlaing, and fifty-two Facebook pages, which had a combined total following of close to twelve million users (Facebook 2018).

A few days later, two Reuters journalists, Wa Lone and Kyaw Soe Oo, were sentenced to seven years in prison under the Official Secrets Act over accusations of holding secret government documents that they intended to share with international media and the ethnic armed group Arakan Army (Sithu Aung Myint 2018). The two were arrested in December 2017 after investigating a massacre of Rohingya men and boys in the coastal town of Inn Din in northern Rakhine State. After responding to a call from police officers, who met them in a restaurant and handed them documents, the journalists were arrested for having the documents in their possession. As they were being taken away from the court after the sentencing, Wa Lone was quoted as saying, "We know we did nothing wrong. I have no fear. I believe in justice, democracy and freedom" (Shoon Naing and Aye Min Thant 2018, ¶22). The arrest and subsequent sentencing were met with national and international condemnation, as was the rejection of their appeal in early 2019. At a public protest to call for their release, organizer Ei Ei Moe, from the pro-democracy youth movement Generation Wave, described their jailing as "blocking the eyes and blinding the ears of the public" (Dunant and Su Myat Mon 2018, ¶15).[2]

These events underscore the complexities of Myanmar's much lauded "transition". Celebrated early on for the release of imprisoned journalists and the end of pre-publication censorship, hopes for increased freedom of expression and media freedom were tempered by the crackdown that followed. Much has happened in the media sector since the controversial elections in 2010 organized by the military junta and boycotted by Aung San Suu Kyi and the National League for Democracy (NLD), including reforms to laws that had repressed the media for decades. Some argue that these changes are a continuation of the military government's Seven Step Roadmap to Disciplined Democracy, announced in 2003 (see the interview with Thiha Saw, this volume; Lall 2016; Rogers 2012). Laws on news media and publishing replaced older ones, allowing private owners to publish print dailies for the first time in five decades, despite enormous financial and resource challenges. Media outlets formerly in exile and in the country's borderlands, including those that identify as ethnic media, were permitted to officially register and to set up offices in the country as early as 2012. Many are now disseminating content — including in historically banned ethnic languages — previously considered too critical and subject to censorship and criminal prosecution. Stop-gap reform measures intended to appease those critical of the ongoing centralized control of the broadcast sector include two-year cooperation agreements between five Myanmar companies and the state-run MRTV that see each company operating as a content provider for one of MRTV's digital free-to-air TV channels.

At a September 2018 public protest in Yangon held in solidarity with the imprisoned Reuters journalists, poet Maung Saungkha donned a beige NLD jacket, topped it with a green military-style jacket, and proceeded to "hit" journalists covering the event with a rolled up copy of state-run newspaper *Kyemon* (Dunant and Su Myat Mon 2018, p. 17).[3] After the NLD's landslide victory in the November 2015 general elections, and despite continued military control over key levers of government power, there were high expectations that the NLD and State Counsellor Aung San Suu Kyi would prioritize and nourish free media and free expression. This demonstration reflects the disappointment and anger of journalists and free expression advocates about these unmet expectations.

Assessments of the NLD's performance thus far have been dismal. In May 2018 the writers and free expression network PEN Myanmar, along with eighteen of its civil society and free expression partners, gave the government a score of two out of sixty possible points for its second-year performance because of restrictive laws, defamation lawsuits and imprisonments, the regression of free expression in the digital sphere, dominance of state and military-owned media, powerful joint-ventures between the state and its business cronies, and a generalized failure to prioritize media reform and free expression; the 2018 score was six points lower than the previous year (PEN Myanmar 2018).

The Telecommunications Law is one of the NLD's weapons. Since 2013 the law has been used widely against online critics. According to Athan (2018), a free expression NGO, as of 9 September 2018, 150 cases had been filed under this law, the vast majority since the NLD came to power. Although a coalition of twenty-two civil society groups called for Section 66(d) of the law — which criminalizes expression — to be abolished, a revised version of the law passed by the Union parliament in August 2017 did not abolish 66(d) or decriminalize defamation. Journalists have also been arrested and charged under colonial-era laws such as the Unlawful Association Act and the Official Secrets Act.

State media have long been criticized for being government mouthpieces, a role they are continuing under the NLD with their focus on Aung San Suu Kyi and other top leaders, their avoidance of controversial topics or bad news, and their publishing of misinformation which, some say, is simply "better written propaganda" than under the military regime (PEN Myanmar 2016, p. 4; see also PEN Myanmar 2017). In high-profile cases, such as accusations of military crackdowns in northern Rakhine, state media also often bury the stories or opt to attack critics. This was very telling on 29 January 2017, when a senior member of the NLD team, the prominent Muslim lawyer and NLD legal advisor Ko Ni, was shot dead at Yangon International Airport upon his return from an official trip to Indonesia. Ko Ni was famed for his work as an advocate for constitutional and legal reform and for religious diversity.[4] Private national media and netizens captured the grief and mourning of NLD party members, civil society activists and ordinary citizens (Thant Sin 2017). In stark contrast, the state media's coverage was subdued, highlighting official news of events and meetings attended by Aung San Suu Kyi and then president Htin Kyaw, and burying news of the assassination and its aftermath on inside pages (Htun Khaing 2017). According to critics, the NLD-led government was reluctant to draw attention to the deep divisions signalled by the assassination of a respected and beloved Muslim lawyer in what is officially and predominantly a Buddhist country (San Yamin Aung 2017). Two years later, the killers have not been brought to justice.

Soon after the assassination, Wirathu, the leader of the radical nationalist Buddhist organization Ma Ba Tha (Committee for the Protection of Nationality and Religion), congratulated Ko Ni's killers on social media. When the award-winning investigative journalist

Swe Win criticized his actions, also on social media, a high-ranking member of the Ma Ba Tha in Mandalay sued him for defamation. A separate case filed in Yangon was later dropped. Myanmar's Ministry of Religious Affairs and Culture publicly defended the journalist, saying he had done nothing wrong (RFA 2017), and Myanmar's highest religious body, the State Sangha Maha Nayaka (Ma Ha Na), banned Wirathu from preaching publicly for one year and then declared Ma Ba Tha illegal (*Straits Times* 2017).[5] The Ma Ba Tha complainant later petitioned the court to withdraw the charge, but the case has nonetheless continued, including the arrest of Swe Win at Yangon's international airport in July 2017 and his subsequent release on bail. In August 2017 the complainant was himself arrested after participating in anti-government protests in Mandalay (Aung Ko Oo 2017). The assassination — and the responses to it — along with many other cases discussed in this chapter, illustrate the complexity and contradictions of Myanmar's ongoing political transition, and the role of media as sites for the playing out of power struggles and as active agents in their own right.

This compilation of work by academics, journalists, writers, media development experts, trainers and civil society activists documents developments in the media sector since the country's political opening. *Myanmar Media in Transition: Legacies, Challenges and Change* offers critical analyses and captures experiences on the ground, moving beyond the common research focus on media "systems" to instead focus on *processes* through which media are engaged as tools by key stakeholders and through which media act as agents themselves. This introductory chapter begins with an overview of existing research and theoretical debates about media in transition in other countries and world regions. This is followed by a history of Myanmar media inside, on the borders and outside of the country, and an overview of the current media landscape and major issues facing reformers. The Epilogue discusses the challenges we faced assembling this volume.

Media and Political Transitions

The wave of democratization in Latin America in the 1980s and Eastern Europe following the collapse of the Soviet Union re-energized the longstanding interest in the role of media in political transitions. This led to the emergence of the "transitions" paradigm, which remains the dominant approach to understanding transitions away from authoritarianism. The transitions paradigm has been critiqued, however, for its assumption of a movement towards liberal democracy (Roudakova 2012, p. 247) and its teleological approach (Carothers 2002). As this period of democratization was wrapping up towards the end of the 1990s, analysts began to discuss regimes combining authoritarian and democratic elements, and the growing consensus in comparative politics now revolves around the notion of such "hybrid regimes" as "the most common form of political organization around the world" (Roudakova 2012, p. 247; Voltmer 2015).

The field of comparative media and political communication has been dominated by the state-centric media "systems" approach since the publication of the highly influential *Four Theories of the Press* (Siebert et al. 1956). An important attempt to update and expand this seminal work is Hallin and Mancini's (2004) *Comparing Media Systems*, which proposes three models of media systems as possible frameworks for comparison. These are the Liberal Model, which they argue prevails in Britain, Ireland and North America; the Democratic Corporatist Model, that characterizes northern continental Europe; and the Polarized Pluralist Model, which they say can be found in the Mediterranean countries of southern Europe. They note that these models are ideal types, more normative than real, and that they may include variations that the authors hope would be revealed by applying these models in various contexts. A more recent edited collection by Hallin and Mancini (2012), *Comparing Media Systems beyond the Western World*, is a conversation with critics of their first book who argue that the three basic models it proposes do not translate well enough to be heuristically useful in most other parts of the world. The newer volume addresses some of these concerns, featuring significant critiques questioning the value of static models of media as "systems" and the lack of attention to *process* in comparative media work and research on political transition (McCargo 2012; Roudakova 2012). Roudakova (2012) calls for a typology that conceptualizes media systems as *processes*, distinguishes between processes that function to maintain and to erode order, and analyses how this shifts over time. She argues that the project by "transitologists" and "hybridologists" to formulate a "typology of hybrid regimes" (p. 247) is unhelpful "when it denotes a lump of features that the researcher does not know how to untangle" (p. 248). Suggesting that researchers focus on media agency, McCargo (2012) argues that modelling "systems" is problematic since "there are so many exceptions to every rule that rules tend to obscure rather than explain the nature of the game itself" (p. 202).

Even those committed to theorizing them admit that "typologies" of democratic media, and their role in transitions, are often limited due to the unique circumstances of each national context (Hallin and Mancini 2004, 2012). Although there has been significant research into media's role in political transitions, and several models developed, no overarching, coherent explanation that applies to all such cases has emerged. This is not particularly surprising, as the role of media in this process has proven to be highly contextual and varied. Reflecting on the case of Indonesia a decade after the fall of the authoritarian regime, Krishna Sen argues for "micro-level careful, empirical studies of media structures, regulations and practices" to explain how media operate in changing political environments (Sen 2011, p. 2).

Since media generally defy ready classification, McCargo (2003, 2012) offers us a useful formulation, urging us to "see media outfits as polyvalent, speaking with forked or multiple tongues, and given to acting in apparently contradictory ways" (McCargo 2012, p. 202). He has offered a framework for understanding media as agents of stability that work to preserve the social order; agents of restraint that provide checks and balances on the political order; and agents of change that help shape political changes during times of instability or crisis (McCargo 2003). This approach also interrogates commonly used terms such as censorship, ownership and partisanship, and the assumption underlying much research that most media can be understood as business enterprises, which does not hold with local realities in several Asian countries (McCargo 2012). McCargo (2012) argues that the tendency to characterize some forms of media using terms such as "clientelism" or "instrumentalism" suggests that they are peripheral deviations, when they are actually far more common than we are led to believe and are perhaps even dominant patterns globally.

Research on media and transition, like many discussions of media and politics, also tends to conflate media with journalism, mentioning only in passing, for example, that "similar processes have been at work in other areas of media and communication practice" (Hallin and Mancini 2012, p. 259; see also Curran 2007; Hallin and Mancini 2004; Zeilonka 2015). Too often transition research ignores the role of the entertainment industries and pop culture and downplays the role of social groups, civil society groups and political parties, as well as the impact of ideology and globalization, moves that disconnect the research from the ways in which contemporary democracies work (Curran 2007; Heryanto 2008). More attention needs to be paid to the non-state and non-commercial efforts that also compel and propel change during transition, a gap *Myanmar Media in Transition* addresses. However, while avoiding state-centrism, we cannot ignore the important role of the state. The available models for thinking about the relationship between media and the state present both useful insights and limitations.

State/Media Relationships

Hallin and Mancini's (2004) Polarized Pluralist Model has been both used and critiqued as a catch-all for societies outside of Europe and the Americas. It emphasizes political clientelism, "in which access to social resources is controlled by patrons and delivered to clients in exchange for deference and various forms of support", and formal rules are less important than personal and political relationships (Hallin and Mancini 2004, p. 58). They note that clientelistic relationships exist to some degree everywhere, and are often the target of reform efforts. Clientelism tends to be associated with lower levels of professionalization, as journalists are integrated into the clientelist networks characterized by private rather than public forms of communication. The process of political communication thus tends to be closed and "to serve the process of negotiation among elites rather than providing information for the mass public", while access to information for journalists tends to depend on their political ties (p. 59). Media that operate in this way function as agents of stability, maintaining the status quo.

In Southeast Asia, clientelism is often indicated by the term "crony", used to define business elites in countries across the region and their close association in many cases with authoritarian regimes, in particular since privatization in the 1980s and after the 1997 financial crisis. It is common to hear such references in Myanmar, where a class of business owners hailed from the military or had close ties with top generals and access to capital and ownership during the time of the junta. Since the country's wave of privatization began in 2008, a new class of oligarchs has emerged that benefited from the earlier patronage of the military, and while they are characterized to a certain degree by political clientelism, they are becoming increasingly autonomous from the political elites and consolidating their own economic power (Ford, Gillan and Htwe Htwe Thein 2016). Functioning as agents of stability, these oligarchs and their media promote the status quo in order to preserve their own footing in the media landscape. The growing concentration of media ownership in the hands of these oligarchs and cronies across Asia has had a negative impact on public participation in political processes (Tapsell 2015). In addition, clientelistic systems have become entwined in an increasingly interconnected global media network. Flew, Iosifidis and Steemers (2016) argue that in this context the role of states has shifted from controlling the media — a key feature in oppressive environments — to managing, coordinating and facilitating developments through the regulatory framework, and sharing power, to varying degrees, with the corporate sector, international bodies and civil society, as well as with the emerging media oligarchs.

Another potentially useful concept is the "new despotisms", a "new spectre" greatly entangled with democracies by doing business with them, selling arms to them, negotiating alliances with them, and mimicking them by experimenting with democratic practices (Keane 2015, p. 249). Keane (2015) defines despotism as "top-down, vertically organized power structured by interconnected patrons and clients" in which both benefit, but under "asymmetries of power" in which "things are stacked in favour of the more powerful" (p. 251). Contemporary despotisms are "governing arrangements mixed with concentrations of private capital" that expand their power through misinformation and spin that threaten actual or emerging democracies (p. 249). The media employed in such a project construct a rhetoric of change while functioning as agents of stability by reinforcing the status quo of power relations. They employ the rhetoric of democracy and make reference to "the people", embracing "the institutional facades of electoral democracy", while excluding undesirable candidates and voters (Keane 2015, p. 250). This concept can help illuminate aspects of Myanmar's transition, including, arguably, assessing the role of those oligarchs that currently control the broadcast sector.

The continued role of the state can be problematic when governments transitioning from authoritarian rule use the powers available to them to curb press freedom and freedom of expression, demonstrating that changing regulatory frameworks is one challenge, but dealing with cultural change is another entirely. Transitions literature refers to the phenomenon of *path dependency*, or the tendency to repeat patterns from the old regime in the organization and behaviour of new institutions and practices in the newly democratizing state (Powers 2016; Voltmer 2013). Those who have been in power will try to remain there, employing media as agents of stability, while contending forces will contest this by working to break free of old cultural patterns, employing media as tools or as partners in their attempts to push for change. Writing about the political changes in post-Communist Eastern European states and the relationship between the political actors and the media, Milton (2001) argues that the democratic forces that came into power after the Communist regimes retained the same media dependence as the regime they were replacing. Regardless of ideology (whether, for example, nationalist, Nazi or Soviet regimes), political actors "will use available political opportunities and resources to pursue their own political goals, and therefore institutional relations of media dependence will persist because this serves the agendas and interests of the political actors charged with granting media independence" (Milton 2001, p. 518). In their chapter on the legal framework for media and expression, Gayathry Venkiteswaran, Yin Yadanar Thein and Myint Kyaw argue that the democratically elected NLD government also uses legal tools as a means to keep itself in power.

Economic Forces of Change

Economic liberalization and promotion of commercial media are creating a global media model that is displacing the national variations of the past, and where journalism, in particular, is being modelled after dominant political and economic powers like the United States (Hallin and Mancini 2012, p. 251). Sen (2002) argues that the liberalization of the broadcast sector was one of the seeds of the political transition in Indonesia, which political economists have often attributed to the 1997 financial crisis. During Soeharto's authoritarian rule, this liberalization of the broadcast sector benefited his family and cronies but also weakened state control of information and news and thus expanded the space for media to function as agents of change (Sen 2002, p. 85). In the countries of Central and Eastern Europe, Price (2009) found two major influences on the direction of media reform: accession to the European Union and its requirements for regional standardization, and the impact of privatization and private forces, factors he argued were far more important than large-scale media development assistance from the United States and Europe.

Nevertheless, media assistance can provide an important impetus for change, with a number of large foundations, organizations and governments often dedicating funds towards media development and reform. Much media assistance focuses on the journalism sector and reforming the legal framework to accommodate the shift from the predominantly government-owned or -controlled media to public (especially in the broadcast sector) or independent private media and self-regulatory mechanisms (Price and Krug 2000; Kumar 2006). Other key initiatives include building professionalism among journalists, supporting media associations and providing funds to set up independent media outlets. The media development "industry" is largely motivated by the belief that a free and independent media environment is key to democratizing society, especially in improving public participation in political and public processes. How these dynamics have shaped historic media development work in Myanmar is discussed by Jane Madlyn McElhone and Lisa Brooten in this volume.

Grass Roots Change Agents

Other uses of media as agents of change include myriad grass-roots efforts to create alternative venues for expression, especially given the incredible technological changes that have recently made participation more accessible, including artistic performances, visual arts and other various forms of locally produced media. These locally produced media range from one-offs, such as performance art, street theatre or event flyers or other leaflets, to ongoing efforts such as small local print publications intended primarily for local communication within groups or small localities (Bailey et al. 2008; Brooten 2008*b*, 2011*b*; Downing 2001, 2011). Activists and reform advocates have also used online platforms to campaign locally and globally for their causes, creating mailing groups, online petitions and setting up alternative sources of information and news (Gan et al. 2004; Abbott 2011). Segura and Waisbord (2016) write that Latin America experienced one of the most active periods of media reform in the 2000s as a result of public mobilization and media movements, public debates, strategic litigation, and leftist governments that were open to reforms. Much of the early literature on the use of digital media in Southeast Asia focuses on efforts to challenge or topple regimes, while later works examine how these media can or do contribute to ongoing efforts to reform and democratize the media sector (Siriyuvasak 2005; Chowdhury 2008; Weiss 2012).

Although many commentators argue that Myanmar's current transition is "top down" — in that it was initiated and is being pushed by the state — this picture makes invisible all of the work done under the radar for two decades prior to the political opening that led to this recent push for change inside the country, and it diverts attention from non-state actors' contributions to the new Myanmar. Lall (2016) argues that activists and external donors promoted under-the-radar development of civil society during the final years of the military regime, particularly from 2005 to 2010, and that these developments played a key role in making the current transition towards the regime's goal of "discipline-flourishing democracy" possible (p. 3). Myanmar's civil society sector has become increasingly active, but along with such changes also come threats and challenges to the momentum for change. In her chapter, Jennifer Leehey explores local media as agents of change and the use of an evocative essay as a form of community resistance against large private interests, at the risk of costly legal challenges. This complex media landscape makes for engaging discussion in this volume, which we hope will jumpstart a long and fruitful exchange between academics, policymakers and media practitioners on these vital topics of participation and change.

Several chapters in this volume focus on individual and group resistance to historic and emerging forms of control and the opportunities being seized to access and share information beyond society's power brokers in order to push for change. State and private interests are far from the only players in this landscape; journalists, writers, filmmakers, musicians and civil society actors are also important in shaping new developments in media, as are audiences. This volume examines a variety of media and their roles in the current transition as agents of change, restraint and stability. Those producing and screening short films and documentaries about human rights, using social media in political debates, promoting change in the music industry, and writing poetry and other literature are all engaging in this work. We recognize, however, that power relations between the different groups and key players are not balanced, and that the influence of culture, interactions between groups, and the impact of fear also affect the direction of this transition. It is key, therefore, that reformers and policymakers have a historical grounding in order to understand recent events in Myanmar and the cultural patterns that have led to the current media landscape.

A History of Media and Free Expression in Myanmar

Developments since the political opening must be understood against the backdrop of struggles for freedom from military rule and the contestations of identities associated with nationhood resulting from decades of dictatorship and prolonged ethnic conflicts throughout the country. A look back at the earliest vestiges of media in Myanmar (then officially called Burma) sheds light on the country's long struggle with official censorship and control — and efforts to counter it — as well as religious and state involvement with media. It also highlights the country's vibrant, yet tumultuous, journalistic past, especially given the historically contentious relationship between the state and the people, and between the different ethnic and religious communities, since the colonial period.

Myanmar is one of the most ethnically diverse countries in the world (Smith 1994), but accessing accurate population figures and data about ethnic identities has always been difficult. Myanmar is estimated to be ninety per cent Buddhist. The majority Burmans (or Bamar people), who primarily reside in the seven regions in the central part of the country, are mainly Buddhists and they have historically dominated politics and the military, and, by extension, narratives in the media and other social and religious institutions. According to the former military junta, and the two governments that have since been in power, there are 135 different indigenous ethnic groups in the country. However, this figure is widely contested; some say there are 135 languages and dialects spoken, not ethnic groups; others say the figure is propaganda, as the military was never able to produce any reliable data or list of the "135 national races of Burma" (Smith 1994, p. 18; see also Cheesman 2017; Lintner 2017). For the first time in more than thirty years, a census carried out in 2014 with UN help calculated the population to be 51,486,253, including an estimated 1,206,353 people who were not counted in parts of Rakhine, Kachin and Kayin States due to conflict and problems of access in those regions (Department of Population 2015). Many ethnic civil society organizations (CSOs) criticized the ethnic coding in the census, claiming it was designed without proper consultation, and they called for the census to be postponed until peace was attained. More than one million Rohingya Muslims were not officially counted unless they agreed to be categorized as Bengalis (Mclaughlin 2014), although the UN did include them in the final population estimate. Millions of Myanmar nationals living outside the country were also not counted. That this issue is contentious can be assessed from the fact that as this volume was going to press the government had yet to release any data on ethnicity collected in the 2014 Myanmar Population and Housing census (San Yamin Aung 2018).

Many of the ongoing, and in some cases increasing, conflicts in Myanmar echo earlier conflicts from the British colonial period. During the post–World War II negotiations for independence, General Aung San, who had backed the Japanese during the war, signed the 1947 Panglong Agreement with several ethnic groups from the north who were pro-British and wanted assurances of self-administration upon independence. But Aung San was assassinated before the agreement could be enforced. Although the concept of federalism was included in the independence constitution, it became a tool for the subsequent Burmese military governments to impose their rule over the ethnic states (Kipgen 2017). The military has been at war with dozens of groups from the ethnic states ever since, and attempts to broker peace over the decades have mostly failed. Aung San Suu Kyi's current leadership in the peace negotiations has been much criticized, and yet the military largely controls the process, which has excluded many of the key players from the ethnic states (Horsey 2017; Min Aung Htoo Nai 2017). The Alliance for Gender Inclusion in the Peace Process (AGIPP) has also pointed to the absence of women in the peace negotiations, reflecting a wider problem of gender inequality and discrimination in the society (AGIPP 2017). Thin Lei Win's chapter in this volume speaks to this exclusion in the media context.

Even though Myanmar is linguistically diverse, this diversity was suppressed for decades under military rule in favour of the Burmese language. As such, information about the seven states and other self-administered areas named after ethnic minorities had in the past tended to be scarce, with the exception of efforts by individuals and communities that managed to produce reports, documentaries and interviews with journalists outside the country. This means that younger generations of ethnic minorities have for the most part been deprived of education and training in their own languages, although some have been educated in rural schools run by ethnic armed groups and therefore have a stronger grasp of their mother tongues, both oral and written. Ethnic nationality communities have nonetheless promoted their languages through their own media, from 'rebel broadcasts' in the 1970s and 1980s to news and religious media today (Lintner 2001, p. 29).[6] Many of these developments stem from patterns established under colonial rule.

The British Colonial Period (1824–1948) and Post-independence Civilian Rule (1948–62)

Education and literacy have always been highly valued in Burma and a source of national pride (Lintner 2001). Newspapers were first published in Burma during British colonial rule, beginning with the English-language newspaper *The Maulmain Chronicle*, founded in 1836 and published by the British administration as a means of communicating with British forces. This was followed by other papers produced by the British administration, Baptist missions and other English merchants

(U Thaung 1995). Burmese King Mindon was impressed with these early papers and their ability to openly critique leaders, and he became a strong proponent of a free press, which he tried to implement (Lintner 2001; U Thaung 1995). The first printing press in Burma was set up in the early nineteenth century by American missionary Adoniram Judson, who also printed the first book, *The Way To Heaven*, which he wrote and then published in 1816 (U Thaung 1995).

The early papers in Burma were published in English, with the exception of two papers produced by the local Baptist mission. One was the *Hsa-tu-gaw* (Morning Star). Launched in 1842 in Sgaw Karen language, it was considered the country's first ethnic language newspaper. It was also the longest-running vernacular newspaper, until its closure by General Ne Win just before he took power in 1962 (San San May 2016; Smith 1991). The other was the Myanmar-language Christian *Dhamma Thadinsa* (Religious Herald), founded in 1843 and considered the country's first Burmese-language newspaper (San San May 2016). In 1853 the ethnic Arakan Weekly Press published a twice-weekly paper called the *Akyab Commercial News* (later called *Arakan News*) in Sittwe, in what is now officially called Rakhine State (San San May 2016). English-language newspapers were published in Rangoon (now officially called Yangon) as early as 1853; the first Burmese-language paper in Rangoon was believed to have been launched in 1869 (San San May 2016).

Censorship rules in Burma were largely determined by the British administration in India (Larkin 2003). Following the Indian Mutiny in 1857,[7] the Governor General of India, Lord Canning, attempted to regulate the press by banning the publication of news without prior approval; his law became known as the "Gagging Act" (De 2013, p. 166). Then, in 1873, two years before the British annexation of Upper Burma, the country's second-to-last reigning monarch, King Mindon, introduced an act ensuring freedom of the press, considered the first indigenous press freedom law in Southeast Asia (*The Irrawaddy* 2016; Lintner 2001). One year later, the king started publishing a weekly.[8] In 1878 he also established the *Burma Herald* to counter what he called the pro-British views of Rangoon newspapers. That same year, the Vernacular Press Act was enacted in British India, of which Burma was a part, banning newspapers from reporting or depicting what it termed defamation of the government.

The media tended to support the nationalist movement that grew during the 1920s, contributing to its radicalization (Linter 2001; San San May 2016). The first cartoon published in Burma was drawn in 1914 by a British railway official, and, in 1917, Shwe Ta Lay's cartoon critiquing British officials for callously wearing shoes in Buddhist pagodas initiated a controversy that stirred early Burmese nationalist consciousness (Leehey 1997). By 1923 there were thirty-one newspapers operating in Rangoon, Mandalay, Moulmein, Sittwe, Bassein and Tharawaddy, including one of the country's longest-running newspapers, the state-owned *Myanma Alin*, launched in 1914 (*The Irrawaddy* 2016).[9] Throughout the 1920s and 1930s, Burmese media and Burmese language cartoons reflected the popular desire for independence (Leehey 1997; Linter 2001).

In 1947, Burma's first constitution guaranteed citizens the right to freely express their opinions and convictions, and ushered in a brief era of parliamentary democracy during which writers and artists had almost total freedom of expression. When the country won independence from the British in 1948, there were thirty-nine newspapers publishing in a variety of languages, including Chinese, Gujarati, Urdu, Tamil, Telegu and Hindi (Tharaphi 2011). During the post-independence period, media in Burma thrived, reinforcing the country's reputation as having one of the liveliest presses in Asia (Leehey 1997). Many of the more than thirty daily newspapers and myriad journals and magazines operating at the time considered themselves watchdogs against corruption, and most had their own cartoonists (Allott 1993; Leehey 1997). Ethnic conflict was rife, and journals emerged in the rural areas of the country that were home to ethnic rebel groups, establishing what Smith (1991) has called an "insurgent press" (p. 69). By the 1950s, the space for free expression was beginning to narrow. Writers began joining various political factions, and literary criticism became politicized despite the inability to write freely (Leehey 2005).

Film-going began around 1906, with films projected on to large sheets hung by scaffolding in the streets because of a lack of equipped theatres. Documentary filmmaking started in 1920 with a short work about the independence hero U Tun Shein (Aung Min 2012). In the post-independence period, the film industry grew, with for-profit companies beginning to produce documentaries, including recordings of the funerals of high-profile student leaders Bo Aung Kyaw and

General Aung San and a popular film on the Karen conflict, the country's longest-running civil war (Aung Min 2012).

During the Cold War, both the United States and Russia engaged in a propaganda war. They poured financial aid into Burma to support the publication of their views and to gain the support of the Burmese. A large influx of U.S. money supported the publication of books on U.S. culture and the dangers of the Russian empire, but it also promoted corruption in the publishing industry (U Thaung 1995). In the ongoing propaganda war, Russia and China also flooded the market with publications, which divided Burmese political forces and the literary field into pro-U.S. and pro-Russian camps (U Thaung 1995).

After only a few years of civilian rule, a 1962 *coup d'état* brought General Ne Win to power. Several name changes and shuffles in personnel notwithstanding, the military retained control of the country for the next half-century.

Military Rule and Censorship: 1962–2010

This period in Burma's history was characterized by strict censorship of all media, including the visual arts and live performances. After seizing power in 1962, General Ne Win targeted the press, imprisoning newspaper editors and establishing two state-run newspapers: *Working People's Daily* and *Forward Weekly* (Smith 1991). He also created the Burma Press Council to promote press freedom through the voluntary observance of a state-imposed code of ethics, revoked all existing press laws, and enacted a new instrument of censorship, the Printers and Publishers Registration Law of 1962. For the first year, General Ne Win allowed private weekly and monthly journals to publish without incident, but in 1964 he nationalized all private publications and arrested editors and journalists, decimating the country's previously vibrant private press (Allott 1993; Lintner 2001). Private newspapers were banned altogether in 1966 (Lintner 2001). Political cartooning also disappeared as a result (Leehey 1997). Those publications that remained became mouthpieces of Ne Win's Burmese Socialist Program Party (BSPP), political content was forbidden, and cartoons were limited to less sensitive topics such as nutrition and agriculture (Allott 1994; Leehey 1997; Smith 1991).

Nevertheless, cartoons remained a vital form of political commentary, allowing for multiple interpretations and thus veiled messages that could get past the censors, and revealing "the critical discourse which cannot be expressed explicitly" (Leehey 1997, p. 154). Filmmaking, on the other hand, was harnessed to the goals of the socialist state, and Burmese filmmakers were isolated and unable to access technical innovations or the creative developments in cinema in the United States and Europe (Aung Min 2012).

With the exception of official publications and school and university textbooks, book publishing remained in private hands, yet all books and periodicals had to be approved by the censorship body, the Press Scrutiny Board (PSB), before publication and distribution. Separate censorship boards existed for film (and later video) scripts and for popular music, and book covers and paintings also underwent scrutiny before publication or exhibition (Allott 1993). Reinforcing its pride in its literacy levels, under the BSPP regime the country twice won UNESCO prizes for its literacy campaigns, in 1971 and 1983 (Smith 1991; Gartner 2011).[10] Nevertheless, the challenge of printing book-length works and the lack of independent reporting contributed to the rise in importance of monthly literary magazines as a forum for serious writing during the 1970s and 1980s (Leehey 2005). Literature and literary debate remained vibrant during this time period, and what Leehey (2005) identifies as "the new style" in Burmese literature emerged, characterized by shifting and elusive meaning, which through its very shifting "captures something important about the subjective experience of everyday life under military rule" (p. 198). The country's historical love of print continues today, as veteran journalist Thiha Saw explains in his interview in this volume.

In 1974 a new constitution granted free expression in accordance with the "Burmese Way to Socialism". The News Agency Burma controlled the flow of information in and out of the country. All foreign correspondents, except those working for the Soviet Tass and China's Xinhua, were expelled, and foreign journalists banned. Burmese writers during the 1970s and 1980s were concerned about the arbitrary nature of the decisions handed down by the PSB, and the fact that publications had to be printed *before* submission and then censored by either ripping out pages or inking over the allegedly offensive bits (Allott 1993).

Burma was the last country in Southeast Asia to establish a television service (McDaniel 2002), yet, despite the censorship, other forms of creative expression prospered. Well before the advent of TV, the first Burmese feature film was released in 1920. And as Jane Ferguson explains in this volume, even during the decades of military dictatorship, film studios continued to produce feature-length movies that entertained audiences in hundreds of cinemas throughout the country. Myanmar Radio was launched in 1960 and MRTV in 1980. The country was for a long time limited to three state-run stations that each broadcast a few hours a day. By 1968 the cinema industry was in decline as cinemas and production houses were nationalized (Zon Pan Pwint 2016). In the 1990s, because of a lack of resources, strict rules on content, and emerging digital technologies, producers shifted to selling their content — largely low-budget dramas and comedies — in VCD format (Lim 2012).

Under military rule it was well known that a blacklist had been created of those writers forbidden to publish (Allott 1993). In another form of blacklist, various parts of the country were designated as white, brown or black areas, corresponding to the degree of control the regime had over each area. White areas designated military control, brown areas were only partially controlled by the military, and black areas were under the control of ethnic nationalist groups (Brooten 2003; Kumar 2014). Visitors to the country were generally confined to white areas, and research on the country was severely restricted. For this reason there are few scholarly works that examine the development of media and communications systems during this period. Restrictions were particularly harsh for ethnic nationalities seeking to preserve and teach their own languages, and many intellectuals from ethnic communities were arrested or went underground (Smith 1991).

1988: Uprisings, the "Democracy Spring", and a Coup

By early 1988 the Press Scrutiny Board (PSB) had relaxed its restrictions and private individuals could obtain magazine publishing licences fairly easily. By the middle of the year, more than ninety different magazines on a variety of topics were being published (Allott 1993). Massive uprisings in August and September led to a hiatus, albeit an extremely brief one, from the censorship that characterized communications under military rule. Started by students, the protests transformed within a short time into a nationwide strike. A large number of newspapers, press sheets and other publications emerged, many with biting satirical commentary on the political scene under General Ne Win and rule by the Burma Socialist Program Party (BSPP). Political cartooning re-emerged, ridiculing General Ne Win and the BSPP, and *Ayaun Thit*, a journal produced by the newly established Artists and Cartoonists Union of Burma, printed cartoons as posters and displayed them at demonstrations (Leehey 1997; Lent 1995). The year 1988 also saw the formation of the Musicians Union (Smith 1991). Evidence of this creative proliferation can be found in the nearly one hundred unofficial, independent publications from this period documented and archived in the British Library, including a lot of information that was unavailable in the mainstream private or state-run media of the time and many courageous statements from older, senior journalists who had long been silenced (Allott 1993). Even the state-run newspapers reported more accurately during this period (Smith 1991). The ban on foreign journalists was temporarily lifted. Students used the available space to organize small group communication structures that later became an underground opposition movement, exemplifying a history of student agitation for change (Brooten 2003).

On 18 September a *coup d'état* brought a new military configuration, the State Law and Order Restoration Council (SLORC), to power, which then imposed martial law and banned all public protests. Newspapers were banned, with the exception of the state-run *Lok-tha Pyei-thu Nei-zin* and its English-language version, the *Working People's Daily* (Allott 1993). Strict censorship was imposed and many editors, journalists and writers were arrested. As a result of the protests and their aftermath, an estimated 3,000 people were killed, 3,000 imprisoned, and 10,000 fled the country, some to ethnic minority controlled areas along the borderlands and others into exile (Guyon 1992). Journalists, cartoonists, writers and other artists were forced to decide whether to stay and give up their independence and their (short-lived) ability to publish freely or to continue their work in exile.

The month following the coup, Burma's favourite comedian and satirist, Zargana, was arrested for participating in the pro-democracy movement. He was imprisoned until April 1990, including seven months in solitary confinement (Human Rights Watch 2009). Hugely popular in the late 1980s, Zargana's name means "tweezers", referring to his ability to "pick out" the irony of political situations. Another well-known satirist and writer at that time was Maung Thawka, known by his pen name U Ba Thaw. He was a popular speaker at evening literary gatherings, where he could "reduce large audiences to fits of laughter with his satirical accounts of VIPs — very important pigs, very important phongvis (monks), very important government officials" (Allott 2001, p. 387). When an unofficial Union of Burmese Writers was launched in 1988, Maung Thawka was elected president. A known supporter of Aung San Suu Kyi, when she was placed under house arrest in July 1989, he was also arrested. Maung Thawka died in prison in 1991 (Allott 2001). These are only a few of the many stories of those who struggled against the military regime, a struggle that continued after the 1988 coup, bubbling under the surface for nearly two decades in this tightly controlled environment.

Brewing Storms: Between a Coup and a Revolution

The newly installed SLORC amended the 1962 Printers and Publishers Registration Act in 1989, increasing fines for infractions. For the press, writers and artists, a new range of topics became taboo, including democracy, human rights, politics, the events of 1988, government officials, and anything to do with opposition leader Aung San Suu Kyi, as well as references to South African freedom fighter Nelson Mandela. Leading writers were arrested, such as Ba Thaw and Win Tin, the chairman and vice-chairman of Burma's Writers' Association. Rising production costs and tightening censorship made publishing more difficult and books and periodicals more expensive (Smith 1991; Hudson-Rodd 2008). Ethnic writers and intellectuals were also arrested or went underground, and fewer books were published in ethnic minority languages under the SLORC than under the BSPP regime (Smith 1991). The SLORC's state-run media also orchestrated a xenophobic campaign against Burma's substantial Indian and Chinese populations, warning against interracial marriage and its resultant racial impurity (Smith 1991).

An additional censorship board was established in 1989 under the Ministry of Home and Religious Affairs to protect Burmese music from foreign influences. Military Intelligence chief Khin Nyunt urged musicians to be patriotic in their work and to cooperate with the state-controlled Myanmar Media Association (Smith 1991). Following a performance of satirical songs, chants and skits at the NLD headquarters during the Thingyan water festival in 1989, arrests of musicians and singers continued (Smith 1991). The SLORC similarly targeted the film and video industry, arresting key industry actors and directors, charging the chairman of Burma's Film Society with treason and launching a "cultural" campaign to coerce actors and directors to work with the Motion Picture Organization, a patriotic institution allied with the SLORC (Smith 1991).

Other performers, including comedians, also faced serious crackdowns during this period. For example, in May 1990, one month after being released from prison, Zargana was rearrested after doing stand-up comedy — telling a joke about the Minister of Information — at the Yankin Teachers Training College Stadium in Rangoon. He was sentenced to five years but released in March 1994. Once released he was banned from using his stage name Zargana and from performing publicly or even attending public events. His jokes were nonetheless said to have continued spreading by word of mouth. Despite these sanctions he was repeatedly invited to appear on military television — invitations that he always refused (Allott 2001; Human Rights Watch 2009).

The Burmese people did not consider the country's state-run media credible (Allott 1994; Smith 1991, 1992) and, as a result, relied on international broadcasters such as the British Broadcasting Corporation (BBC), the Voice of America (VOA) and Radio Free Asia (RFA) (Fink 2001; Lintner 1989). Aware of their influence, the military regime targeted foreign media. Two books in particular, *The Conspiracy of Treasonous Minions within the Myanmar Naing-Ngan and Traitorous Cohorts* and *A Skyful of Lies* [sic], attacked the foreign media for their reporting during 1988. Smith (1991) counted more than a hundred cartoons attacking the BBC in the state-run *Working People's Daily*, a campaign which he argued "conjured up the image of a network of foreigners secretly working together to seize control of Burma" (p. 72). In addition, a black market trade in pirated videotapes from Thailand, Singapore and Malaysia emerged in the early 1980s. Despite the low penetration of television, villagers often collaborated to purchase video players, and communal watching was common. Western news reports and video footage of NLD or other protest rallies were keenly-sought-after items (Smith 1991).

In the years following the 1988 protests, media continued to be used as tools in the struggle for power. Shortly after assuming control in 1988, the SLORC began signing ceasefire agreements with as many ethnic minority groups as it could, and the discourse and promise of peace and development in the ethnic regions became especially prevalent in state-run media (Brooten 2003). The NLD won elections in 1990 but was prevented from assuming power. Many of its leaders were subsequently arrested or went into exile, and the military retained its rule of the country. In 1995, in a largely symbolic but devastating blow to the ethnic opposition, the Burmese military captured the ethnic minority alliance headquarters at Manerplaw, just across the border from Ban Tha Song Yang in northwestern Thailand, a hub for visiting journalists and dignitaries meeting with opposition ethnic nationalist leaders (Brooten 2003). The hub then shifted to the Thai town of Mae Sot, across the Karen State border.

The 1988 coup had little effect on media already being published in the ethnic-controlled rural areas, home to myriad opposition forces, yet it spawned other media, including outlets established by students who had fled the country (Brooten 2003; Smith 1991). Opposition ethnic minority radio stations emerged intermittently. Several writers and journalists who fled the country established writers and artists clubs in the "liberated area" of the border, and they began publishing magazines that offered an important forum for young writers and cartoonists (Smith 1991). And while media produced in exile rarely made it to Rangoon, opposition groups did manage to smuggle information into the country periodically in order to counteract the regime's media representations of the opposition activists and the various ethnic nationality groups and to raise awareness of the plight of ethnic minorities in rural areas (Brooten 2003; Smith 1991).

During the 1990s the emergence of private monthly magazines was an important development, starting with business-oriented magazines that told stories of Burmese living abroad that would not have previously been allowed (Allott 1993). These magazines featured articles, cartoons, poems, foreign news features and eye-catching photographs, as well as many short stories, which Allott (1993) argues was "the most popular and important literary genre in Burma" (p. 23; see also Allott 1994; Brooten 2003; Kumar 2014). Many were fanzines focused on Myanmar celebrities. These monthlies were a refreshing alternative to the dry state-run newspapers, and the short stories they contained often used metaphor, allusion and irony to express ideas indirectly to avoid the censors. Nevertheless, like all non-state publications, including novels and other books, they had to undergo review by the Press Scrutiny Board *after* they were printed, creating strong pressure for authors and publishers to self-censor to avoid having to alter existing physical copies, especially given the increasing cost of paper (Allott 1993). This eventually changed with the introduction of computers in the 1990s, when pre-publication review and censorship replaced the older system (Leehey 2005). These private monthlies set the ground for the private weeklies that appeared in the early 2000s, and the newsweeklies that later followed in the mid-2000s. The first private weekly was a soccer journal, because soccer was a very popular sport and an easy money maker. *The Myanmar Times* was one of the prominent newsweeklies, launched in 2000 by Sonny Swe, the son of military intelligence head Brigadier General Thein Swe, in partnership with Australian businessman Ross Dunkley. Despite criticism that it was able to operate due to its close ties with the military, it quickly became one of the standard-bearers of journalism inside the country. Perhaps more than any other outlet, it has had a tempestuous history, including in 2004 when Sonny Swe was thrown into prison for nine years, ostensibly for violating censorship regulations. His father was also imprisoned as part of a military purge that saw military intelligence disbanded.

After 1988 the broadcast sector remained largely controlled by the government, but expanded to include the military and a few select private interests. In addition to state-run broadcasting, which began in 1936 during the colonial period and was named the Burma Broadcasting Service (BBS)[11] in 1946, the military launched Myawaddy TV on 27 March 1995, Burmese Armed Forces Day. In 2004 the regime entered into a joint venture with Forever Group to launch MRTV-4, and in 2010 established another lucrative broadcast joint venture with Shwe Than Lwin Media Co Ltd., the owner of the pay TV network

SkyNet, a direct-to-home satellite service. In 2005 the exiled Democratic Voice of Burma (now called DVB Multimedia Group) became the first Burmese satellite broadcaster, beaming into the country from exile. Government control was also undermined by the emergence of black market satellite dishes (Reporters Without Borders 2010a). The nationwide state broadcaster, Myanmar Radio, was launched in 1960 as an AM station and remained the only radio service in the country until the launch of Yangon City FM in 2001. Yangon City FM was one of seven FM stations which were established as joint ventures between the government and private companies (business cronies) over the next ten years. Additional state-controlled stations were later launched, including Thazin FM in 2008 by the Ministry of Defence and Myanma Radio Athan by MRTV and the Ministry of Information (Nwe Nwe Aye 2012; UNESCO and IMS 2016).

Documentary filmmaking was challenging in the aftermath of the 1988 uprisings. The craft was not developed inside the country and, given the pervasive climate of censorship and fear, foreign filmmakers had difficulties getting visas, let alone accessing people willing to talk with them. Those who were able to get a permit to film inside the country were stuck with a government "minder" who controlled where they could travel and what they could film, and, even if the filming was successful, it was challenging to get the film safely out of the country, past the eyes of the customs agents (Schlaefli 2016). A new surge of documentary filmmaking began to emerge in the mid-2000s, however, with classes and workshops offered at the Yangon Film School (YFS) and the Alliance Française (Aung Min 2012; Schlaefli 2016). YFS, established in 2005 by Anglo-Burmese filmmaker Lindsey Merrison, is officially a Berlin-based non-profit organization but was established to support young Myanmar filmmakers. Since its founding, YFS has produced almost two hundred films — including several award-winners — that have screened in film festivals around the world. YFS also creates films for local and international development organizations working in Myanmar, and trains their students to help local people in marginalized communities shoot their own films (Schlaefli 2016). A more detailed history of the Myanmar film and video industry and the impact of the transition are the focus of the chapter by Jane Ferguson in this volume.

In the late 1990s and early 2000s, local punk and hip-hop bands emerged on to the Burmese music scene. Punk rock lyrics were overtly anti-establishment, performed by bands like No U-Turn and Side Effect. The first ever hip-hop group, ACID, was formed in 2000 by Zayar Thaw (who would later be elected as an NLD legislator) and three other musicians — Annaga, Hein Zaw and Yan Yan Chan. The band had to submit their lyrics, demo tapes, finished recordings and cover art for the approval of the censors (Denby 2012), and they got into trouble for lyrics that were pro-democracy and pro-social justice.[12] The punk bands later used their performances to counter hate speech (Hindstrom 2015), while members of Generation Wave used hip-hop and other art forms to engage young people in politics during the transition (Freemuse 2011). In this volume, Heather MacLachlan provides an overview of changes in the music industry during the early transition period.

The internet's development in Burma was slow and from the start highly controlled. In 1996 the military regime launched its own website, Myanmar.com, as well as a Computer Science and Development Law which wielded an automatic seven to fifteen years' jail term for anyone who set up or had links to a computer network without the prior approval of the state Myanmar Posts and Telecommunications (MPT) service.[13] The MPT began providing an email service in 1997 and launched the first dial-up internet service in 1999, but the use of these services was limited by their exorbitant cost and access remained out of reach for most Burmese (Chon 2001; Zarny Win 2001). In early 2000 the regime listed a series of regulations for internet users, including prohibiting any writings "detrimental to the interests of the Union of Myanmar" or related to politics, making account holders responsible for all activity on their accounts, prohibiting hacking or other misuse, and requiring permission to publish web pages ("Regulations for Internet Users" 2000).

The government was clearly concerned about the impact of new information technologies. Despite allowing citizens access to email accounts, all messages had to pass through a central server controlled by the military, where they could be held up for hours waiting for the censors to read them (Neumann 2002; Zarny Win 2001). Early internet cafes in Rangoon only allowed access to members, and services were limited to an "Intranet" of government-approved sites. Membership fees and monthly service charges kept these off-limits to all but the country's elite. Several studies in the mid-2000s found that the regime was actively using filtering and surveillance tools to monitor and censor the internet through its two internet service providers — MPT and the first private provider, Bagan CyberTech (OpenNet Initiative 2005; Villeneuve 2007). The early development of the internet and the rise of Myanmar blogging culture is further detailed in this volume by Kamran Emad and Erin McAuliffe, in the context of privacy risks, as well as by Htaike Htaike Aung and Wai Myo Htut for the telecommunications sector.

2007 Saffron Revolution and 2008 Cyclone Nargis

In September 2007 an estimated hundred thousand monks, students and activists marched in the streets of more than twenty-five Burmese cities and towns calling for democracy, and the protests gained worldwide attention. The military regime declared martial law, banned foreign journalists and suppressed news of the protests. Yet citizen reporters and bloggers used their cell phones and digital cameras to upload information and images to the internet, where they were picked up by exiled media and transnational news networks. The amateur video of the fatal shooting of Japanese journalist Kenji Nagai at close range by a Burmese soldier attracted worldwide attention when it was aired on Japanese and other international television networks. Additional footage of violence against unarmed protestors was smuggled out and aired internationally. In response the military junta shut down official internet access and soldiers began targeting those with cameras (Brooten 2008a). The exiled broadcaster Democratic Voice of Burma used a BGAN (broadband global area network) satellite terminal to access the internet inside the country, thus circumventing the junta's attempts to control information flows (Khin Maung Win, personal communication, 11 September 2017). More than 6,000 people were arrested, including approximately 1,400 monks, between August and October 2007 (ALTSEAN Burma 2007). The figures for the death toll differ; the government claimed only 13 people were killed, the UN human rights envoy on Burma said 31 people had died, while the *Democratic Voice of Burma* reported that 138 people had been killed (Zarni Mann 2013).

Less than a year later, in May 2008, an estimated 130,000 people lost their lives during the devastating Cyclone Nargis, the largest natural disaster in the country's recorded history. The official government death toll was grossly underestimated from the start, as the junta attempted to reduce the catastrophe's political impact, preventing aid workers from reporting on the extent of the damage by keeping them out of the affected areas (Brooten 2008a). The UN estimated that 2.4 million people were affected by the devastation and that by early June 2008 only 1.3 million of these people had received even the most basic assistance, which was inadequate and below minimum requirements (UN 2008). The junta was criticized for its secrecy and obsession with security that delayed responses to the humanitarian crisis by keeping many aid workers and aid out of the country for weeks following the cyclone (Brooten 2008a). Despite the devastation and calls to postpone the nominal constitutional referendum — the first step in the regime's "Seven-Step Roadmap to Democracy" — the vote was held on 10 May in all but the five hardest-hit regions. For these five regions the referendum was postponed, but only until 24 May.

The Saffron Revolution and Cyclone Nargis both had an impact on the media sector. Audiences for Burma's exiled media skyrocketed, and the editors of the more established media — such as Aung Zaw of *The Irrawaddy*, Soe Myint of *Mizzima*, and Aye Chan Naing and Khin Maung Win of the Democratic Voice of Burma (DVB) — took on new roles as analysts for international news outlets (Brooten 2011a). There was almost no reporting of the Saffron Revolution inside Burma, but during Cyclone Nargis the regime started relaxing its controls.

These two events also triggered an increase in aid and development efforts. In 2008, Myanmar's first indigenous adult training and research institute, Myanmar Egress, founded an in-house media-training centre (IMS 2012). Donor support to many of Burma's exiled media increased, and with it the ability of these media to continue building networks inside the country. This expanded support, along with the transnational pro-democracy movement and technological advances, continued to strengthen the media inside and operating in exile and along the country's borderlands. Nevertheless, this did not happen uniformly, and the larger, more developed groups tended to benefit most, rather than the smaller, ethnic or community-based media (Brooten 2003). These efforts are explored in more detail in Jane Madlyn

McElhone and Lisa Brooten's chapter on media development in this volume.

Many actors, musicians and performers responded to the cyclone by carrying out fundraising initiatives. In August 2008 the Burmese band Iron Cross performed in a concert at the Thuwanah Sports Stadium in Rangoon to raise money for the victims. The audience of fifty thousand was said to be the largest ever in the history of Burma (*The Irrawaddy* 2008). The junta allowed certain artist associations to organize concerts and shows to raise funds, but other groups were banned, such as the Moustache Brothers, a comedy troupe from Mandalay known to be supportive of the pro-democracy movement and whose members had served time in jail for their stinging critiques of the military (Cho 2008; Menendez and Hodgson 2013). A well-known *a-nyeint* comedy troupe, Thee Lay Thee and Say Yaung Zon, toured several countries telling jokes and performing skits that mocked the junta. The junta banned a recording of their performances that became a huge hit after being circulated outside of the country as well as clandestinely inside it on VCD (*The Irrawaddy* 2008).

This overview provides some indication of the historical events and patterns that shaped the country before the quasi-civilian Thein Sein administration began its legislative changes in 2010 and 2011. Contemporary events cannot be fully understood without some knowledge of how this history and its legacies have created both opportunities and challenges for those working to develop, diversify and democratize Myanmar media.

The Media Landscape Today: 2010–Present

When the current period of reform began, the media sector was vibrant but significantly restricted. There were about two hundred weekly and monthly journals and magazines in the private print market, covering news, sports and lifestyle. Many privately owned publications were associated directly or indirectly with high-ranking members of the army, including some individuals who also held cabinet positions (Nwe Nwe Aye 2012). Even then, few were spared the pre-publication censorship rules, and in this environment it was difficult to find truly independent publications. The government, military and a few select business partners retained control over the broadcast sector. Significant restrictions continued to limit artistic freedoms. The telecommunications sector was stagnant, with exorbitant prices for SIM cards and very little infrastructural development. The internet was less regulated than other media in the country, but access was limited to less than one per cent of the population (Crouch 2016).

It is not surprising that media are now functioning as agents of change, reflecting internal divisions within the country, but their roles remain varied. The military and its former foes in the NLD-led government are struggling to define new power relationships and to change the old ways of doing things, but have challenged many media's efforts to act as agents of restraint, and have in many ways encouraged media to act as agents of stability, reproducing persistent old patterns and habits. At the same time, other media resist change as agents of stability, reproducing persistent old habits and patterns. And while new opportunities are opening up for Myanmar media, there remain significant barriers to their development as agents of restraint and change, independent of state and corporate interests. These include problematic laws, government control of infrastructure, economic challenges, bureaucratic hurdles, restricted access to information, and the rise of online bullying and hate speech. Much of this has been exacerbated by the meteoric nature of recent change, perhaps most obvious in the rapid growth in telecommunications in the country.

Growth in Telecommunications

In 2011 only one per cent of the population was online, but by 2015 Myanmar was the fourth fastest growing telecommunications market in the world (Trautwein 2015). By 2016 the telecommunications sector was the single most important draw for foreign direct investment in the country, raising concerns about other sectors of the economy (Samarajiva 2016). Myanmar was in 2017 considered the fastest-growing smartphone society in the world — an estimated 95 per cent of the population has access to mobile services and 85 per cent of the phones they are using are smartphones (Heijmans 2017). These figures, however, are based on the number of SIM cards purchased. The number of towers that extend mobile penetration is much more limited, particularly in remote regions (Aung Kyaw Nyunt 2016; Heijmans 2017). As such, only an estimated 40 per cent of the population actually has access to the internet, either through mobile or broadband, although that number is rapidly increasing (Internet in Myanmar 2017). Broadband penetration initially lagged behind mobile but it is now growing quickly. Nevertheless, wired broadband may become increasingly irrelevant as mobile continues to proliferate and prices continue to drop.

This rapid growth in mobile services has largely replaced the need for internet cafes for online communication, although they still function in some areas so that people can charge their phones and connect to wireless internet, as explained by Htaike Htaike Aung and Wai Myo Htut in this volume. In rural areas, many people are now getting their news through online sources, especially Facebook, displacing radio as a primary source of information. Facebook and Viber have become Myanmar's most popular news dissemination and messaging sites. The number of digital media has grown, with popular online news aggregators attracting large audiences. Access to social media on mobile phones has for the first time given people direct access to politicians and other high-profile people, as discussed in this volume by Yan Naung Oak and Lisa Brooten, who explore the use of Facebook by high-profile figures in Myanmar and assess the platform's role in efforts to develop a more diverse public sphere. The rapid rise in social media use has led more people to express their political views, at the cost of promoting intolerance against ethnic and religious communities (Lee 2016), an issue discussed by Sarah Oh and Eaint Thiri Thu in this volume. Another concern is the lack of basic literacy about privacy rights and risks in this new digital age, as discussed in the chapter by Kamran Emad and Erin McAuliffe.

Political Economy of Myanmar Media

To a large measure, the Myanmar media landscape is controlled by military and political figures and their business allies, especially the broadcast and daily newspaper sectors. Which forms of ownership regulation will be introduced and to what extent the state will retain control over infrastructure such as broadcast towers, printing stations and distribution networks remains to be seen. Key needs include increased transparency regarding media ownership, mechanisms to establish and maintain a source of public information about media operations, opportunities for public input and feedback about the role of media in Myanmar, and regulation that serves the public interest. The Myanmar people have embraced the information age and the recent opening and, despite recent setbacks, many groups are working hard to keep these new forms of access open.

Notwithstanding the dominance of the state and military in the Myanmar media landscape, private media have existed for some time, even though many are owned by cronies of army officials, families of high-ranking ministers or generals, or by people known to be close to them. The political opening has done little to transform the established patterns of highly concentrated ownership. This is demonstrated by the private and independent media outlets that struggle to sustain their operations against the dominance of state-run media and those owned by business elites. Assessing the political economy of Myanmar media is a difficult task because each of the government-crony joint ventures was established without any form of reporting requirement regarding ownership structure or revenues, and because various secondary sources and government websites often report inconsistent information (Smith 1991). This is a research lacuna that needs to be addressed in much greater detail as soon as possible to promote transparency in the media sector. We endeavour here to map the prominent players. In doing so, we distinguish between state-run media, which until recently were military controlled, and private sector media, although these categories are far from exclusive, as already indicated, and their many intersections and relationships need to be mapped out with much more clarity.

One example of the blurring of the state-run/private distinction is in the telecommunications sector. Telecommunication services were first provided by the state-owned MPT, but they were controlled, expensive, and limited to certain areas, much like the subsequent initial access to mobile services and the internet. Until 2013, internet connections were provided by Yatanaporn Teleport, RedLink and SkyNet MPS, joint ventures with the regime that depended on MPT's communications infrastructure (Song 2013). The two sons of

Shwe Mann, the former chairman of the lower house in parliament from the military-backed USDP — Toe Naing Mann and Aung Thet Mann — founded the second private internet service provider, RedLink Communications, in 2008.[14]

In 2013, after the sector was liberalized, two foreign private companies entered the market: Norway's Telenor AS and Qatar's Ooredoo QSC. In January 2017 a fourth licence was awarded to a joint venture between Vietnam's military-run Viettel and two local companies, one of which belongs to the Myanmar army (Reuters 2017). By the end of 2016 there were more than fifteen internet service providers in the country (Internet in Myanmar 2016).

State-run Media

For a long time the military *was* the state in Burma. More recently, however, the state-run media have come under the control of the government, and they need to be considered separately from the military-run media. In the print sector the government owns two national dailies — the Myanmar-language *Kyemon* (The Mirror) and *Myanma Alinn* — and has a joint venture with Global Direct Link to run the English-language *Global New Light of Myanmar*. The government runs and manages the state broadcaster MRTV as well as a variety of state-private joint ventures. Its most notable broadcast joint ventures are with Skynet, started in 2010 and owned by Shwe Than Lwin Media Co Ltd, and with Forever Group, which has run MRTV-4 since 2004 (Nwe Nwe Aye 2012).[15] The government also runs AM radio stations and has joint ventures with a variety of companies that run FM stations, including Zaykabar Co, Shwe Taung Group of Companies and Htoo Group of Companies (Nwe Nwe Aye 2012). The five companies awarded two-year digital television channel contracts in April 2017 to run joint ventures with the Ministry of Information include DVB Multimedia Co Ltd, Mizzima Co Ltd, Young Investment Group Co Ltd, Fortune International Co Ltd and Kaung Myanmar Aung Co Ltd.

The military publishes two dailies — the national *Myawaddy Daily* and the *Yadanabone Daily* in Mandalay — and owns its own television channel, Myawaddy, and radio station, Thazin FM (Nwe Nwe Aye 2012). It also publishes several magazines.

Private Media

The country has seven private national dailies: *7Day*, *Daily Eleven*, *The Voice Daily*, two editions of *The Myanmar Times* (English language and Myanmar language), *The Standard Time Daily* and *Democracy Today*. *Daily Eleven* is part of the Eleven Media Group established by Than Htut Aung in 2000. The group began by publishing sports journals and, since 2005, newsweeklies and bi-weeklies. It was one of the first media outlets to publish a daily, in May 2013 (Meston 2013). The *7Day* daily and weekly publications are owned by Thaung Su Nyein through his media company Information Matrix Co Ltd, which started with a magazine on information technology and now includes a series of popular journals. He is the son of Win Aung, the late foreign minister (BBC 2013). The *Voice Daily* is part of the stable of publications owned by the Myanmar Partners Think Tank Group affiliated with the development organization Myanmar Egress, which first published the *Living Color* business magazine in 1995. The *Voice Weekly* was launched in 2004 and began publishing a daily in 2015. Myanmar Egress founding member, the late Nay Win Maung, was the son of a military officer and was known to be close to the lower house chairman Shwe Mann. He later, however, handed over *Living Color* magazine to Ye Naing Win, whose father is the ex-military intelligence chief General Khin Nyunt (Aung Din 2011).[16]

Set up in 2000 by Australian Ross Dunkley and Sonny Swe, *The Myanmar Times* has had various owners with military and government connections. It has also had a tumultuous history, with both its founders serving stints in prison. In February 2014, business tycoon Thein Tun, widely known as the man who brought Pepsi to Myanmar, became the majority shareholder of the company (*Mizzima* 2014). From the start the company was perceived as pro-establishment, and at times pro-junta, due to its connections with prominent figures in the government. But under the junta it also faced tremendous pressure and censorship (Gleeson 2017). Since Sonny Swe's release from prison in 2013, he has had an active presence in the media sector; first as deputy CEO of Myanmar Consolidated Media Ltd, the owner and operator of *The Myanmar Times*, then as CEO of *Mizzima* and majority shareholder, and now as founder and CEO of Black Knight Media, the owner of Frontier Media. Frontier has steadily become one of the most respected journalism outfits in Myanmar, with a reputation for tackling taboo topics. Sonny says people still think of him as the son of a general, but that the military has always hated him "for pushing boundaries and revealing the truth".[17]

Shwe Than Lwin owns SkyNet and *Democracy Today*. The publisher for *Democracy Today* is listed as Ko Ko, who is chairman of the Yangon Media Group and also publisher of the *Yangon Times* (Burrett 2017). Meanwhile, a construction company — Three Friends Construction — is a newcomer to the media business, publishing *The Standard Times* (Sandar Lwin 2013).

There are also hundreds of other weekly and monthly journals and magazines. The owner of *Popular Journal* and *Popular News Journal*, Nan Kalayar Win, is the daughter of former Secretary 3 of the SLORC, Lt-Gen Win Myint. The owners of *Snapshot Journal* (Myat Khaing) and *Envoy Journal* (Maung Maung) were close allies of the former Minister of Information and Culture from the State Peace and Development Council (SPDC), Brigadier General Kyaw Hsan (Aung Din 2011).

In the broadcast sector, two private companies — Forever Group and Skynet — have well-established joint ventures with the state and, along with state-run broadcasting, dominate the sector. The private broadcast company DVB Multimedia Co Ltd, referenced earlier, continues to broadcast via satellite from Thailand, and is considered the country's only independent news broadcaster. This status, however, may change, as the DVB Multimedia Group is one of five entities to have been awarded digital broadcasting contracts in 2017. These companies' permits will need to be renewed in two years or once the by-laws for the Broadcasting Law have been approved and implemented. The concern is that this partnership may jeopardize DVB's editorial independence.

A unique aspect of Myanmar's media landscape is the presence of formerly exiled media entities that have returned to the country to continue their work. One of the most prominent is the DVB Multimedia Group, along with *The Irrawaddy* and *Mizzima*. Supported, historically, and in some cases currently, by institutional donors, these media are now tackling the challenges of sustainability in a competitive playing field with other private media that had already been established inside the country, and where state, military and crony media have significant advantages.

Mingalar Company Ltd is the largest film distributor in the country, reportedly controlling eighty per cent of the domestic cinema trade (Buncombe and Htusan 2012). It owns six of Yangon's most popular cinemas. Mingalar entered the business in 1999, securing three cinemas in Yangon and two in Mandalay when the military regime eased economic restrictions on some sectors and privatized the ownership of cinema halls (AP 1999). The property developer Shwe Taung Group controls most of the remaining market, along with other newcomers that offer newer and better-equipped cinemas (Nandar Aung 2017). The push to refurbish old cinemas and build new ones has partly been due to the re-entry of U.S.-based 20th Century Fox International. The company pulled out of the country after the 1962 coup. It subsequently struck a deal in 2012 with Mingalar as its local distributor (Buncombe and Htusan 2012). Jane Ferguson analyses the current state of the film and video industry in her chapter in this volume.

The transition has seen some realignment of media ownership, although many of the players remain the same as in the junta era. The overall environment for media and expression, however, has not improved since the election of the National League for Democracy. By most accounts, it has worsened when compared with the initial changes made under the Thein Sein administration.

Thein Sein Administration

After the quasi-civilian government was installed by the military junta in 2011, with Thein Sein as president, changes in the media sector began in earnest. That year, local publications were allowed for the first time to publish articles, interviews and photographs of Aung San Suu Kyi, as well as articles written by her. Pre-publication censorship was abolished in August 2012, along with the censorship body and sixteen loosely worded guidelines for content that had held editors accountable for "sensitive" content deemed harmful to national security or "the dignity of the state" (Kumar 2014, p. 76). Journalists began reporting on previously taboo topics, and the digital space opened up with the liberalization of the telecommunications sector. An Interim Press Council was created. In April 2013 the first private daily newspaper licences — twenty-six in total — were handed out. And in 2014 thirteen dailies entered the market. International news agencies opened offices inside the country with their own foreign correspondents, although visas were becoming more difficult to obtain and local journalists working with foreign media have come under threat while covering the crisis in Rakhine State (Brooten and Verbruggen 2017; Crispin 2018; Dickinson 2017). The majority of exiled media returned. Susan Banki and Ja Seng Ing provide an analysis of the changes faced by one of these outlets — *The Irrawaddy* — as it made the move back to the country. Ethnic media in the borderlands also began moving back, alongside nascent start-ups publishing and broadcasting in Myanmar and ethnic languages, a transformation which Jane Madlyn McElhone overviews in this volume.

The abolition of pre-publication censorship benefitted the artistic industries. Myanmar hosted its first independent international literary festival in February 2013 (VOA 2013). Filmmakers highlighted themes that were formerly off-limits, including politics and social justice. The film industry had been limited by the 1996 Television and Video Law that required all films and videos to be vetted prior to exhibition, but in December 2011 the Minister of Information and Culture, Kyaw San, announced that censorship of film and video would be relaxed. Films that were previously restricted in the country were subsequently permitted to screen, including *Burma VJ*, about the video journalists who reported on the 2007 Saffron Revolution and the government's response, and *Nargis*, by a group of young filmmakers from the Yangon Film School about the aftermath of the 2008 cyclone and the plight of its victims (Aung Min 2012; Harris 2013). Yet, nudity and sex remained off limits, and the horror genre was often banned (Harris 2013). In this volume, Mon Mon Myat discusses the impact of the Human Rights Human Dignity Film Festival, including films blocked by the film censorship board such as *Sittwe* and *Twilight over Burma*, the latter after the NLD came into power.

The partial relaxing of pre-exhibition censorship for artistic works created a new openness and a freer space for music, comedy and traditional forms of satirical critique that were previously banned, yet bureaucratic hurdles and the highly restrictive legal framework have continued to present challenges (Harris 2013). For example, live music performances required advance permits from multiple levels of government, while public performances have often been controlled through the use of Section 505 of the penal code and Section 18 of the Peaceful Assembly and Peaceful Procession Law (Harris 2013). The often broad and arbitrary interpretations of the law have muddied the terms by which art has been judged political or offensive. Heather MacLachlan brings to this volume a discussion of changes in the music industry during the transition period. Reflecting on the opening of space for writers and poets, Ma Thida highlights the lingering culture of fear that challenges efforts to promote and defend freedom of expression.

Coverage of the 2015 parliamentary elections, while flawed, was fairer and more transparent than coverage of the 2010 nominal elections staged by the military junta, yet journalists had to contend with significant problems in gaining access and reporting freely. The military regime conducted elections on 7 November 2010, the fifth step of its so-called Roadmap to Democracy. However, the Union Election Commission (UEC), which was directly appointed by the regime, issued restrictions on opposition political parties and media (SEAPA 2011). Political parties not contesting the election were deregistered, including the NLD. In March 2010 the Press Scrutiny and Registration Board issued directives to the media to not publish interviews with opposition leaders or discuss the electoral laws (Kumar 2014, p. 73). Commentary about the 2008 constitution was added to the list of restrictions in July 2010, and in October the regime announced it was not granting press visas to foreign journalists who wanted to cover the elections (Kumar 2014). Local journalists working for foreign media reported being followed and photographed by Myanmar police and security agents (Kumar 2014). Those who tried to evade the authorities were arrested and deported, including Toru Yamaji, the head of the Tokyo-based news agency APF (Reporters Without Borders 2010b). Aung San Suu Kyi was released six days after the elections, on 13 November, an event which was widely attended by the media. But at least ten publications were suspended for between one and three weeks for what the censors claimed was overly extensive coverage of the opposition leader (Nay Thwin 2010). The pre-election coverage of the November 2015 parliamentary elections faced fewer restrictions than in 2010 but it was still lacking in many ways. In her chapter, Carine Jacquet discusses the interactions between the Union Election Commission and journalists during the elections.

A rollback on media freedom and free expression began in 2014 under the Thein Sein administration, a few scant years after the political opening. Many people were charged that year under internet or peaceful assembly and association laws, and the Committee to Protect Journalists included Myanmar in its 2015 list of the world's ten most censored countries (CPJ 2015). Chapters in this volume on the legal framework and media in the ethnic states highlight the risks journalists face from the military, as demonstrated by the killing of freelance reporter Aung Kyaw Naing (also known as Par Gyi) while in military custody in 2014. That same year, the CEO and four journalists from the weekly *Unity Journal* were convicted under the Official Secrets Act for reporting on a military facility. They were subsequently pardoned in a political prisoner amnesty when the NLD formed the government in April 2016.

NLD-led Government

Despite the change in government, private media continue to struggle to survive in the market. Many outlets have closed down due in part to competition from highly subsidized state media, as well as inexperience and a lack of access to capital. The situation is particularly dire in the ethnic states and regions (MDIF 2018). More advertisers are moving to state media in search of larger audiences and closer ties with the NLD government. The rush to set up new dailies following the country's political opening has been dampened by the harsh realities of sustaining media businesses (Downing 2015). By the end of 2016, the number of dailies had shrunk to six, and a seventh daily was launched in early 2017.

Digital freedom has suffered, with Section 66(d) of the Telecommunications Law being used to silence critics of the government and the military, while threats against journalists have increased. The media community and observers were shocked when a journalist was murdered in December 2016, despite the NLD being in power. Soe Moe Tun, who worked for *Daily Eleven News* in Monywa, Sagaing Region, was killed while reporting on illegal logging (ARTICLE 19 2016). Access to conflict zones has been restricted, preventing independent coverage of the humanitarian crisis in northern Rakhine State and limiting coverage of the growing conflicts in Kachin and Shan States. Self-censorship remains entrenched. In this volume, journalist Lawi Weng writes about his experiences reporting from the conflict areas, while journalism trainer Ye Naing Moe shares his observations with interviewers Nai Nai and Jane Madlyn McElhone about the challenges facing journalists in the new political environment.

Apart from the state apparatus, non-state actors — in particular, Buddhist hardliners — have also used the laws to harass individuals. Journalist Swe Win of *Myanmar Now* is among those who have been targeted by the radical Buddhist organization Ma Ba Tha, in his case using Section 66(d) of the Telecommunications Law. In March 2017, members of the punk band Rebel Riot were pressured to apologize to Ma Ba Tha over a photo posted on their Facebook page that showed them dressed up as Jesus, Shiva and Buddha during their performance. Band member Kyaw Thu Win was quoted as saying that they had been criticized online for "insulting" Buddhism (Hpraw Pan Lee 2017).

The most high-profile case under the NLD administration by far, however, has been the arrest and conviction of the two Reuters journalists Wa Lone and Kyaw Soe Oo, discussed at the beginning of this chapter. No other case has so clearly encapsulated the disappointment of the media community in the elected NLD representatives. This case demonstrates as well that the biggest test so far of the Thein Sein and NLD governments has undoubtably been the Rohingya crisis.

Media and the Rohingya Situation

More than any other crisis, the communal violence in Rakhine State that first erupted in 2012, and then intensified in 2017, has exposed tensions and schisms in the country and tested the extent and integrity of the political opening, including media freedom, free expression, and journalistic ethics and professionalism. This is especially the case when journalists tackle taboo issues such as religion, ethnic rights, the military and charges of ethnic cleansing and genocide. Journalists' access to the affected areas in Rakhine State has been restricted, leading to reliance on official sources and distorted or incomplete coverage (Brooten and Verbruggen 2017; *Frontier Myanmar* 2016). Few Myanmar media outlets have covered violence committed against the Rohingya, and there is a widespread lack of self-critique among Myanmar journalists who merely repeat the official line (Ye Naing Moe, personal communication, 20 September 2017; see also Myanmar Institute for Democracy 2017). Myanmar media have been highly critical of foreign media, accusing them of an overemphasis on human rights and not enough on national security. Local and foreign journalists who report critically about the military's operations in Rakhine State face accusations from their peers for exaggerating or false reporting. In her chapter in this volume, Eaint Thiri Thu reflects on how military rule has affected reporting of the plight of the Rohingya and the difficulties journalists face in accessing the truth.

Social media platforms, especially Facebook, have been used to spread rumours and hate speech, provoking violent reactions. The spread of hateful messages and their consequences for the safety of journalists and civilians are especially evident in the violence in Rakhine State, where most of the messages tend to be anti-Muslim or anti-Rohingya (Davis 2017; Wade 2017). Evidence now demonstrates that Facebook was used in a systematic campaign by military personnel (Mozur 2018). Wade (2017) documents the use of seminars and local media to propagandize against the Rohingya, and assesses how the propaganda, "not just in leaflets and statements [by Ma Ba Tha and other nationalist monks], but in domestic media of all stripes, state-owned and private — left little mental space within the Buddhist communities of Rakhine State to consider the Rohingya as anything but menacing" (p. 118). Journalists who use Facebook or Twitter to provide live reports from an incident or press briefing have been subject to online harassment and attacks by those who think the content is sympathetic to the Rohingya. Even journalists from Rakhine working with local media have encountered hostile responses and death threats from the public when covering the conflict on the ground, as they are perceived to be biased (Mratt Kyaw Thu 2017). Sarah Oh writes in this volume about individuals and campaigns that emerged in response to the communal conflict and the surge in hate speech.

Facebook's role in the violence has been much critiqued. During an interview in April 2018, the platform's founder, Mark Zuckerberg, acknowledged that he was concerned about the potential dangers of Facebook misuse in Myanmar (Klein 2018). The interview shed light on his lack of awareness of the situation on the ground. He referenced an attempt to thwart an incitement of communal violence between Buddhists and Muslims in Myanmar, and praised the effectiveness of Facebook's systems (he specifically used the phrase "our systems") for monitoring such attempts to incite violence. In fact, this particular case was identified and reported by civil society in Myanmar, and it took several days for Facebook to take action. The civil society groups in Myanmar who initially identified and reported this incident sent an open letter to Zuckerberg, criticizing Facebook's over-reliance on third parties, absence of a proper mechanism for emergency escalation, reticence to engage local stakeholders around systemic solutions, and lack of transparency (Phandeeyar et al. 2018). While Facebook is reportedly continuing efforts to improve its ability to respond to notifications of abuse and to monitor and remove hate speech proactively (Facebook, 15 August 2018), civil society activists remain unconvinced that the company's commitment to improving the situation and ending the resulting violence is on par with its commitment to improving its own reputation.

Capturing the complex and fast-moving Rakhine and Rohingya situation and the media's response to it has been one of the more challenging aspects of compiling this volume.

Assembling This Volume

Assembling *Myanmar Media in Transition* presented many challenges, notably the concern that the information would become outdated by the time of publication. Events and decisions are unfolding rapidly as we pen this introductory chapter, especially involving legal cases against the media and other civil society actors, as well as developments in the Rakhine and Rohingya crisis. But we must at some point stop updating and acknowledge that this work, like all works, is partial. We offer this volume as a panoramic snapshot of the Myanmar media landscape at this point in time, with a level of detail and depth useful as a baseline for building comparative research around the many themes raised. We discuss Myanmar media scholarship in greater detail in the Epilogue.

A significant limitation facing us is that there are few media scholars focused on Myanmar. The country's isolation during military rule had a direct impact on the kinds of research scholars were permitted to undertake, which has resulted in limited academic analysis of media. The academic literature that does exist is scattered and piecemeal. Information on ownership and cross-ownership of media, as well as informal agreements between parties that have characterized the media sector in the country, are difficult to come by. Myanmar journalists acknowledge that writing about media ownership brings with it the risk of criminal defamation (Human Rights Watch 2016). As a result, literature on the subject is sparse, even in print media. In-depth analyses in English of Myanmar-language media are also rare. This volume is the first in English to bring together empirical and theoretical contributions by scholars on different aspects of Myanmar media. These are complimented by more descriptive pieces by experienced media professionals and reform advocates, whose work helps fill the gaps in the academic literature and provides context. Several chapters are collaborative efforts by academics and practitioners. Despite the political opening, there were interviewees — both local and foreign — who were reluctant to share information on the record, in order not to jeopardize relationships, including with donors or organizations working in the area, as well as out of a fear of reprisals. This is an indication that while legislative change may be possible in the short term, the deeper cultural patterns, such as the culture of fear around speaking openly, will take more time to overcome.

The main purpose of this volume is to document and theorize the changes occurring since the political opening. But, more importantly, the intention is to spark conversations between academics, policymakers and media practitioners and to provide a historical foundation for reflections on the media landscape of Myanmar today and for the future. After decades of forced silence on topics of vital importance, Myanmar media now offer platforms for greater discussion and engagement, yet they are also being used for repressive purposes. This volume amply illustrates that, while media act as agents of change, and are themselves affected by change, they can also act as agents of restraint, holding officials to account, keeping an eye out for corruption. And, as agents of stability, some media, such as Myanmar's state-run outlets, are maintaining the status quo rather than promoting a structural or cultural transition away from business-as-usual. This volume explores all of the phenomena in action during this current period of transition.

Notes

1. The ICC has begun a preliminary examination of the forced displacement of the Rohingya and the international mission's findings on gross human rights violations. The UN Human Rights Council passed a resolution on 27 September 2018 to create an independent mechanism to collect evidence of alleged crimes committed against the Rohingya. See Keaten (2018).

2. Generation Wave is a high-profile political activist youth group.
3. Maung Saunghkha was at the time founding director of the Research Team on the Telecommunications Law and is now the founding director of the free expression non-governmental organization Athan.
4. Ko Ni was also responsible for helping the NLD identify the new position of State Counsellor for Aung San Suu Kyi, who is barred by the constitution from becoming president (Beech 2017).
5. After it was declared illegal, the Committee for the Protection of Nationality and Religion (Ma Ba Tha) changed its name to the Buddha Dhamma Charity Foundation and continued its operations.
6. The members of Burma News International (BNI), who represent ethnic identities, produce content in Myanmar and their own languages, as well as in English. See https://www.bnionline.net.
7. The Indian Mutiny of 1957–58 was one of the biggest, but unsuccessful, uprisings organized by the sepoys (soldiers) against the British East India Company.
8. The paper shut down when the British annexed Upper Burma in 1885.
9. The names of Rangoon, Moulmein and Bassein were changed in 1989 along with the change in the country's name. They are now referred to as Yangon, Mawlamyine and Pathein, respectively.
10. Despite the country's historically high literacy rate, in 1987 the previously reported literacy rate of over 78 per cent was suddenly reduced to 18.7 per cent, ostensibly so that Burma could meet the strict requirements to be considered for least developed country (LDC) status at the United Nations (Smith 1991).
11. The BBS was renamed Myanmar Radio and Television (MRTV) in 1997.
12. Zayar Thaw was imprisoned for three years in 2008 for founding the youth organization Generation Wave in the wake of the 2007 uprising known as the Saffron Revolution.
13. The text of the law is available at http://www.wipo.int/edocs/lexdocs/laws/en/mm/mm012en.pdf.
14. Since the political opening, Shwe Mann has been seen as an ally of Aung San Suu Kyi, especially after he was removed as USDP party chairman before the 2015 elections (BBC 2015).
15. Forever Group was established in 1996 as a graphics training centre and collaborated with the Information Ministry on e-learning and e-book initiatives beginning in the early 2000s (*Mizzima* 2016). Its founder and CEO, Win Maw, is known to be close to the former information minister Kyaw Hsan, who was reportedly also a shareholder of the company (Foster 2013). The owner of Shwe Than Lwin, Kyaw Win, is known to be close to the former president Thein Sein and the military (Foster 2013).

16. Ye Naing Win was arrested after his father Khin Nyunt was ousted from power in 2004. In the 1990s, Ye Naing Wing was made director of the country's first internet provider, Bagan Cyber Tech, which was later renamed Myanmar Teleport.
17. Interview with Sonny Swe, 13 July 2018 in Yangon.

References

Abbott, J.P. 2011. "Cacophony or Empowerment? Analysing the Impact of New Information Communication Technologies and New Social Media in Southeast Asia". *Journal of Current Southeast Asian Affairs* 30 (4): 3–31.

AGIPP (Alliance for Gender Inclusion in the Peace Process). 2017. *Analysis of Myanmar's Second Union Peace Conference – 21st Century Panglong from a Gender Perspective by Alliance for Gender Inclusion in the Peace Process (AGIPP)*. https://www.agipp.org/sites/agipp.org/files/agipp_upc_analysis_paper.pdf.

Allott, A. 1993. *Inked Over, Ripped Out: Burmese Storytellers and the Censors*. New York: PEN American Center.

———. 1994. "Burmese Ways". *Index on Censorship* 23 (3): 87–105.

———. 2001. "Burma: Popular Culture, Zargana (Maung Thura) and Other Comedians". In *Censorship: A World Encyclopedia*, edited by D. Jones, p. 387. London: Routledge.

ALTSEAN Burma. 2007. "Saffron Revolution: Update". 15 October 2007. http://www.altsean.org/Docs/PDF%20Format/Thematic%20Briefers/Saffron%20Revolution%20-%20Update.pdf.

AP. 1999. "Myanmar's Rat-Infested Cinemas Seek Salvation in Private Hands". *Utusan Online*, 26 February 1999. http://ww1.utusan.com.my/utusan/info.asp?y=1999&dt=0226&pub=Utusan_Express&sec=Features&pg=fe_05.htm.

ARTICLE 19. 2016. "Myanmar: Journalist Investigating Illegal Logging Killed". 14 December 2016. https://www.article19.org/resources.php/resource/38596/en/myanmar:-journalist-investigating-illegal-logging-killed.

ATHAN. 2018. "The Number of Cases under the Telecommunications Law Rises to 48 after the Amendment". Press statement, 9 September 2018.

Aung Din. 2011. "Partial List of Cronies Who Provide Political and Financial Support for Burma's Ruling Regime". *US Campaign for Burma*, June 2011. http://www.burmapartnership.org/wp-content/uploads/2011/06/The-Regime_s-Cronies-List-June-27_-2011_-Final.pdf.

Aung Ko Oo. 2017. "Myanmar Now Chief Editor Swe Win Appears before Court for the Third Time". *Mizzima*, 22 August 2017. http://www.mizzima.com/news-domestic/myanmar-now-chief-editor-swe-win-appears-court-third-time.

Aung Kyaw Nyunt. 2016. "Ministry Puts Mobile Penetration at 90 Percent". *Myanmar Times*, 19 July 2016. https://www.mmtimes.com/business/technology/21466-ministry-puts-mobile-penetration-at-90-percent.html.

Aung Min. 2012. "The Story of Myanmar Documentary Film". https://www.guggenheim.org/blogs/map/the-story-of-myanmar-documentary-film.

Bailey, O., B. Cammaerts, and N. Carpentier. 2008. *Understanding Alternative Media*. Maidenhead: McGraw Hill/OUP.

BBC. 2013. "My Business: Running a Newspaper in Burma". 4 September 2013. http://www.bbc.com/news/business-23901922.

———. 2015. "Aung San Suu Kyi Hails Shwe Mann as an 'Ally'". 18 August 2015. http://www.bbc.com/news/world-asia-33974550.

Beech, H. 2017. "The Murder of an Honorable Lawyer in Myanmar". *New Yorker*, 7 March 2017. https://www.newyorker.com/news/news-desk/the-murder-of-an-honorable-lawyer-in-myanmar.

Brooten, L. 2003. *Global Communications, Local Conceptions: Human Rights and the Politics of Communication among the Burmese Opposition-in-exile*. PhD dissertation, College of Communication, Ohio University.

———. 2008a. "Burmese Political Cartoons and the Transnational Public Sphere in Times of Crisis". *International Journal of Comic Art* 10 (2): 254–81.

———. 2008b. " 'Media as Our Mirror': Indigenous Media in Burma (Myanmar)". In *Global Indigenous Media: Cultures, Practices and Politics*, edited by P. Wilson and M. Stewart, pp. 111–27. Duke University Press.

———. 2011a. "Media, Militarization and Human Rights: Comparing Media Reform in the Philippines and Burma". *Communication, Culture & Critique* 4 (3): 312–32.

———. 2011b. "Independent Media of (Burma/Myanmar)". In *Sage Encyclopedia of Social Movement Media*, edited by John D.H. Downing, pp. 242–46. Thousand Hills, CA: Sage.

Brooten, L., and Y. Verbruggen. 2017. "Producing the News: Reporting on Myanmar's Rohingya Crisis". *Journal of Contemporary Asia* 47 (3). https://doi.org/10.1080/00472336.2017.1303078.

Buncombe, A., and E. Htusan. 2012. "Burma's Film-lovers Celebrate a Titanic Taste of Freedom". *The Independent*, 17 August 2012. http://www.independent.co.uk/news/world/asia/burma-s-film-lovers-celebrate-a-titanic-taste-of-freedom-8057198.html.

Burrett, T. 2017. "Mixed Signals: Democratization and the Myanmar Media". *Politics and Governance* 5 (2): 41–58.

Carothers, T. 2002. "The End of the Transition Paradigm". *Journal of Democracy* 13 (1): 5–21.

Cheesman, N. 2017. "How in Myanmar 'National Races' Came to Surpass Citizenship and Exclude Rohingya". *Journal of Contemporary Asia* 47 (3): 461–83. https://doi.org/10.1080/00472336.2017.1297476.

Cho, V. 2008. "Burmese Celebrities Try to Help Survivors". *The Irrawaddy*, 31 May 2008. http://www.burmanet.org/news/2008/05/31/irrawaddy-burmese-celebrities-try-to-help-survivors-violet-cho/.

Chon, G. 2001. "Waiting to be Wired". *Asiaweek*, 20 July 2001.

Chowdhury, M. 2008. "The Role of the Internet in Burma's Saffron Revolution". Berkman Center Research Publication no. 2008-08. The Berkman Center for Internet & Society at Harvard University.

CPJ (Committee to Protect Journalists). 2015. "10 Most Censored Countries". https://cpj.org/2015/04/10-most-censored-countries.php.

Crispin, S. 2018. "Threats, Arrests, and Access Denied as Myanmar Backtracks on Press Freedom". Committee to Protect Journalists, 12 February 2018. http://cpj.org/blog/2018/02/threats-arrests-and-access-denied-as-myanmar-backt.php.

Crouch, E. 2016. "Myanmar Was Off the Grid for Decades – Now it's Catching Up Fast". *Techinasia*, 19 January 2016. https://www.techinasia.com/myanmar-internet-revolution-startups.

Curran, J. 2007. "Reinterpreting the Democratic Roles of the Media". *Brazilian Journalism Research* 3 (1): 31–54.

Davis, A. 2017. "How Social Media Spurred Myanmar's Latest Violence". Institute for War and Peace Reporting, 12 September 2017. https://iwpr.net/global-voices/how-social-media-spurred-myanmars-latest.

De, S. 2013. "Marginal Whites and the Great Uprising: A Case Study of the Bengal Presidency". In *Mutiny at the Margins: New Perspectives on the Indian Uprising of 1857*, vol. 2, *Britain and the Indian Uprising*, edited by A. Major and C. Bates, pp. 165–81. Sage.

Denby, K. 2012. "The Hip Hop Artist Who Dreams of Democracy. *The Times*, 30 January 2012. https://www.thetimes.co.uk/article/the-hip-hop-activist-who-dreams-of-democracy-g78576v28r7.

Department of Population. 2015. "The 2014 Myanmar Population and Housing Census. Highlights of the Main Results. Census Report Volume 2-A". Ministry of Immigration and Population, May 2015. http://myanmar.unfpa.org/sites/default/files/pub-pdf/Census%20Highlights%20Report%20-%20ENGLISH%20%281%29.pdf.

Dickinson, E. 2017. "As Mistrust Grows amid the Rohingya Crisis, Myanmar Tightens Restrictions on Foreign Media". *The Splice Newsroom*, 21 December 2017. http://www.thesplicenewsroom.com/myanmar-crackdown-press-freedom-foreign-media/.

Downing, J. 2015. "Fourth Estate Feels the Pinch". *Frontier Myanmar*, 19 November 2015. https://frontiermyanmar.net/en/features/fourth-estate-feels-the-pinch.

Downing, J.D.H. 2001. *Radical Media: Rebellious Communication and Social Movements*. Thousand Oaks: Sage.

———, ed. 2011. *Sage Encyclopedia of Social Movement Media*. Thousand Hills, CA: Sage.

Dunant, B., and Su Myat Mon. 2018. "Yangon Youth Protestors Demand the Release of Jailed Reuters Journalists". *Frontier Myanmar*, 16 September 2018. https://frontiermyanmar.net/en/yangon-youth-protestors-demand-the-release-of-jailed-reuters-journalists.

Facebook. 2018. "Removing Myanmar Military Officials from Facebook". Facebook Newsroom, 27 August 2018. http://newsroom.fb.com/news/2018/08/removing-myanmar-officials/.

Fink, C. 2001. *Living Silence: Burma under Military Rule*. London: Zed Books.

Flew, T., P. Iosifidis, and J. Steemers. 2016. *Global Media and National Policies: The Return of the State*. Palgrave Macmillan UK.

Ford, M., M. Gillan, and Htwe Htwe Thein. 2016. "From Cronyism to Oligarchy? Privatisation and Business Elites in Myanmar". *Journal of Contemporary Asia* 46 (1): 18–41.

Foster, M. 2013. *The Business of Media in Myanmar*. Internews.

Freemuse. 2011. "Generation Wave (Burma/Myanmar)". 11 February 2011. http://freemuse.org/freemuseArchives/freerip/freemuse.org/sw39821.html.

Frontier Myanmar. 2016. "On Confirmation Bias". 1 December 2016. https://frontiermyanmar.net/en/on-confirmation-bias.

Gan, S., J. Gomez, and U. Johannen. 2004. *Asian Cyberactivism: Freedom of Expression and Media Censorship*. Friedrich Naumann Foundation.

Gartner, U. 2011. "Education in Myanmar: A Concise Abstract of Educational Policy". Southeast Asian Studies, University of Passau. http://www.phil.unipassau.de/fileadmin/dokumente/lehrstuehle/korff/pdf/publications/Education_in_Myanmar_WP15.pdf.

Gleeson, S. 2017. "The Muzzling of the Myanmar Times". *Frontier Myanmar*, 27 February 2017. https://frontiermyanmar.net/en/the-muzzling-of-the-myanmar-times.

Guyon, R. 1992. "Violent Repression in Burma: Human Rights and the Global Response". *Pacific Law Journal* 10 (2): 410–59. https://escholarship.org/content/qt05k6p059/qt05k6p059.pdf.

Hallin, D.C., and P. Mancini. 2004. *Comparing Media Systems: Three Models of Media and Politics*. Cambridge: Cambridge University Press.

———, eds. 2012. *Comparing Media Systems beyond the Western World*. Cambridge: Cambridge University Press.

Harris, M. 2013. *Burma: Freedom of Expression in Transition*. Index on Censorship, 15 July 2013. https://www.indexoncensorship.org/wp-content/uploads/2013/07/Burma-Freedom-of-Expression-in-Transition.pdf.

Heijmans, P. 2017. "The Unprecedented Explosion of Smartphones in Myanmar". *Bloomberg Businessweek*, 11 July 2017. https://www.bloomberg.com/news/

features/2017-07-10/the-unprecedented-explosion-of-smartphones-in-myanmar.
Heryanto, A. 2008. *Popular Culture in Indonesia: Fluid Identities in Post-authoritarian Politics*. London: Routledge.
Hindstrom, H. 2015. "Myanmar's Punk Rockers Challenge Anti-Muslim Rhetoric". Al-Jazeera, 3 November 2015. http://www.aljazeera.com/indepth/features/2015/10/myanmar-punk-rockers-challenge-anti-muslim-rhetoric-151028102356467.html.
Horsey, R. 2017. "Myanmar's Peace Conference Leaves Talks on Uncertain Path". *Nikkei Asian Review*, 31 May 2017. https://asia.nikkei.com/Viewpoints/Richard-Horsey/Myanmar-s-peace-conference-leaves-talks-on-uncertain-path?page=2.
Hpraw Pan Lee. 2017. "Punk Band Apologizes to Ma Ba Tha for Posting Facebook Photos Allegedly Insulting Buddhism". *Mizzima*, 30 March 2017. http://www.mizzima.com/news-domestic/punk-band-apologizes-ma-ba-tha-posting-facebook-photos-allegedly-insulting-buddhism.
Hudson-Rodd, N. 2008. "'Not a Rice-Eating Robot': Freedom to Speak in Burma". In *Political Regimes and the Media in Asia*, edited by K. Sen and T. Lee, pp. 85–105. London: Routledge.
Human Rights Council. 2018. "Report of the Independent International Fact-Finding Mission on Myanmar". A/HRC/39/64. http://www.ohchr.org/Documents/HRBodies/.../FFM-Myanmar/A_HRC_39_64.pdf.
Human Rights Watch. 2009. *Burma's Forgotten Prisoners*.
———. 2016. *"They Can Arrest You Any Time": The Criminalization of Peaceful Expression in Burma*. https://www.hrw.org/sites/default/files/report_pdf/burma0616web.pdf.
IMS (International Media Support). 2012. *An Assessment of Media Development Challenges and Opportunities in Myanmar: Change is in the Air*. https://www.mediasupport.org/wp-content/uploads/2012/11/ims-change-myanmar-2012.pdf.
Internet in Myanmar. 2016. "Internet Service Providers Overview in Myanmar". https://www.internetinmyanmar.com/isp-overview-myanmar/.
———. 2017. "Internet Users in Myanmar Increased by 97% in 1 year, 70% Are Mobile Users". https://www.internetinmyanmar.com/internet-users-myanmar-2017/.
The Irrawaddy. 2008. "From Rock to Romance". December 2008, vol. 16 (12). http://www2.irrawaddy.com/article.php?art_id=14749&page=1.
———. 2016. "Burma's Media Landscape through the Years". 4 May 2016. https://www.irrawaddy.com/news/burma/burmas-media-landscape-through-the-years.html (accessed 9 March 2017).

Keane, J. 2015. "Mediated Despotism — A World beyond Democracy". In *Media and Politics in New Democracies: Europe in a Comparative Perspective*, edited by J. Zielonka, pp. 248–61. New York: Oxford University Press.

Keaten, J. 2018. "UN Human Rights Body Creates Team to Document Myanmar Abuses". *Washington Post*, 27 September 2018. https://www.washingtonpost.com/world/asia_pacific/un-rights-body-sets-up-new-team-to-document-myanmar-crimes/2018/09/27/76b3fc6c-c265-11e8-9451-e878f96be19b_story.html?utm_term=.7606408bd4e6.

Kipgen, N. 2017. "The Continuing Challenges of Myanmar's Peace Process". *The Diplomat*, 6 June 2017. http://thediplomat.com/2017/06/the-continuing-challenges-of-myanmars-peace-process/.

Klein, E. 2018. "Mark Zuckerberg on Facebook's Hardest Year, and What Comes Next". *The Ezra Klein Show*, 2 April 2018. https://art19.com/shows/the-ezra-klein-show/episodes/0d5f503d-80d0-4e98-aa08-d29599957459.

Kumar, K. 2006. "International Assistance to Promote Independent Media in Transition and Post-conflict Societies". *Democratization* 13 (4): 652–67.

Kumar, M. 2014. *Media in an Authoritarian State: A Study of Myanmar*. New Delhi: Atlantic.

Lall, M. 2016. *Understanding Reform in Myanmar: People and Society in the Wake of Military Rule*. London: Hurst.

Larkin, E. 2003. "The Self-Conscious Censor: Censorship in Burma under the British, 1900–1939". *Journal of Burma Studies* 3:64–101.

Lee, R. 2016. "The Dark Side of Liberalization: How Myanmar's Political and Media Freedoms Are Being Used to Limit Muslim Rights". *Islam and Christian-Muslims Relations* 27 (2): 195–211.

Leehey, J. 1997. "Message in a Bottle: A Gallery of Social/Political Cartoons from Burma". *Southeast Asian Journal of Social Science* 25 (1): 151–66.

———. 2005. "Writing in a Crazy Way: Literary Life in Contemporary Urban Burma. In *Burma at the Turn of the Twenty-first Century*, edited by M. Skidmore, pp. 175–205. Honolulu: University of Hawai'i Press

Lent, J. 1995. *Asian Popular Culture*. Boulder, CO: Westview Press.

Lim, David C.L. 2012. "Introduction: Southeast Asian Film as a Site of Cultural Interpretation and Social Intervention". In *Film in Contemporary Southeast Asia: Cultural Interpretation and Social Intervention*, edited by David C.L. Lim and H. Yamamoto. Routledge.

Lintner, B. 1989. *Outrage: Burma's Struggle for Democracy*. Hong Kong: Review Publishing.

———. 2001. "Burma: Denial of Access". In *The Right to Know: Access to Information in Southeast Asia*, edited by S. Coronel. Philippine Center for Investigative Journalism.

———. 2017. "Book Review: Myanmar's Enemy Within: Buddhist Violence and the Making of the Muslim 'Other'". *The Irrawaddy*, 4 September 2017. https://www.irrawaddy.com/culture/books/myanmars-enemy-within-buddhist-violence-making-muslim.html.

McCargo, D. 2003. *Media and Politics in Pacific Asia*. London: Routledge.

———. 2012. "Partisan Polyvalence: Characterizing the Political Role of Asian Media". In *Comparing Media Systems beyond the Western World*, edited by D.C. Hallin and P. Mancini, pp. 201–23. Cambridge: Cambridge University Press.

McDaniel, D. 2002. *Electronic Tigers of Southeast Asia: The Politics of Media, Technology and National Development*. Ames: Iowa State University Press.

Media Development Investment Fund. 2018. *An Unfavorable Business: Running Local Media in Myanmar's Ethnic States and Region*. New York: MDIF.

Menendez, J., and K. Hodgson. 2013. "Burma: Moustache Brothers Keep on Telling Jokes". *BBC Magazine*, 5 January 2013. http://www.bbc.com/news/magazine-20528893.

Meston, A. 2013. "Dr Than Htut Aung, 2013 Golden Pen Laureate – Biography". WAN-IFRA. http://www.wan-ifra.org/articles/2013/06/03/dr-than-htut-aung-2013-golden-pen-laureate-biography.

Milton, A. 2001. "Bound But Not Gagged: Media Reform in Democratic Transitions. *Comparative Political Studies* 34 (5): 493–526.

Min Aung Htoo Nai. 2017. "'Talks Did Not Become Reality': UPJDC Secretary Bemoans Lack of Progress in Peace Process". Mon News Agency/Burma News International, 31 August 2017. http://www.bnionline.net/news/mon-state/item/3441-talks-did-not-become-reality-upjdc-secretary-bemoans-lack-of-progress-in-peace-process.html.

Mizzima. 2014. "Tycoon U Thein Tun Buys Majority Share in The Myanmar Times". 3 March 2014. http://archive-3.mizzima.com/mizzima-news/media/item/10959-tycoon-u-thein-tun-buys-majority-share-the-myanmar-times/10959-tycoon-u-thein-tun-buys-majority-share-the-myanmar-times.

———. 2016. "Forever Group Signs New Deal with Thaicom Satellite". 6 April 2016. http://www.mizzima.com/business-domestic/forever-group-signs-new-deal-thaicom-satellite.

Mozur, P. 2018. "A Genocide Incited on Facebook, with Posts from Myanmar's Military". *New York Times*, 15 October 2018 <https://www.nytimes.com/2018/10/15/technology/myanmar-facebook-genocide.html>.

Mratt Kyaw Thu. 2017. "'That Guy Should Be Killed': Escaping a Mob in Maungdaw". *Frontier Myanmar*, 11 September 2017. https://frontiermyanmar.net/en/that-guy-should-be-killed-escaping-mob-maungdaw#.WbYYcFtmPQw.twitter.

Myanmar Institute for Democracy (MID). 2017. *Interim Report on Coverage of Myanmar Media on Rakhine Conflict*, 12 October 2017. https://www.dropbox.com/s/75xxsitut08bn89/Rakhine%20Report.pdf?dl=0.

Nandar Aung. 2017. "Myanmar's Biggest Movie Screen on the Way". *Myanmar Times*, 15 March 2017. https://www.mmtimes.com/lifestyle/25339-myanmars-biggest-movie-screen-on-the-way.html.

Nay Thwin. 2010. "Journals Suspended for Suu Kyi Coverage". *Democratic Voice of Burma*, 22 November 2010. http://www.dvb.no/news/journals-suspended-for-suu-kyi-coverage/12986.

Neumann, L. 2002. "Special Report: Burma under Pressure". Committee to Protect Journalists. https://cpj.org/reports/2002/02/burma-feb02.php.

Nwe Nwe Aye. 2012. "Role of the Media in Myanmar: Can It Be a Watchdog for Corruption?" In *Myanmar's Transition: Opening, Obstacles, and Opportunities*, edited by N. Cheeseman, M. Skidmore, and T. Wilson, pp. 186–203. Singapore: Institute of Southeast Asian Studies.

OpenNet Initiative. 2005. *Internet Filtering in Burma – A Country Study*. October 2005. https://opennet.net/studies/burma.

PEN Myanmar. 2016. *November 2016 Scorecard Assessing Freedom of Expression in Myanmar*. https://pen.org/sites/default/files/PEN%20Myanmar%20-%20Freedom%20of%20Expression%20Scorecard%20-%20December%202016.pdf.

———. 2017. *Scorecard Assessing Freedom of Expression in Myanmar*. https://pen.org/wp-content/uploads/2017/05/May-2017-Scorecard-English.pdf.

———. 2018. *Scorecard Assessing Freedom of Expression in Myanmar*. https://pen.org/wp-content/uploads/2018/05/Freedom-of-Expression-Scorecard-1May2018-FINAL-laid-out.pdf.

Phandeeyar, MIDO, et al. 2018. "Myanmar – Open Letter to Mark Zuckerberg". 5 April 2018. Available at https://drive.google.com/file/d/1Rs02G96Y9w5dpX0Vf1LjWp6B9mp32VY-/view.

Price, M., and P. Krug. 2000. *The Enabling Environment for Free and Independent Media*. Programme in Comparative Media Law & Policy, Oxford University.

Price, M. E. 2009. "Media Transitions in the Rear-View Mirror: Some Reflections". *International Journal of Politics, Culture, and Society* 22 (4): 485–496.

Powers, M. 2016. "NGO Publicity and Reinforcing Path Dependencies: Explaining the Persistence of Media-Centered Publicity Strategies". *International Journal of Press/Politics* 21 (4): 490–507.

"Regulations for Internet Users Issued". 2000. TV Myanmar (from BBC Summary of World Broadcasts), 20 January 2000. Available at http://archive.hrea.org/lists/huridocs-tech/markup/msg00416.html.

Reporters Without Borders. 2010a. "Burmese Media Combating Censorship". 22 December 2010. https://rsf.org/en/reports/burmese-media-combating-censorship.

———. 2010b. "Japanese Journalist and Two Burmese Journalists Freed". 10 November 2010. https://rsf.org/en/news/japanese-journalist-and-two-burmese-journalists-freed.

Reuters. 2017. "Myanmar Awards Fourth Telecoms License as Mobile Market Heats Up". 12 January 2017. http://www.reuters.com/article/myanmar-telecoms-idUSL4N1F24KI.

RFA (Radio Free Asia). 2017. "Prominent Myanmar Journalist Released on Bail until Trial on Defamation Charges". 31 July 2017. http://www.rfa.org/english/news/myanmar/prominent-myanmar-journalist-released-on-bail-until-trial-on-defamation-charges-07312017161821.html.

Rogers, B. 2012. *Burma: A Nation at the Crossroads*. London: Rider Books.

Roudakova, N. 2012. "Comparing Processes: Media, 'Transitions', and Historical Change". In *Comparing Media Systems beyond the Western World*, edited by D.C. Hallin and P. Mancini, pp. 246–77. Cambridge: Cambridge University Press.

Samarajiva, R. 2016. "Telecom is Biggest Attractor of FDI in Myanmar". 25 December 2016. *LIRNEasia*. http://lirneasia.net/2016/12/telecom-is-biggest-attractor-of-fdi-in-myanmar/.

San San May. 2016. "Early Newspapers in Burma". Southeast Asia Library Group Newsletter, no. 48 (December). http://www.sealg.org/pdf/newsletter2016.pdf.

San Yamin Aung. 2017. "Journalists Weigh in on Front Page Omission of U Ko Ni's Death in State Media". The Irrawaddy, 1 February 2017. https://www.irrawaddy.com/news/burma/journalists-weigh-in-on-front-page-omission-of-u-ko-nis-death-in-state-media.html.

———. 2018. "Still No Date for Release of Census Findings on Ethnic Populations". *The Irrawaddy*, 21 February 2018. https://www.irrawaddy.com/news/burma/still-no-date-release-census-findings-ethnic-populations.html.

Sandar Lwin. 2013. "Daily Papers Make Debut". *Myanmar Times*, 8 April 2013. https://www.mmtimes.com/national-news/6396-daily-papers-finally-make-debut.html.

Schlaefli, S. 2016. "We're Much More Than Just a Film School". *Myanmar Times*, 25 November 2016. https://www.mmtimes.com/lifestyle/23888-we-re-much-more-than-just-a-film-school.html.

SEAPA. 2011. "Burma – Restraint and Punishment during Election Year". *SEAPA Annual Press Freedom Reports*. Thailand.

Segura, M., and S. Waisbord. 2016. *Media Movements: Civil Society and Media Policy Reform in Latin America*. London: Zed Books.

Sen, K. 2002. "Indonesia: Media and the End of Authoritarian Rule". In *Media Reform: Democratizing the Media, Democratizing the State*, edited by M.E. Price, B. Rozumilowicz, and S. Verhulst, pp. 69–88. London: Routledge.

———. 2011. "Re-forming Media in Indonesia's Transition to Democracy. In *Politics and Media in Twenty-first Century Indonesia: Decade of Democracy*, edited by K. Sen and D.T. Hill, pp. 1–10. Routledge.

Shoon Naing and Aye Min Thant. 2018. "Myanmar Court Jails Reuters Reporters for Seven Years in Landmark Secrets Case". Reuters. https://www.reuters.com/article/us-myanmar-journalists/myanmar-court-jails-reuters-reporters-for-seven-years-in-landmark-secrets-case-idUSKCN1LJ09E.

Siebert, F.S., T. Peterson, and W. Schramm. 1956. *Four Theories of the Press*. Urbana: University of Illinois Press.

Siriyuvasak, U. 2005. "People's Media and Communication Rights in Indonesia and the Philippines". *Inter-Asia Cultural Studies* 6 (2): 245–63.

Sithu Aung Myint. 2018. "Crafting a Case to Secure a Conviction". *Frontier Myanmar*, 16 September 2018. https://frontiermyanmar.net/en/crafting-a-case-to-secure-a-conviction.

Smith, M. 1991. *State of Fear: Censorship in Burma (Myanmar)*. London: ARTICLE 19.

———. 1992. "Confronting Fear with Laughter". *Index on Censorship* 21 (1): 8–10.

———. 1994. *Ethnic Groups in Burma: Development, Democracy and Human Rights*. No. 8 in ASI's Human Rights Series. London: Anti-Slavery International.

Song, S. 2013. "Internet in Myanmar Remains Slow, Unstable, and Affordable to Less than 1% of the Population". *International Business Times*, 9 April 2013. http://www.ibtimes.com/internet-myanmar-remains-slow-unstable-affordable-less-1-population-1402463.

Straits Times. 2017. "Faced with Ban, Myanmar Hardline Ma Ba Tha Monks Change Name". 28 May 2017. http://www.straitstimes.com/asia/se-asia/faced-with-ban-myanmar-hardline-ma-ba-tha-monks-change-name.

Tapsell, R. 2015. "Indonesia's Media Oligarchy and the 'Jokowi Phenomenon'". *Indonesia* 99: 29–50.

Thant Sin. 2017. "U Ko Ni, Respected Legal Adviser of Myanmar's Ruling Party, Assassinated". *Global Voices*, 1 February 2017. globalvoices.org/2017/02/01/u-ko-ni-respected-legal-adviser-of-myanmars-ruling-party-assassinated (accessed 3 February 2017).

Tharapi Than. 2011. "Understanding Prostitutes and Prostitution in Democratic Burma, 1942–62". *South East Asia Research* 19 (3): 537–65.

Trautwein, C. 2015. "Myanmar Named Fourth-fastest-growing Mobile Market in the World by Ericsson". *Myanmar Times*, 20 November 2015. http://www.mmtimes.com/index.php/business/technology/17727-myanmar-named-fourth-fastest-growing-mobile-market-in-the-world-by-ericsson.html.

U Thaung. 1995. *A Journalist, a General and an Army in Burma*. Bangkok: White Lotus.

UNESCO and International Media Support. 2016. *Assessment of Media Development in Myanmar: Based on UNESCO's Media Development Indicators*. Bangkok: UNESCO; Copenhagen: International Media Support.

United Nations. 2008. "Cyclone Nargis OCHA Situation Report No. 27". 4 June 2008. UN Office for the Coordination of Humanitarian Affairs. http://ochaonline.un.org/OchaLinkClick.aspx?link=ocha&docId=1090625.

Villeneuve, N. 2007. "Evasion Tactics". *Index on Censorship* (magazine) 4:71–85.

VOA. 2013. "International Writers Converge in Rangoon for Literature Festival". 4 February 2013. https://www.voanews.com/a/international_writers_converge_on_rangoon_for_literature_festival_irrawaddy_literary/1596985.html.

Voltmer, K. 2013. *The Media in Transitional Democracies*. Cambridge: Polity.

———. 2015. "Converging and Diverging Pathways of Media Transformation". In *Media and Politics in New Democracies: Europe in a Comparative Perspective*, edited by J. Zielonka, pp. 217–30. New York: Oxford University Press.

Wade, F. 2017. *Myanmar's Enemy Within: Buddhist Violence and the Making of Muslim 'Other'*. London: Zed Books.

Weiss, M. 2012. "Politics in Cyberspace: New Media in Malaysia". *fesmedia Asia* series. Friedrich-Ebert-Stiftung.

Zarni Mann. 2013. "Recalling Monk Beatings That Sparked the Saffron Revolution". *The Irrawaddy*, 6 September 2013. https://www.irrawaddy.com/news/burma/recalling-monk-beatings-that-sparked-the-saffron-revolution.html.

Zarny Win. 2001. "Junta Allows New Email Accounts". *The Irrawaddy*, 17 September 2001. http://www2.irrawaddy.com/print_article.php?art_id=3464.

Zielonka, J. 2015. "Introduction: Fragile Democracy, Volatile Politics, and the Quest for a Free Media". In *Media and Politics in New Democracies: Europe in a Comparative Perspective*, edited by J. Zielonka, pp. 1–21. New York: Oxford University Press.

Zon Pan Pwint. 2016. "Vanishing Act: Myanmar's Lost Movie Palaces". *Myanmar Times*, 4 March 2016. http://www.mmtimes.com/index.php/lifestyle/19303-vanishing-act-myanmar-s-lost-movie-palaces.html.

Part I
Structural Constraints and Opportunities

2

Legal Changes for Media and Expression: New Reforms, Old Controls

Gayathry Venkiteswaran, Yin Yadanar Thein and Myint Kyaw

In 2012, Yangon was abuzz with meetings and conferences on media development — something unheard of during the military regime. These meetings followed public announcements by the quasi-civilian Thein Sein government installed in March 2011 of a reform agenda that would include improvements to the media laws. According to the former information minister Ye Htut, these planned reforms date back to 2007, under the former military dictator Than Shwe, when the junta studied options for legal reform (Mclaughlin 2014), while Kean (2018) places the start of the change in 2004 after a high-profile purge of military intelligence. When the National League for Democracy (NLD) formed the government in 2016, expectations were high that technical and procedural problems with the laws and their enforcement would be reviewed and addressed (Htet Naing Zaw 2016). Yet civil society has been disappointed by the lack of political will to bring the laws in line with international norms and standards. Instead, the NLD-led government has continued to use criminal laws to silence journalists and critics. Globally, the media development sector has adopted a rather formulaic approach regarding reform, placing faith in problematic legislative and judicial systems as the arbiters of the practices and regulation of speech and expression. The emphasis that national and international actors in Myanmar place on laws as fundamental to the transition is thus not uncommon, yet it is questionable, especially in a country where the judicial process has been used to imprison critics and censor the media.

This chapter provides an overview of the laws related to media and free expression introduced or changed in Myanmar since 2011. We begin with a review of the literature on media legal reforms during transitions, followed by a mapping of the media laws in Myanmar and issues related to the reform process. We argue that the legal framework, while attempting to undo the controls of the past, has not been radically transformed. The paradigm of control has prevailed during this transition period, and the use of criminal laws has rendered some of the legal changes inadequate to support freedom, public interest, diversity and pluralism in relation to media and expression.

At the start of the political transition, under the Thein Sein administration, the Ministry of Information played a dominant role in driving the agenda, in collaboration with a few select international media-assistance organizations. This coalition influenced how others participated in, or were excluded from, the process of reforming the laws. We argue that despite the top-down structure, growing networks of individuals and activists are raising significant challenges in the form of campaigns and protests against the legal harassment of critics and against poorly drafted laws, resulting in greater public awareness of press freedom and freedom of expression.

Our overview of laws and cases is supplemented here with interviews with journalists and media activists. We also draw from our personal experiences and observations as free expression advocates during the transition period. As part of our work, we have attended, participated in and organized various formal and informal meetings related to media freedom and reform, which has provided insights into the legal reform process we discuss here.

Media Legal Reforms during Political Transitions

Media laws refer to the formal, specific and legally binding tools shaped or driven by a broader set of media policy goals that establish the structure and behaviour of media systems. Legal frameworks for the media are needed for several reasons: the media are a key economic sector, they act as agents of social reproduction that play a constitutive role in the development of social and political formations, and the public role of media cannot be guaranteed by market forces alone (Freedman 2006; McChesney 1998; McQuail 2010). From a rights perspective, the legal framework for media is based on Article 19 of the Universal Declaration of Human Rights and the International Covenant on Civil and Political Rights, which guarantee rights for the media and free speech, while at the same time providing guidelines for permissible restrictions (such as limits to protection based on the rights or reputations of others, national security, public order, public health and morals).[1] In societies undergoing political transition, legal reforms of media are generally included as part of the overall reform agenda. An enabling environment for media is one where the state does not regulate journalists, has limits on its ownership or control of media, and is restricted in its use of laws on criminal defamation, libel or sedition that can impede the work of media (Price and Krug 2000).

Discussions about media reform and the explosion of digital technologies have acknowledged the challenge of addressing digital media convergence. Scholars argue that it is important to recognize public interest and how the public is mediated at the heart of these policies (Cuilenburg and McQuail 2003). Others say that the pervasiveness of information technologies make the boundaries in the field of media policy difficult to discern. As such, media policies and laws should move beyond regulating media types to also deal with the structures of ownership and how content is created, processed, transported, stored and distributed (Braman 2004). Policymakers should also consider whether the conduct and performance of media take public interest into account (McQuail 2010). Attempts to adapt legal frameworks to the revolutionary nature of digital technologies have, however, encountered challenges due to the lack of expertise among policymakers (Braman 2004; Dragomir and Thompson 2014).

But beyond laws and regulations, there are also non-binding rules, conventions and accountability mechanisms that informally govern the media, such as professional codes of ethics, public opinion and political lobbying (McQuail 2010). Studies on media policies have documented two other strategies — policy inaction and policy silences. Policy inaction is the absence of policy. Examples can include not intervening in media editorial decision-making, which can be positive, or creating unintended consequences such as anomalies between the traditional and new media (Papathanassopoulos 2016). Policy silence is a strategic decision taken by elites, through state mechanisms, to promote their hegemonic interests, which could result in the exclusion of certain agendas, stakeholders or real options for the legal framework (Freedman 2014).

The process of lawmaking then raises questions about who benefits from these changes. These are fundamentally political concerns, and do not merely constitute technical or neutral processes that can democratize old repressive legal regimes (Freedman 2006). Law- and policymaking represent the battleground for contrasting interests and the legitimation of ideologies of various actors, including the state and its institutions, political parties, interest groups, media businesses, journalists' associations and international donors and aid agencies. The interaction between different actors, the institutional structures within which they work and the objectives they pursue determine how the different groups get involved in, or are excluded from, the lawmaking process (Freedman 2006). Inevitably, the state and its institutions hold more power than the other stakeholders because they dominate the lawmaking structures and processes.

Literature on media transition point to the challenges facing the new political forces that replace authoritarian regimes and to the interest of the new entrants in retaining control over the media (Voltmer 2013). Weak states are more likely to derail reform because of the inability of the government to provide the conditions necessary for the political expression of the people (Rotberg 2004). The classification of states as strong, weak or failed is based on the ability of the nation-states to deliver political goods that citizens are unable to achieve on their own. These include safety and security, rule of law, respect for human rights, sustainable economic development, and human development (Rotberg 2004). Voltmer (2013) argues that in the process of democratization, the state is strengthened by becoming "capable of implementing and enforcing legislation and the allocation of resources" while at the same time restraining itself so that it "is willing to devolve power and to tolerate and encourage public spaces where divergent views and dissent can be expressed" (p. 135). Often, media policies formulated by new governments, based on promises of reforms and democratization, are mere improvement or succession, "whereby an existing policy or program is succeeded by another" (Papathanassopoulos 2016, p. 2). In a study of selected countries in post-Communist East Central Europe, Milton (2001) found that democratic leaders eventually opted out of their own media reform agenda in favour of their political survival, which included retaining control of the media.

Despite the power and influence of the state in the legal reform process, civil society participation is also significant and can lead to successful media reforms (Rothman 2015; Segura and Waisbord 2016). Policies can be affected by acts of resistance by consumer groups, activists and citizens (Freedman 2006), and this is especially important because the process can be used to raise public consciousness about the value of free speech in a democratic society (Price and Krug 2000). Political openings give civil society an opportunity to form new alliances and initiate campaigns to engage the public and legislators to repeal problematic legal obstacles. It is common for non-governmental organizations or movements that advocate democratization to be supported by international organizations that allocate funds for training and for participation in lawmaking processes to improve the legal frameworks governing freedom of expression and the media (Kumar 2006).

Political and Legal Framework for Media and Expression in Myanmar

This section examines the laws related to media and expression that have been introduced, repealed or amended thus far during the transition. Many attribute the changes taking place in Myanmar to the Seven Step

Roadmap to Disciplined Democracy introduced in 2003, as discussed in the introductory chapter. Some argue that the form Myanmar's democracy will take will be similar to the semi-democracy style with dominant-party rule of Malaysia or Singapore (Min Zin and Joseph 2012) that preserves the role of the military (Jones 2014). Others say the changes are part of the military's strategy for survival and that it intended to control the process of reform "with or without civilian window dressing" (Croissant and Kamerling 2013, p. 122). Because of the military's strong influence, the old mindset has framed the policies and laws being reworked during this transition.

At the outset, several factors have already constrained the reform process and its outcomes. Foremost is the controversial 2008 Constitution of the Republic of the Union of Myanmar.[2] On the one hand, it includes provisions for freedom of expression under Article 354(a) ("to express and publish freely their convictions and opinions"), together with Article 365 on the rights to develop literature, language, culture, art, traditions and religion. On the other, these two constitutional provisions, like many others addressing fundamental civil liberties in Myanmar, are subject to laws on national security, public order, community peace and tranquillity, public morality and, in the case of cultural rights, the preservation of national solidarity. Second, the constitution has concentrated power in the hands of the military.[3] Against this backdrop, the process of lawmaking has been fundamentally dominated by the military junta and, until 2015, by the Union Solidarity and Development Party (USDP) government. The NLD, as the opposition party until it won the November 2015 elections, was less invested in the media reform process, although it had endorsed the military's transition plans (Min Zin and Joseph 2012). It was only when transitioning to form the government that party representatives appeared in public to share their limited plans regarding the media (Kohn 2016).

The administrative or procedural nature of the judicial system also restrains the reform process; the courts go through the motions of hearings and judgements during trials, but with no regard for the principles of the rule of law (Cheesman 2015). Designed to support state institutions, the judiciary has not been a major consideration in ongoing discussions about media reform. Reformers have treated the courts and access to justice as procedures that will have to correct themselves in the new environment (Cheesman 2015). The judiciary in Myanmar is subordinate to other state institutions — namely, the military — and maintains law and order largely through what Cheesman (2015) describes as a "quietening project" (p. 276), or the use of court procedures to immobilize and silence people. Given the country's historically limited judicial independence, laws were applied selectively and arbitrarily by the junta (Hudson-Rodd 2008). As such, the weakness of the system today renders ineffective even the best-designed laws.

The reform process is affected by the broader dynamics of the transition itself, which some observers have described as a fragile power-sharing arrangement between the military and the civilian government (Fuller 2015). In addition, there is a general lack of capacity in the NLD — as well as in the ethnic parties — to engage with civil society, despite the party drawing its legitimacy from the pro-democracy movement (Stokke et al. 2015). This political context not only hinders genuine reform but also deepens the divide between those who have power over and access to the media and information systems and those who do not.

Media and political activists in Myanmar have had to deal with various restrictive laws and regulations, many enacted during the British colonial period. Among them are the Penal Code of 1860 (India Act XLV),[4] the Unlawful Association Act 1908 and the Official Secrets Act 1923. The use of these laws has continued during the transition and will be discussed later in the chapter. For the print media, the junta-era Printers and Publishers Registration Law 1962 — introduced under Ne Win — was notorious for its total control of the sector, as it was used to silence journalists and writers and dictate censorship rules. The law was often used in conjunction with other laws such as the 1950 Emergency Provisions Act (Lintner 2001). It served as a sword of Damocles suspended over the heads of publishers and journalists for more than five decades, until it was replaced by the News Media Law and the Printing and Publishing Enterprise Law, which, as we will see, are significant milestones but which have their own challenges.

Media Laws during the Political Opening

One of the early changes introduced following the political opening was the removal of pre-publication censorship for the print media in August 2012, along with plans to repeal the 1962 Printers and Publishers Registration Law. The first draft law to replace the draconian ordinance was the Media Law written by the Ministry of Information in 2012 with support from UNESCO.[5] However, journalists and publishers resisted the first draft, which they argued was prepared without consultation. The task of coming up with a new draft was then given to the Interim Press Council (IPC). The revised draft, known as the News Media Law,[6] incorporated input from representatives of journalists' associations. While the new draft was an improvement, there was again little meaningful consultation, and the ministry had the final say on its content. As the discussions on the law progressed, the ministry caught the IPC and the rest of the media community by surprise by bulldozing the Printing and Publishing Enterprise Bill through parliament in July 2013 (Brooten 2016). Civil society and the journalists' associations organized a public campaign to reject the law (discussed later in this chapter). However, both the News Media Law and the Printing and Publishing Enterprise Law (PPEL) were eventually passed by the upper and lower houses with little public input or participation from NLD lawmakers.[7]

The News Media Law signals a departure from the old regime by ensuring no pre-publication censorship (Article 5), journalists' right to public information (Art. 6), and recognition of the importance of journalists' safety (Art. 7). It recognizes the role of the media as the fourth estate with full freedoms and rights (Art. 3), including the right to critique the executive, legislative and judicial institutions (Art. 4). However, the law is problematic as it only nullifies orders, directives, notices and declarations made under the 1962 law that restrict freedom of expression and contradict the new law (Art. 32) — it does not prevent the use of other laws to criminalize speech (Human Rights Watch 2016). The law defines news media as "print media, broadcasting media, internet media and other public media services", which is vague and does not recognize the need for different legal structures or regulatory frameworks for the different aspects of content production and dissemination (ARTICLE 19 2014). And while the law provides for the creation of a self-regulatory body, the president and the upper and lower houses of parliament also nominate candidates to this body, in addition to media and civil society representation. The law lacks clarity as to how the council can maintain and assert its independence in such a set-up.

A press council was established early in the transition, even before the media law was enacted, but it attracted controversy. In 2012 the government, under Information Minister Kyaw Hsan, announced the establishment of the twenty-member Myanmar Core Press Council (MCPC) under Article 354 of the constitution. Many journalists shunned the council, which was made up mainly of pro-establishment individuals (Kyaw Su Mon and Ei Ei Toe Lwin 2012). When Aung Kyi was appointed as the new minister of information in August 2012, he dissolved the MCPC and replaced it with an Interim Press Council (IPC) with more members from the journalists' associations (Nyein Nyein 2012). This IPC was tasked with preparing the draft media law, a code of ethics for media and a plan for the safety of journalists; adjudicating complaints against the media; and developing the professional capacity of journalists through training. The IPC became the main body tasked with negotiating with the government in deliberations about the draft laws, even though journalists' associations wanted to engage directly with the state. But the IPC's willingness to accept funds from the government amounting to 50 million kyat (equivalent to US$36,600) drew strong criticism. Some media actors still insist the council lacks independence, even though it transitioned into a permanent structure, now known as the Myanmar Press Council, in 2015 (Ye Mon 2015). Under Article 19(a) of the News Media Law, part of the council's income is sourced from the government budget. Given the history of state control of media, some journalists view this provision as an attempt by the government to use its financial allocation to influence the council. Another criticism is that the council is sidelined by institutions like the military that tend to take their complaints to court instead of seeking council mediation (Kyaw Ye Lynn 2016).

The Broadcast Law, passed in August 2015, was also introduced as one of the media-related legal reforms. Given the smaller number of players in this sector, all of whom have close ties to the military junta, it was not surprising that discussions about the law were confined to those with vested interests. This included the Ministry of Information and its state broadcasters, as well as the private companies that have joint broadcasting ventures with the ministry, namely, Forever Group and SkyNet, the latter owned by Shwe Than Lwin Co Ltd. Apart from state and commercial broadcasters, the Broadcast Law introduced two new categories: public service broadcasting and community media. The former was envisaged vis-à-vis a transformation of the state media into public service broadcasters, while the latter was intended to provide more opportunities for media at the local level, particularly in the ethnic states.[8] However, there is little information regarding how these media will eventually be established. While the law allows for more private broadcasters to operate in the market, the state broadcaster retains an unfair advantage over any new entrants or independent players. Observers have expressed frustration over the delay in approving by-laws or regulations which would operationalize the law (Lun Min Mang 2016). In June 2018 the law was amended to prevent monopolies in the broadcast sector, which is a positive change, but another amendment on the creation of temporary licences will increase the risk that broadcasters will self-censor and underinvest in their channels. As mentioned in Chapter 1 in this volume, five private companies have won temporary bids to broadcast television, but only through joint ventures with the Ministry of Information as content service providers for the state's MRTV digital free-to-air channels.

The Public Service Media Bill, tabled in parliament in March 2014, sought to clarify the role of public service broadcasting by legislating state support not only for its broadcasters but also for state-owned newspapers: the Myanmar language *Myanmar Alin* and *Kyemon* (The Mirror) and *Global New Light of Myanmar* (in English). The proposed law drew much criticism, especially for its inclusion of state newspapers, and for its weak guarantees of editorial independence, content diversity and pluralism, or public participation in the governance mechanism (ARTICLE 19 2013). The bill was withdrawn in March 2015 due to public pressure (DVB 2015). The ministry claimed the withdrawal would allow it to improve the draft (MNA 2015). This was the first time a government bill was withdrawn after it was tabled in parliament. Journalists' associations and members of the Myanmar Press Council say state media should be privatized and not given any special privileges, and that they would only support the idea of a public service broadcaster if it was fully independent of the state (Pyae Thet Phyo 2017).

The Telecommunications Law is the most controversial new media law. It was drafted under the Thein Sein administration with support from the World Bank, but fewer groups got involved in the process than with the media laws. Representatives of non-governmental organizations (NGOs) criticized the drafting process, as well as the World Bank, for favouring private and state interests over the protection of human rights (Igoe 2014).⁹ The law sets the framework for the liberalization of the sector, allows private sector operators an allocation of spectrum, and establishes rules regarding competition and access. The Telecommunications Law regulates the licensing, numbering, competition, spectrum allocation and interconnectivity targets in the sector. The law has been widely criticized for the scope of violations related to content and content distribution and its aggressive use during the transition against journalists, activists and ordinary individuals, especially under Section 66(d). Section 66(d) is a criminal law provision that permits penalties of up to three years in prison for "extorting, coercing, restraining wrongfully, defaming, disturbing, causing undue influence or threatening any person using a telecommunications network". The law initially did not allow for bail but this was changed in August 2017.

Other Laws under Review during the Transition

Apart from media-specific laws, the Thein Sein government also amended other laws that affect the work of journalists, activists and the creative industries. The 2004 Electronic Transactions Law, another legal tool used by earlier regimes against bloggers, activists and journalists, was amended in 2014 to reduce the severity of punishments to three to seven years (from the earlier seven to fifteen years). Although the law had been criticized in the past for its overly broad and ill-defined offences, which included sending or receiving information detrimental to national security, law, order, public tranquillity, national solidarity, the national economy and national culture, these offences were retained in the 2014 amendment (Freedom House 2014). The new Peaceful Assembly and Peaceful Procession Law enacted in 2011 was considered an improvement, but it has been selectively enforced. Protests led by monks against the international community on issues related to the crisis in Rakhine State and the award of a telecommunications licence to Qatar-based Ooredoo were allowed to proceed, while those organized by student activists campaigning on education reform or farmers fighting against land grabs — and journalists covering these protests — were targeted by the authorities (Phuong Nguyen 2012; *The Irrawaddy* 2014). Media workers who protest in public have also been threatened under this law, as we will show later. Prompted by the NLD's repealing of two security laws in 2016 (Law Safeguarding the State from the Danger of Subversive Elements [State Protection Law] and the Emergency Provisions Act 1950), which demonstrates it has the means and power to fix repressive and undemocratic laws, supporters expected to see further reforms. Yet subsequent changes to the law on assembly were more restrictive and they were met with considerable push-back from civil society and even the Tatmadaw representatives in parliament (Pyae Thet Phyo 2018). In March 2017 the government introduced the Law Protecting the Privacy and Security of Citizens, which is vaguely worded and does not spell out how privacy will be protected. Privacy risks are discussed in more detail by Kamran Emad and Erin McAuliffe in this volume. Even more worrying was the inclusion of criminal defamation in this privacy law, as Article 8(f) can be used for silencing critics. The article states that "no one shall act in any way to slander or harm [a citizen's] reputation", and anyone found guilty under this article is liable to a prison sentence between six months and three years and a fine between 300,000 and 1.5 million kyat (approximately US$200–1,000). Section 66(d) of the Telecommunications Law was amended to remove filing of third-party complaints, meaning that only those affected by a case are allowed to bring suit. Article 8(f) of the privacy law, however, allows for third-party complaints. There are nearly ten cases under this provision, and it now numbers among the laws that include criminal defamation. The others are the Penal Code, News Media Law, Telecommunications Law and the Electronic Transactions Law.

 Discussions on laws on the right to information and anti-hate speech were initiated early in the transition. That Myanmar signed on to the Extractive Industry Transparency Initiative (EITI) in 2014 could have led, as a logical next step, to the development of a right to information law (World Bank 2014b). For journalists and the public, one of the main barriers to access to public information is the Official Secrets Act 1923 that is still in use and which protects state institutions and public officials from scrutiny and disclosures. Activists say the government invited civil society groups to discussions on a law providing for the right to information which was shared with them in late 2017. There has not, however, been a final draft or an official announcement of its tabling. Journalists could potentially use the News Media Law to seek information, but they say that public and military officials remain unwilling to provide information. The environment supports a culture of favouritism among media, in which state-owned and government-friendly media have unfettered access to regional parliamentary sessions and government departments and their activities, while others (mostly private media) do not. Meanwhile, the draft law against hate speech, known as the Interfaith Harmonious Coexistence Law, was submitted to parliament in September 2017 (DVB 2017), but as of this writing in late 2018 there have been no further announcements or debates on the law. Human rights groups say enacting a law against hate speech can be contentious because of the challenge of determining the rights and offences and of providing clear definitions of hate speech and how it spreads on social media. Furthermore, those minorities whose citizenship is not recognized, in particular the Rohingya, will be excluded from any proposed protection (CIVICUS 2017).

Unshackled but Not Free

While welcoming the government's removal of some legal barriers facing media, practitioners and advocates for freedom of expression have criticized the lack of guarantees to rights and protection, especially as other laws are still being used to stifle expression (see Table 2.1 for a timeline of the cases related to media and free expression). Pre-publication censorship may have been removed but the current media laws cannot shield media workers from contempt of court, criminal defamation, intellectual property infringement or incitement to hatred, among other charges. Even though the Printing and Publishing Enterprise Law (PPEL) has a less prohibitive licensing regime than the law it replaced, it still gives the government the power to control press licences, news websites and foreign news agencies, and to ban reports said to be

TABLE 2.1
Timeline of Policy Announcements, Legal Changes and Criminal Cases Related to Media and Free Expression

Period	Information Ministers	Laws Passed and Policy Announcements	Examples of the Use of Laws against Media, Activists and Politicians during the Transition
Military Regime and Quasi-civilian Government			
13 Sept 2002 – 27 Aug 2012	Brig. General Kyaw Hsan	• Media reform announcements by President Thein Sein in March 2011. • Peaceful Demonstrations and Gathering Law 2011. • Myanmar Core Press Council (MCPC) formed (lasts only a few months).	**Penal Code** • Ministry of Mines threatens criminal defamation against *The Voice* in March 2012 over its report based on the Auditor General's Report on misappropriation of funds (Article 499).
27 Aug 2012 – 29 July 2014	Rtd. Major General Aung Kyi	• Press Scrutiny and Registration Division and pre-publication censorship abolished in August 2012. • Parliament passes Printing and Publishing Enterprise Law (2013). • Parliament passes Telecommunications Law (2013). • Interim Press Council set up in September 2012 to replace the MCPC.	**Penal Code** • Reporter Ma Khine of *Eleven Media* sentenced to three months imprisonment in December 2012 for defamation, trespassing, and "using abusive language" in Kayah State (Article 500 [defamation], Article 451 [trespassing], Article 294 [using abusive language]). • In April 2014 a court in Magway sentenced DVB reporter Ko Zaw Pe and the parent of a student to a year in prison on charges of trespassing and disturbing a civil servant over an interview seeking information about a Japanese-funded scholarship scheme in the Magway Region Education Department.

Legal Changes for Media and Expression

			• Arrest and conviction of five staff members of the *Bi Mon Te Nay Journal* in July 2014 over an article which mistakenly claimed opposition leader Aung San Suu Kyi and ethnic opposition leaders had formed an interim government (Article 505[b] on incitement against the State). **Official Secrets Act 1923** • Four reporters and the chief executive of the (now-defunct) *Unity Journal* sentenced to ten years imprisonment with hard labour in July 2014 after reporting on a military chemical weapons factory on land confiscated from local farmers in Magwe Region. They were eventually given amnesty in 2016. **News Media Law** • The first case filed under the law, for ethical breach under Article 25(b) in November 2014 against *Myanmar Thandawsint*. **Penal Code** • Htin Lin Oo, a writer and former information officer for the NLD, received a two-year jail term for blasphemy for a speech said to have condemned religious extremism in the country (Article 295[a], known as the blasphemy provision, and Article 298). • Students protesting against a proposed education bill faced a brutal crackdown in March 2015. Journalists covering the crackdown also faced similar threats (unlawful assembly, rioting etc.).
1 Aug 2014 – 30 Mar 2016	Lt. Col. Ye Htut (also spokeperson for President Thein Sein since February 2013 until March 2016)	• Parliament passes News Media Law (2014) and Broadcasting Law (2015). • Electronic Transactions Law is amended (2014). • Peaceful Assembly Law amended in 2016 (known as Peaceful Assembly and Peaceful Procession Law). • Election of members to the News Media Council in October 2015, as provided for under the News Media Law. Some media and journalist representatives boycott the elections.	

TABLE 2.1 (continued)

Period	Information Ministers	Laws Passed and Policy Announcements	Examples of the Use of Laws against Media, Activists and Politicians during the Transition
			• The editor Than Htaik Thu and deputy chief reporter Hsan Moe Tun of *Myanmar Post* were sentenced to two months in prison with hard labour in March 2015 over a story said to have taken a swipe at the military representatives in parliament (Article 500 on defamation). **Printing and Publishing Enterprises Law, Article 4** • In November 2015, five men were charged for publishing a 2016 calendar which contained the term "Rohingya" on the grounds of threatening public order and tranquillity. They were eventually fined an amount equivalent to US$800 each, although the Penal Code was applied to arrest them for a short period. **Telecommunications Law, Section 66(d)** • Activist Patrick Kum Ja Lee was one of the first to be charged under the Telecommunications Law. He was arrested in October 2015 for his Facebook post mocking the military. • Within days, Chaw Sandi Htun was arrested for posting a montage on her Facebook page showing that the Myanmar military's re-designed uniform matches the colour of Aung San Suu Kyi's dress. • A month later, poet Maung Saungkha was arrested in connection with a verse he posted on social media suggesting that he had a tattoo of the president (Thein Sein) on his penis. • Each of the three was sentenced to six months in prison.

Elected Government under the NLD			
April 2016 –	Pe Myint	• Emergency Law and State Protection Law repealed in 2016. • Regulations for the Broadcasting Law pending. • Parliament passes Citizens Personal Privacy and Personal Security Law (2017). • Telecommunications Law 2013 amended in August 2017.	**Telecommunications Law, Section 66(d)** • The army filed a complaint against the chief editor and a senior reporter of *7Day Daily* in June 2016 for publishing a story quoting former general Shwe Mann's message to graduates of the Defense Service Academy urging his former colleagues to work for the country's newly elected democratic government. The military claimed the article could lead to disunity in the army and encourage treason. The complaint was later dropped after the newspaper published an apology to the military in a state-owned media as part of a negotiated settlement (charges were also filed under the Penal Code [Article 131 on offences related to the army, navy etc.]). • *Eleven Media* chief executive Than Htut Aung and chief editor Wai Phyo were sued by the Yangon Division chief minister Phyo Min Thein in November 2016 over an editorial accusing him of taking bribes. The two were released on bail after being detained for nearly two months. • Police arrested *The Voice Daily* chief editor Kyaw Min Swe and satirist British Ko Ko Maung in June 2017 for allegedly defaming the military over a satirical article that questioned the country's peace process. They were first charged under the Telecommunications Law but additional complaints were filed under the News Media Law. The charges were eventually dropped. • *Myanmar Now* editor-in-chief Swe Win faced two charges filed by followers of the Buddhist monk Wirathu, who alleged his comment had insulted the ultranationalist monk. As of September 2017, one of the complaints was dropped; the other, in Mandalay, continues.

TABLE 2.1 (continued)

Period	Information Ministers	Laws Passed and Policy Announcements	Examples of the Use of Laws against Media, Activists and Politicians during the Transition
			Electronic Transactions Law, Article 34(d) • *Eleven Media* filed a complaint in July 2016 against *Mizzima* editor-in-chief and managing director Soe Myint, columnist Sithu Aung Myint and the editor-in-charge of the Myanmar edition, Myo Thant, over an article criticising *Eleven Media*'s reportage about the Myanmar Peace Centre. The case was later dropped. **Unlawful Associations Act 1908** • In June 2017, *The Irrawaddy*'s senior reporter Lawi Weng (aka Thein Zaw) and DVB's Aye Nai and Ko Pyae Phone Aung were arrested by the military, along with four other civilians, on their way back from a reporting trip about drug burning in an area in Shan State controlled by the Ta'ang National Liberation Army. They were held at the Hsipaw Prison for over two months before the charges were dropped. **Official Secrets Act 1923** • Two Reuters journalists, Wa Lone and Kyaw Soe Oo, were arrested on 12 December 2017 while they were investigating how the Myanmar military looted and burned a Rohingya village, killed ten men and then buried the bodies in a mass grave. They were arrested after a dinner with two police officers who handed documents to them, which were then used to accuse them of breaching the law for possessing alleged confidential documents. The trial exposed inconsistencies in the testimonies by the police witnesses, including one who admitted the two journalists were framed. The Myanmar military admitted to its role in the killings that were highlighted in Wa Lone and Kyaw Soe Oo's investigative report, and seven soldiers have been jailed. Despite international pressure, the two were found guilty and sentenced to seven years in jail. Their appeal was rejected in January 2019.

harmful to national security, public order and the rule of law, or that insult religion or violate the constitution (Art. 7). Together with the Penal Code, the PPEL still subjects printers and publishers to punitive action.

Journalists say the guarantees to access public information and to safety in the News Media Law have yet to materialize. Nai Kasauh Mon, chief editor of the Mon News Agency and a former executive director of Burma News International (a network of independent ethnic news media outlets), said in an interview that those working in the ethnic states face particular challenges when they need to get information from the military or local officials. "There are no spokespersons who can talk to the media, and when we go to the government departments, the officials say they have no authority to make statements. This happens despite the guarantee in the law" (personal communication, 8 June 2017). Seng Mai, a chief editor based in Myitkyina, Kachin State, says she fears cronies of the military regime will quickly try to buy and establish TV or radio stations, especially in the ethnic states, posing a challenge for smaller ethnic media outlets (personal communication, 16 February 2016).

Although it abolished pre-publication censorship in August 2012, the Thein Sein administration did not adopt a hands-off approach for the news media. The promise of media freedom rang hollow when several media outlets and journalists have been subjected to harsh laws for their reportage. In February 2014, four reporters and the chief executive of the (now-defunct) *Unity Journal* were arrested for violating the Official Secrets Act 1923 for their report about a military chemical weapons factory, allegedly built on land confiscated from local farmers in Magwe Region. The five were sentenced in July 2014 to ten years imprisonment with hard labour. The sentences were eventually reduced and in April 2016 they were released under a presidential pardon, soon after the NLD took office. The law was used again in the high-profile arrests and convictions of two Reuters journalists, Wa Lone and Kyaw Soe Oo, who were investigating the military's role in the killings of Rohingya in Rakhine state following the military crackdown in August 2017. News outlets, including Reuters, reported the witness testimony of a police officer that the reporters were framed when the police handed them documents later said to be confidential. Yet on 3 September 2018, Wa Lone and Kyaw Soe Oo were sentenced to seven years imprisonment, minus time already served. Their first appeal at the regional court was rejected in January 2019.

Article 505(b) of the Penal Code was used in the case of three editors and two publishers of the *Bi Mon Te Nay Journal* arrested in July 2014 on charges of inciting against the state for an article which mistakenly claimed then opposition leader Aung San Suu Kyi and ethnic opposition leaders had formed an interim government. The defendants were first charged under the Emergency Provisions Act for "causing public alarm and undermining security of the state", but these charges were later dropped and replaced by charges under the Penal Code (Lun Min Mang and Ye Mon 2014, ¶7). The five were convicted and sentenced to two years in jail, but they were subsequently released as part of a mass amnesty by President Thein Sein in July 2015. The journal has since shut down.

In November 2014 the first case was filed under the News Media Law. The Information Ministry filed charges against eleven staff members of *Myanmar Thandawsint*, for describing then president Thein Sein's words as "gibberish, irrational, cheap and inconsistent ... completely nonsensical, absurd and insane" (AFP 2014, ¶5) in their 9 October issue. These comments were attributed to political scientist Myo Yan Naung Thein and NLD co-founder and patron Tin Oo in an interview. The ministry said the publication had breached ethical standards as stipulated in the law. However, press freedom advocates argued that the ministry's action forced a narrow interpretation of the law where protection of reputation is concerned, and that the law could easily be abused to silence the media (SEAPA 2014). Nine of the staff were acquitted, but the chief editor Kyaw Swa Win and deputy editor Ant Khaung Min were fined one million kyat (US$855) each for the charges under Article 25(b) of the law (Naw Noreen 2015).

Self-regulation as a New Layer of Control?

In theory the role of a press council is to promote press freedom and ethical practices among journalists as well as to mediate public complaints. But the Myanmar Press Council has largely been ignored by government authorities and the military, which have resorted to using criminal laws against individuals they allege have criticized them.

Several council members believe that once cases are filed in the courts, mediation cannot proceed for fear of facing contempt of court. Yet, even if the council is faced with contempt, as a body with the mandate to adjudicate complaints against the media, it should challenge any such court ruling. Given Myanmar's weak judiciary, cases that do end up in court related to criminal defamation or other national security breaches are always decided in favour of the complainants, especially military and government officials. All individuals charged under Section 66(d) of the Telecommunications Law have been convicted by the courts (Free Expression Myanmar 2017). The military's insistence on pursuing legal charges point to its disregard of the media's self-regulatory mechanism. The case of the *Myanmar Post* editor Than Htaik Thu and deputy chief reporter Hsan Moe, who were sentenced to two months in prison with hard labour under the Penal Code for criticizing the military, and the arrest, trial and sentencing of the two Reuters journalists discussed earlier, highlight the power of the military as a stumbling block to the effectiveness of the press council as a self-regulatory mechanism. Furthermore, there are concerns that the council could be another layer of control over the media, as the government and legislature can nominate names to the council (Htike Nanda Win 2018).

In the broadcast sector, two regulatory bodies will be created once by-laws are enacted under the Broadcast Law. The first is the National Broadcasting Development Authority, an inter-agency body composed of heads and senior officers from ministries responsible for information, home affairs and defence. The authority will determine the overall plans for broadcasting development and management of the spectrum, allocate broadcasting services and supervise broadcast-related activities. The second, the National Broadcasting Council, will be comprised of members nominated by the president and the speakers of the two houses in parliament; each of them will nominate six candidates, nine of whom will be appointed (Art. 12). The nominees should be those with expertise or backgrounds in broadcasting, telecommunications, law, business management and finance, or consumer protection and citizens' rights (Art. 7). The duties of the appointed members will include licensing, the creation of policies, rules and regulations for the law based on consultations, supporting human resources and professional development, and publishing and adopting broadcasting codes of conduct. While the role of the council is close to what is needed in terms of a regulatory body, the status of the National Broadcasting Development Authority is unclear, and it has been given powers to issue notification orders, directives and procedures (Art. 106[b]) that could conflict and interfere with those of the council. The president also wields significant power over the council in terms of appointments and removals, a situation that could be open to abuse. Scholars studying the outcome of media reforms in Western Balkan states note that because the processes there have mainly been top-down initiatives, laws intended to promote public service broadcasting and self-regulatory mechanisms increased the risk of these institutions being politicized or re-taken by the state (Irion and Jusic 2013).

Silencing Critics

Censorship of online content and expression has increased significantly during the transition. Activist groups such as Athan have documented 150 criminal defamation cases under the Telecommunications Law for online expression as of 9 September 2018.[10] Eleven of these were filed during the Thein Sein administration (from the law's enactment in 2013 until March 2016), and five resulted in convictions and sentences. The bulk of the cases have been reported since the NLD came into power in April 2016 and the party is among the chief complainants, along with public officials, the military and other individuals. Journalists are among those accused of defamation under Section 66(d) of the law, including staff of *7Day Daily*, *Eleven Media*, *The Voice Daily* and *Myanmar Now*. Monitoring by Free Expression Myanmar (2017) shows that over two-thirds of the defendants were political party members, human rights defenders, journalists and others actively involved in criticizing or monitoring those in power. *Myanmar Now* editor-in-chief Swe Win faces criminal defamation charges following an accusation by a follower of the radical Buddhist organization Ma Ba Tha for his criticism of radical monk Wirathu, who had praised those behind the assassination of prominent lawyer Ko Ni (Lawi Weng 2017). As of September 2018, Swe Win has had to make thirty-four appearances at the court in Mandalay where the police report was first lodged against him. "The constant reporting is meant to harass me by making me appear in court over and over again even when nothing happens. They are psychologically attacking me."[11] While there have been public campaigns against Section 66(d) of the law (see the chapter by Htaike Htaike Aung and Wai Myo Htut in this volume), Swe Win worries that public support for him is diminishing over time as the court case drags on.

The Telecommunications Law initially made it easy for anyone to lodge complaints, and the cases observed during the transition appear to have been processed speedily by the police and the courts in a manner consistent with the years under military rule when dissidents were denied counsel or had their cases resolved after short hearings (Cheesman 2015). Even though the law was amended in August 2017 to make the offences bailable, and to restrict the complainants to those directly affected by the alleged offences, it retains the criminalization of defamation. Analysis of the use of the law showed that no complaints were lodged under the three grounds that were eventually removed by the amendment: bullying, wrongful restraint, and exerting undue influence (Free Expression Myanmar 2017). Critics say the amendments merely "played around the edges" of the law and that the NLD was deliberate in preventing wider improvements or a total repeal (Spencer, Zar Chi Oo and Yin Yadanar Thein 2017, ¶4). The government's justification for keeping the law is the perceived higher impact of online defamation and hate speech compared to offline expression (Reuters 2017).

In this environment it is not surprising that journalists and activists resort to self-censorship and avoid public interest issues that could implicate powerful institutions such as the military and the ultra-nationalist Buddhist organization Ma Ba Tha. In a case that drew international criticism in June 2017, three journalists and four other civilians were detained by the military on their return from a reporting trip about drug burning in an area in Shan State controlled by the Ta'ang National Liberation Army. They were accused under the Unlawful Associations Act 1908 of associating with groups declared illegal by the state. They were held at Hsipaw Prison for more than two months before the charges were dropped. The military stated in a letter to the Myanmar Press Council that the withdrawal of the charges constituted "wiping the slate clean" (*The Irrawaddy* 2017, ¶2), although some journalists felt this was done to curry the media's favour in light of the crisis in northern Rakhine state.[12]

Journalists' lives have also been threatened because of their work. In 2014, freelance reporter Aung Kyaw Naing (Par Gyi), who reported on the conflict area at the Thai border, was murdered by military officers while in their custody (CPJ 2014). Two soldiers were acquitted by the military court, and the family's petition to the Supreme Court for a proper investigation into the murder was rejected, raising suspicion about the military's influence over the judiciary. Another journalist, Oo Oo Nyein, who reported on allegations relating to security forces in Kachin State for *Hot News*, was repeatedly harassed under Article 500 of the Penal Code, under Article 25(b) of the News Media Law in 2016, and Article 17(1) of the Unlawful Association Act in 2017. The complaints were initiated by members of the security forces (Paing Soe 2017).

Overall, the much-lauded legal reform of the media has seen many of the restrictions from the period of the military junta and the administration of Thein Sein retained and new restrictions introduced under the NLD government. Using both the old and new laws, the NLD government, the military and other non-state actors target journalists and activists for work that is vital to the democratization process. As state counsellor, Aung San Suu Kyi has repeatedly mentioned the importance of peace and national reconciliation. For her, this seems to mean gaining the support of the military and ethnic armed groups at any cost. This could explain her silence on the military's violations of freedom of expression and her lack of public commitment to improving laws on media and expression. Despite Aung San Suu Kyi's rhetoric on the rule of law, neither she nor her government has provided a holistic plan for the reform of the legal and judicial systems. On the contrary, she has undermined the rule of law in cases involving the media and expression, the latest involving the prosecution and jailing of the two Reuters journalists. She not only prejudiced the court by publicly stating that the journalists were guilty, but she also supported the court despite the multiple violations of rule of law throughout (Goldberg 2018). In this case the country under the NLD government appears to constitute a weak state as described by Rotberg (2004) and Voltmer (2013), as the government has not stopped the abuse of laws by institutions such as the military, and it is also itself a perpetrator of human rights violations. For the most part, human rights groups have reported not being adequately consulted in the lawmaking processes. In response, they have organized several campaigns and actions to resist these repressive laws and to protest against the crackdowns on media and activists.

People's Campaigns against Repressive Laws

When Myanmar began to open, activists and media outlets both inside and outside the country became more open with their work and found opportunities to establish new alliances and to stake a claim in the reform agenda. In the beginning, due to long-held suspicions and a mutual lack of trust, most grass-roots and civil society organizations kept a safe distance from political parties, even if they may have collaborated on specific issues (personal communication with Aung Myo Min, 7 February 2016). Civil society was divided on various issues, but the culture of mistrust has been slowly changing. In October 2014, for example, more than six hundred NGOs came together to discuss the challenges of the transition at a civil society forum, forming coalitions on specific issues such as the right to information. To respond to the spate of arrests under the Telecommunications Law, twenty-two civil society groups came together in late 2016 to protest against and lobby for the repeal of Section 66(d) of the law.

During the drafting of the media laws, journalists' associations organized signature campaigns and protests when they disagreed with the draft texts or when their positions had been excluded from the deliberations. In 2013 the Myanmar Journalists Network (MJN), Myanmar Journalists Association (MJA) and Myanmar Journalists Union (MJU) organized a campaign to raise public awareness about the Printing and Publishing Enterprise Law. They launched a petition to prevent the adoption of the law and travelled to media houses across the country to collect signatures. Although the law was eventually passed, the parliamentary committee responsible delayed its debate and responded to the complaints from the media community. These efforts also made clear that journalists from various media outlets had a common cause and could be organized to defend their rights. Senior editor and media reformer Thiha Saw considered the formation of these journalists' associations a significant part of the transition. "This was the first time we ever saw these types of associations in the country. Myanmar journalists had never before had independent associations to represent them.... The associations have pushed through a number of results, working not only alone, but also together" (International Media Support 2015). When editors and journalists were targeted by the Telecommunications Law, they formed, in June 2017, the Protection Committee for Myanmar Journalists, to focus on the welfare of media personnel.

In 2012, journalists formed an ad hoc committee to tackle press freedom issues. One of its most visible early actions was to organize a march to several locations in Yangon, with the marchers wearing black T-shirts bearing the slogans "Stop Killing Press". The protest was in response to the suspension of two publications — *The Voice Weekly* and *The Envoy* — that the government said had published stories that had been censored by the Press Scrutiny and Registration Division. More than a hundred journalists conducted a sit-down protest outside the Myanmar Peace Centre in Yangon. Half of the members of the crowd were later threatened with charges of violating the Peaceful Assembly and Peaceful Procession Law. In 2014, freelance journalist Yae Khe was arrested for violating Article 18 of the law after organizing a protest in Bago in support of greater media freedom and the release of jailed journalists. The police had not given him permission to hold the protest, but a hundred people turned up to it and Yae Khe was arrested the following day. Similar protests in other areas, reportedly, were allowed, pointing to the arbitrary application of the law.

In March 2015, during an international media conference, freelance journalist Soe Yazar Tun held up a placard in the main conference hall to protest against the detention of two journalists who were covering student protests in Letpadan, Bago region. The MJN had boycotted the conference because the host, the Ministry of Information, refused to take responsibility for the detentions and arrests of two other journalists who were covering students protesting against a controversial education bill. Soe Yazar Tun's action took many journalists by surprise, but their wide support for it indicated their disappointment with the ministry. In response to another case of harassment by the military, journalists and photographers changed their Facebook profile pictures on 29 June 2016 in solidarity with the newspaper *7Day Daily*. After the military filed a complaint under Section 131 of the Penal Code over an article they alleged cast them as being disloyal to the country, *7Day* published an apology, a move that was criticized by the media community. The provision relates to abetting mutiny and carries a maximum sentence of ten years imprisonment. Following the sentencing of Wa Lone and Kyaw Soe Oo of Reuters, activists and journalists planned a march for 6 September 2018 in solidarity with the two. At first the organizers were informed they would not be able to proceed, but then a day before the event they were told that they could go ahead. The risks associated with public protests continue to be a real threat for civil society actors who challenge the state, including for journalists who join the protests or report on them.

Representatives of journalists' organizations have been frustrated with the Thein Sein and NLD governments, both of which have reneged on promises to include civil society recommendations for improvements to such laws as the News Media Law. To some extent the old model of dealing with a "recognized" body has been maintained; i.e., the government has formally engaged with the body it created — the Interim Myanmar Press Council, now known as the Myanmar Press Council — but it is only for show. On a number of occasions when journalists' groups have raised issues directly with the government or the military, formal responses have only been sent to the press council for dissemination to the media community.[13] Journalists have also complained about the lack of meaningful consultation related to the Broadcast Law. As the sector is dominated by state television and radio stations through direct state ownership or as joint ventures with select private companies, neither the public nor media NGOs are adequately consulted or given the opportunity to provide feedback on the laws. On the contrary, the new laws that have been introduced have for the most part been drafted by the state with the help of foreign consultants, and only then presented to civil society groups for their feedback. On the one hand, media groups, including the formerly exiled ones, have been invited to meetings to discuss media reforms and to the annual media development conferences (held for the first time in 2012), but, on the other hand, these groups say the processes — including setting the conference agenda — are dominated by the Ministry of Information, UNESCO and a small number of international media development organizations. Local journalists and activists are excluded from many of the discussions on draft legislation. Former editor and press council vice-chair Pe Myint noted that the media community was relatively weaker than the state and politicians in power. He said the media failed to influence the bargaining and negotiation process involving the laws that directly affect their work.[14] Little has changed since then to enable civil society and media involvement.

The absence of meaningful engagement is more pronounced for civil society actors from the ethnic states when confronting state institutions, particularly if the representatives are women. Women activists have reported in interviews that they are sometimes excluded from discussions, or that their voices are drowned out by those expressing Yangon-centric interests. Women editors say the discussions have failed to take into account how the draft laws would benefit them or the kinds of impact they could have (Cunningham 2016). To remedy this situation, a group of women journalists formed the Myanmar Women Journalists' Society in 2016 to counter gender-based discrimination and raise awareness of the experiences of women journalists. Similarly, networks of journalists have been formed in different ethnic states — such as the Southern Myanmar Journalist Network and the Chin Media Network — so that journalists can organize themselves in order to engage with other stakeholders. With the growing number of associations representing journalists, it is important to critically analyse their motives, their effectiveness in advocacy, whether the presence of many groups reflects diversity of voices or divisions in the media community, and how these will influence media reforms.

Conclusion: Change without Reform

There have been clear changes to Myanmar's media laws. The removal of pre-publication censorship rules in 2012 was not merely a symbolic act; it was a significant step towards freeing the media and creating self-regulatory mechanisms. However, given that historically the country has had an over-legislated environment and a weak judiciary, the attention placed on legislation by the Ministry of Information, international experts and media development organizations without the concurrent transformation of relevant institutions is problematic. This is especially true because Myanmar is a weak state; the junta was a repressive regime, and all predictions point to the military remaining a defining institution in legal reform of the media due to its aggressive attempts to prevent the media from performing their duties. During the many high-profile examples of action taken by the military against journalists, the government has tended to remain silent.

The NLD government has not found the right balance between strengthening its capacity to enforce protection and restraining itself from being an agent of repression. *Myanmar Now*'s Swe Win, reflecting on his need to regularly report to the courts since early 2017, concludes that legal reforms have thus far failed, citing the example of the Telecommunications Law. "The law was enacted by the former government and then amended by the current government two months after my lawsuit started. But they didn't decriminalize [defamation] and there is still a heavy punishment. Both governments have failed." This sentiment highlights the stark reality that the NLD does not prioritize media reform and, worse still, that it uses the laws to silence dissent.

Myanmar journalists may be able to report more freely and may have access to information and areas that used to be off-limits, but post-opening coverage is still risky. In this volume the interview with journalism trainer Ye Naing Moe, the chapters by Eaint Thiri Thu, Lawi Weng, and Susan Banki and Ja Seng Ing echo the aforementioned cases in demonstrating how such risk is especially true when covering conflicts in the ethnic states or accessing information that implicates the military or the government. Nevertheless, journalists and activists are able to express their concerns about the laws and their abuses through various means, including exhibitions, protests, petitions, through journalists' organizations and meetings with officials and elected representatives.

There are some advantages to focusing on laws during the transition. For one, it forces people with different interests, agendas, expertise and concerns to engage in conversations and debates about the norms and standards they want, given the country's social, cultural, historical and political contexts. At another level, while the laws may not be ideal or adequately meet international human rights standards (PEN Myanmar 2017), they can be used to lobby for further change and to push the boundaries of freedom and rights.

The ability to transform the recent changes into real reform in the future will depend on at least four factors. The first is whether the NLD government will consider a moratorium on the criminalization of journalism and free speech in order to demonstrate its commitment to democratization and the rule of law. The current trend shows the persistent use of both old and new laws against the media and critics of the government or military, which has the effect of silencing healthy discussion. Next, there has to be meaningful consultation with civil society and other key players to allow for substantial input from the public on policy decisions. The government's practice of only engaging with select groups should be replaced by a more open and inclusive outreach. State and civil society actors should also consider interventions outside the legal framework, especially when it comes to countering hate speech. Thirdly, it is important that the legal framework better reflects media convergence given the dynamic growth of new technologies in Myanmar. There is a need to more narrowly define criminal offences related to speech and the media, and at the same time expand the safeguards available for the public. Finally, it will be incumbent on the media community and civil society to keep up the momentum and pressure on the government to ensure that the gains made are not rolled back in the years to come.

Notes

1. See the UN Office of the High Commissioner on Human Rights website for the detailed provisions of the International Covenant on Civil and Political Rights: http://www.ohchr.org/EN/ProfessionalInterest/Pages/CCPR.aspx.
2. The text of the constitution can be accessed at http://www.burmalibrary.org/docs5/Myanmar_Constitution-2008-en.pdf.
3. The armed forces are headed by the commander-in-chief, who is not obliged to report to the president or parliament, and who holds key cabinet posts (home ministry, defence, and border affairs). Other aspects of the constitution that embolden the military's position are (i) its right to take

power in the event of an emergency and (ii) the shield clause protecting the institution from being tried for past crimes (Tarabay 2017).
4. Provisions that criminalize speech include unlawful assembly (Art. 141); insulting religion or anti-blasphemy (Arts. 295, 295[a] and 298); trespassing (Art. 451); defamation (Arts. 499–502); and publishing or disseminating content that could cause offences against the state or against public tranquillity (Art. 505[b]). The full text of the Penal Code can be accessed at http://www.wipo.int/wipolex/en/text.jsp?file_id=181185.
5. Throughout the opening, the Ministry of Information sought assistance from international experts from UNESCO or from media development organizations such as International Media Support and the Center for Law and Democracy (the work of international organizations is discussed in the chapter on media development by Jane Madlyn McElhone and Lisa Brooten).
6. Although officially known as the News Media Law, most people have come to refer to it simply as the Media Law.
7. Unofficial translations of the News Media Law, the PPEL and the Broadcast Law can be found at http://www.burmalibrary.org/docs17/2014-Media_Law-en.pdf; https://www.article19.org/data/files/medialibrary/3679/Printing-and-Publishing-Enterprise-Law-Bill.pdf; and http://www.burmalibrary.org/docs21/2015-08-28-Broadcasting_Law-en-red.pdf.
8. Information Minister Ye Htut speaking at the Myanmar Media Development Conference in Yangon on 10 December 2015.
9. The World Bank allocated funds of US$31.5 million for the country's reform project for the telecommunication sector in 2014 "to improve the enabling environment for the telecommunications sector and extend coverage in selected remote pilot locations. [The World Bank] also established priority eGovernment technological foundations and institutional capacity for the government to embark on its public sector reform program" (World Bank 2014a, ¶10).
10. The figures are from a press statement issued by Athan on 9 September 2018 titled "The number of cases under the Telecommunications Law rises to 48 after the amendment".
11. Personal interview by volume co-editor Jane Madlyn McElhone in June 2018 in Yangon.
12. Personal experience of and encounters by co-author Myint Kyaw.
13. Personal experience of co-author Myint Kyaw.
14. Pe Myint was speaking on behalf of the Myanmar Press Council at the 4th Myanmar Media Development Conference, Yangon, 10 December 2015. In March 2016 he was named information minister by the NLD government.

References

AFP. 2014. "Myanmar Govt to Sue Newspaper over 'Insane' President Jibe". 4 November 2014. https://sg.news.yahoo.com/myanmar-govt-sue-newspaper-over-insane-president-slur-081623717.html.

ARTICLE 19. 2013. "Statement: Myanmar – Public Service Media Needed but Proposed Bill Inadequate". 26 June 2013. http://www.article19.org/resources.php/resource/37123/en/myanmar:-public-service-media-needed-but-proposed-bill-inadequate.

———. 2014. "Myanmar: News Media Law – Legal Analysis". http://www.article19.org/data/files/medialibrary/37623/News-Media-Law-Myanmar-EN.pdf.

Braman, S. 2004. "Where Has Media Policy Gone? Defining the Field in the Twenty-First Century". *Communication Law and Policy* 9 (2): 153–82.

Brooten, L. 2016. "Burmese Media in Transition". *International Journal of Communication* 10:182–99.

Cheesman, N. 2015. "That Signifier of Desire, the Rule of Law". *Social Research* 82 (2): 267–90.

CIVICUS. 2017. "Deepening Humanitarian Crisis Now Coined a 'Catastrophe'". *Monitor*, 30 October 2017. http://monitor.civicus.org/newsfeed/2017/10/30/deepening-humanitarian-crisis-now-coined-catastrophe/.

CPJ (Committee to Protect Journalists). 2014. "Journalist Killed in Military Custody in Burma". 24 October 2014. http://cpj.org/2014/10/journalist-killed-in-military-custody-in-burma.php.

Croissant, A., and J. Kamerling. 2013. "Why Do Military Regimes Institutionalize? Constitution-making and Elections as Political Survival Strategy in Myanmar". *Asian Journal of Political Science* 21 (2): 105–25.

Cuilenburg, J., and D. McQuail. 2003. "Media Policy Paradigm Shifts towards a New Communications Policy Paradigm". *European Journal of Communication* 18 (2): 181–207.

Cunningham, S. 2016. "Women Journalists Numerous but Still Stymied by Stereotypes". *Mizzima News*, 12 November 2016. http://www.mizzima.com/development-news/women-journalists-numerous-still-stymied-stereotypes.

Dragomir, M., and M. Thompson, eds. 2014. *Mapping Digital Media: Global Findings*. New York: Open Society Foundations.

DVB. 2015. "MoI Withdraws Public Service Media Bill". 18 March 2015. http://www.dvb.no/news/moi-withdraws-public-service-media-bill-burma-myanmar/49303.

———. 2017. "Anti-Hate Speech Draft Law Submitted to Myanmar Parliament". 28 September 2017. http://coconuts.co/yangon/news/anti-hate-speech-draft-law-submitted-parliament/.

Free Expression Myanmar. 2017. "66(d) No Real Change: An Analysis of Complaints Made before and after the 2017 Legal Amendment". http://freeexpressionmyanmar.org/wp-content/uploads/2017/12/66d-no-real-change.pdf.

Freedman, D. 2006. *The Politics of Media Policy*. Polity Press.

———. 2014. *The Contradictions of Media Power*. Bloomsbury Academic.

Freedom House. 2014. "Freedom of the Press: Myanmar". https://freedomhouse.org/report/freedom-press/2014/myanmar.

Fuller, T. 2015. "Myanmar Military Still Big Power Despite Opposition Victory". *New York Times*, 10 November 2015. http://www.nytimes.com/2015/11/11/world/asia/myanmar-military-aung-san-suu-kyi-election.html.

Goldberg, J. 2018. "Jailed Reporters' Wives 'Devastated' by Aung San Suu Kyi Response". *The Guardian*, 5 September 2018. http://www.theguardian.com/world/2018/sep/04/jailed-reporters-wives-devastated-aung-san-suu-kyi-response.

Htet Naing Zaw. 2016. "Incoming Info Minister Pe Myint: 'I Will Ensure Press Freedom'". *The Irrawaddy*, 28 March 2016. http://www.irrawaddy.com/in-person/interview/incoming-info-minister-pe-myint-will-ensure-press-freedom.html.

Htike Nanda Win. 2018. "Press Council Plans Elections in 2018". *Myanmar Times*, 11 April 2018. https://www.mmtimes.com/news/press-council-plans-elections-2018.html.

Hudson-Rodd, N. 2008. "'Not a Rice-Eating Robot': Freedom to Speak, in Burma". In *Political Regimes and the Media in Asia*, edited by K. Sen and T. Lee, pp. 85–105. London: Routledge.

Human Rights Watch. 2016. *"They Can Arrest You Any Time": The Criminalization of Peaceful Expression in Burma*. 29 June 2016. http://www.hrw.org/report/2016/06/29/they-can-arrest-you-any-time/criminalization-peaceful-expression-burma.

Igoe, M. 2014. "Is Myanmar Ready for a Telecommunications Revolution?" *Devex*, 16 May 2014. http://www.devex.com/news/is-myanmar-ready-for-a-telecommunications-revolution-83498.

International Media Support. 2015. "Government and Media Must Learn to Change Their Ways". 7 January 2015. http://www.mediasupport.org/media-reform-myanmar-government-media-must-learn-change-ways/.

Irion, K., and T. Jusic. 2013. *International Assistance and Media Democratization in the Western Balkans: A Cross-National Comparison*. Working paper 1/2013 prepared in the framework of the Regional Research Promotion Programme in the Western Balkans (RRPP). Sarajevo: Analitika – Center for Social Research.

The Irrawaddy. 2014. "Journalists Charged for Leading Unauthorized Protest". 29 April 2014. http://www.irrawaddy.com/news/latest-news/journalist-charged-leading-unauthorized-protest.html.

———. 2017. "Military Withdraws Cases against Detained Journalists". 1 September 2017. http://www.irrawaddy.com/news/burma/military-withdraw-cases-detained-journalists.html.

Jones, L. 2014. "Explaining Myanmar's Regime Transition: The Periphery is Central". *Democratization* 21 (5): 780–802.

Kean, T. 2018. "Public Discourse". In *Routledge Handbook of Contemporary Myanmar*, edited by A. Simpson, N. Farrelly, and I. Holliday, pp. 145–57. New York: Routledge.

Kohn, A. 2016. "Myanmar: Government Discusses Media Strategy". *DW Akademie*, 12 February 2016. http://www.dw.com/en/myanmar-government-discusses-media-strategy/a-1904479.

Kyaw Su Mon and Ei Ei Toe Lwin. 2012. "Questions over Press Council Formation". *Myanmar Times*, 13 August 2012. http://www.mmtimes.com/national-news/170-questions-over-press-council-formation.html.

Kyaw Ye Lynn. 2016. "Military Continues to Put Pressure on Media". Southeast Asian Press Alliance. 28 June 2016. http://www.seapa.org/military-continues-to-put-pressure-on-media/.

Kumar, K. 2006. "International Assistance to Promote Independent Media in Transition and Post-conflict Societies". *Democratization* 13 (4): 652–67.

Lawi Weng. 2017. "Ma Ba Tha Takes Aim at the Media". *The Irrawaddy*, 9 March 2017. http://www.irrawaddy.com/opinion/commentary/ma-ba-tha-takes-aim-at-the-media.html.

Lintner, B. 2001. "Burma: Denial of Access". In *The Right to Know: Access to Information in Southeast Asia*, edited by S. Coronel, pp. 21–41. Philippine Center For Investigative Journalism.

Lun Min Mang. 2016. "MOI Chief to Push for Broadcasting Law Reform". *Myanmar Times*, 4 May 2016. http://www.mmtimes.com/national-news/20102-moi-chief-to-push-for-broadcasting-law-reform.html.

Lun Min Mang and Ye Mon. 2014. "'Bi Mon Te Nay' Staff to Appeal". *Myanmar Times*, 17 October 2014. http://www.mmtimes.com/national-news/11979-bi-mon-te-nay-staff-to-appeal-two-year-jail-terms.html.

McChesney, R. 1998. "Making Media Democratic". *Boston Review* (Summer). http://bostonreview.net/archives/BR23.3/mcchesney.html.

Mclaughlin, T. 2014. "U Ye Htut: From Military to Ministry". *Myanmar Times*, 23 July 2014. http://www.mmtimes.com/home-page/editor-s-pick/10937-in-internet-age-a-soldier-takes-up-a-new-fight-2.html.

McQuail, D. 2010. *McQuail's Mass Communication Theory*. London: Sage.

Milton, A. 2001. "Bound but Not Gagged: Media Reform in Democratic Transitions". *Comparative Political Studies* 34 (5): 493–526.

Min Zin and B. Joseph. 2012. "The Democrats' Opportunity". *Journal of Democracy* 23 (4): 104–19.

MNA (Myanmar News Agency). 2015. "Information Ministry Withdraws Proposed Public Service Media Bill". *Global New Light of Myanmar*, 18 March 2015. http://www.globalnewlightofmyanmar.com/information-ministry-withdraws-proposed-public-service-media-bill/.

Naw Noreen. 2015. "Myanmar Herald Editors Fined for Insulting President". DVB, 22 July 2015. http://www.dvb.no/news/myanmar-herald-editors-fined-for-insulting-president-burma-myanmar/55016.

Nyein Nyein. 2012. "New Interim Press Council Formed". *The Irrawaddy*, 17 September 2012. http://www.irrawaddy.com/news/burma/new-interim-press-council-formed.html.

Paing Soe. 2017. "Burmese Journalist Sued, Threatened after Logging, Cattle-rustling Reports". DVB, 13 February 2017. http://www.dvb.no/news/burmese-journalist-sued-threatened-logging-cattle-rustling-reports/74100.

Papathanassopoulus, S. 2016. "Media Policy". In *The International Encyclopedia of Political Communication*, edited by G. Mazzoleni, pp. 1–9. Wiley.

PEN Myanmar. 2017. *Scorecard Assessing Freedom of Expression in Myanmar*. 3 May 2017. http://pen.org/wp-content/uploads/2017/05/May-2017-Scorecard-English.pdf.

Phuong Nguyen. 2012. "Myanmar's Peaceful Assembly Law: A Big Step forward but a Long Way to Go". *cogitASIA*, 27 November 2012. Center for Strategic & International Studies. http://www.cogitasia.com/myanmar%E2%80%99s-peaceful-assembly-law-a-big-step-forward-but-a-long-way-to-go/.

Price, M., and P. Krug. 2000. *The Enabling Environment for Free and Independent Media*. Programme in Comparative Media Law & Policy, Oxford University.

Pyae Thet Phyo. 2017. "Public Service Media Revival in the Works". *Myanmar Times*, 1 May 2017. http://www.mmtimes.com/national-news/nay-pyi-taw/25802-public-service-media-revival-in-the-works.html.

———. 2018. "Amendments to Assembly Bill Approved by Amyotha Hlutaw". *Myanmar Times*, 8 March 2018. http://www.mmtimes.com/news/amendments-assembly-bill-approved-amyotha-hluttaw.html.

Reuters. 2017. "Myanmar Mulls Change to Defamation Law". *The Irrawaddy*, 6 July 2017. http://www.irrawaddy.com/news/burma/myanmar-mulls-change-defamation-law.html.

Rotberg, R. 2004. "The Failure and Collapse of Nation-States: Breakdown, Prevention, and Repair". In *When States Fail: Causes and Consequences*, edited by R. Rotberg, pp. 1–50. Princeton University Press.

Rothman, P. 2015. *The Politics of Media Development: The Importance of Engaging Government and Civil Society*. Center for International Media Assistance and National Endowment for Democracy.

SEAPA (Southeast Asian Press Alliance). 2014. "Government Using New Media Law to Stifle Criticism". 13 November 2014. http://www.seapa.org/government-using-new-media-law-to-stifle-criticism/.

Segura, M., and S. Waisbord. 2016. *Media Movements: Civil Society and Media Policy Reform in Latin America*. London: Zed Books.

Spencer, O., Zar Chi Oo, and Yin Yadanar Thein. 2017. "The 66(d) Amendment: Tinkering at the Edges". *Frontier Myanmar*, 15 September 2017. http://frontiermyanmar.net/en/the-66d-amendment-tinkering-at-the-edges.

Stokke, K., Khine Win, and Soe Myint Aung. (2015). "Political Parties and Popular Representation in Myanmar's Democratisation Process". *Journal of Current Southeast Asian Affairs* 34 (3): 3–35.

Tarabay, J. 2017. "Myanmar's Military: The Power Aung San Suu Kyi Can't Control". CNN, 24 September 2017. http://edition.cnn.com/2017/09/21/asia/myanmar-military-the-real-power/index.html.

Voltmer, K. 2013. *The Media in Transitional Democracies*. Polity Press.

World Bank. 2014a. "Press Release: Myanmar Moves Toward Connectivity for All". 6 February 2014. http://www.worldbank.org/en/news/press-release/2014/02/06/myanmar-moves-toward-connectivity-for-all.

———. 2014b. "EITI Candidacy Approval is a Transparency Breakthrough for Myanmar". 14 July 2018. http://www.worldbank.org/en/news/feature/2014/07/14/eiti-candidacy-approval-is-a-transparency-breakthrough-for-myanmar.

Ye Mon. 2015. "Press Council Confirmed, Eyes Media Law Changes". *Myanmar Times*, 28 October 2015. http://www.mmtimes.com/national-news/17240-press-council-confirmed-eyes-media-law-changes.html.

3

Whispered Support: Two Decades of International Aid for Independent Journalism and Free Expression

Jane Madlyn McElhone and Lisa Brooten

> *In March 2012, at Myanmar's[1] first national media development conference at the Chatrium Hotel in Yangon, Yangon Journalism School's founding director and lead trainer Ye Naing Moe asked which editors and journalists had been trained by the Indochina Media Memorial Fund (IMMF) during the long years of the military junta. I looked around as a sea of hands filled the room. It was the first time the IMMF's cross-border and underground training had been acknowledged in public, and the first time Burmese editors and journalists publicly admitted they had been trained.*[2]

These reflections by Jane Madlyn McElhone begin to clarify the inextricable connection between the two decades of international aid during the military junta and the struggle to protect and increase the space for free expression and free media inside the country since the political opening. Although plans for top-down, government-led media reforms began shortly after a purge of military intelligence in 2004 (Kean 2018), media development efforts in, and for, the country have a much longer history. Empowered by decades of aid support — in the form of educational opportunities, training, and funding — editors, journalists, writers and free expression advocates from inside the country, the borderlands, and exile have seized the unprecedented opportunities presented by the political opening. They are pushing the boundaries of independent journalism, advocating and fighting for free expression and free media, and playing leadership roles, including mentoring what Ye Naing Moe affectionately calls "our new generation of watchdogs" (Interview 30; see appendix). They say these historic aid opportunities have provided an important impetus for change, and that they have helped them navigate the new media development narrative which some aid recipients, including some contributors to this book, argue too often prioritizes state media development and foreign policy agendas above local ownership and decision-making, public service, diversity and access for all.³ As they have always done, these media practitioners are working within, and pushing against, the constraints of the shifting space allowed for free media and free expression established by the government, the military and their cronies.

Against the comparative backdrop of international media development, we examine the dynamics that drove this historic support in Burma. By telling the stories of the aid recipients and the choices they have made since the political opening, including in response to the Rakhine crisis, and sharing the reflections of donors, we assess the legacy of this quarter century of aid.

This chapter is drawn primarily from Jane Madlyn McElhone's thirteen years of in-field experience in Myanmar and other nations in transition, as well as key informant interviews she conducted in 2017 and 2018. A list of interviewees and a brief description of their media development roles are provided in the appendix. Quotations from the interviews are identified in the chapter text by their number in the appendix, so, for example, (1) refers to Ahr Mahn from *7Day Daily*.

Our discussion is driven by a series of interlinked questions. Who were the key media development actors during the time of the military junta, what kind of support did they offer, and who benefited from it? What were the assumptions driving the aid? With hindsight, what are the lessons learned that can be applied to Myanmar's contemporary media development sector, and to regional and international media development efforts? What is the legacy of the many years of pre-transition aid? What have we learned from the response to the Rakhine crisis? As the experiences in other countries provide additional context for understanding the historical and current changes in Myanmar, we begin with an overview of research on media development and free expression in countries in transition.

Media Development and Political Transitions

The emergence of media development as a subfield of the development industry can be traced back to a 1980 proposal taken up by UNESCO to use voluntary contributions from developed nations to support media in developing countries (Berger 2010). UNESCO, however, had been involved in global media issues well before this 1980 initiative, and the field of international development, since its emergence and promotion of "modernization" after World War II, had debated the role of media in reducing poverty and improving living conditions in what were then newly independent former colonies. These early approaches to the use of media to promote modernization conceptualized media as disseminators of ideas and innovations, often employing techniques such as social marketing and "edutainment" (Berger 2010). The 1980s saw a media development focus on Latin America, but the fall of the Berlin Wall in 1989 caused a shift in focus to Eastern Europe and the former Soviet republics, a focus which was again redirected in the 2000s towards Asia and Africa, and, since the attacks of 11 September 2001, especially, towards the Middle East (Hume 2004).

Arguably lacking a coherent and agreed-upon definition, media development is generally conceptualized as both a process and an outcome, two concepts often conflated in development goals, creating "incoherence" (Berger 2010, p. 550). In general, however, media development is recognized as more narrowly focused than the use of media or communications in pursuit of broader development goals; instead, it tends to refer to the advancement, diversification and democratization of the media themselves (Berger 2010; Paneerselvan and Nair 2008). Nevertheless, this focus on the development of media is also seen as contributing to broader development goals, including the promotion of good governance, institutional reform, economic development, nation building, policy issues and public participation (Voltmer 2013). The Center for International Media Assistance (CIMA) at the United States' National Endowment for Democracy distinguishes between "media development", a process initiated within a country, albeit often with donor support, and externally initiated "support/assistance to media development" (CIMA 2018, p. 3). Some definitions of media development explicitly identify a focus on journalism, while others conflate "media" and "journalism" without comment. The strong association made in policy discourse between a free press and democracy results in a focus on journalism training, journalists' safety, freedom of the press, professionalism, access to information, investigative journalism, support for media associations, media law reform, and legislative and regulatory reforms. Other areas of concern include financial sustainability and the transition of state-owned media to public service and private media (Berger 2010; Price and Krug 2000; Kumar 2006). More recently, digital initiatives include information and communication technology for development (ICT4D), technology for transparency and accountability, and open government data (Kalathil 2017).

While research on media development has been defined as "nascent at its very best", media development efforts have been understood over the years as both a manifestation and a key component of the transition from "traditional" to "modern" societies, but also more recently as a key component of regime change in countries in transition (Brownlee 2017, p. 2278). Price (2015) defines media development as "soft interventions by external governments and NGOs to shape a media system" (p. 115). "Media mobilization" as promoted by bilateral government aid agencies, government organizations, international governmental organizations and other groups is not neutral, but rather a kind of "foreign policy of media space" (Price 2001, ¶11). Governments, militaries, private interests and other powerful players, he argues, "design communication infrastructures to optimize achievement of their own strategic goals" so that "transition-produced systems look the way they do as a result of a competition among parties interested in the future of the media market and, at times, the future of the country" (Price 2015, p. 112).

This is not to say that individual media development practitioners consciously promote their country's foreign policy or attempt to shape aid recipients' foreign or domestic policy, but rather to recognize that development aid is determined by large-scale foreign policy objectives and other global constraints and opportunities that affect local practitioners. These objectives include protection of human rights, promotion of democratic transitions, prevention of conflict and genocide, stability, provision of a sympathetic media environment for the sending state, and the enhancement of trade relations (Berger 2010; Hume 2004; Price 2001).

Media development has historically connoted specific forms of intervention, originating for the most part externally, usually involving northern developers and southern development recipients — Myanmar is no exception — and projects with a functionalist intent, such as improving healthcare or reducing corruption (Berger 2010; Deane 2011). Yet critics argue that the dominant Western model is flawed in that it is neocolonial, top-down, both in its conception and implementation, and project driven (Waisbord 2008). They point to the ways in which mainstream media development organizations tend to emphasize physical and legal infrastructure and the business aspects of media development, such as skills development and financial sustainability, at the expense of democracy, issues related to free expression, or "the conceptual world of media, dialogue and discourse" (Paneerselvan and Nair 2008, p. 3; see also Berger 2010). Media development organizations have been criticized for imposing a Western approach on training (Brooten 2006; Miller 2011) and for using a one-size-fits-all, overly normative approach that ignores country and region-specific complexities and is based on the overly simplified belief "that a free and plural media will always achieve positive democratic outcomes" (Deane 2011, p. 238). This proved problematic in Bosnia and Kosovo, for example, where "millions of Western development dollars converted some contractors into media moguls" (Hume 2004, p. 23) and in much of the former USSR, where "millions of dollars in aid have not produced a viable independent media" (Hume 2004, p. 11).

Externally driven and not-for-profit media development is today "a multi-million dollar undertaking involving hundreds of US and European organizations" (Hume 2004, p. 21). Although it represents a tiny portion of overall development funding (less than one per cent), is often fragmented and its impact challenging to document (Kalathil 2017), it is clear that media development assistance by Western aid agencies has significantly increased since the early days. Only rough estimates are available, but these suggest that at least US$600 million, and probably much more, was spent on global media development during the decade of the 1990s (Hume 2004). A 2018 CIMA report estimates that US$454 million per year of official development assistance currently targets the media sector (Meyers and Angaya Juma 2018). Yet, given the challenges of interpreting inconsistent donor reporting, if you take into account all governments and private donors around the world, CIMA senior director Mark Nelson estimates that over the past decade (since the mid-2000s) the figure is probably close to US$600–700 million *annually* (16). According to the 2018 CIMA report, the level of donor support for media remains steady, but also very small: on average, 0.3 per cent of total official development aid between 2010 and 2015 (Meyers and Angaya Juma 2018). When considering whether aid is going where it is needed most, the authors note that the Middle East region and countries including Myanmar, Belarus and Tunisia seem to be privileged by donors, "probably on account of their genuine needs and opportunities in the realm of free expression" (Meyers and Angaya Juma 2018, p. 27). At nearly US$53 million, Myanmar was the fifth largest media support recipient country between 2010 and 2015 (Meyers and Angaya Juma 2018, p. 25).

Information about non-European and non-American aid for media development is gradually becoming more available. China, for example, is now a significant global donor, largely in the form of loans, and with a focus on infrastructure development — choices that do not necessarily "enshrine the values of pluralism, independence, and democratic dialogue that are core to media development" (Meyers and Angaya Juma 2018, p. 4).[4] The top ten media support funders between 2010 and 2015 were Germany, the United States, Japan, the United Kingdom, Sweden, France, EU institutions, the Netherlands, Norway and Switzerland (Meyers and Angaya Juma 2018).

Media development organizations and networks, such as the Global Forum for Media Development and CIMA, tend to interpret "media development" in line with the values of Western-style democracy (Berger 2010; Brooten 2006; Brownlee 2017; Kalathil 2017; Price 2001, 2015). Price (2015) describes this as "a kind of world view of the normal", and one of the most enduring assumptions influencing its tone and agenda is that free and independent media are a key part of democracies and democratization (p. 112). The assumption is not that media are themselves democratic; rather, that professional, independent, ethical media have value as a democratic cornerstone (Voltmer 2013). Other assumptions are that broad access to the internet is necessary for democratization and that community broadcasting should be allocated frequency space (Price 2015). Norris (2006) points to a strong correlation between liberal media landscapes and democracy and good governance, yet says that this does not mean that one causes the other; Singapore, for example, has restricted press freedom yet also promotes a public perception of low levels of corruption (Transparency International 2017). At its best, media development aid has arguably helped to hold public officials accountable, including through investigative journalism and ensuring citizens have the news and information they need to participate in democratic processes. The aid has also helped develop inclusive platforms so people can tell their stories and voice their opinions, and has mobilized people to fight for change (Voltmer 2013).

The literature suggests that the various approaches to media development have important policy implications. Paneerselvan and Nair (2008) note the dangers of state-centrism and the importance of distinguishing between media pluralism and the proliferation of media, as a proliferation of media outlets does not guarantee a pluralistic environment, and may merely reinforce the dominant narrative or a particular position. They also urge policymakers to recognize the intrinsic value of media outside of their instrumental value as vehicles for information. Critiques of the top-down nature of much early media development work led to calls for new approaches that delink media development from exclusively external interventions, prioritizing local initiatives instead and establishing common and explicit "denominators … for defining what, at minimum, constitutes 'media development'" (Berger 2010, p. 553). As Price (2001) argues, "No foreign policy of information space can be wholly credible or meaningfully sustained unless there is a domestic policy that fosters a civil society. Enlarging and enriching the public sphere at home is a necessary prerequisite — especially for a free people — as they cope with the challenges of an endlessly changing, complex, and terrifying world" (¶46).

Media Development and Myanmar's Political Transition

Since 2012, many new media development organizations have entered the scene with the stated intention of building an infrastructure to improve journalism in order to "bolster democratic tendencies" (Price 2015, p. 116). While private media actors have sought to close, or at least limit, the space for state involvement in the media sector, international media development organizations and some of the formerly exiled media outlets collaborated with the Ministry of Information early on and were thus perceived to be supporting and extending the space for state engagement and state-owned media. International Media Support (IMS), the British Broadcasting Corporation (BBC), Voice of America (VOA) and Deutsche Welle (DW) numbered among the former critics of the regime that formed partnerships early on (Foster 2013). UNESCO, IMS and the Centre for Law and Democracy worked with the Ministry of Information under the former Thein Sein administration to draft media laws and policies. In 2013 the U.S. State Department financed trips abroad for lawyers to review draft laws and other pieces of "industry-defining legislation" (Price 2015, p. 126). IMS provided funding for a ministry delegation to travel to several Asian and Scandinavian countries to study models and laws related to broadcasting (IMS 2012). A number of international organizations have supported the state broadcaster, MRTV, in a variety of ways. The debate over state involvement in the media sector continues. In a 2018 media development report published by UNESCO, private media and media development actors state categorically that the Myanmar government should not be in the print media business, although opinions are mixed about the state broadcaster and efforts to transform it into a public broadcaster (UNESCO 2018).

There are significant dangers in taking as a default those "external prefabricated designs" that have evolved regarding free and independent media systems, argues Price (2015), which "if applied in an automatic, template-like fashion ... can deter consideration of complex issues of institution-building" (p. 118). In Myanmar's case, this may mean recognizing the ways in which standard approaches to democratizing media might inadvertently reinforce control by the military (Price 2015), such as prioritizing support for government involvement in the media sector with the assumption that state-run media can be transformed into public service media.

Another concern is the potential for civil society (including media) to become dependent on donors and to allow donor interests rather than training needs to drive the topical agenda for training (UNESCO and IMS 2016). Opening Myanmar's media market too widely is also viewed as a risk, as it is certain to lead to even greater commercialization, a further entrenched oligarchic ownership structure, and "content that weakens values of local history and culture" (Price 2015, p. 118). Such an oligarchic ownership structure is already apparent in Myanmar's media system (Brooten 2016; UNESCO and IMS 2016). This is consistent with research on business elites — or the new oligarchs — in the current political climate, who are "no longer reliant on a sole patron-client relationship" but have benefitted from the recent privatization, giving them "incentives and motives for asserting themselves directly as political actors" (Ford et al. 2016, pp. 37–38). These concerns have not been alleviated in the years since the political opening. On the contrary, while there is more media content available, the oligarchic ownership structure is still a primary concern, particularly in the broadcast sector. There has, by contrast, been visible change in Myanmar's local media sector, with dozens of outlets now operating in the country's fourteen ethnic states and regions. Nevertheless, as the Media Development Investment Fund (MDIF) describes it, these local media "exist in a perfect storm of undermining forces, which together create an almost impossible environment for achieving commercial sustainability", including in some cases a significant dependency on international donor support and a resulting NGO mindset that is difficult to change (Settles 2018).

One important means of avoiding the dangers of "prefabricated designs" is to understand Myanmar's history and the legacies from which it now draws to shape the contemporary media development landscape. Researchers and policymakers will be more effective today if they can benefit from the lessons already learned by media practitioners and development advocates, in many cases, under the radar. In this chapter, therefore, we focus on this essential yet often overlooked part of the story.

Whispered Support: Media Development in a Closed Society

Key donors and implementers supported Burmese media development for two decades prior to the country's political transition. In this section we learn about their strategies and priorities, the assumptions that drove their decision-making, and the lessons they learned — and continue to learn — that can be applied today.

The Supporters

The story of Burmese media development spans more than twenty-five years, starting in the late 1980s and early 1990s, primarily outside of the country (11). This time period coincides with historic events inside Burma, notably the 1988 student uprising. According to consultant Lyndal Min, it was in the jungles along the Thai-Burmese border that Burmese media development got its start. Thousands of students fled to these areas, controlled by ethnic armed organizations, following the brutal military crackdown in 1988. At the time, their discourse of democracy and human rights coincided with U.S. foreign policy interests, in particular U.S. president Ronald Reagan's ostensible mission to promote freedom and democracy around the world (Brooten 2011). The Burmese government-in-exile had set up operations on the border. Ethnic armies had been gaining ground in their struggles against the regime, and rumours that they could take Rangoon had increased international interest.

> That is where advocacy, media and communications became useful tools for the revolutionaries fighting the Burmese military junta. In the beginning, people came out of the jungles to the border areas, including Mae Sot, Thailand, to make calls to international media and to pass on their news, much in the way of citizen journalists. But they were untrained and it was difficult to cross-check their information

unless you had extremely good personal connections. International journalists also found it difficult to go inside.... Then international broadcasters such as the BBC, VOA and RFA began bringing their stringers to Mae Sot for training. Ex-combatants began crossing the border looking for new work, including as journalists. That was the start of Burma's media development story. (11)

For two decades, international media development work targeting Burma predominantly took place across the border in Thailand. In the early days, non-governmental organizations (NGOs) conducting regional training, such as Images Asia based in Chiang Mai, Thailand, focused on media advocacy and development. International journalism trainers also came in periodically for brief visits, but Lyndal Min questions whether their training had an impact, as the students were primarily interested in learning advocacy to support their efforts to defeat the junta, especially in the early days (11). Over time, Burmese media operating in exile, and ethnic media along the border, were offered more sustained institutional and project support and training (Brooten 2003, 2011), and scholarship programmes were established for overseas studies for journalists and writers.

The number of donors, media development organizations, training courses and advocates for free expression and legal protection supporting Burmese media development gradually increased. The key players included the National Endowment for Democracy (NED),[5] which started its media work in 1992; the Open Society Foundations (formerly called Open Society Institute), which started in 1994; the Indochina Media Memorial Foundation (IMMF), which started in 1996 and was funded by a variety of donors, including OSF and the Swedish International Development Cooperation Agency (Sida); Sida, which started in 1998; Burma Relief Centre, which started in 1999 and was funded by Sida and Global Affairs Canada (formerly called CIDA); and Internews, which started in 2001 and was funded by USAID (3).[6]

From 1998 to 2011, Sida spent SEK 46 million (approximately US$5.5 million based on today's exchange rates). The vast majority went to exiled media outlets — Democratic Voice of Burma, *The Irrawaddy* and *Mizzima* — and the remainder for projects inside the country, including the Yangon Film School (5). OSF spent approximately

US$6 million from 1994 to 2011, primarily on the aforementioned Burman-run exiled media outlets and, on a more modest scale, small ethnic media working in the borderlands in areas controlled by ethnic armed organizations, as well as private media operating inside the country and training, scholarships and fellowships (28). Burma Relief Centre spent an estimated US$1.5 million on its work with ethnic media from 1999 to 2011 (21). U.S. government funding for democracy and human rights during this period was channelled primarily through NGOs, with the majority going to NED, notably for exiled groups and the collection and dissemination of information on human rights and democracy. NED estimates it spent US$9.3 million on 137 Burmese media-related projects from 1992 to 2011 (7). USAID also supported the strengthening of independent media, improved access to information, and the development of technical skills for ethnic and exiled journalists, including via the media development organization Internews, which began its work in Burma in 2001.

These figures provide a glimpse of the monies spent by key players in the media development field prior to the transition, yet they do not capture the full picture. Sida, OSF and other donors also supported regional and international organizations that worked on Burma, including the Southeast Asian Press Alliance, ARTICLE 19, PEN International, Committee to Protect Journalists, Human Rights Watch, International Federation of Journalists and the International Freedom of Expression Exchange. A more extensive, although not exhaustive, list of donors, implementers and advocates that also supported media and free expression during this period (and, in some cases, continue to do so) includes (in alphabetical order) the American Center (Rangoon), the British Council (Rangoon), Civil Rights Defenders, the Dutch government, Fojo/Sweden, Index on Censorship, the International Center for Journalists, the Independent Journalism Foundation, the PEN Centers, People in Need, Reporters sans Frontières, and Rights and Democracy (Canada).

Operating out of Chiang Mai, Thailand, the Indochina Media Memorial Foundation (IMMF) began training journalists from Cambodia, Vietnam and Laos in 1994; Burma was added to its roster in 1996. Until 2009, IMMF conducted regular month-long journalism training courses on non-political topics such as the environment and migrant labour, often with human rights angles. As then IMMF executive director Sarah McLean explained in 2017,

> Our mandate was to teach journalists living inside Burma — to try to change things inside the country — and our philosophy was that journalism was not learned entirely in the classroom. So on every training course we sent all of the participants out into the field to do interviews. Not everyone pursued journalism afterwards — the well-known Myanmar woman writer Ju continued to write novels, but focused largely on gender and environmental issues, while Aye Mye Htet became a filmmaker. Pe Myint, our very first participant from Myanmar in 1996, who at that time wrote environmental stories for a science journal, is now Minister of Information. Most of the young journalists who attended IMMF courses benefitted in some way, and learned valuable lessons about reporting and writing news. (10)

From the start of its work with Burmese media, Internews focused on strengthening the professional capacities of small, border-based publications run by exiled and ethnic groups, as well as underground training inside the country. The journalism school it founded in Chiang Mai in 2004, known as the J-School, provided a wide range of workshops and training over the years, notably ten-month residential journalism courses funded by the Dutch government. Up until its closure in 2012, the school trained more than one thousand journalists from both sides of the Thai-Burmese border (3).

According to Gary Rozema, a project manager for the Burma Relief Centre (BRC), his organization was inspired by ethnic youth to broaden its work in 1996 to include ethnic media, in addition to its humanitarian efforts with internally displaced peoples. When the Burmese army seized lands governed by ethnic armed organizations, the young people living there sought new opportunities to support their struggle for a democratic federal union, and they set up civil society groups working on human rights, the environment, and media. At the time there were large Burman-run exiled media, Rozema notes, but it was difficult to get information about local ethnic communities back to the communities in their local languages (21). Created out of the ethnic armed struggle, Shan Herald Agency for News (SHAN) was at that point the only independent ethnic media in operation. As its model seemed viable and international media were using it as a source, in 1999 BRC gave funding to SHAN so it could train other ethnic groups, thus contributing to the formation of new ethnic media outlets. The Karen Information Center also existed at that time but functioned as the official information department of the ethnic armed organization, the Karen National Union (KNU), and it took some time before the KNU agreed to it becoming independent. The BRC media development programme gradually expanded to other ethnic states to help existing media incubate new outlets, and to promote the practice of ethic media groups mentoring and training each other (21). This helped lay the ground for the creation of the ethnic media network, Burma News International (BNI), in 2003. For the next eight years, until the political transition, BNI provided its members with wide-ranging training, often targeting women journalists (28).

Although it was risky to support the media sector inside Burma, journalism training was quietly conducted, most frequently at the American Center and the British Council in Rangoon (28). Sarah McLean notes that it was harder to bring women journalists out to Thailand, but that they managed to reach a lot of them by offering periodic covert training at the American Center (10). In 2005 the Yangon Film School was launched inside the country to assist young filmmakers. According to Sida donor David Holmertz, the school battled censorship and took risks, but its work was considered less sensitive than journalism and therefore was allowed some space (5). In 2008, following the 2007 Saffron Revolution, Myanmar Egress, the country's first indigenous adult training and research institute, founded an in-house media-training centre (UNDEP 2013). Myanmar Egress had been established two years earlier, in 2006, by a group that saw themselves as a "third force", including Nay Win Maung who founded *Living Colour* magazine and *The Voice* journal (Lall 2015, p. 8). Myanmar Egress trained more than thirty thousand students and strove to avoid direct affiliation with either the military regime or the opposition NLD, and to navigate the constraints of working inside the country towards "the development of good governance ... through the development of civil society, civic education and advocacy skills" (UNDEP 2013, p. 1; Nan Tin Htwe 2012). However, their connections and willingness to work with the regime made them controversial and the target of attacks by activists in exile (Lall 2015; Nan Tin Htwe 2012). Many believe the Myanmar Egress media training centre was allowed to operate and to receive international funding, including from the EU, because Egress promoted the passage of the 2008 constitution and participation in the 2010 nominal elections (Lall 2015).

Funding Priorities

In the early days, donors primarily regarded Burmese media as tools for achieving their goals: support for the democracy movement, respect for human rights (Brooten 2003, 2011), and improved free access to independent news and information. The Open Society Foundation's Burma Program, for example, focused its support on marginalized groups — including ethnic communities, women and youth — with the hope, according to the stated mission on its website, that it would "foster a generation of civil society and media leaders who would represent one of the best hopes for a peaceful transition to democracy" (OSF 2013, ¶1). Sida assisted the democracy movement by supporting groups inside the country, along the border and in exile, initially routing funding through the Olof Palme International Center, the umbrella organization for the Swedish labour movement that works for democracy, human rights and peace (6).

Throughout the years of rule by the military junta, the vast majority of international media development aid went to media outlets and journalists working and studying outside of Burma. This is one of the main criticisms that has been levelled at donors. Yet, according to OSF's former country director Liz Tydeman, it was, for most, the only safe choice:

> First of all, it was extremely difficult and risky to provide support inside the country, so it would have been irresponsible for donors to start funding inside if they didn't know the situation very well. Even signing agreements with groups inside was risky. Also, it was so restricted, what could journalists actually write? Many of the journalists we knew inside sent their stories to exiled media outside because they couldn't publish them themselves. (28)

A long-time donor with the National Endowment for Democracy (NED), John Knaus, concurs.

> It's a valid criticism that most of the money didn't get inside, but it was a question of access. We couldn't get to journalists inside because we weren't allowed in. Also, what were they really publishing? What could they get past the censors? And what was their institutional capacity to manage international aid? That said, the target audience of exiled media was predominantly inside the country and many of the journalists came out of the country for training. (7)

Until the political opening, Knaus says that 85 to 90 per cent of NED's funding went to projects outside of the country, and that the intention was for groups outside to support journalists inside and to disseminate news inside. That was deemed a safer way to navigate the restrictions and to ensure journalists did not get into trouble (7). Kenneth Van Toll, the former deputy-director of Free Voice Netherlands (since 2011 known as Free Press Unlimited), tells a similar story. FVN didn't have a dedicated Burma programme or a Southeast Asian office, so they could not risk working inside the country. They decided, however, that Burma was the priority, and tried to work with Burmese journalists via regional networks like the Southeast Asian Press Alliance (29). One of the big challenges was that donors and media support groups could not advertise anything inside the country and instead relied almost entirely on participants recommending other potential participants, and on alumni recruiting people they knew. This raises the question of whether everything went to a small group of people outside, or if the intended trickle-down effect inside the country was actually successful.

Conversations with donors also make clear that grantees could sometimes get mixed messages from the people offering them assistance — on the one hand, from supporters who wanted them to distribute their products for free, and on the other, from supporters who wanted them to start making money and become sustainable. For John Knaus of NED, it was a question of mission.

> We weren't trying to make our grantees self-sustaining. We were trying to get information out of the country and circulating around the entire country, including the ethnic states, so people knew what

was going on under the junta. That was a very different mindset than wanting to develop leading journals. We wanted information to be free and available to everyone. (7)

Knaus adds that even now very few of the media inside the country are financially independent — on the contrary, many are donor or crony funded, or dependent on other sources of income raised by the companies that support them — and that this situation is not unique to Myanmar. Liz Tydeman concurs, although she thinks donors should have pushed for more sustained institutional and business development. "One of the problems", she admitted, "was that not many of us were media or business experts" (28). Kenneth Van Toll agrees: "We were an NGO. We knew a lot about media but we didn't really have any business sense. If we had had that kind of background and experience, then maybe we would have done things differently" (29). Donor decision-making was thus to some extent determined — and curtailed — by the sectoral knowledge, sometimes limited, of the people making the decisions.

These reflections strike a chord with Media Development Investment Fund (MDIF) Southeast Asia Program director Tessa Piper. MDIF is running a multi-year business coaching programme in Myanmar for thirteen national and local media partners to strengthen their business and organizational capacity. Piper says that one of the biggest challenges has been tackling a dependence on donor funding that was inadvertently fostered by media development support.

> The Myanmar media sector is unusual. They were all operating under incredibly difficult circumstances during the junta, whether inside or out, and couldn't run as regular businesses. And no one wanted to be publicly associated with them, so the traditional means of making money were unavailable. As well, most of the [formerly exiled] media grantees were committed to producing content. They were not nascent businesspeople.... And no one even knew if and when the situation inside the country would change and if business skills would even be needed. So it is understandable that changing the mindset will take time. (20)

While it is difficult to fully address the issue of sustainability in exile or to operate an independent business in a closed society, Piper recommends integrating institutional development, management and ethics into pre-transition media development projects (20). Gary Rozema of Burma Relief Centre argues, however, that media development projects are not enough, as sustainability in the ethnic states, for example, will remain elusive, if not unattainable, until there is a devolution of political and economic powers within a peaceful federal union (21). And whatever the repercussions in terms of sustainability and resilience, some media choose not to go the business route, and to remain NGOs or community-based organizations.

Lessons Learned

There are many lessons to be learned from the two decades of media development work prior to Myanmar's political opening that can usefully inform current work inside the country, and potentially in other closed and transitional countries around the world. Here we focus on the lessons raised by interviewees linked to education and training, and to trust and responsibility.

Several of the donors highlighted education. Although Liz Tydeman admits that she worried that scholarship recipients would not want to go back home, one of her biggest regrets is not investing in more master's programmes for journalists. She adds, for the record, that most, if not all, of the media workers who received scholarships did return (28). Tessa Piper recommends longer-term training and mentoring programmes, including institutional development, and cautions that the training needs of smaller ethnic media should not be ignored (20). Sarah McLean points to two of the recognized strengths of the IMMF training programme: that it had a small number of quality trainers who engaged over the long-term and who the Burmese came to trust, and that it trained local journalists from each country to be trainers. With hindsight, though, she says IMMF should have brought the most promising people back for further training rather than always looking for new participants. The decision-making was often driven, however, by IMMF's donors, who wanted to see higher numbers (10).

The lessons linked to trust and responsibility, donors say, are complex. During those early years it was very difficult to measure the impact of projects, especially those inside the country, as there was little or no data, and evidence was largely anecdotal. That meant that donors often had to monitor projects unseen and depend on their grantees for accurate information. There was no real choice but to trust them, says Liz Tydeman, even in Rangoon: "We supported three media organizations that were based there, but it was too risky to meet with them and to discuss their projects, and they were understandably afraid" (28). Yet donors also needed to ensure that grantees had the tools and skills they needed to do the job and to handle the money, and to be ever mindful of corruption.

It was a hard lesson for many donors — just as the country was opening up — when one of the best-funded exiled media, the Democratic Voice of Burma (DVB), became mired in an embezzlement scandal (DVB 2011).[7] With hindsight, their donors now realize that they should have asked more questions, not assumed that grantees' advisory boards would provide effective governance and oversight, and not have limited communication to the top managers. "We trusted them too much", John Knaus said, "and they trusted their people too much. But without the rapid increase in exiled media funding around the time of the 2007 Saffron Revolution, it might not have happened. We and other donors wanted to offer support and to respond quickly. In hindsight, though, the structures in place were not adequate to absorb this large increase. That is when mistakes happen" (7). Yet many of the donors had been supporting DVB for years and were long-time Burma watchers. The embezzlement scandal thus said as much about the inadequacy of international donor decision-making and oversight as it did about DVB's inadequate management and operating structures, as well as the shortcomings of its international advisory board.

These are only a few of a long list of the challenges faced by donors and media implementers during two decades of pre-transition support. But did these challenges turn into lessons learned, and did they affect subsequent donor funding? What impact are they having now during the political transition? How do the aid recipients view media development work, and what have they learned from their own experiences? The fact that DVB experienced another much talked about financial crisis in 2018, while continuing to receive substantial donor funding, might suggest that little has changed on either front, despite the opportunity for donors and media development support organizations to work more closely with their grantees and to more attentively monitor the money trail. This speaks to a highly sensitive issue that deserves closer analysis: how to enable and respect grantees' autonomy while ensuring transparency and always looking out for mismanagement and corruption.

Following the Aid Trail

The stories of the people who received media development aid during the years of military rule, and the choices they have made during the political transition, shed light on the legacy of international support. Many are leaders, trendsetters, mentors, trainers, educators, journalists, editors, writers, filmmakers and advocates of free expression. They say that media development assistance during the junta era helped them get their start. Their narratives do not always fit neatly into log frames or other quantitative measurement tools used to assess impact, but they do demonstrate the legacy of the aid and provide an opportunity for the recipients themselves to teach us how it has affected their lives and work.

Two contributors to this volume, Ye Naing Moe and Mon Mon Myat, are among the many aid beneficiaries. They grew up in the same town in Magway Township in central Myanmar and took part in the local student uprising in 1988. Ye Naing Moe's access to international media education and training — from the Independent Journalism Foundation, Indochina Media Memorial Foundation, and as a visiting scholar at the University of California Berkeley Graduate School of Journalism, supported by OSF — was transformative. Well before the country's political opening, Ye established himself as a respected trainer and mentor, as well as a reporter and photographer. He started training journalists inside the country in 2003, and then in 2009 founded the Yangon Journalism School, followed by its sister school in Mandalay in 2015. The schools are, for him, the legacy of IMMF (30). Ye is also a weekly columnist at the private *7Day Daily*, where many other editors were also trained by IMMF. These include Nyein Nyein Naing, the editor-in-chief of *7Day Digital* who discovered journalism when she was 18 years old via covert training offered by IMMF at the American Center in Rangoon (18), and Ahr Man who attended IMMF training courses in Thailand and is now editor-in-chief of *7Day Daily* (1). Both are now in their thirties. Other IMMF-trained editors and journalists include William Chen, founding editor-in-chief of *Modern* and *Kumudra* journals (4), and Nyan Lynn, founding editor and owner of the investigative magazine *Maw Kun* (17).

With an undergraduate economics degree in hand from the University of Rangoon, 30-year-old Mon Mon Myat left Burma in 2000, twelve years after the student uprisings, to pursue a Master of Business Administration degree in Thailand. Although she did not know anyone involved in media development, journalist friends from inside the country, including Ye, would come out from time to time for training with IMMF. Ye told her about the Internews J-School in Chiang Mai, and in 2003 she completed a basic journalism programme, while also working as the school's administrator. This was followed in 2004 by a Mekong Media Fellowship, a six-month reporting project with Inter Press Service, a news agency that focuses on the global south, and then in 2006 a distance master's in journalism from Ateneo de Manila University in the Philippines. In 2007 she returned to Burma, worked as a stringer for Agence France Presse, *Bangkok Post*, and other news agencies, and then in 2011, with help from Internews, co-founded Yangon Press International, which Ye Naing Moe describes as the first uncensored online news agency inside the country (30). As she discusses in her chapter in this volume, it was those opportunities that gave her the experience she needed to co-found Myanmar's annual Human Rights, Human Dignity Film Festival in 2014 (12).

Many were able to travel and study outside the country with the assistance of international aid. Like Ye Naing Moe, veteran journalist, trainer and press council member Myint Kyaw was a visiting scholar at the University of California Berkeley Graduate School of Journalism in 2008/9 (13), as was Kyaw Zwa Moe, *The Irrawaddy* English editor, in 2004/5. Imprisoned from 1991 to 1999 for his links to an underground political journal, Kyaw Zwa Moe joined *The Irrawaddy* in 2001 in Chiang Mai, the journal founded by his brother Aung Zaw. He says that the underground political journal that got him into trouble was not journalism — a fact he only really grasped after leaving prison and being trained by IMMF, doing a SEAPA fellowship in Cambodia, and then spending four years writing and reporting from conflict zones. "From a donor's perspective, the money invested in me was not wasted, because I never quit journalism. Also, I had four years in the field before I went to Berkeley, so I was able to absorb more" (8).

OSF offered scholarships for the prestigious four-month international writers programme at the University of Iowa (28). Myanmar's current Minister of Information, Pe Myint, took part in that programme, as did the woman writer and feminist Ju (Dr Tin Tin Win), and the regional parliamentarian, blogger and former political prisoner Nay Phone Latt, who notes,

> I read a book by U Kyaw Winn about the writing programme while I was in prison, and it was my dream to attend. The international community took on my case and they offered me a scholarship when I got out, but I didn't have a passport. Yet I was lucky — they waited for six months till I was ready. What an opportunity to be exposed to so many writers and thinkers from around the world. (15)

Nay Phone Latt went on to co-found PEN Myanmar, alongside other former political prisoners and leading free expression advocates and writers, including Ma Thida, also a contributor to this volume. He is now an NLD MP representing Yangon region.

The Internews J-School has also had a lasting impact on Myanmar media. Burmese who lived in the country under the junta remember listening to broadcaster Michael Pan on the BBC Burmese Service. Pan later became the Internews J-School resident journalism advisor in Chiang Mai, where he mentored many of the journalists currently working in Myanmar, and then moved inside during the transition to manage Internews' projects (19). Brang Mai, the founding CEO of *Myitkyina News Journal* in Kachin State, and Mai Naing Naing Oo, the founder of *Marnagar* journal in Lashio in northern Shan State, are just two of the editors working in the ethnic states who graduated from the J-School; Brang Mai worked at the school for eight years before setting up his own media in Kachin State (2, 9). Now a journalism advisor at Internews, Sein Win says he was transformed by the journalism training he was offered in exile, both at the J-School and during a six-month training course in Cambodia.[8]

"When we started our work, we were engaged in an information campaign to overthrow the regime. Then I was exposed to journalism education outside of the country and it taught me professionalism and changed my attitude. It didn't happen overnight but it was the starting point. It opened my eyes to what it means to be a real journalist" (22).

In June 2011 a group of independent journalists working inside the country founded the first independent Burmese online news agency, Yangon Press International (YPI), with financial assistance from Internews. The YPI team was composed of Mon Mon Myat, Nyan Lynn (co-founder and owner of *Maw Kun*), Zayar Hlaing (co-founder and editor of *Maw Kun*, press council member and trainer), Myint Kyaw and Aung Htun U (board member and trainer at the Yangon and Mandalay Journalism Schools). The team produced independent news stories for YPI's Facebook page and for international and exiled media with assistance from stringers around the country, including Seng Mai, the founding chief editor of *Myitkyina News Journal* in Kachin State (23), and Soe Soe Myar, who runs the *Kantarawaddy Times* local office in Dee Maw Soe, Kayah State. With a degree in electronic communications from Mandalay University and three months of training from the Internews J-School in Chiang Mai, Soe Soe Myar met the founder of the *Kantarawaddy Times* in a refugee camp along the Thai-Burmese border, was trained by him and then started working for the *Kantarawaddy Times* and as a Yangon Press International stringer (25).

Scholarships were also provided to journalists inside Burma. One of the first went to Min Htet. Now with the BBC Burmese Service, at the time he was employed by the state-controlled English-language daily *New Light of Myanmar*, so the decision was controversial (8). Another went to award-winning investigative journalist and *Myanmar Now* editor-in-chief Swe Win. Imprisoned from 1998 to 2005 for distributing anti-junta material, upon his release Swe Win worked for a few months at the *Myanmar Times* and did a two-year online course with Indiana University before winning an OSF scholarship to study journalism at the University of Hong Kong in 2008/9. He then worked for a variety of regional media, including *Asia Times* and *The Irrawaddy*, and as a freelancer for international media, including the *New York Times* and *Al Jazeera*, before setting up his own website called *Yangon Globe* and then, in 2015, the investigative journalism outlet *Myanmar Now* (26).

Prior to the 2007 Saffron Revolution, aid agencies were openly debating whether or not to move their focus and funding inside the country. Kyaw Zwa Moe recalls many donors feeling that the exiled media organizations were not capable of changing anything, and thus trying to push for change inside. It was during that period that the European Union (EU) gave money to the development organization Myanmar Egress (8).

While a wide range of individuals benefited from international aid during the military junta, the most significant portion of media development funding by far went to exiled media and, of that, the largest chunk to three Burman-run exiled media operations in Thailand, India and Norway: *The Irrawaddy*, *Mizzima* and DVB. *Mizzima* was launched in 1988 by Burmese exiles living in New Delhi, while *The Irrawaddy* was established in 1990 by Burmese exiles in Thailand. DVB began broadcasting via shortwave radio in 1992 from Oslo, Norway, and then in 2005 launched its satellite television service. From the start, all three received international media development assistance, although this funding ebbed and flowed for more than twenty years, often linked to political events and natural disasters inside the country. DVB's former founding deputy director Khin Maung Win[9] says the 2007 Saffron Revolution — and the monks who started the protests — saved them by attracting international interest and increased support (6), as did Cyclone Nargis that devastated the country the following year. All three exiled media opened up offices inside the country in 2012, yet only *Mizzima* decided to stop accepting donor funding that same year. *Mizzima* CEO Soe Myint says he knew it would be a risk but that he wanted to compete like everyone else in the marketplace. It has been a bit of a roller coaster ever since, he says, launching new products, partnering with different investors and, at times, picking up the pieces from ventures that have not succeeded; for example, the daily he launched in 2014 that shut down one year later (24). The key figures who founded the once-exiled media operations, and many of their staff and stringers, have for the most part stayed in the journalism field during the transition, with varying degrees of professional and financial success, although some have moved on to other more lucrative jobs at competing media operations, launched their own media outlets or joined international NGOs.

Whether or not the pre-transition support has had a structural impact on the national mainstream media landscape is debatable, but the long list of Burmese who benefited from international support during the military dictatorship nonetheless reads like a who's who of Myanmar's independent media, media development and free expression sectors. Their current work, many say, would have been unimaginable without the provision of aid and training that is helping them navigate the new media development narrative inside the country. Ye Naing Moe says the Yangon Journalism School would not even exist: "It was the regular, systematic support outside the country during the junta that ratcheted up the more recent media development inside" (30). Mon Mon Myat agrees, stressing that it was also a matter of local ownership and decision-making. "Before the opening, donors and media implementers tried to support what the Burmese wanted. After the opening, though, it was often what the donors wanted, driven by their policies rather than by need and local decision-making" (12). There was definite room for improvement, though, according to Myint Kyaw, during those pre-transition years, particularly with regards to training and safety. During the junta, he says, training was often focused on oppositional groups fighting for democracy, and on technical skills such as writing stories, conducting interviews, and structuring news, but did not focus sufficiently on ethics and professionalism. That makes it more challenging now, he says, to teach those skills. Safety was also a concern. Donors often supported media in exile and on the borders because there was no one to support inside or because it was risky. Yet the exiled media did not do enough to ensure the safety of the journalists living and working inside who helped them, often at great personal risk (13). These observations and lessons, the aid recipients say, have relevance during Myanmar's current transition, as well as for other countries experiencing political transitions.

The Political Opening: New Voices, More Whispers

> Until the political opening, I did not truly understand the level of discretion — the whispering and the silence — that characterized the two decades of international aid for the Burmese media sector under the junta, particularly when it came to working inside the country. The transition brought with it a brand new media development narrative, with unfamiliar rules and players, and it took considerable time before the longer-term donors and implementers felt they could trust the newcomers and feel comfortable speaking openly and collaborating. It some ways, the two groups still exist in different media development worlds.

Jane McElhone made this observation in early 2012 when OSF and Internews met in Chiang Mai, Thailand, to discuss the unprecedented changes inside Burma. The two organizations had never before spoken openly about what they had been doing inside the country. Fearing repercussions for grantees inside, they had not wanted to take the risk, even with trusted partners. This reticence, coupled with scepticism vis-à-vis the political opening on the part of the longer-term donors, was tinged with a desire to help grantees capitalize on the opening, according to OSF's Liz Tydeman. "Out of all our civil society partners, journalists and media organizations were the quickest to respond to Burma's political changes, so we desperately wanted to support them" (28). Nai Kasauh Mon, chief editor of Mon News Agency and former executive director of the ethnic media network Burma News International (BNI), compares this approach with those of newcomers to the media aid landscape. "After the opening the old media development players stuck with their partners out of a desire to maintain independent media, whereas the new players tended to offer support for the state and for capacity-building" (14). The changes provoked debate about where funding priorities should lie and what kind of relationships should be established with Thein Sein's government, and now with the NLD.

For the media development sector, 2012 was a transformative year, and along with unprecedented media reforms, including the abolition of pre-publication censorship, came a new cluster of international media donors and implementers. The Ministry of Information's rising media star (and future minister) Ye Htut heralded the planned reforms at the first national media development conference in March 2012 when he jokingly stated that Myanmar journalists who still wanted to be censored would have to go to China.

In many ways, the 2012 Conference on Media Development in Myanmar exemplified the sudden shift in the sector. Instead of the many familiar faces that had been quietly collaborating for years, the stage was filled with new faces talking about a country in which many of them had just begun to work. At one point, a newly arrived donor shocked long-term donors by announcing that he wanted to support training but that he could not find any existing projects. These new arrivals felt an urgency to carve out their own territory, but without necessarily having the time, or inclination, to learn about the two decades of work that had come before.[10] Their sense of urgency was often at odds with the caution and scepticism of many of the longstanding donors and media implementers who were waiting for their Burmese partners and grantees to set the agenda, but who were also criticized for reacting too slowly to the unexpected opportunities.

A key case in point is the UNESCO *Assessment of Media Development in Myanmar* report, released in 2016, and published jointly with International Media Support/Denmark (UNESCO 2016). With the exception of a brief reference to some of the groups that had conducted pre-transition journalism training along the Burmese-Thai border and inside the country, the report does not cite pre-transition aid and development work. It also does not include interviews with many of the key actors included in this chapter, who for the most part continue to work actively in the media development sector, including the National Endowment for Democracy, Open Society Foundations, Indochina Media Memorial Fund, and Burma Relief Centre. This represents a research gap in their report and a missed opportunity to document and assess the lessons of Myanmar's media development history most applicable to the ongoing development of the sector.

As a result of the 2012 reforms, donors and media implementers redirected the vast majority of their funding inside the country. Nevertheless, the main assumptions and motivations remained largely the same; notably, the promotion of democracy and human rights. What is different, however, is that donors and media implementers are no longer supporting the democracy movement in solidarity with the journalists inside the country and in exile against a common enemy, but are often now incorporating the state into their efforts to build democracy and to promote human rights. For many of the new arrivals, this meant collaborating with Thein Sein's former quasi-civilian administration, and working now with the NLD-led government. The new wild card in the media development community is therefore the state, which in significant ways has become the centre and focus of media development attention during the transition. Yangon Journalism School director Ye Naing Moe remembers the collective feeling of surprise on the part of independent journalists and editors inside the country at seeing government officials seated at meetings and conferences with their former foes in the exiled media community and a cluster of new media development actors. "There we were trying to protect our very small space for independent expression that we had carefully and creatively carved out during the junta", he explains, "when suddenly we looked up and saw these new actors — donors, NGOs and formerly exiled media — flying over our heads and into the laps of the authorities" (30).

Those relationships between media developers and the government were arguably at their closest during the early media reform years — 2012 and 2013. Now that the NLD are in power, however, they are arguably and ironically at their weakest. That private media, independent journalism, and media development are not priorities for this government is slowing, if not thwarting, the development of the sector. At the same time, the government has expanded the state media sector and safeguarded its privileges. International media developers and donors have nonetheless continued to support state media, much to the consternation of private media actors. Yet given the government's stance vis-à-vis the Rakhine crisis and the imprisonment of the Reuters journalists, the justification for this continued support is now, more than ever, in question.

The changes that at first seemed an opportunity for increased exchange and frank dialogue with a growing number of diverse voices have now been constrained by a return to whispers on sensitive topics, and by the wave of nationalism that surfaced in May 2012 and intensified in August 2017, resulting in renewed violence in Rakhine State and the mass exodus of Rohingya from the country.

The Rohingya Situation

While the legacy of two decades of media development aid during the military junta cannot be viewed and analysed through a single lens, the coverage of the Rakhine crisis by independent Myanmar media, particularly since August 2017, has triggered a number of unpleasant questions about the effectiveness of media development efforts. The conflicts in Kachin State and Shan State, where the UN alleges that Myanmar armed forces are responsible for war crimes and crimes against humanity, have been covered in some Myanmar media (United Nations Human Rights Council 2018). Yet on Rakhine many have chosen to remain silent or to publish the military and government's narratives with little or no critical analysis (Myanmar Institute for Democracy 2017). Media development efforts have supported the building of a multiplicity of outlets and platforms for the expression of diverse views, which, along with social media, have contributed to a disturbing degree of nationalist and racist discourse, and in some cases hate speech and incitement. International reactions to local Myanmar media coverage, and local media's counter-accusations of bias, have created a chasm between many local media actors and the international agencies that have long supported them.

While this trend was also visible during the communal violence that flared up in 2012, in the early days of the political transition, coverage by some of the recently arrived exiled media was at that point deemed less nationalistic than that of the media inside the country. That demonstrations to protest their coverage were organized in May 2012 outside of the DVB office, as well as the offices of some international media, is a case in point (McElhone 2012; Reporters Without Borders 2012). Yet much has changed in five years. When violence again erupted in August 2017, there was this time little difference in coverage. With a few rare exceptions, the majority of media adopted the official military and government stance, and some formerly exiled media joined in the blanket condemnation of international media coverage. The impact these developments will have in the longer term on Myanmar journalism — and on Myanmar journalists' relationships with international donors and media implementers — remains to be seen. According to Ye Naing Moe, in his interview in this volume, the sentencing of the two Reuters journalists to seven years in prison in August 2018 has prompted media coverage that is now more critical of the government. This is something to monitor.

Looking Forward

The legacy of two decades of pre-transition aid is playing out now as the current chapter of Myanmar's media development story is being written and reported. While a significant portion of that funding went to exiled media outlets, many individual actors both inside and outside the country also benefited. The story of the exiled media outlets is certainly better known internationally, yet which funding approach had the greatest influence in preparing media, journalists and free expression advocates for the transition deserves closer examination. In his interview in this volume, Thiha Saw argues, for example, that despite their international funding, formerly exiled media did not really affect the structure of the print media sector inside, as they were late to the game and media businesses had already been built inside the country. The impact of international aid on the legal and regulatory structures of media, as well as the culture of news values and media content, does deserve closer study, although direct causal links between this aid and its impact are not easy to document.

At the moment it is hard to be hopeful that the cultural legacy of decades of silence and secrecy in Myanmar, especially around sensitive and divisive topics, can be countered so that dialogue can remain open, and that public interest journalism can trump nationalism, populism and hatred. As the Myanmar media landscape continues to develop, media developers and donors must think carefully about which media are best positioned to promote public discussion and debate on key issues through independent, diverse and pluralistic coverage. They may not be those traditionally supported by external aid.

Yet despite the myriad challenges, there has been positive change, and some strong and younger voices have emerged, no longer satisfied with whispering, whatever the repercussions. The desire for freedom of expression and strong public service and investigative journalism remains clear in Myanmar, and grass-roots efforts have emerged to promote peace and tolerance and to counter divisive narratives. These are the efforts that should be prioritized for continued support.

Notes

1. In keeping with the style employed in the book and explained in the preface, in this chapter the authors use Burma/Rangoon for the period when the military junta was in power, and Myanmar/Yangon for the period of political transition.
2. The primary author has attended the annual conferences on media development in Myanmar since they began in 2012.
3. See also Meyers and Angaya Juma (2018); Miller (2009).
4. The CIMA report database indicates nearly $2.1 billion worth of China-financed projects in the media sectors of developing countries. It also shows that new donors are investing in media. For example, several new countries have joined the OECD's Development Assistance Committee since 2013, including Slovakia and Iceland, which for the first time appear as media supporters. The Gates Foundation is also included for the first time. Other new donor countries in the study include the United Arab Emirates, India and Brazil.
5. NED was founded in 1983 during the Reagan administration to support democratic movements around the world and to combat communism (https://www.ned.org/about/history/).
6. Representatives from four donor and media development groups, including the National Endowment for Democracy, Open Society Foundations, Free Voice Netherlands (now known as Free Press Unlimited) and Media Development Investment Fund participated in a focus group discussion about the two decades of pre-transition aid on 9 September 2017 in Yangon.
7. The co-author of this chapter, contributing editor Jane McElhone, was working as a donor at OSF during this time and closely monitored the embezzlement issue.
8. Sein Win notes that other leading journalists and editors took the same course in Cambodia, including Kyaw Min Swe from *The Voice*, now serving as executive director of the Myanmar Journalism Institute, and Kamayut TV founder Nathan Maung.
9. Khin Maung Win left DVB in 2017 and is now working as a media consultant.
10. We notice a similar trend among some scholars and journalists new to Myanmar, who write as though media and journalism have just emerged in the country as a result of the political opening.

References

Berger, G. 2010. "Problematizing 'Media Development' as a Bandwagon Gets Rolling". *International Communication Gazette* 72 (7): 547–65.

Brooten, L. 2003. "Global Communications, Local Conceptions: Human Rights and the Politics of Communication among the Burmese Opposition-in-Exile". Doctoral dissertation, Ohio University.

———. 2011. "Media, Militarization and Human Rights: Comparing Media Reform in the Philippines and Burma". *Communication, Culture & Critique* 4 (3): 312–32.

———. 2006. "Political Violence and Journalism in a Multi-ethnic State: A Case Study of Burma (Myanmar)". *Journal of Communication Inquiry* 30 (4), 354–73.

Brownlee, B.J. 2017. "Media Development in Syria: The Janus-faced Nature of Foreign Aid Assistance". *Third World Quarterly* 38 (10): 2276–94

Deane, J. 2011. "Media Development". In *The Handbook of Development Communication and Social Change*, edited by K.G. Wilkins, T. Tufte, and R. Obregon, pp. 226–41. Wiley Blackwell.

DVB. 2011. "Statement: Possible Embezzlement of DVB Funds". http://www.dvb.no/uncategorized/press-statement-misappropriation-of-dvb-assets-in-the-news-network-inside-burma/19320.

FOJO: Media Institute. 2013. "Media in Exile: Problems and Solutions". https://fojo.se/our-stories/281-media-in-exile-problems-and-solutions.

Ford, M., M. Gillan, and Htwe Htwe Thein. 2016. "From Cronyism to Oligarchy? Privatization and Business Elites in Myanmar". *Journal of Contemporary Asia* 46 (1): 18–41.

Foster, M. 2013. "The Business of Media in Myanmar, 2013". A report commissioned by Internews. https://www.internews.org/sites/default/files/resources/Internews_Burma_Business_Report2014.pdf.

Hume, E. 2004. "The Media Missionaries: American Support for Journalism Excellence and Press Freedom around the Globe". Miami: Knight Foundation.

Humphries, R. 2009. "Saffron-Robed Monks and digital Flash Cards: The Development and Challenges of Burmese Exile Media". In *Development in Asia: Inter-disciplinary, Post-neoliberal, and Transnational Perspective*, edited by D. Nault, pp. 237–58. Boca Raton: Brown Walker.

IMS (International Media Support). 2012. "Myanmar: Creating Media in Service of the Public". 28 September 2012. https://www.mediasupport.org/myanmar-creating-media-in-service-of-the-public/.

Kalathil, S. 2017. "A Slowly Shifting Field: Understanding Donor Priorities in Media Development". Center for International Media Assistance. 12 June 2017. http://www.cima.ned.org/publication/slowly-shifting-field/ (accessed 15 June 2017).

Kean, T. 2018. "Public Discourse". In *Routledge Handbook of Contemporary Myanmar*, edited by A. Simpson, N. Farrelly, and I. Holliday, pp. 145–57. New York: Routledge.

Kumar, K. 2006. "International Assistance to promote Independent Media in Transition and Post-conflict Societies". *Democratization* 13 (4): 652–67.

McElhone, J. 2012. "Exiled Media's Coming of Age: Setting the Stage for a Shared Burmese Identity Based on Inclusive Citizenship and Human Rights". Msc dissertation, School of Oriental and African Studies (SOAS).

———. 2018. "Mapping Media Development in Myanmar". Available at https://bangkok.unesco.org/content/mapping-media-development-myanmar-myanmar-and-english-versions>.

Miller, J. 2009. "NGOs and 'Modernization' and 'Democratization' of Media: Situating Media Assistance". *Global Media and Communication* 5 (1): 9–3.

———. 2011. "Questioning the Western Approach to Training". *Niemann Reports* 65 (1): 38–41.

Myanmar Institute for Democracy. 2017. "The Interim Report – Summary of Media Coverage on Rakhine Conflict and Recommendations". Available at https://view.publitas.com/mid/report-eng/page/1.

Myers M., and L. Angaya Juma. 2018. *Defending Independent Media: A Comprehensive Analysis of Aid Flows*. Washington DC: Center for International Media Assistance (CIMA). https://www.cima.ned.org/publication/comprehensive-analysis-media-aid-flows/.

Norris, P. 2006. "The Role of the Free Press in Promoting Democratization, Good Governance, and Human Development". Paper for UNESCO meeting on World Press Freedom Day: Media, Development, and Poverty Eradication. Colombo, Sri Lanka, 1–2 May 2006. Available at http://www.gsdrc.org/document-library/the-role-of-the-free-press-in-promoting-democratization-good-governance-and-human-development/.

Open Society Foundations. 2013. "Explainers: Burma and Open Society". https://www.opensocietyfoundations.org/explainers/burma-and-open-society.

Panneerselvan, A.S., and L. Nair. 2008. *Spheres of Influence*. Panos South Asia. http://archive.panosa.org/pdf/Spheres%20of%20influence%20final%20pdf.pdf.

Price, M.E. 2001. "Journeys in Media Space. Global Media and National Controls: Rethinking the Role of the State". Graham Spry Memorial Lecture. http://www.fondsgrahamspryfund.ca/previous-conferences/conference-2001/transcript-of-journeys-in-media-space-global-media-and-national-controls-rethinking-the-role-of-the-state-2001/.

———. 2015. *Free Expression, Globalism and the New Strategic Communication*. New York: Cambridge University Press.

Price, M., and P. Krug. 2000. *The Enabling Environment for Free and Independent Media*. Programme in Comparative Media Law & Policy, Oxford University.

Reporters Without Borders. 2012. "Crisis in Arakan State and New Threats to Freedom of News and Information". https://rsf.org/en/reports/crisis-arakan-state-and-new-threats-freedom-news-and-information.

Settles, R. 2018. "The Media Market: Obstacles to Local Media Sustainability". In *An Unfavorable Business: Running local media in Myanmar's Ethnic States and Regions*, edited by T. Piper and J. McElhone. New York: Media Development Investment Fund (MDIF). Available at https://www.mdif.org.

Transparency International. 2017. *Corruptions Perception Index 2017*. https://www.transparency.org/news/feature/corruption_perceptions_index_2017#table.

UNESCO and IMS. 2016. *Assessment of Media Development in Myanmar*. http://www.unesco.org/new/en/communication-and-information/resources/publications-and-communication-materials/publications/full-list/assessment-of-media-development-in-myanmar.

United Nations Human Rights Council. 2018. "Report of Independent International Fact-Finding Mission on Myanmar". https://www.ohchr.org/EN/HRBodies/HRC/MyanmarFFM/Pages/ReportoftheMyanmarFFM.aspx.

USAID (United States Agency for International Development). n.d. *USAID Assistance to Burma from 2008–2012*. https://www.usaid.gov/sites/default/files/documents/1861/USAID_Burma_assistance_2008-2012_fact_sheet.pdf.

Voltmer, K. 2013. *The Media in Transitional Democracies*. Cambridge: Polity.

Waisbord, S. 2008. "The Institutional Challenges of Participatory Communication in International Aid". *Social Identities* 14 (4): 505–22.

Appendix: List of Interviews

1) Ahr Man, editor-in-chief of *7Day Daily*. (Personal communication on 30 November 2017.)
2) Brang Mai, founding CEO of the *Myitkyina News Journal* in Myitkyina, Kachin State. Studied at the Internews J-School in Chiang Mai, Thailand. (Interviewed in Loikaw, Kayah State on 26 June 2017.)
3) Allison Campbell, Internews vice-president for global initiatives. Founded the Internews Burma Project in 2001, set up its J-School (for exiled Burmese journalists in Thailand), and transitioned the project to Yangon in 2013. (Email correspondence on 24 July and 1 December 2017.)
4) William Chen, CEO of *Modern* and *Kumudra*. (Interviewed in Yangon on 2 November 2017.)
5) David Holmertz, head of Support Unit for Asia and MENA, Department for Asia, Middle East and Humanitarian Assistance, Swedish International Development Cooperation Agency (Sida). He has supported Burmese

media since 2007. He was based in Yangon from 2014 to 2017. (Interviewed in Yangon on 13 June 2017; email correspondence on 2 November 2017.)
6) Khin Maung Win, co-founder and deputy director of DVB Multimedia until March 2018. (Interviewed in Yangon on 13 September 2017.)
7) John Knaus, associate director with the National Endowment for Democracy (NED). He has been supporting Myanmar media and civil society since 1990. (Interviewed in Yangon on 9 September 2017; email correspondence on 14 November 2017.)
8) Kyaw Zwa Moe, English editor at *The Irrawaddy*. (Interviewed in Loikaw, Kayah State on 26 June 2017.)
9) Mai Naing Naing Oo, founding chief editor of the *Marnagar Journal* in Lashio, Shan State. (Interviewed in Loikaw, Kayah State on 26 June 2017.)
10) Sarah McLean, formerly executive-director of the Indochina Media Memorial Foundation (IMMF). Yangon Journalism School board member. (Interviewed in Mandalay on 6 November 2017.)
11) Lyndal Min, consultant who has worked on Myanmar for more than twenty-five years and who was in the media development field in Myanmar and Southeast Asia from 1998 to 2008. (Interviewed in Yangon on 8 July 2017.)
12) Mon Mon Myat, co-founder of the Human Rights, Human Dignity Film Festival. Studied at the Internews J-School in Chiang Mai, Thailand. (Interviewed in Yangon on 12 July 2017.)
13) Myint Kyaw, Press Council member and trainer. (Interviewed in Loikaw, Kayah State on 26 June 2017.)
14) Nai Kasauh Mon, executive director of the ethnic media network BNI and chief editor of Mon News Agency. (Interviewed in Hpa-An, Kayin State on 27 September 2017.)
15) Nay Phone Latt, Yangon regional parliamentarian, former blogger, political prisoner, and co-founder of Myanmar IT for Development and PEN Myanmar. (Interviewed in Yangon on 12 July 2017.)
16) Mark Nelson, senior director, Center for International Media Assistance (CIMA). (Email correspondence on 28 September 2018 and 2 November 2017).
17) Nyan Lynn, Mawkun co-founder and publisher. Second year doctoral student in the Journalism & Mass Communications Program at the University of Kansas. (Series of interviews in 2016 and 2017 and email correspondence on 14 September 2018.)
18) Nyein Nyein Naing, editor-in-chief of 7Day Digital. (Interviewed on 5 November 2017 in Mandalay.)
19) Michael Pan, Internews Myanmar country director. Formerly journalist in residence at the Internews J-School in Chiang Mai, Thailand. (Interviewed in Yangon on 12 July 2017.)

20) Tessa Piper, Asia director of the Media Development Investment Fund, including the Myanmar Media Program. (Interviewed in Yangon on 9 September 2017.)
21) Gary Rozema, Burma Relief Center programme manager, who has worked on Myanmar for twenty-seven years and with ethnic media for eighteen years. (Interviewed on the border on 13 November 2017.)
22) Sein Win, lead trainer, Myanmar Journalism Institute. (Interviewed in Loikaw, Kayah State on 27 June 2017.)
23) Seng Mai, founding chief editor of the *Myitkyina News Journal* in Myitkyina, Kachin State. (Email correspondence on 30 November 2017.)
24) Soe Myint, chief editor of the formerly exiled *Mizzima News*. (Interviewed in Yangon on 20 June 2017.)
25) Soe Soe Nyar, managing editor, the *Kantarawaddy Times*, Dee Maw Soe, Kayah State. (Interviewed in Loikaw, Kayah State, on 27 June 2017.)
26) Swe Win, *Myanmar Now* editor-in-chief. (Interviewed in Yangon on 28 June 2018.)
27) Thiha Saw, veteran journalist, Press Council member, secretary of the Myanmar Journalists Association, executive director of the Myanmar Journalism Institute. (Interviewed in Yangon on 16 July 2017.)
28) Liz Tydeman. Worked for the Open Society Institute Burma Program for fifteen years, including four years as Myanmar country director (2013–16). She is currently working with the Swedish – Burma Committee. (Interviewed in Yangon on 9 September 2017; email correspondence on 29 November 2017.)
29) Kenneth Van Toll, formerly deputy-director of Free Voice Netherlands. (Interviewed in Yangon on 9 September 2017.)
30) Ye Naing Moe, founding director and lead trainer of the Yangon and Mandalay Journalism Schools. (Interviewed in Yangon on 20 September 2017 and in Mandalay on 5 November 2017.)

4

The Changing Face of Print Media: An Interview with News Veteran Thiha Saw

Interviewed by Jane Madlyn McElhone and Gayathry Venkiteswaran

The publication in 2013 of Myanmar's first private daily newspapers in half a century was one of the most important and exciting moments for journalists and editors since the country's political opening. Thiha Saw launched one of those first private newspapers — the English-language *Myanmar Freedom Daily*. He has been part of the country's print media sector since 1979, most recently as executive editor at Myanmar Consolidated Media (MCM), where he oversaw the country's only English-language daily, *Myanmar Times*, a Myanmar-language weekly, and MCM's online team. *Myanmar Media in Transition* contributing editors Jane Madlyn McElhone and Gayathry Venkiteswaran interviewed veteran publisher, journalist and editor Thiha Saw in 2017 and 2018 to talk about his experiences and his expectations of the political opening.

Q: You are one of Myanmar's print media veterans and a vocal champion of the private media sector. You got your start, though, during the military regime working for state-controlled print media until an unexpected chance came along to do independent journalism.

TS: Yes, I started at one of the two English-language state papers, *Working People's Daily*, in the late 70s, and then moved to the state-controlled Myanmar News Agency in the early 80s. Then, in August 1988 [during the student-initiated uprising], we got our chance. A group of young and mid-career editors, including me, took over six Burmese- and English-language newspapers and ran a free press for about three weeks. We told the chief editors to go away and had a brief, amazing, period of press freedom. Then a new military government took over and they sent me a letter saying I was allowed to "retire" prematurely.

Despite the new military regime and your own so-called retirement, that's when you started witnessing slow change in the print media sector.

Well, there was strict pre-publication censorship, so there was no possibility of having a private daily newspaper, but there were dozens of private monthlies run by journalists and writers. So in 1990 I launched my first private publication — a monthly business journal called *Myanmar Dana*. To publish on time, we had to send our content to the censors at least one week before deadline. We also had to find someone who would lease us a licence. In those days licences were issued to government departments or officially recognized groups, like writers' groups or associations for retired police officers. The private monthlies set the ground for the private weeklies that appeared in early 2000, starting with a soccer journal. It was a really popular game in Myanmar, so you could make money with it. The newsweeklies, like *Eleven*, *The Voice* and *Flower*, followed in mid-2000.

So how did you get your licence?

I actually tried applying myself, but they said sorry, you're a blacklisted journalist. Yet they were actually quite nice, saying we know you're a serious journalist and you want to do this kind of publication, so go ask your father. My father had retired in 1987 from the Ministry of Information. He was a chief accountant and then some kind of deputy-director with the ministry's literary publishing house. [It was founded as the Burma Translation Society in the 1950s, but was then nationalized by Ne Win in the mid 1960s.] So I said, "Dad please help me", and that's how one licence ended up belonging to my family.

Were the Saffron Revolution [in 2007] and Cyclone Nargis [in 2008] game changers?

By Saffron and Nargis, the weekly journals were already quite popular. They were critical events, but given pre-publication censorship [that remained until 2012], the journals had to send their news to exiled media friends to be broadcast or published online so the world would know what was going on. There was no local reporting inside the country at all, although with Nargis things changed a little bit. The first couple of weeks there was a huge taboo and we could not cover it at all. So there we were with a huge cyclone and we could not write about it. But then reporting started inside. Yet the change did not come from the local journalists who were always deeply involved in all kinds of news stories. It came from the way the regime handled the censorship process, relaxing it to some extent along the way.

Were these changes part of the military's so-called 7-Step Roadmap to Democracy?

Yes. They had a plan, even if we didn't believe it at the time. We thought it was propaganda. But there were these gradual changes along the way, including a new constitution in 2008, and then the elections in 2010, and then relaxation of censorship.

And what about coverage of Aung San Suu Kyi?

When Aung San Suu Kyi was still under house arrest, could we write her stories? No way. And she was only released after election day [the elections were held on 7 November 2010; Aung San Suu Kyi was released on 13 November]. Maybe to prevent her from participating, or maybe not — we don't know. But just before her release there were rumours, so reporters and all kinds of other interested people wanted to be there. The road was blocked with barbed wire until the very last day, so we sat beside it until the way was cleared and then we ran to the gate of her residence and started taking pictures. Everybody wrote stories and published her photo, but what about the huge crowds? I took their photos and published them in my weekly journal *Open News*. For that I was summoned to the censorship board. I had broken one regulation — I didn't submit the content and pictures before printing. But she was released on a Saturday and my paper was published on Monday, so what could I do? I wanted to reach my readers immediately. So I said to my team — let's forget about the process and let's publish the story. You go to prison for five years or ten years, whatever. Let's go ahead. And there was a second problem — I was the publisher and editor-in-chief of *Open News Weekly* and wrote a satirical piece every week. They knew this, and they also knew the licence didn't belong to me. They wouldn't give me one under my name, as they didn't think I was pro-regime. Yet the person I leased it from happened to be the wife of the cousin of Minister of Information Kyaw San, so they didn't want to touch her. She was a friend of my wife's, and we paid her 20,000 kyat every week. So they decided they couldn't take action against her, and instead told her to fire me. Yet I was the publisher and the editor-in-chief, so I had to fire myself.

So were you then blacklisted?

No. But my name wasn't on the paper for six weeks. I was there the whole time but my name wasn't, and I continued that paper until I launched that stupid [laughing] English-language *Myanma Freedom Daily* in 2014. At that point I had to suspend both my monthly and weekly and put all of my energy into publishing a daily paper.

Tell us about what you call that *stupid daily paper*.

It was crazy. We lost a lot of money — almost everything. But I didn't do it out of stupidity. I felt at the time — and I still feel — that Myanmar needs a private independent English-language daily. Not the state *New Light of Myanmar* but a real voice of Myanmar people. Our first cover story was the twenty-fifth anniversary of 1988. That was my idea — my ambition. No other English paper had it. But I was warned the market wasn't ready, wasn't mature, so people said they couldn't assist me. And most of the advertising market went to the broadcast sector. But I still went ahead and got a licence. It was the first time I was granted a licence under my own name. And we ran for a year, before we suspended the paper. It was an exciting year, but few dailies lasted longer than that. Then I was asked to join the *Myanmar Times*, so I went there and created their English-language daily.

And in 2012 and 2013 the ground was set for the private dailies.

Yes. In 2012 they scrapped the pre-publication censorship process and established the Press Council. Then, in 2013, the new laws started coming in, including the News Media Law and the Printing and Publishing Enterprises Law. To a certain extent, licences and processes relaxed. We wanted to scrap the special media licensing, but they said no, no, no. Yet we knew the trick — that they could control us through that process. But what they did was relax the rules and decentralize. Now you could apply for a licence in any district all over the country and even apply online. That made it easier. And then the second big thing — they got rid of the yearly renewal process. Now you were OK for five years. That was a huge change for print media. And then came the daily papers.

What lessons have you learned moving from a monthly to a weekly and then to a daily from 1990 to 2014, and then back again to a daily and weekly in 2017?

There are at least a couple of lessons. Number one: don't ever look away from the real market and the changing dynamics. Whether a monthly, weekly or daily, you need to pay attention. Number two: to have a media reform process, there needs to be political will. The state is still the major media player. State-owned entities need to be shut down. The big advertising money goes to them, as do public subsidies. That means they are using taxpayers' money, selling at low prices, and making a lot of money, especially the two Burmese-language state papers. Private people are not happy about it. It is time to scrap them or privatize them. That would create a level playing field. Private media is independent but not really strong, so I have also been suggesting setting up a Myanmar media fund. There is funding from international organizations, so why not from the government?

Did the return of exiled media impact the print media sector?

No, not really. We welcomed them back of course. But they were late to the game. *7Day*, *Eleven* and others had already built their media empires on their own and they knew how to manage businesses in the local markets. The exiled media had international funding but couldn't compete. *Mizzima* launched a daily and *The Irrawaddy* a weekly, but, like many other print media, they did not survive.

What do you think the print media sector will look like in five years time?

I don't know. But take a look at India or Japan. They still have very strong daily print newspapers. Despite technological changes, some people still want to read print. In Myanmar we are leapfrogging from print to broadcast to social media. More and more people are getting their information from mobile online platforms. Now we have more than fifty million mobile phones, and they are getting cheaper. But I am pretty sure we will have newspapers in five years time — that is if the government makes changes, including getting rid of state papers.

But given its performance during its first three years in power, is it likely the current government will shut down state media?

Honestly, even though we keep talking to them and explaining why they need to shut down state media, they haven't budged. So we don't expect to have a level playing field for a long time. That means opportunities are limited. We know we can't compete with state media and we know we can't compete with the speed and reach of digital media with regards to breaking news. But what about in-depth and investigative reporting? Print media still has the advantage for that.

So, knowing what you know, what made you take the risk of jumping back into the print media sector?

I always said I'd be willing, even in the current environment. I knew what to expect. I knew that media were struggling and losing money. And I was no longer only thinking in terms of print. I had said I wanted to set up a multimedia house — print, digital, online TV or maybe radio — and when I went back to *Myanmar Times*, that is what I planned to do. So, yes, I was pressured to go back to revive, to save, the English-language daily. But I think my role was to be a multi-platform change catalyst.

5

Privacy Risks in Myanmar's Emerging ICT Sector

Kamran Emad and Erin McAuliffe

Before the long-awaited 2015 general election, a cyber-group operating under the name Union of Hacktivists[1] became infamous for launching several DDoS (distributed denial of service)[2] attacks on Burmese media sites, including *The Irrawaddy* and *Eleven Media*. Unleashed Research Labs, a cybersecurity firm, traced the origins of these attacks to a military-operated network run by the Defense Services Computer Directorate, attributing the attacks on independent media outlets to the work of government — namely military — employees (Hindstrom 2016). Although the intention was simply platform and content defacement, these attacks emphasize the risks individuals, institutions and corporations face in storing and sharing information online. As more content is exchanged online and more information, particularly personal information, is stored by mobile providers, such risks are likely to shift from defacement attacks to identity theft and privacy violations. Given Myanmar's weak central regulations and the government's ability to access consumer and provider information under the 2013 Telecommunications Law, individuals and organizations are increasingly at risk of privacy violations.

Myanmar's transition is unique. Not only is the country emerging from the longest modern-day military government but the political transition also parallels the introduction of affordable smartphones and mobile technologies available for public consumption across the country. This availability and affordability of information and communications technologies (ICTs) is certainly exciting for the Myanmar public; however, security and privacy risks are high due to a patchwork regulatory framework and rapid growth in mobile penetration. During military rule, modern ICT infrastructure and services were largely unavailable to the public because of high prices. Alongside high economic barriers to entry, punitive regulations emphasized the government's ability to restrict an individual's usage of ICTs while failing to provide a coherent strategy for addressing macro-level issues in the sector. These issues range from cyber-attacks to data collection standards imposed on industry stakeholders. Today, the ICT regulatory framework remains largely unrestricted by laws or institutions, with the exception of the 2013 Telecommunications Law, which allows the government to seize information on ICT users and disable communications services based on broad legal language that is highly unspecific (MCRB, IHRB and DIHR 2015). While the government did enact the Law Protecting the Privacy and Security of Citizens in 2017, the law's ambiguous language provides little clarity or assurance to individuals. This existing legal environment protects the government while putting the public at risk of unwanted surveillance. It also places companies in a precarious position; by complying with the laws, they could infringe on the human rights of their customers.

Ethnic discrimination and the sensitivity of identity documents in Myanmar pose additional risks to individuals as ICTs continue to collect and store personal information through software and product sales. Many individuals lack official documentation, and others are not considered full citizens. Their designation in a "lesser" category — as associate or naturalized citizen — often stipulates membership in an undesirable and racially discriminated-against group. In many countries, individuals are required to register SIM cards using official documents. Such practices are also emerging in Myanmar. The Ministry of Transport and Communications has required mobile phone users to register their SIM cards since March 2017 by providing their mobile operator with their personal identification documents and current address. This is an ad-hoc process intended to attribute individual users to SIM cards (and thus telecommunications activity) while allowing law enforcement to identify individuals in emergencies or criminal investigations; however, the benefits of this approach are disputed (MCRB 2014). If registration requirements expand, individuals could be denied services by local distributors based on their citizenship status and become susceptible to discrimination when personal communications data is improperly used by law enforcement.

The Data Revolution and the Explosion of Digitally Stored Data in Myanmar

The ICT sector in Myanmar has expanded significantly since the Posts and Telecommunications Department (PTD) under the Ministry of Communications and Information Technology (MCIT) permitted foreign operators to enter the market in 2013. Estimates place mobile penetration in Myanmar at around fifty million people (*Mizzima* 2018), with Google's Android operating system dominating mobile market share in the country. As more citizens gain access to affordable wireless services, usage of mobile apps and third-party services has increased well outside of major population centres in Mandalay, Naypyidaw and Yangon. As is the case globally, the demand for mobile data is growing exponentially and, with it, the quantity of user-generated data stemming from the usage of ICT devices and software. Increased connectivity is already affecting a variety of sectors, including healthcare, financial services and transportation/logistics. However, while ICTs are certainly transformational, additional focus is needed to ensure that positive outcomes are maximized, particularly in the context of human rights. This includes the right to privacy.

Myanmar's digital revolution comes at a time when mobile devices have become gateways to distribution platforms for apps and multi-media, revolutionizing communications through traditional telephony, Voice over Internet Protocol (VoIP),[3] IP-based messaging apps[4] and social media. With more people connected than ever before, a flurry of new businesses are establishing additional data touch points with Myanmar users. Businesses are also working to accommodate customer demand for more profitable mobile data services, instead of traditional telephony and SMS services (Lee and Slodkowski 2016). Given the newness of ICTs in Myanmar, there is a knowledge gap between ICT users and companies providing ICT services. Many users are unaware of what information they are sharing when using ICTs and are uninformed as to how they can manage their data footprint online. This includes a general lack of awareness of existing grievance mechanisms and options for remedy in the event of digital dangers such as revenge pornography, hate speech or cyber-bullying.[5]

The amount of data being generated by ICT usage and then transmitted, stored and analysed is massive. Collecting this immense amount of information is a priority for mobile network operators (MNOs) and over-the-top (OTT) service providers[6] for two primary reasons: (1) regulatory compliance, including the ability to fulfil information requests made by law enforcement and government security agencies; and (2) to leverage user data for business insights and/or as a component of a broader monetization strategy. In the context of ICTs, "data" can refer to a variety of information, including communications data, metadata and personally identifiable information. All this information can be utilized to affirmatively identify an individual user and associate him or her with specific communications occurring on a network.[7] When individuals register their SIM cards or create accounts through various services provided by MNOs, their information can be stored anywhere from a filing cabinet to an electronic database, depending on the relative sophistication of the entity storing the information. Depending on how this information is stored and protected, there can be risks of misuse, often with the original provider of the data unaware of how their information is being utilized across the public and private sectors.

Currently, the only relevant privacy law in the country is the Law Protecting the Privacy and Security of Citizens, enacted by the government in March 2017. The law is vague and ill conceived. Although it stipulates that citizens have the right to privacy and security as well as protection of these rights, the definitions of key terms remain ambiguous. The law also fails to outline a clear process for how information can be obtained and how it will be protected and regulated.[8] Without clear and strong privacy regulations, the government's ability to access user data stored by ICT companies and relevant third parties is codified in both the Telecommunications Law and Electronic Transactions Law (MCRB, IHRB and DIHR 2015). The lack of coherent privacy regulations is not unique to Myanmar and is not surprising given the history of the country's information environment and the absence of a definition of privacy in Myanmar's cultural and linguistic contexts. However, large scale private investment combined with rapid public connectivity during the early stages of the country's political transition indicates a strong need for a national and regional focus on necessary legal reforms that protect individuals and foster positive relations between the government, the private sector and the public.

Some larger multinational corporations (MNCs) operating in the country have turned to international standards for data privacy regulation, but most companies face barriers in guaranteeing the protection of personally identifiable information (PII) and informing users when their data are collected or transferred to a third party. However, even MNCs with privacy regulations cannot fully guarantee the safety of their users' information in an environment that grants the government unchecked ability to access and use such data. In the absence of a clear data regulatory framework and in an environment of low user awareness, companies have a responsibility to carefully manage user data, particularly PII, and to make valiant efforts to promote information literacy among users.

Myanmar's ICT Sector and Current Regulatory Framework

Former president Thein Sein's 2012–15 Framework for Economic and Social Reform (FESR) identified the need to improve telecommunication services as a key policy concern for the country and set an ambitious target of eighty per cent mobile phone penetration by 2015 (Government of Myanmar 2013).[9] Broader market liberalization has led to improved connectivity, but there are numerous gaps in Myanmar's legal framework. The existing legal framework includes broad legal authority for the government to access private data. Article 75 of the 2013 Telecommunications Law favours the national security interests of the government and fails to specify safeguards for companies or individuals. Article 76 allows the government to enter and inspect telecommunications services and relevant data when it is "in the public interest" or an "emergency". In addition, both the 2004 Electronic Transaction Law (Sections 33[a] and [b]) and the 1996 Computer Science Development Law (Section 35) allow the government to imprison individuals they perceive to be using electronic technologies or computer networks to engage in activity that undermines state security and national unity (MCRB, IHRB and DIHR 2015, pp. 78–80). Furthermore, the central body of the Electronic Transactions Control Board has the right to acquire any identification documents from individuals suspected of violating the 2004 law. These provisions exist in the absence of a rights-respecting model to limit government surveillance,[10] further threatening user privacy. While there are numerous laws in place that pose serious human rights risks to users, there is no existing framework outlining requirements for businesses collecting and storing user/customer data. Ideally, these requirements would include specific information about how users are informed (via terms of use or otherwise) in their local language of data collection policies and minimum standards for data encryption.[11]

Risks to human rights are amplified by the generally low levels of digital literacy among users, including a limited understanding of how to appropriately manage personal information online. In addition to the issue of users not understanding options for remedy in digital spaces, it can also be challenging for users to differentiate between companies collecting and sharing data. As the Myanmar government has not taken steps to protect human rights through a cohesive legal framework, private sector stakeholders must align their operational policies with the UN Guiding Principles on Business and Human Rights. Dialogue between the government, civil society and the private sector will be critical as policies are developed and refined (MCRB and MIDO 2015). Forums for stakeholder engagement should be operated transparently, with limited barriers to entry for those interested in participating. Civil society can help private companies expand their human rights due diligence and policy design based on front-line expertise and knowledge of the local environment. During the 2013 telecommunications rollout, many community members had a difficult time discerning subcontractors from network operators or understanding the difference between network operators and OTT service providers. This resulted in misunderstandings within the community regarding who was responsible for addressing community concerns and providing grievance mechanisms. In the context of privacy, transparent communication can help clarify to customers/users when their data are collected, how they are stored, and practical steps users can take to manage their digital footprint online.

Risks and Opportunities

In the year following the introduction of services by two additional foreign providers — Ooredoo and Telenor — mobile penetration surpassed half of the country's population, smartphones with 3G-enabled SIM cards became the norm for users, and the price of SIM cards dropped from a few hundred dollars to approximately US$1.50 apiece (Htoo Thant 2015). Both Telenor and Ooredoo introduced 4G services in late 2015, and Mytel[12] — Myanmar's fourth operator — began services in 2018 with 4G coverage (Aung Kyaw Nyunt 2018; "Viettel to Launch" 2018). The arrival of faster networks could parallel such development in more developed nations such as the United States, where 5G is projected to arrive by 2020. With fixed-line internet rates still out of reach for the average Myanmar citizen, most people in the country access the internet via 3G or 4G wireless networks on Android smartphones. Messaging apps that use Wi-Fi or 3G connectivity — such as Viber, LINE and Facebook Messenger — have become quite popular and are largely the norm for everyday communication. And, lastly, Niantic's augmented reality game Pokémon Go landed in Myanmar in August 2016, allowing youth (and adults) to partake in their first augmented reality experience.

Telecommunication companies have also strived to meet the needs and demands of Myanmar's rural and impoverished population by introducing cost-free data services and services to facilitate financial transactions. In 2016, MPT began offering Facebook Flex, allowing users to switch between a free mode and data mode when using Facebook, and Facebook Free Basics, or internet.org, a platform run by Facebook that allows registered mobile phone users of partner MNOs (mobile network operators) to access information on a variety of topics provided by different service providers (Trautwein 2016). Although Facebook argues that Free Basics provides many offline communities with opportunities for accessing information, the service has been heavily criticized, particularly in India, for allegedly disrespecting net neutrality and crafting the internet into a "walled garden" of information (Trautwein 2016). Financial technology companies are emerging, working to provide alternative methods for financial transactions and services for the unbanked — approximately 90 per cent of Myanmar's population (Oxford Business Group 2016). In Kenya, the mobile money service M-PESA has expanded financial inclusivity, making storing and exchanging money quicker and safer and extending participation to the unbanked. In similar ways to the service in Kenya, mobile money has the potential to become a leading financial service for individuals in Myanmar, given the low percentage of people using banks and the growth of mobile phone accessibility (McGee 2016). Although such services and opportunities are provided with good intentions, they introduce several new risks for various stakeholders, predominantly individuals, in this evolving data environment. Notably, government access to information increases the surveillance of individuals and potentially exposes them to more discrimination. In addition, the absence of protection and responsibility mechanisms to regulate the actions of individuals, businesses and the government means there could be risks of theft or the mishandling of money stored in or transferred through a mobile money service.

In Myanmar, Facebook remains largely unregulated except in situations when the government deems content threatening to national security or the government's security, as stated in the 2013 Telecommunications Law. This, however, leaves a mobile avenue open for users to share personal content and information — their own or the data of others — with relative impunity (Hynes 2016). As of 2016 there were already several cases where women either had Facebook accounts created with their name and phone number advertising sexual intercourse or had received threats that individuals were going to Photoshop their photos to appear nude and share them online (*Myanmar Now* 2016). Facebook has also become the "go-to" for daily information, and mobile network operators have begun promoting zero-rated Facebook use or specific data packages catering to heavy social media users. MPT customers also have access to services provided through Facebook Free Basics. In addition to free access to Facebook, Free Basics provides access to health, education and business sources. *Maya* and *BabyCenter*, websites for women's health and pregnancy, respectively, and *SmartBusiness*, an entrepreneur website, receive heavy daily traffic through Free Basics users ("Free Basics" 2015). Although this does disseminate useful information to largely offline audiences, it reiterates the widespread dilemma in Myanmar that the internet is equivalent to Facebook and reinforces Facebook as the main source for obtaining information. This is hindering the efforts of those attempting to increase avenues for credible information sources.

In Myanmar's developing ICT sector, a regulatory framework that protects the right to privacy is essential. The absence of adequate data privacy regulations and the existence of current laws that allow the government to access user information increase the possibility of misuse. As Myanmar's political transition continues, companies must work proactively to protect human rights. With the help of trusted local civil society organizations, companies can analyse their operational policies and grievance mechanisms through a local lens to ensure they are protecting the human rights of their users/customers. From a business standpoint, companies can leverage data privacy and transparent disclosure as a differentiator in the marketplace, and incentivize the adoption of standards across the industry. Companies must step to the forefront and ensure their users are informed and protected.

Notes

1. The name under which a group of cyber hacktivists that emerged in 2015 claimed responsibility for cyberattacks against Burmese independent media outlets.
2. In a DDoS attack, one system is targeted and made unavailable by multiple systems (computers and internet connections) that temporarily disrupt its service.

3. VOIP delivers voice communications and multimedia over the internet.
4. IP-based messaging applications exchange text-based communication and multimedia over the internet.
5. See Chapters 3.C and 4.2 in MCRB, IHRB and DIHR (2015) for further information on digital dangers.
6. OTT refers to services provided by telecommunications service providers through the public internet or cloud services.
7. See Chapter 4.3 in MCRB, IHRB and DIHR (2015) for further information on data privacy and international best practices.
8. See Union Parliament 2017.
9. The target was achieved in 2017.
10. See Lawful Interception Annex of MCRB, IHRB and DIHR (2015, p. 35).
11. See Chapter 4.3 in MCRB, IHRB and DIHR (2015) for further information on data privacy and international best practices.
12. The network is a collaboration between Vietnam's Viettel and two partners in Myanmar — Star High Public Company and Myanmar National Telecom Holding Public Ltd. "Mytel" is the brand name of this collaborative network, Telecom International Myanmar.

References

Aung Kyaw Nyunt. 2018. "Mytel Enters Myanmar's Telecoms Mart". *Myanmar Times*, 26 March 2018. https://www.mmtimes.com/news/mytel-enters-myanmars-telecoms-mart.html.

"Free Basics Platform – English". 2015. https://info.internet.org/en/story/platform/.

Government of Myanmar. 2013. "Framework for Economic and Social Reform – Policy Priorities for 2012–2015 towards the Long-Term Goals of the National Comprehensive Development Plan (FESR)". Available at https://mdricesd.files.wordpress.com/2015/10/paper-fesr-2012-15-jan-2013.pdf.

Hindstrom, H. 2016. "Is Myanmar's Military behind Shadowy Cyber Attacks?", *The Diplomat*, 27 February 2016 <https://thediplomat.com/2016/02/was-myanmars-military-behind-shadowy-cyber-attacks/>.

Htoo Thant. 2015. "Mobile Penetration Reaches Half the Country". *Myanmar Times*, 2 June 2015. http://www.mmtimes.com/index.php/business/technology/14815-mobile-penetration-reaches-half-the-country.html.

Hynes, C. 2016. "Fintech Holds the Key to Myanmar's Future". *Forbes*, 31 October 2016. https://www.forbes.com/sites/chynes/2016/10/31/fintech-key-myanmar-future/#758976d44880.

International Finance Corporation. 2010. "M-Money Channel Distribution Case – Kenya: Safaricom M-Pesa". IFC Mobile Money Toolkit. International Finance Corporation.

Lee, Y., and A. Slodkowski. 2016. "Telenor Shifts Myanmar Focus to Data Services as 'Hyper Growth' Era Ends". Reuters, 2 November 2016. http://www.reuters.com/article/us-myanmar-telenor-idUSKBN12X1NU.

Long, K. 2016. "Govt, Firms Dismiss Hacking Report". *Myanmar Times*, 26 February 2016. http://www.mmtimes.com/index.php/national-news/19200-govt-firms-dismiss-hacking-report.html.

McGee, Harry. 2016. "How the Mobile Phone Changed Kenya". *Irish Times*, 14 May 2016. http://www.irishtimes.com/news/world/africa/how-the-mobile-phone-changed-kenya-1.2646968.

MCRB (Myanmar Centre for Responsible Business). 2014. "MCIT-PTD Public Consultation on a Code of Practice for Mobile Customer Registration: Submission from Myanmar Centre for Responsible Business". http://www.myanmar-responsiblebusiness.org/news/code-of-practice-for-mobile-customer-registration.html.

MCRB, IHRB (Institute for Human Rights and Business), and DIHR (Danish Institute for Human Rights). 2015. *Myanmar ICT Sector-Wide Impact Assessment*. Available at http://www.myanmar-responsiblebusiness.org/pdf/SWIA/ICT/complete.pdf.

MCRB and MIDO (Myanmar ICT for Development Organization). 2015. Letter to H.E. U Thaung Tin, Deputy Minister, Ministry of Communications and Information Technology (MCIT), 10 June 2015. Available at http://www.myanmar-responsiblebusiness.org/news/mcrb-and-mido.html.

Mizzima. 2018. "Mobile Phone Usage in Myanmar Increases 110 Percent". 23 May 2018. http://www.mizzima.com/business-domestic/mobile-phone-usage-myanmar-increases-110-percent.

Myanmar Now. 2016. "As Tech Spreads, Myanmar Women Suffer Online Abuse, 'Revenge Porn'". 10 June 2016. http://www.myanmar-now.org/news/i/?id=e7abeaa2-3f3e-497e-a0db-210bf599a82e.

Nyunt, Aung Kyaw. "Mytel Enters Myanmar's Telecoms Mart". *Myanmar Times*, 26 March 2018. https://www.mmtimes.com/news/mytel-enters-myanmars-telecoms-mart.html.

Oxford Business Group. 2016. "The Report: Myanmar 2016". https://oxfordbusinessgroup.com/myanmar-2016.

Thant, Htoo. 2015. "Mobile Penetration Reaches Half the Country". *Myanmar Times*, 2 June 2015. http://www.mmtimes.com/index.php/business/technology/14815-mobile-penetration-reaches-half-the-country.html.

Trautwein, Catherine. 2016. "Facebook Free Basics Lands in Myanmar". *Myanmar Times*, 6 June 2016. http://www.mmtimes.com/index.php/business/technology/20685-facebook-free-basics-lands-in-myanmar.html.

Union Parliament. 2017. *Law Protecting the Privacy and Security of Citizens* [unofficial English translation]. http://www.myanmar-responsiblebusiness.org/pdf/Law-Protecting-Privacy-and-Security-of-Citizens_en_unofficial.pdf.

"Viettel to Launch 4G Service in Myanmar". 2018. *Viet Nam News*, 28 May 2018. http://vietnamnews.vn/economy/448759/viettel-to-launch-4g-service-in-myanmar.html#DHIjpMsFMetUTGz8.97.

Part II
Journalism in Transition

6

Silencing a Snakehead Fish: A Case Study in Local Media, Rural-Based Activism, and Defamation Litigation in Southern Myanmar

Jennifer Leehey

With the installation of a semi-civilian parliamentary system in 2011, Myanmar cast off its long-standing international "pariah-state" status and created conditions conducive to economic expansion. As the country increasingly gears its economy towards large-scale, land- and resource-intensive development, there are serious, negative consequences for the majority rural population, long subject to land confiscations and other abuses under the military state.

At the same time, political liberalizations since 2011 have expanded the space for civil society and media, creating opportunities for forms of public contestation and political engagement that would have been impossible in previous eras. All over Myanmar, smallholder farmers in alliance with urban-based activists, volunteer lawyers' groups, media workers and others have been mobilizing against land grabs, forced displacements and other threats. High-profile campaigns have emerged to challenge large investment projects. These movements are not without risk: violent crackdowns, threats of violence, and imprisonment of protesters continue in Myanmar, where the state is intertwined with powerful business interests, and authoritarian mentalities and practices persist. Still, the rollback of the most overt forms of state repression — together with new discourses of state accountability, democracy and rule of law — have encouraged diverse actors to test the possibilities for protest and political activity.

My focus in this chapter is on civil society mobilization in Tanintharyi Region in southern Myanmar, and particularly in Kanbauk, a village of about 1,500 households in the Tanintharyi Hills, eighty kilometres north of the regional capital, Dawei. In recent years, Kanbauk villagers have contended with Delco Ltd, a Yangon-based company that runs a tin and tungsten mine in their area in a production-sharing agreement with the government-owned Mining Enterprise No. 2. Villagers have been seeking to assert some influence over company practices, especially regarding the release of wastewater into local streams. Tensions intensified after an accident in September 2015 in which a tailing pond embankment collapsed causing a flash flood that led to the death of a child and the destruction of many villagers' houses. I discuss the resistance effort that emerged in the village and the company's strategies to suppress and dismiss it. Specifically, I focus on the work of a Kanbauk writer and activist, Aung Lwin, and an evocative essay he wrote, published in May 2016 in *Tanintharyi Weekly*, a small regional publication. Written from the perspective of a fish dying in a stream polluted by mining waste, Aung Lwin's essay offers a sardonic view of events in the village and hints at a possible arrangement between the company and local government officials. As part of its larger effort to quash local resistance to the mine, Delco filed (and won) a lawsuit against Aung Lwin for criminal defamation under Article 500 of the Myanmar Penal Code.

The case reveals the complexities of the current moment in Myanmar and the uncertain spaces in which actors in civil society are operating. It reveals as well the fraught dynamics of media, as authoritarian forces remain active and unpredictable. Although this particular lawsuit was brought against the writer rather than the publication, it has wider implications for Myanmar media, especially for smaller, more vulnerable, regional outlets.

Field research for this chapter in September 2016 and February 2017 included in-depth interviews in Dawei and Yangon with Aung Lwin, his editors at *Tanintharyi Weekly* (Thurein Hlaing and Myo Aung) and his lawyers, with follow-up by email. I attended the final hearing of Aung Lwin's first trial at Yephyu Township courthouse in September 2016 and met supporters from his village. In 2014 I visited Kanbauk with Aung Lwin while he was a research fellow with Chiang Mai University in Thailand, carrying out a study of the social impact of oil and gas pipeline construction near Kanbauk. I visited him in my capacity as coordinator for the fellowship programme.[1] I conducted in-depth interviews with key figures in the Dawei Development Association (DDA), an organization advocating sustainable development and land rights. Secondary research sources include news articles and NGO reports.

Before turning to the villagers' mobilization and the defamation lawsuit, I review the history of the "Dawei Watch Media Group", which produces *Tanintharyi Weekly* and the *Dawei Watch* website. The development of independent media coverage in Tanintharyi is bound up with the larger story of civil society actors mobilizing in response to plans for the Dawei Special Economic Zone (SEZ) megaproject, taking advantage of emerging opportunities for contestation in the early phases of Myanmar's equivocal transition.

Civil Society and Media in Tanintharyi

While many areas in Myanmar are undergoing economic transformation, resource-rich Tanintharyi Region has been especially targeted. Plans for the Dawei SEZ, first unveiled in 2008, are moving forward, now with trilateral Thai, Myanmar and Japanese investment (Sekine 2016). The SEZ, when completed, is expected to be one of the largest industrial zones in Southeast Asia, covering approximately 200 square kilometres. Plans include a deepwater port on the Andaman coast, one or more power plants, a petrochemical complex, heavy and medium industries, and a 140-kilometre road to the Thai border. It is estimated that between twenty and thirty-six villages (22,000 to 43,000 people) will be displaced or otherwise directly affected by the SEZ and associated projects such as reservoirs and resettlement areas (DDA 2014, p. 16).

Elsewhere in the region, and partly in anticipation of the SEZ, investors are pursuing ventures in mining, oil and gas development, agriculture (especially rubber and palm plantations) and construction.

News of the planned SEZ began trickling into the Dawei area following the signing of a memorandum of understanding between the Myanmar government and Thailand's Italian-Thai Development Company Ltd in 2008. At that time, the authoritarian controls of the State Peace and Development Council (SPDC) military government were fully in force. Information was limited; people in Dawei learned of the plans mostly via reports in the English-language Thai newspaper the *Bangkok Post*, brought over the border. Space for civil society was quite constrained, although some "social welfare" organizations were permitted. An important early venue for Dawei youth activists was the Art and Language Center (ALC), established in 2007 to teach Thai, English, and creative arts to children and youth. On the margins of these activities, ALC organizers conferred about regional issues, especially the social and environmental implications of the impending SEZ project. Individuals and groups — including youth activists and some academics from Dawei University — organized as a loose consortium. Around 2010, a few intrepid Dawei-based activists also began organizing villagers in the planned project area, particularly in the twenty-four villages slated for resettlement. The activists reached out to local leaders, such as monks, village committees and the youth leaders of community-based organizations.

Independent media coverage in Tanintharyi also began covertly. In July 2010, two Dawei youth, Thurein Hlaing and Myo Aung, began producing a monthly online newsletter, *Ba Htoo*, named after a nationalist-era military hero from their region. The newsletter, produced in Yangon, was intended for a small circle of like-minded urban youth with access to the internet and email — then extremely limited in Myanmar. *Ba Htoo* aggregated news pieces about Tanintharyi Region published in the *Bangkok Post* or in exile-based Burmese media like *The Irrawaddy*, and included some original reporting. Anticipating scrutiny by Special Branch police, the editors and contributors protected their anonymity. The newsletter ran for about ten months.

In this period, several Dawei-based activists had opportunities to attend training programmes in Thailand, gaining exposure to transnational activist networks and global frameworks of human rights and sustainable development.² Myo Aung participated in a programme run by Earthrights International (ERI) in Chiang Mai, and Thurein Hlaing — an editor with the *Voice Weekly* in Yangon — took a course in Bangkok on "Business Reporting" sponsored by the international non-profit organization, Internews. These experiences deepened their determination to develop independent media in Tanintharyi.

Following the installation of the semi-civilian government in 2011, civil society groups in Dawei (and elsewhere in Myanmar) stepped up their activities. President Thein Sein was keen to indicate that his administration represented a real break from the past. As Thurein Hlaing put it, "We knew we had to take advantage of this time" (interview, 18 September 2016).

Grass-roots organizing and networking increased as government surveillance eased. The ban on political associations, in place since 1962, was lifted. In August 2011, Dawei activists hosted a large, closed-door meeting to discuss the planned Dawei megaproject with such stakeholders as villagers from Nabule (the main SEZ site), Karen-area activists, Yangon-based civil society figures, and representatives from several Thai land rights and environmental organizations.³

Dawei activists recognized the need for national media attention and, in December 2011, held a press conference in Yangon to launch a research report on local people's understanding of the SEZ project (DDA 2012). The event founded the Dawei Development Association. It was also the first press conference held by ordinary civilians — not government officials or academics — in Myanmar in decades. National media outlets like *Voice Weekly*, *7Day*, *Eleven* and *Myanmar Messenger* covered it.

In 2012, censorship restrictions gradually eased. Building upon their experience with *Ba Htoo*, Thurein Hlaing and Myo Aung began producing a two-page newsletter, *Dawei News*, distributing it as a supplement to the *Voice Weekly*. As the latter was already registered with the Press Scrutiny and Registration Division, there was no need to apply for a new licence. *Dawei News* was distributed in Tanintharyi Region and Naypyidaw. The journalists' dual goals were to improve information flows in Tanintharyi, where people were "living in the dark", and to target policymakers who likely had little understanding of what was actually unfolding in remote Dawei (Thurein Hlaing, interview, 18 September 2016). Articles included stories of villagers losing their land, unclear communication from SEZ officials, and other problems, along with lighter pieces about local culture and food. Myo Aung, Thurein Hlaing and Aye Aye Zin established a Facebook page, *Dawei Watch*, to reach an online audience. The group also began selling their news stories to other media houses in Yangon, functioning as a professional outlet in their own right.

Liberalizations in Myanmar's media sphere included the granting of licences for a variety of new independent publications, and in 2013 the *Dawei Watch* journalists received a permit to publish *Tanintharyi Weekly*. Aimed at a local audience, *Tanintharyi Weekly* carries some longer articles with background information on regional issues, news from diverse areas and ethnic communities, a letters-to-the-editor section, and an "opinion/perspective" section with essays, history or short-fiction. It currently has a circulation of four thousand copies and about twenty regular contributors.

At the same time as media coverage became more professional, civil society actors became more sophisticated in using media in their advocacy campaigns. An important early success was the movement in January 2012 against the SEZ's planned 4,000-megawatt coal-fired power plant. Activists raised awareness with pamphlets and fact sheets, fed information to media outlets, and staged a one-day beach-cleaning event, where they collected litter and handed out stickers against "dirty industry". They carefully framed it as a pro-enviromental conservation "movement", rather than a "protest", trying to avoid the connotations of political opposition. Following several weeks of media attention to the issue, in mid-January 2012 the Thein Sein administration announced that the 4,000-megawatt coal-plant project would be cancelled, or significantly reduced in size, citing environmental concerns. Civil society and media workers recognize that they have distinct but complementary roles. Media professionals provide readers with information to be able to assess regional and national issues, while activists seeking to advance causes gain protection from being in the media eye.

The events I discuss here suggest a trajectory of improving conditions, with media workers and activists responding to emerging opportunities in the political context, pushing the authorities to make good on their rhetoric of government accountability. In the post-2011 period, civil society actors have pursued strategies of "rightful resistance" — O'Brien and Li's (2006) term for a mode of contention in which actors seek to hold the powerful to their legal and rhetorical commitments. It is resistance in a paradigm of "reform" rather than "rebellion". Activists contesting the SEZ, for example, often refer in their campaigns to official positions on "environmental conservation" and "sustainable development", as laid out in the 2008 constitution and government policy frameworks.[4]

To some extent these strategies have yielded results. Sekine (2016) presents a fairly optimistic picture in her study of rural-based collective actions against land confiscations in Tanintharyi. In these rural mobilizations, and in the alliances and networks that support them, she sees growing legitimacy for farmers' claims in the national context and, arguably, an incipient movement for more democratic land governance (2016, p. 6). The Dawei SEZ project has been scaled back from the original plan and progress has been hindered, partly due to coordinated civil society resistance — including, in one notable case, a village refusing to relocate from a site where developers intended to build a reservoir to supply SEZ industries (Zaw Aung and Middleton 2016).

But it is also clear that spaces for political engagement are still limited in fundamental ways. As Jones (2014) and others have pointed out, the transition in 2011 was, in many respects, a top-down, military-managed affair that left important social relations and institutions intact. Jones's analysis highlights the key role played by a "state-linked oligarchic elite" — a business class that was fostered by the military after the dismantling of the Burma Socialist Program Party (BSPP) state in 1988, and which continues to enjoy "considerable economic dominance and close relations with military and state officials" (2014, p. 151). Jones argues that the dynamics of state-facilitated crony capitalism, and "political-business complexes", especially in Myanmar's long-conflicted borderland areas, have set broad structural constraints on the country's reform process. These dynamics — along with Cheesman's (2015a and 2015b) analysis of persistent authoritarianism in Myanmar's legal institutions — are fully evident in the case study that follows.

Mining in Kanbauk

In the resource-rich Kanbauk area, creeks flow out of thickly forested hillsides. Along with farming and fishing, generations of residents have relied on tin and tungsten mining, whether as employees of the local mine or as small-scale independent miners. The Kanbauk mine, first established by a British concern in 1911, has passed through several owners. In the early 1970s, under Burma's system of state socialism, the mine became an asset of state-owned Mining Enterprise No. 2 under the Ministry of Mines. In the 1990s, the State Law and Order Restoration Council (SLORC) military junta instituted a series of economic reforms to promote private investment, and in 1998 a private company, Delco Ltd, owned by military-linked businessman Win Oo, entered into a joint venture with Mining Enterprise No. 2 to run the medium-scale mine.

In 2007, Delco was acquired by a Kachin businessman, Ding Ying, also known as Zakhung Ting Ying. A notorious warlord, he was the founder and long-time leader of the New Democratic Army-Kachin (NDAK) militia, which made a ceasefire agreement with the SLORC military authority in 1989. He and his immediate circle have profited from timber and mining concessions in northeastern Kachin State and from cross-border trade with China, exemplifying the "rapacious frontier capitalism" (Jones 2014, p. 152) that has emerged in Myanmar's borderlands in the context of ceasefire negotiations. Under a 2010 contract with the Myanmar Investment Commission, Delco was granted a production-sharing agreement with Mining Enterprise No. 2, specifying that the government would receive 33 per cent of what is mined (MEITI 2015, p. 49). The mine was reclassified as a "large-scale operation" with permission to excavate in a larger area with heavier equipment.

Meanwhile, Win Oo, the former Delco owner, was elected member of parliament for Yephyu Township with the military-linked Union Solidarity and Development Party (USDP) in the 2010 election. In parliament, he served on the "Investment and Industrial Development Committee" and was involved in developing mining laws. Curiously, he also retained a managerial position with Delco in its Yangon office (*Myanmar Times*, 29 June 2014).

Villagers became aware of the mine's expanding reach only when bulldozers and other heavy equipment arrived. To improve its water supply, Delco built a small dam on a stream on Ye-kan ("reservoir") mountain. As a consequence, many waterfalls dried up. The company built a road from the mine site up the mountain to a colonial-era reservoir, felling many trees. Villagers had previously enjoyed the waterfalls and collected firewood on the mountain, but now the company blocked their access. Delco also released wastewater from the mining operation into the Yeh-yint ("fearless") stream that passed through the village.

In late 2014, four or five villagers, including Aung Lwin, the protagonist of this story, went to speak to Delco's managing director and other officials about protecting the forests and local streams. They voiced concerns about a tailing pond that held waste from the mine — the pond was weakly constructed with mud rather than proper concrete embankments. The Delco managers responded that they had a contract with the Ministry of Mines to expand their operations and that the tailing pond was safe.

The Accident

About ten months later, in the middle of the night of 23 September 2015, the embankment of the tailing pond collapsed, releasing a surge of polluted wastewater.[5] As it gushed downstream, the sludge overflowed the Yeh-yint, destroying homes and gardens. A twelve-year old boy was caught underwater in the wreckage of a house, and later died, while his mother was carried downstream, eventually catching on to a bridge. Many elderly residents were injured. Some two hundred villagers had to be evacuated to the local monastery. About twenty houses were destroyed and another fifty or sixty damaged.

Furious villagers gathered spontaneously at the Kanbauk central monument, calling for action against local Delco managers and for the closure of the mine (DVB, 24 September 2015). The regional police chief, arriving from Dawei, stepped in and asked the protesters to select five representatives. That night, the company's managing director agreed to suspend mining operations pending an investigation, to provide compensation, and to meet with local leaders to discuss closure of the mine.

In the following weeks the company paid 7 million kyat (approximately US$5,450) compensation to the family whose child had died —

an out-of-court settlement negotiated in consultation with Tanintharyi Region officials who had investigated the incident. Some in the village encouraged the family to sue and offered to help find a pro-bono lawyer, but the family was poor and fearful of the legal system. They concluded (probably correctly) that a trial would just complicate their lives. Many villagers were angry when they learned how little compensation the company had paid.

In media statements, Delco and Ministry of Mining officials began to downplay the disaster, signalling their intention to resume mining. The official position was that the 23 September accident had not affected the village, rather only an area along the riverbank inhabited by "squatters" without proper title to the land (*Myanmar Times*, 1 October 2015). Still, Delco agreed to build nineteen new houses for the families whose homes had been destroyed and to provide compensation to others whose houses were damaged, presenting this as corporate benevolence rather than any legal obligation.

Channelling Anger into Rightful Resistance

About forty local residents organized the "Kanbauk Region Resources Survival Network" (Bse. *kan-bau? dethá ăyìn-myi? shin-than-yè kun-ye?*) to mobilize a coherent community response. Aung Lwin, 29, and Khin Soe, a former political activist from the 1988 era in his mid-50s, emerged as leaders. Initially, members of the group wanted to petition the government to close the mine, but given the mining ministry's 33 per cent stake in the operation, difficulties accessing government agencies and the expense of travel to meet with officials, the group opted to engage with the company and regional authorities.

The Resources Survival group organized two workshops, in October and November, to collect testimony from villagers regarding the mine's impact and to disseminate information about relevant laws, including the notoriously weak 1994 Mining Law and the somewhat more stringent legislation promulgated during the Thein Sein administration, such as the 2012 Environmental Conservation Law and 2015 Environmental Impact Assessment Procedure Law. Representatives from the Dawei Pro-bono Lawyers Group and the Dawei Development Association provided legal and strategic advice. About fifty villagers attended each event.

The group invited four local Delco managers, including the managing director, to attend the first meeting. (Aung Lwin recounted how afterwards they said, "This is the first time we ever participated in a meeting like this to discuss mining laws.") The Resources Survival group invited mine employees to the second workshop — an office worker, a foreman and three mine labourers attended.

The organizers drafted a set of twelve demands (Bse. *tàung-hso-kyeʔ-mya*),[6] with reference to company legal obligations. Villagers asserted, for example, that the company should prevent rubble from sliding on to farmer's fields and garden plots, stop releasing wastewater into streams, and mitigate the impact of explosives that were destabilizing hillsides. Another section demanded that Delco prepare proper environmental and social impact assessments and develop an environmental management plan, or, if they already had such a plan, make it available to the public as specified in the 2015 Environmental Impact Assessment Procedure Law. There was a section on working conditions at the mine and the need for sufficient drinking water, proper safety equipment and labour contracts in line with International Labour Organization standards.

Several sections dealt with land tenure issues. Villagers wanted Delco to provide compensation to those who lost fields and garden plots. As noted, Delco's position was that villagers living and planting near the mining area had no legal title and thus no right to compensation; however, the Dawei Pro-bono Lawyers' Group claimed that villagers could assert land rights based on customary use, a principle that was gaining some currency in land claims disputes and public consultations on the Draft National Land Use Policy (2014). Villagers also objected to the company's enclosure of the area around the mining site, demanding the right to freely access the reservoir and forests that they had previously enjoyed as communal resources.

Using the rhetoric of sustainable development, and making their claims, as far as possible, with reference to Myanmar laws, Kanbauk villagers were pursuing "rightful resistance". O'Brien and Li (2006) have shown that, in rural China, such "within-system" contention can be effective in curbing the exercise of power while avoiding the risks of more direct defiance. In the Kanbauk case, however, rightful resistance efforts have proven less than successful.

As the Resources Survival group held workshops and organized, Delco carried out a series of community development projects (Bse. *lu-hmu-yè loʔ-ngàn*), apparently to improve public relations. The company made a donation to the local monastery, oversaw some renovations at the Kanbauk high school and improved the local road between Kanbauk and the hamlet of Paya. To many in the village it seemed that Delco was trying to diminish the Resources Survival group's influence.

In December, the Resources Survival group leaders requested a meeting with Delco representatives to begin negotiating a formal "community benefit agreement". The meeting, which was attended by two Delco representatives and about fifty villagers, turned contentious. Five individuals who had been coordinating with Delco on local projects were present and they took the side of the company, arguing that Delco had a contract with the Ministry of Mines, so no further agreement was necessary. Nothing was concluded, except that Delco representatives agreed to hold another meeting with the Resources Survival group.

That meeting never occurred, despite the group's multiple efforts. On 5 January, in the middle of the night, the company released more wastewater into Yeh-yint stream, infuriating residents. The Resources Survival group led a demonstration on 18 January. Several hundred villagers participated — not only from Kanbauk but also from surrounding villages. A number of people spoke at the demonstration: a farmer who could no longer irrigate his fields because of the polluted stream; a fisherman who had lost his livelihood because the Heinze River, downstream from Kanbauk, no longer had fish; a young woman whose family had lost their garden. Khin Soe spoke about the laws being violated, while Aung Lwin served as master of ceremonies. National media outlets came to cover the event.

The placards prepared for the demonstration — printed white-on-red in the tradition of Myanmar state propaganda signboards from the military era — proclaimed villagers' demands in distinctly "rightful" language (translated here from Burmese): "In order to not destroy the natural environment, follow the law"; "No trust in the irresponsible and unaccountable Delco mine"; and "Holders of executive and legislative authority: don't neglect us". The language was submitted in advance to the General Administration Department authorities in accordance with regulations under the 2012 Peaceful Assembly and Procession Law.

In conjunction with the demonstration, the group sent a formal letter laying out their twelve demands to Mining Enterprise No. 2 under the Ministry of Mines, with a copy to the Tanintharyi Region chief minister. The local Delco office received a copy via the village administrator. No office replied.

On 27 January, Delco announced that they would resume mining. The announcement referred to the company's construction of nineteen new houses, each costing 2.8 million kyat (approximately US$2,200), and asserted Delco's commitment to "expanding community development" (*Myanmar Times*, 28 January 2016). It also referred to Delco's upgrading of infrastructure and safety plans "in collaboration with the Ministry of Mines, the regional government, and Kanbauk residents". The company, in other words, projected an image of responsible compliance with the state and engagement with the community, while, in fact, assiduously avoiding villagers' efforts to initiate meaningful consultation.

As Delco resumed mining, villagers assumed a position of watchful waiting. Some hope had been kindled with the November 2015 national elections, which saw a resounding victory for the National League for Democracy (NLD). Kanbauk villagers awaited the accession to power of the new NLD-led government in April 2016, hopeful that the shift in personnel across various levels of government — and, locally, the ushering out of USDP officials believed to be financially involved with Delco[7] — would create more conducive conditions for their campaign.

Aesthetic Engagement

Aung Lwin's essay "The Lament of a Snakehead Fish" was produced in this period and expresses the frustration and despair of the moment.[8] Written from the perspective of a fish dying in a stream that has been polluted with mining waste, the essay refers to the history of the Kanbauk area, the expansion of industrial-scale mining after 2010, and recent events, including the September 2015 accident and villagers' efforts to negotiate an agreement with the company. The company is not named, but Delco is clearly the referent. In the essay, the story of progressive ecological devastation, with which the fish-narrator has intimate experience, is joined with details of the villagers' struggles with the mining company, which he claims to understand only partly ("since I am a snakehead fish").

The figure of an anthropomorphic animal is familiar in Burmese traditions. In Jātaka tales — the semi-canonical stories that describe the previous lives of Gautama Buddha — the Buddha-to-be often appears in animal form, exhibiting a particular virtue. Although not explicitly moralistic like a Jātaka tale, Aung Lwin's essay recalls that tradition as well as the Buddhist notion that all sentient beings are linked in cycles of karmic existence. One also thinks of Burmese editorial cartoons in which a talking fish, cow, bird or buffalo offers an ironic comment on human social behaviour.

Aung Lwin told me that he wrote the essay after observing a snakehead fish languishing in a small creek under a footbridge in Kanbauk. "It is a real fish, not just imagination", he said (interview, 24 September 2016).[9]

Most broadly, the "Lament" essay is a commentary on the folly of human short-sightedness regarding the environment. A key theme is that the human and animal realms are entwined. The essay is about trauma and loss and evokes feelings of sympathy and horror. But there is also humour, as when the snakehead fish refers, absurdly, to a "fish-national registration card" that hasn't been issued yet, or, more poignantly, fish tears that no one can see.

It is useful to consider the piece in relation to the rational discourses of rightful resistance. The "Lament" essay appeals to the senses and emotions and draws on specific knowledge of local history and ecology to condemn environmental devastation. The text conveys an immanent moral critique that, arguably, exceeds the legalistic arguments presented in documents such as the villagers' twelve demands to Delco. The essay confirms the fundamental legitimacy of the villagers' resistance, while pointing to the limitations of their rightful approach.

Throughout, the snakehead disavows his agency ("this is not something that I can understand, as I am a snakehead fish"), but, of course, the point is that the narrator's distinctive voice has emerged at this moment when the villagers' reasonable efforts to assert their agency have been systematically stymied. He is a figure of their denied aspirations.

Aung Lwin's essay was published in *Tanintharyi Weekly* on 9 May 2016. Within a few days he realized there would be a problem. The five Kanbauk villagers who had worked with Delco on development projects objected to a passage in which they are characterized as "so-called community leaders" (more literally, "swear-to-god community leaders"; Bse. *hpǎyà-sù yaʔ-mí-yaʔ-hpaʔ*) involved in "for-show development projects" (Bse. *han-pyá-kyè ywa-hpún-hpyò-yè-loʔ-ngàn*). These five sent a letter to Aung Lwin's employer, the French oil company Total's Corporate Social Responsibility head office in Yangon. They also came to his workplace in Kanbauk to speak with his manager, asking the company to control their employee. The Total office in Yangon responded that Aung Lwin was free to do as he wished in his private life. Aung Lwin was not surprised when, a few days later, he received notice that Delco Ltd — specifically, the company's Communications and Public Relations Manager, Win Oo[10] — was suing him for criminal defamation under Article 500 of the Myanmar Penal Code. He was ordered to report to the Yephyu Township court for the first hearing on 24 May.

Law and Order

In his analysis of Myanmar's legal institutions, Cheesman (2015a, 2015b) argues that although successive regimes in Burma-Myanmar have professed commitment to the "rule of law" (Bse. *tǎyà úbǎde sò-mò-yè*), and the phrase is certainly prominent in official rhetoric currently, the country's juridical institutions are actually animated by ideas of "law and order" (Bse. *nyein-wuʔ-pí-byà-yè*), a wholly different conception of political association, "whereby people are subdued so they might be protected ... [and] administrative immobilising mechanisms quieten people" (2015a, p. 35).

Cheesman shows how, after 1962, courts became subordinated to the delivery of purportedly socialist policy. The dismantling of rule-of-law procedures stripped citizens of rights. After 1988 and the official rejection of socialism under the unambiguously named "State Law and Order Restoration Council" military junta, "rule of law" was semantically conflated with the law-and-order principle. Features of the system included the state's identification of "public enemies" and the use of judicial torture. Endemic corruption — the buying and selling of case outcomes — naturally ensued in a system where the appearance of orderliness outranked adherence to law (2015a, pp. 168–76).

In the present post-junta, constitutional era, rule-of-law rhetoric is prominent, but Myanmar's legal institutions are still animated by law-and-order principles. Courts continue to function as part of the government administration; the judiciary is formally subordinate to the military-controlled Ministry of Home Affairs and works in tandem with the police department and the prison system. An important corollary of judicial subordination is that "many matters that fall within the purview of courts in rule-of-law settings do not come within their domain in Myanmar" (2015b, p. 281), thus impunity for military and government officials is assured.

One can readily observe "law-and-order" ideology at work in the details of the case explored here. When the accident occurred in September 2015, an orderly administrative process foreclosed consideration of legal questions regarding, say, company criminal negligence. The compliance of the dead boy's family in accepting the meagre compensation illustrates that poor Myanmar farmers, habituated to military rule, do not typically look to the legal system for recourse. Delco's identification of accident victims as illegal squatters (Bse. *kyù-kyaw ne-htain-thu*) exemplifies law deployed in "quietening".

Likewise, Delco's defamation suit against Aung Lwin was intended to punish and silence him. As Myo Aung, co-editor at *Tanintharyi Weekly*, put it:

> Aung Lwin is a strong community leader, with good network, good education. He is part of the new generation of leaders. So the company thinks: "we must cut down this young tree". Or if they cannot cut him down, they will at least put pressure, so that he cannot grow straight. (interview, 20 September 2016)

Tanintharyi Weekly editors noted that, actually, they had published more strident criticism of Delco in their editorials, including phrases such as "Delco is not following the law" and "Delco doesn't care about the people", but the company did not sue their publication.

Several informants noted that officials in Tanintharyi region dislike environmental activists, seeing them as impeding development of the region, from which the officials also profit. Aung Lwin is considered a "destructionist" (Bse. *ăhpyeʔ-thămà*), a term commonly used during the era of military rule to vilify opposition figures. Aung Lwin is aware of how he is seen and of the larger ideological framework it implies:

> In Myanmar, people are confused about "opposition" [Bse. *ătaiʔ-ăkhan*]. It is a neutral word in democracy. In fact, democracy needs to have an "opposition". But in a military dictatorship, opposition is something to be defeated.

He continued:

> In our history we have never had a chance to say "no". Also, in this transition we never have a chance to express our opinion. Why don't we dare to say "no"? Our thinking is limited; we are still inside the box. (interview, 24 September 2016)

It is precisely Aung Lwin's clear conception of the principles of local self-determination, sustainable development and rule of law that make him a threat to the power structure and their plans for resource extraction.

Lawsuits function punitively, partly through the stress they induce. In Aung Lwin's case, the first trial in Yephyu consisted of a dozen hearings spread out over four months, followed by an appeal process that carried on for more than a year. As Myint Kyaw with the Myanmar Press Council observed, "Even if Aung Lwin wins his case, he will be reluctant to write like this again; that is what the company thinks" (interview, 14 September 2016).

I asked Aung Lwin's lawyers and supporters what particular pressures there might be on the Yephyu Township judge to deliver a guilty verdict, given that Delco Ltd is owned by a reputed warlord with long-standing military ties. "A judge in a small township court knows who has power in the area", explained Than Zaw Aung of the Myanmar Media Lawyers Group. "Maybe the judge thinks, 'If I favour this person [Aung Lwin], he can do nothing to protect me'" (interview, 4 October 2016). Chief General Administration Department officers in townships commonly hold weekly meetings with local officials to give instructions, and judges are usually invited. At such a meeting, the chief officer might make a suggestion about a preferred verdict for a case.

Still, supporters expressed hope that Aung Lwin would have "a fair-minded judge". Myint Kyaw suggested that the verdict would depend on "how the judge understands the role of media in society" (interview, 14 September 2016).

Media Reforms and Defamation Laws

Since 2011, international observers have lauded policy changes relating to freedoms of expression, association and assembly as a hallmark of Myanmar's transition. However, from the start, rights advocates, especially inside the country, have worried about inadequate legal protections for media workers and civil society (see Gayathry Venkiteswaran and Yin Yadanar Thein's chapter in this volume). Among the various laws that may entangle journalists are those invoking criminal defamation. Several such laws are in force from various periods in Myanmar's history, resulting in a "stacked" system fraught with duplications and inconsistencies (Mark 2016).[11] By imposing criminal penalties, Myanmar's defamation laws violate the international standard that civil penalties are sufficient to protect reputations. Defamation laws are also supposed to be unambiguous, so that individuals can have a reasonable certainty regarding the legality of their actions (ARTICLE 19 2000, p. 7).

Aung Lwin was charged under Article 500 of the Myanmar Penal Code, an instrument of colonial control, revised in 1957. Defamation cases involving media were pursued under this law in the 1950s, before the imposition of state censorship, and the law has re-emerged for use against media in the post-2011 period. The penalty is imprisonment for up to two years, a fine, or both. Unlike other defamation-related statutes in Myanmar, it lays out ten exceptions, including for a statement or imputation that is true and in the public interest.[12] Technically, an institution or government department cannot sue a person. However, in practice, the stipulation is bypassed through the use of proxy plaintiffs. There have been several cases in which named government officials have charged journalists or media houses on the government's behalf. "[A]part from the criminal sentencing, the real problem lies less with the wording of the defamation law and more with its improper interpretation by [the] judiciary" (IMS and UNESCO 2016, p. 28).

It is useful to reflect on local conceptions of "defamation". In the Myanmar Penal Code, the word for defamation, *ăthăye-hpye?-hmú*, incorporates the word *ăthăye*, a fairly abstract term of Pali origin that means reputation, dignity or honour — something that, arguably, every human being possesses. However, in conversations with Aung Lwin's lawyers and supporters, I noted that people easily slipped to the near-synonym *gon-thăye-hpye?-hmú*, using the more familiar word *gon-thăye*, which translates as honour or prestige — a *relative* attribute, possessed to a greater degree by those who are higher in the social hierarchy. The usage suggests a tendency to see defamation as an injury to higher status individuals. Reforming the legal environment for free expression in Myanmar may require changing not only laws but also prosecutorial practices and, indeed, frameworks of mind. Aung Lwin's trial serves as a case in point.

The Trial

Upon learning that he would be sued, Aung Lwin sought advice from his editors at *Tanintharyi Weekly*, who, in turn, contacted the Myanmar Press Council in Yangon, the Southern Myanmar Journalists' Network, the Myanmar Media Lawyers Group and others. Aung Lwin's defence strategy was developed as a group effort among supporters and colleagues in civil society. Tin Tin Thet, with the Dawei Pro-bono Lawyers Group, agreed to lead the defence at the Township Court level, but as she was more experienced with land-tenure issues than defamation cases, she would consult with Than Zaw Aung of the Myanmar Media Lawyers Group in Yangon. Than Zaw Aung took over as lead attorney after the case went to appeal. Myint Kyaw, of the Myanmar Press Council, served as a witness to advise the court on how grievances should be handled according to the News Media Law and the role of a free media in a democracy.

Kanbauk villagers also showed their support. On nine or ten occasions the community organized a rental vehicle and about twenty villagers made the trip to the Yephyu courthouse, an hour south of Kanbauk, to observe proceedings. There was a group from Kanbauk at the hearing I attended on 21 September 2016. At the teashop near the courthouse, they cheerfully consumed plates of rice and curry and cups of tea. At the hearing, they filled the benches at the back of the courtroom and stood quietly by the open doorway.

Delco's case against Aung Lwin focused on three phrases in the essay. The company objected to the narrator's comments on the non-responsiveness of the company to the villagers' demands following the September 2015 accident: "the company just did some for-show village development projects in cooperation with a group of so-called community leaders". The phrase "for-show development projects" (Bse. *han-pyá-kyè ywa-hpún-hpyò-yè-loʔ-ngàn*) was defamatory, according to the plaintiff, because Delco Ltd "has done many good things" for the community, and had "spent 500 million kyat" (approximately US$400,000) on health, education, religion, and infrastructure projects. To say "for show" belittled this work, they claimed. The phrase "so-called community leaders" ("swear-to-god community leaders"; Bse. *hpăyà-sù yaʔ-mí-yaʔ-hpaʔ*) was defamatory, they claimed, because it implied that the company "did not work with the community in a proper way".

The third and probably most critical point concerned the snakehead fish's reference to USDP government officials. The passage (translated here) reads:

> The people who live near my creek say that this [USDP] government's term is ending soon ... [and] that is why the officials don't want to get very involved in this case. Whether it is because their term is ending and they don't want to trouble their minds with this matter before they leave, or because there is give and take between the company and this government, this is not something that I can understand as I am a snakehead fish.

Delco attorneys said the phrase "give and take" (Bse. *ăbè-ăyu*) implied collusion, corruption or an "improper relationship" between the company and officials in the previous USDP-led government.

As the plaintiff in a defamation case is supposed to be an individual rather than an institution, Delco put forward a proxy, the company's Communications and Public Relations Manager, Win Oo. As evidence that harm had occurred, Win Oo testified that he had had a conversation with a friend in a Kanbauk teashop shortly after the publication of the essay in *Tanintharyi Weekly*. Reportedly, the friend said to him: "Ko Win Oo, you said your company was benefitting the community, but when I read this article, it sounds like you are not!" Thus the plaintiff claimed he had "lost face".

Aung Lwin's team constructed their defence around the critical exception that a statement is not defamation if it is true and in the public interest. Tin Tin Thet emphasized the fundamental truthfulness of the essay as a reflection of Kanbauk villagers' experiences and feelings. She noted that media workers have a right and responsibility to report on what is happening in society. Additionally, she highlighted Aung Lwin's main purpose: to support environmental protection and local livelihoods. Thus, the essay was written in good faith and in the public interest.

The fact that Aung Lwin's piece was written from the perspective of a fish complicated matters. The team did not want to argue that the creative, imaginative qualities of the text somehow protected the author from a defamation charge, as that would be a weak defence. *Tanintharyi Weekly* frequently included essays, historical pieces, short stories and poetry in the "opinion/perspective" section of the paper, set off from the reporting in the "news articles" section. The paper had published the snakehead fish's lament assuming that the usual standards for media applied. Still, several villagers called as witnesses for the defence, when asked about their understanding of the essay and the three allegedly defamatory phrases, observed that a snakehead fish could not know much about such issues as "give and take" between company and government officials; thus, in their view, the comments of the fish did not amount to defamation.

The defence's main strategy was to draw the court's attention beyond the text to the larger context of environmental problems in Kanbauk. Meanwhile, the plaintiff's lawyers pointed to Aung Lwin's role in the demonstration against the company in January 2016, presenting this as evidence of an oppositional attitude.

On 30 September, the Yephyu Township Court found Aung Lwin guilty of criminal defamation and imposed a fine of 30,000 kyat (about US$24) or three months in prison.[13] Aung Lwin's supporters suggested that the light sentence might indicate that the judge, while obliged to deliver a guilty verdict, had some sympathy for Aung Lwin. Perhaps he was hoping to resolve the matter quietly with a fine the defendant could readily pay. The four-month trial had also served as punishment — to put the young writer-activist in his place.

However, the case did not end there. Both the company and Aung Lwin chose to appeal; Delco because they considered the sentence too light, and Aung Lwin because he maintained his innocence. He explained:

> It is not about the fine, it's about dignity — not just my dignity, but also the dignity of our village. If we accept the decision, it means the company can do whatever they want without criticism. It is also about the dignity of our regional news media. If I go silent, then that has a bad implication for *Tanintharyi Weekly*. (interview, 1 October 2016)

Subsequently, the case proceeded through two more levels in the court system. For the defence, Than Zaw Aung continued to argue that Aung Lwin's essay was written in the "public interest", referring also to citizens' express duty under the 2008 constitution "to assist the Union in environmental conservation".[14] On the plaintiff's side, the lawyers emphasized the "many good things" the company had done for the community, asserting that Aung Lwin had defamed their "good will".

At the Dawei District Court in December 2016, Aung Lwin was again found guilty and given a somewhat higher penalty — a fine of 50,000 kyat (about US$40) or three months imprisonment. Again, both sides appealed. In May 2017 the Tanintharyi Regional High Court maintained the District Court's decision — neither voiding it nor imposing a higher penalty — and Aung Lwin and his supporters began making plans for appeal to the Supreme Court in Naypyidaw.

The lawsuit against Aung Lwin — together with other defamation cases involving media — highlights the ambivalence of Myanmar's new media "freedoms". In purportedly liberalizing Myanmar, some real reform is taking place, but deeply entrenched illiberalism persists. Courts are not independent and prosecutorial practices are fraught — a situation that emboldens those who want to silence critics and activists. The case illustrates that "the pursuit of enemies, people who decline to be quieted when ordered or urged to do so, continues through the courts in a manner largely consistent with earlier periods" (Cheesman 2015b, p. 277).

Aung Lwin's case has received less attention than some other defamation suits involving larger media houses or pursued under the more punitive Section 66(d) of the Telecommunications Law (2013). Still, his case is important, not least for what it suggests about the pressures on smaller, regional outlets like the Dawei Watch Media Group. Such outlets, with their close links to communities, have in-depth knowledge of local elites and their activities, and the details of local injustices. Although this lawsuit was brought against Aung Lwin personally, rather than the publication, it was also a signal to the Dawei Watch group not to criticize local power-holders too effectively, and especially not to allege corruption.[15]

Ironically, Delco lawyers underscored the ambivalence of media liberalizations in Myanmar when they asserted in their opening arguments that the company supported the principle of a free media — that it was pointedly not suing media outlets that had reported on the tailing pond accident and other events, but rather suing Aung Lwin for his specific transgressions. In making this claim, Delco was aligning itself with the narratives of reform-era Myanmar, in which press freedom is a hallmark of transition to normal governance. The snakehead fish, with his keen eye for hypocrisy, would likely find the assertion amusing.

***

Epilogue

In January 2018 the Myanmar Supreme Court rejected appeals from Aung Lwin and Delco Ltd, maintaining the earlier verdict and sentence, and closing the case. In Kanbauk, villagers continue to try to press Delco to obey environmental regulations. The Resources Survival group has reorganized as the Kanbauk "Mine Monitoring Committee", which is formally recognized by the regional government. When Delco releases wastewater illegally (as it continues to do), the committee files a report with the Ministry of Natural Resources and Environmental Conservation, so that authorities can take action. Regional authorities are paying more attention than in the past.

Notes

1. The research fellowship programme on "Understanding Myanmar's Development" is administered by the Regional Center for Social Science and Sustainable Development (RCSD) at Chiang Mai University, funded by the International Development Research Centre (IDRC) of Canada.

I would like to acknowledge IDRC support for that project, which planted the seeds for this one.
2. Several Dawei activists I interviewed had attended EarthRights International's Mekong School in Chiang Mai or the Community Development and Civic Empowerment (CDCE) programme run by Vahu Institute at Chiang Mai University. These programmes cover such topics as community development, human rights documentation, and national and international advocacy strategies.
3. The groups from Thailand included SEM (Spirit in Education Movement), HPPF (Healthy Public Policy Foundation), TERRA (Toward Ecological Recovery and Regional Alliance) and Eastern People's Network.
4. The 2008 constitution specifies that the government "shall protect and conserve the natural environment" (Chapter 1, Section 45). Relevant policy frameworks include Myanmar's National Sustainable Development Strategy (2009) and the Framework for Economic and Social Reforms (2012).
5. My account of these events draws on English-language news media reports at the time and interviews with Aung Lwin in 2016 and 2017.
6. *Tàung-hso-kye?* translates as "demand" or "request", depending on context.
7. Win Oo, the former Delco owner, lost his seat as MP for Yephyu Township in the 2015 election. He remains a managing director at Delco's Yangon office (*Myanmar Times*, 27 May 2016).
8. An English-language translation is available on Jennifer Leehey's academia.edu page.
9. Aung Lwin's comment suggests a "magical realist" orientation. Elsewhere I have written about magical realism in Myanmar, a topic of earnest teashop discussions among Yangon literati in the 1990s (Leehey 2005).
10. There is no relation between this person and the former Delco owner and USDP MP with the same name.
11. Mark (2016) uses Roquas's term to analyse Myanmar's legal framework relating to property rights. I suggest that Myanmar's media laws are similarly layered, with ambiguities that can be used strategically by power holders.
12. However, one may be guilty of defamation if one's statement is true but *not* in the public interest.
13. The strange discrepancy between the fine and the obviously more punitive jail sentence seems to be an artefact of outdated sentencing guidelines that were drafted in an earlier era when the kyat was more highly valued.
14. Chapter 8 of the 2008 constitution details "Fundamental Rights and Duties of Citizens", including the duty of every citizen to assist the Union in

"environmental conservation" and "protection and preservation of public property".

15. In a separate case, in late 2017, *Tanintharyi Weekly* was sued by the Tanintharyi regional government for allegedly undermining the dignity of the regional chief minister and regional government. Filed under Article 25(b) of the Media Law (2014), the case concerns a satirical column titled "A Smile for the Election Campaign", which describes the feelings and actions of a fictitious village administrator as she manages the village. The piece has been interpreted as an attack on the chief minister's inability to solve the region's electricity problems. The Dawei Township Court decided in favour of the government in October 2018, but *Tanintharyi Weekly* is appealing the decision.

References

ARTICLE 19. 2000. *Defining Defamation: Principles on Freedom of Expression and Protection of Reputation*. International Standards Series. London: Article 19.

Cheesman, N. 2015a. *The Rule of law: How Myanmar's Courts Make Law and Order*. Cambridge: Cambridge University Press.

———. 2015b. "That Signifier of Desire: The Rule of Law". *Social Research* 82, no. 2 (Summer): 267–90.

DDA (Dawei Development Association). 2012. "Local People's Understanding of the Dawei Special Economic Zone" (English version). (March).

———. 2014. "Voices from the Ground: Concerns over the Dawei Special Economic Zone and Related Projects". (September).

DVB Multimedia Group. 2015. "One Dead, Several Injured as Mine Accident Floods Village". 24 September 2015.

IMS (International Media Support) and UNESCO (United Nations Educational, Scientific and Cultural Organization). 2016. "Assessment of Media Development in Myanmar Based on UNESCO's Media Development Indicators". Bangkok: UNESCO; Copenhagen: IMS.

Jones, L. 2014. "The Political Economy of Myanmar's Transition". *Journal of Contemporary Asia* 44 (1): 144–70.

Leehey, J. 2005. "Writing in a Crazy Way: Literary Life in Contemporary Urban Burma". In *Burma at the Turn of the 21st Century*, edited by Monique Skidmore. University of Hawai'i Press.

Mark, S. S. 2016. "Are the Odds of Justice 'Stacked' against Them? Challenges and Opportunities for Securing Land Claims by Smallholder Farmers in Myanmar". *Critical Asian Studies* 48 (3): 443–60.

MEITI (Myanmar Extractive Industries Transparency Initiative). 2015. "EITI Report for the Period April 2013–March 2014; Oil, Gas, and Mining Sectors". MEITI & Moore Stephens, LLP. (December).

Myanmar Times. 2014. "Re-writing the Mining Law 'Waste of Time': Lawmaker". 29 June 2014.

———. 2015. "Delco to Resume Mining after Paying US$5450 for Child's Death". 1 October 2015.

———. 2016a. "Delco Resumes Mining Operations". 28 January 2016.

———. 2016b. "Former MPs: Where are They Now?" 27 May 2016.

———. 2017. "Mines Rules to be Submitted for Government Review this Month". 13 January 2017.

O'Brien, K.J., and L.J. Li. 2006. *Rightful Resistance in Rural China*. New York: Cambridge University Press.

Sekine, Y. 2016. "Land Confiscations and Collective Action in Myanmar's Dawei Special Economic Zone Area: Implications for Rural Democratization". Global Governance/Politics, Climate Justice & Agrarian/Social Justice: Linkages and Challenges, an International Colloquium. Colloquium paper no. 59. The Hague: International Institute of Social Studies (ISS).

Zaw Aung and C. Middleton. 2016. "Social Movement Resistance to Accumulation by Dispossession in Myanmar: A Case Study of the Ka Lone Htar Dam near the Dawei Special Economic Zone". In *Water Governance Dynamics in the Mekong Region*, edited by D. Blake and L. Robins. Strategic Information and Research Development Centre: Petaling Jaya.

7

Precarity and Risk in Myanmar's Media: A Longitudinal Analysis of Natural Disaster Coverage by *The Irrawaddy*

Susan Banki and Ja Seng Ing

In the mid-2000s, journalists from Burma working in exile in neighbouring countries faced constant safety challenges, be it intimidation from local police or surveillance by the Burmese military intelligence. In 2017, journalists from these same publications, now back in the country, faced new challenges: intimidation by government officials and arrests *within* the country. Given the uneven pace and patterns of change in Myanmar (see the introductory chapter to this volume) and the importance of media in covering these developments, it is useful to investigate how collecting and reporting news about Myanmar have evolved in line with the promises of that change.

In this chapter we use the twin concepts of precarity and mobilization to explore the tensions associated with media reporting about Myanmar over time, analysing the reporting of the (formerly) exiled media publication *The Irrawaddy*. The chapter explores coverage through an examination of the sources utilized and the substantive content and tone of the articles. We begin by reviewing *The Irrawaddy*'s history and then position it through the lenses of mobility and precarity. After a discussion of methods, we compare the coverage in *The Irrawaddy* of three natural disasters, in both the English and Burmese editions, and supplement our analysis with interviews with members of staff. Our findings indicate that risks associated with reporting have lessened considerably, but tension remains as *The Irrawaddy* is hamstrung by conflicting goals that influence its coverage.

The Irrawaddy: Outside-In

The story of Myanmar's incomplete reforms would itself be incomplete without a discussion of *The Irrawaddy*, whose role as a publisher, in turn, of a monthly magazine, weekly print journal, video content, and now digital media has secured its place in the country's media history. Founded in exile in 1993 by Aung Zaw and other exiled journalists, *The Irrawaddy* went from an "amateurish, four-page newsletter" (Cochrane 2006, p. 87) to a website that reaches millions.[1] Operating as exiled media from Thailand for its first two decades, *The Irrawaddy*'s position — simultaneously out-of-reach from Myanmar's restrictive government but proximate to events in Myanmar at a time, prior to the internet, when information was not as easy to share across restrictive borders — allowed it to offer credible counter-narratives to official government sources. Its readership has included people both inside and outside the country, both English and Burmese speakers, and both military and opposition leaders (the latter while in prison), as well as other stakeholders.[2]

Its founders' involvement in the democracy movement against Burma's authoritarian rule notwithstanding, from its inception *The Irrawaddy* claimed to be independent. This is partially because it was able to capitalize on student activist founders who tapped into foreign pro-democracy funders (Brooten 2016). Nevertheless, myriad difficulties endured for *The Irrawaddy* staff: visa restrictions on its journalists, which meant operating in semi-legal conditions, with frequent visa runs to neighbouring countries and the ever-present possibility of being detained there;[3] military surveillance and threats;

and harassment from Thai authorities (Aung Zaw 2001; Cochrane 2006).

In 2012 *The Irrawaddy* opened its offices in Yangon following the promise of political reforms coupled with a push for removing censorship laws and protecting not only freedom of expression but also "the security and rights of the media community" (*The Irrawaddy* 2012). As we explore below, such security remains aspirational.

Media Actors as Social Mobilizers

An extensive literature on social movements and contentious politics explores why and how people and organizations engage in collective action to effect change. These *social mobilizers* — the individuals, groups and coalitions who advance particular issues — may have as their targets governments or corporations or even ideologies themselves, and they employ various strategies in their attempts to, for example, highlight the dangers of climate change or demand rights for migrants or promote democratic reform in a country.

Traditionally, social mobilizers have generally been depicted as grass-roots activists who mount protests or advocates who lobby politicians — actors whose position on an issue is clear from the outset. But a case can be made that media play a role as social mobilizers themselves, or agents of change, as McCargo (2003) calls them, although they may not see themselves as such. This may be a controversial assertion in the context of charges of "fake news" and alternative facts emanating from all sides of the political spectrum, but there is a truth to it: to the extent that collective action is frequently spurred through the stories that media cover, they serve as agents for collective action.

Recent writers have started to acknowledge media as social mobilizers. One impressive effort is that of Carroll and Hackett, whose analysis of democratic media activism demonstrates that, while such media activism is embedded in nearly every contemporary social movement, it can be differentiated from others by a strategic focus on communication that "render(s) collective action more reflexive" (2006, p. 99). In the case of Myanmar, Brooten has noted that media can play the role of shaping identities through "cultural activism" (2013, p. 690) and as a component of civil society itself (2016, p. 196).

Much of the scholarship about social mobilizers examines the factors that drive their behaviour and decisions. Most prominently, it has been argued, *opportunity structures* and *resource mobilization* explain mobilization. First, the concept of *opportunity structures* has been used to explain the dynamics that, in shifting, offer openings for protest (Tilly and Tarrow 2007). Traditionally, these dynamics have been considered external: a wall of boulders prevents people from passing through, but an outside shock to the system (an earthquake, perhaps) shifts the boulders and openings are created, allowing people to pass through without changing themselves. Likewise, there are forces exogenous to protestors themselves, such as shifts in political alignment or changing demographics in a region, that create openings for protesters to take action.

The presence of media or coverage of a particular issue can be one of the elements that facilitates mobilization. For example, it has been found that sit-in protests during the 1960s U.S. civil rights movement tended to follow the path of newspaper circulation. That is, where the news of protests cropped up, sit-ins soon followed, attesting to the media as a factor in growing mobilization forces (Andrews and Biggs 2006). There is also a burgeoning literature addressing the effects of social media on protest action more contemporarily (Gleason 2013; Wolfsfeld, Segev and Sheafer 2013). Through the selection (and exclusion) of issues and through their framing, the media have the potential to promote particular political agendas and drive policy change, as well as engender symbolic recognition of an issue (Walgrave and Van Aelst 2006).

Second, scholars have used *resource mobilization* to explain why and when collective action takes place. The shape and intensity of social movement action is influenced by the resources to which social mobilizers have access (McAdam, McCarthy and Zald 1996). It may appear self-evident that better-funded organizations have the means to pay for space, rent office equipment and travel to the sites of protest and lobbying, and these of course help explain which organizations mobilize and how. But resources also include moral resources, such as legitimacy and solidarity; human resources, such as skilled workers and volunteers; tacit knowledge, such as the know-how to organize a petition drive; and social networks, through which strategies and narratives can spread (Edwards and Gillham 2013). It has also been widely recognized that media (and media savvy) is a critical resource for social mobilization, which has its roots in early social movement literature where media events were already considered among the important tactics that activists deployed (Smith 2007; Tilly 1978).

Media, then, have been considered a dual actor, both as an external force that gives social movements public exposure and as a resource from within the movement that ignites action. This is implicitly noted in Clifford Bob's (2001) work comparing successful and unsuccessful social movements in Nigeria and Mexico, where he points to media coverage as one of the indicators of success for two of the movements and explains this partially by the initial media support these movements received. While the article thus contains circular reasoning (media is listed both as evidence of and an explanation for a movement's success), Bob's work highlights the multifaceted role of media in their relationship with social movements.

Precarious Actors: Media Organizations as Institutionally Precarious

A growing literature examines how the forces of globalization and neoliberal economic policies have created a labour system that renders the masses precarious, unable to secure the promise of consistent and sufficiently paid work. The "precariat" who face "systematic insecurity" (Standing 2011, p. 156) range from agricultural labourers where seasonal work precludes full-time wages, to academic casual workers, to creative workers (e.g., artists, actors, musicians, etc.) who cannot count on consistent wages (Ross 2008).

The literature has, of late, recognized different forms of precarity that are not just about earning a living. A more holistic view recognizes that deficits in livelihoods inform other aspects of our lives, including possible social isolation (Lewis, Dwyer, Hodkinson and Waite 2015, p. 160) and difficulties forming and maintaining identities (Neilson and Rossiter 2008). Precarity can also describe an individual's condition stemming from insecure residence, wherein migrants, refugees and stateless people experience differing levels of permission to remain where they are and thus experience "precarity of place" (Banki 2013a). What becomes clear is that precarity is an intersectional problem for many: precarity in the workplace can lead people to migrate without secure residence in order to seek livelihoods. At the same time, those with less than full citizenship are more easily exploited in labour markets and may also have difficulty showing up for work every day. This is because the precarious are limited in their micromobility, and hence lose access to jobs, sources of information, and information networks, all of which rely to a great extent on the ability to move from place to place (Banki 2013b). For journalists, a restricted sense of micromobility plays out in diminished access to accurate sources of information.

These considerations become additionally relevant to our examination when we consider the broader phenomenon of *institutional precarity*, which describes the ways that organizations, companies and other institutions are rendered systematically insecure and exploitable. Institutional precarity accurately describes the situation for media organizations working in countries that limit press freedom, where the ability to operate and survive is dependent on structural forces that go far beyond readership and advertising potential.

In the case of Myanmar, exiled media mitigated a large degree of the institutional precarity that they would have endured within the country, allowing operations to continue outside the country during the decades of an oppressive era inside. Much has been written about how exiled media, based in neighbouring countries of Thailand and India and further afield in Norway, used stringers both inside and outside the country to create transnational exchanges of information (Buck 2007; Cho 2011; Pidduck 2012). Detailed coverage of issues such as the treatment of political prisoners or the military's stronghold in ethnic areas would not have been possible without an exile outlet.

Yet, both in exile and upon return, it has been noted that the strength and survival of formerly exiled media outlets in Myanmar also depend on discourses that are appealing to international funders and investors (Brooten 2006; Pidduck 2012), the ability to pay salaries and supply costs at non-subsidized rates (unlike state-run media outlets, which are subsidized) and laws that protect the freedom of the press (Brooten 2016).

How do these shifting modes of risk and precarity for (formerly) exiled media manifest themselves through media expression? We now turn to an analysis of one exiled media outlet and its coverage of three different natural disasters in three different time periods. We compare how *The Irrawaddy* covered three events in terms of *sources* and *coverage*, and what this tells us about institutional precarity for the media in Myanmar today.

Methods

Our primary tool for analysis was a comparison of *The Irrawaddy*'s coverage of three significant natural disasters, supplemented by interviews with members of *The Irrawaddy* staff. We have focused on Cyclone Nargis in 2008, before the political transition; the earthquakes in Shan State in March 2011, at the inception of transition, when a nominally civilian president was elected by the country's current leaders and the promise of change was being heralded; and the floods throughout Myanmar in July and August 2015, in the lead-up to parliamentary elections and following some reforms, such as the release of some political prisoners, the re-instatement of the National League for Democracy as a political party, labour laws permitting unions, and, as noted, some improvement in media freedom. While the magnitude of the disasters varied considerably (with Cyclone Nargis being the most severe), all three were notable enough to garner sufficient articles for analysis. Further, our analysis measured not the quantity of coverage but the substantive content of the articles, so the difference in the scope of the disasters was unimportant to the analysis. Altogether, we analysed 228 articles: 125 in English and 103 in Burmese. The appendix to this chapter explains our search techniques for selecting articles.

We elected to focus on non-political events (to the extent that natural disasters can be rendered non-political) in order to maintain focus on the reporting of news rather than on the news itself. If we had chosen to report on political events, it would have been difficult to separate the coverage of those events from the concurrent political changes. Our hope is to eliminate that bias by focusing on natural disasters.

Given what we have asserted about the structural and resource influences on media, it is clear that we are less interested in the veracity of *The Irrawaddy*'s claims than in how the news is collected and presented. As such, we follow Atkinson and Coffey's attribution of documents as "social facts" (2004, p. 58), which allows us to examine the contexts in which *The Irrawaddy* has considered the risks and opportunities of its actions. With this as a model, we engage in critical discourse analysis to draw out two important themes that are relevant to our theoretical positionings: we analyse the *sources* of *The Irrawaddy*'s news items, and we analyse the *coverage* of the items for their tone and their content.

Findings

In this section we compare the coverage of the three natural disasters — Cyclone Nargis in 2008, the earthquakes in Shan State in March 2011, and the floods throughout Myanmar in July and August 2015. Cyclone Nargis hit land on 2 May 2008, and the resulting storms and massive flooding in the Irrawaddy Delta resulted in an estimated 140,000 deaths (UN-OCHA 2008). On 24 March 2011, a 6.8 magnitude earthquake hit the northeastern part of the country, Shan State, bordering Laos and Thailand, killing seventy-five people and injuring thousands (BBC 2011). And in 2015, flooding during the rainy season in July and August led to the deaths of more than a hundred people and harm to more than a million across all but two of Myanmar's fourteen regions and ethnic states (BBC 2015).

Sources of Information

From 2008 to 2015, one very clear trend in both English and Burmese editions of *The Irrawaddy* was that the sources of information for disaster coverage increased in diversity and decreased in anonymity over time. Nargis articles contained significant unnamed sources, including villagers who suffered losses, aid workers (both local and foreign) and local traders. There were also many named sources, but these were most often people outside the country with an interest in the crisis, such as the CEO of Save the Children (*The Irrawaddy*

2000c) and interviews with outside "Burma watchers" such as Debbie Stothard, director of Altsean (Stothard 2008).

Perhaps surprisingly, some people "inside" the country agreed to be named in 2008, but these were victims of Nargis who were not critical of the government and who only shared their devastating personal losses. This included the sad story of Khin Hla, who lost twelve members of her family (*The Irrawaddy* 2000d), and the difficulties encountered by Ma Thein, a government official whose entire family worked full time but who could not feed herself or her family with prices rising post-Nargis (Kyi Wai 2008).

Notably, voices critical of the regime during Nargis were by and large located outside of the country, with the exception of one article about the role of media in reporting the disaster, which identified several journalists inside by name and revealed that eight had been arrested for reporting on Nargis. This draws a direct link between the risks associated with reporting and micromobility: "The real work of uncovering the truth about Cyclone Nargis has been left to those reporters who have already taken substantial risks to travel to the most affected areas and convey what they've seen and heard to the rest of the world", said Yeni, the Burmese language editor of *The Irrawaddy* (Yeni 2008). This quotation highlights the institutional precarity of media organizations in particular, because of the need for media to collect facts by remaining micromobile — or, more simply, to move around on the ground.

In 2011, at the inception of transition, *The Irrawaddy*'s use of unidentified sources indicated that local residents and local officials were still nervous about being openly critical of the regime. Nearly all sources inside Myanmar who were critical of the government in 2011 remained unidentified. One article, "Mae Sai, Tachilek Residents Still Shaky After Quake", demonstrated a clear divide between identified sources from Mae Sai, Thailand, who suffered in the earthquake (such as Kae, the owner of a gold shop, or Wasana who worked in the local 7-Eleven) and the unidentified sources quoted who lived in Tachilek, just across the border (where a "motorbike taxi driver" was only identified as such) (Saw Yan Naing 2011b). In one Burmese article, an unidentified local resident asserted that General Aung Than Htut and the social welfare minister gave specific orders for military personnel not to tell their superiors about deaths in the military. The resident further claimed that the military moved patients to a military camp so that they would not be interviewed by foreign reporters (*The Irrawaddy* 2011b). The English equivalent included the names of several sources from inside Myanmar, such as a local government official, a village chairman, and the local manager of World Vision International (Saw Yan Naing 2011a), but these sources offered no criticism, only commentary. One local resident bucked this trend: Ca Mu, a Lahu resident of Yanshin village, offered critiques of the government across two different articles, asserting that the junta stole humanitarian aid and that local people would have been better off without the soldiers coming in at all (Saw Yan Naing 2011c, 2011d). The fact that this behaviour was so rare reveals much about how risky revealing names was considered. Of course, it is difficult to understand the motivations of those experiencing individual precarity, but in explaining the decision of some local people to give their full names, Yeni noted that "People revealed their names because they had nothing to lose."[4] It is also notable that the critiques that Ca Mu offered were only printed in an English article; no Burmese article contained such critiques or mentioned the Lahu situation whatsoever. And in both 2008 and 2011, the Burmese edition of *The Irrawaddy* did not identify their journalists by name.

One significant change between 2008 and 2011 was the diversity of sources on which *The Irrawaddy* relied. By 2011, in addition to sources such as officials from the Myanmar Red Cross Society and World Vision International (Saw Yan Naing 2011d), *The Irrawaddy* included occasional quotes from government officials at both local and national levels, such as a clerk from the local Ward Peace and Development Council (Yan Pai 2011) and a member of parliament (Wai Moe 2011), neither of whom were identified. Perhaps even more interesting is a critique from Khin Maung Hla, a member of the local People's Militia, who directed his criticism not at the government but at local militias, who, he speculated, were to blame for the government's inability to deliver aid to the local village of Chakuni (Saw Yan Naing 2011a; Yan Pai 2011). (The nuanced dynamic between ethnic armies and the quasi-civilian government, which sat in a fragile and often shifting opposition that defied dichotomous explanation, is not explored here.) This same critique is offered in the Burmese edition but without attribution (*The Irrawaddy* 2011b). In the Burmese edition, even when a local authority noted a positive initiative about Naypyidaw helping to build roads to improve access, he asked that his identity remain confidential (*The Irrawaddy* 2011b).

By 2015, quotes from, interviews with, and even text messages from government officials at all levels were commonplace (Nobel Zaw 2015), including from the Union Solidarity and Development Party (USDP) (Yen Saning and Kyaw Hsu Mon 2015), indicating that, at the very least, media in 2015 had relatively easy access to sources that were unavailable prior to this. Further, the use of unidentified sources was much less frequent, in both the English and the Burmese editions. A few examples of unnamed sources were still noted, however, such as an official from Sagaing Division who requested not to be named even though he had said nothing critical about the government (Zarni Mann 2015), or a local Rakhine resident who asserted that the government response had thus far been weak and that the public had a right to know the actual damage that the floods had wrought (ခင်ဦးသာ [Khin Oo Tha] 2015).

Coverage: Tone and Content

Over time there have been changes to the tone of *The Irrawaddy*'s critique. The newspaper moved from an unmoderated and often aggressive stance during Nargis in 2008 to a less strident tone when covering the floods in 2015. For example, one article in the Burmese edition used strong words to disparage, without reference, (former) Senior General Than Shwe for his mishandling of the emergency phase of the crisis, calling him a "စိတ်ဖောက်ပြန် အာဏာရူးနေသူ", which can roughly be translated as a "power-mad person with a mental disorder" (*The Irrawady* 2000a). In an article in the English edition, General Than Shwe's neglect of the hardest-hit regions in Nargis was suggested to be "deliberate and calculated" (Aung Zaw 2008). In 2011 the phrasing of articles shifted to that of a cynical chiding of the government, as when the government "abruptly", in an English article, took over the provision of humanitarian aid or when it appeared as if the motivation for local authorities to clean up a damaged area was to please Naypyidaw officials rather than help the earthquake victims (Htet Aung 2011). In an article noting that the government prohibited foreign doctors or locals from accessing an area where the hospitals remained full, the article concluded: "Meanwhile, cleaners are busy tidying up the compound of the hospital in Tachilek in anticipation of a visit by junta officials from the capital" (Saw Yan Naing 2011e). Notable here is the continued use of "junta" in 2011, when a quasi-civilian administration was in power. In contrast, the tone of articles covering the 2015 floods was factual and moderated, and the military are referred to without sarcasm or stridency.

In terms of the content of the coverage, the most striking difference over time is that, while criticism of the government remained, increasingly it was accompanied by a greater diversity of perspectives. Further, over time the commentary on the government offered fewer structural critiques that took aim at the regime *writ large*. In 2008, articles with a critical slant, for example, drew links between the government's mishandling of the crisis and its relationship with ethnic minorities (Aung Zaw 2008), its propensity to divert Myanmar's resources into the pockets of army generals (Turnell 2008), and its focus on the upcoming referendum while people could not access food and water (*The Irrawaddy* 2000b).

In 2011, coverage of the earthquakes in Shan State also contained strong critiques of the government, and criticism remained structurally targeted. For example, one article in both English and Burmese tied the actions of the government very directly to a pre-transition period. In English (and similarly in Burmese), the article quoted a "Burmese staffer with a foreign NGO in Shan State who spoke on condition of anonymity" as saying, "When I see the government action in Shan State, I remember the authorities' relief mission in Cyclone Nargis.... The military generals used the catastrophe for photo opportunities and propaganda while people were dying" (*The Irrawaddy* 2011a; Wai Moe 2011).

By 2015, criticism of the government lessened considerably. No editorials placed the government at fault, and while critiques of flood response remained, there were certainly fewer of them, and they were not structural in nature: they were productive complaints about the lack of first-aid classes (*The Irrawaddy* 2015) or food running out (Salai Thant Zin 2015). In one instance of structural critique, where anti-mine activists in Letpadaung linked flooding to a copper-mining project, the report also covered a response about the incident from the Chinese company Wanbao, which claimed its employees were stopped from distributing rice and water to villagers by "a handful of extremists" (Nyein Nyein 2015). The fact that *The Irrawaddy* printed Wanbao's charge of extremism indicates an increasing diversity of viewpoints.

By 2015 there were also some positive commentaries on government action, such as an acknowledgement that the township's Forestry Department helped rescue animals in the flood (Lawi Weng 2015), or the recognition from UN Human Rights Envoy Yanghee Lee of the government's efforts to handle the food crisis associated with the floods (coupled with "regret" that she was not able to access Arakan State to evaluate the most recent problems with the Rohingya) (Solomon 2015). By contrast, in 2008 *The Irrawaddy* included virtually no positive comments — the only slightly moderate comment was an observation from a foreign aid worker who insisted that "the regime is not monolithic" (Lawrence 2008).

It is important to note that *The Irrawaddy* has always critiqued actors other than the government, although the breadth of those targets may have increased over time. But even in 2008, articles quoted people who pointed out the disunity among the opposition (Kyaw Zwa Moe 2008) or the lack of spine of the West (Zarni 2008) and of relief organizations (Zarganar 2008). Comedy served as a way to offer such broad-based critiques; through the comic trope of young men idly chatting (The Barber's Shop in English and "ချင်းမိုင်ရကွစိုးနှင့် ထွေရာလေးပါး" or "Chit-Chat Session" in Burmese), the newspaper's barbs speared many and spared none. In the English edition, customers in a barber shop pointed out that the international community's long-term strategy was to "kiss the general's backsides" (Shwe Yoe 2008). In the Burmese, the state-run media was mocked for falsely reporting on the progress of the regime's relief implementation process, when they used the word "ရှန်းရှန်းဝေ", or "effusively", with sarcasm: "The government's newspaper 'effusively' states that the relief plans are promising and in progress" (*The Irrawaddy* 2000e).

Analysis

Changes in the political landscape in Myanmar are reflected in *The Irrawaddy*'s coverage of natural disasters. First, over time, *The*

Irrawaddy relied on a greater diversity of sources and increasingly identified those sources by name, including government sources and even the military. "Nowadays we call the military spokesperson to respond to reports we want to expose.... And we give them credit when they are trying to reform, like 2–3 cases where the military sent their soldiers to military court for human rights violations and abusing power", confirms Yeni of *The Irrawaddy*.[5] This demonstrates a widening of its resource base, as the company has worked to build information networks that were formerly off-limits and to improve its verification of sources, something that was quite challenging in the past. Viewing *The Irrawaddy* as a social mobilizer — or, in McCargo's (2003) terminology, agents of change — foregrounds one of the primary tools of social movements everywhere and offers a compelling reason for *The Irrawaddy*'s return to Myanmar: micromobile journalists with access to "on the ground" information. Here, the credibility of *The Irrawaddy* was mobilized through the resource of information. Yet, while *The Irrawaddy* as an organization was able to access more and richer sources, it was still the case that some sources remained too nervous to reveal their identity, even in 2015 — an indication that individual precarity remained.

It is also notable that in both 2008 and 2011, the Burmese edition of *The Irrawaddy* included many more unidentified sources than in the English. Just as advocates direct specific tactics to specific target audiences, *The Irrawaddy* differentiated the aims of its Burmese readers (which likely included more Burmese government officials, hence the need to protect sources more rigorously) and its English readers (which included a greater number of international Burma watchers, transnational activists and donors).

Second, the tone of *The Irrawaddy*'s coverage grew noticeably less strident from 2008 to 2011 to 2015. Social mobilizers have frequently adapted their strategies and structures to mirror, or reject mirroring, the institutions or governments they hope to reform (Sawer and Groves 1994; Weeks 1996). In the same way, *The Irrawaddy*'s changing tone has followed Myanmar's reform process. This is confirmed by Yeni, who noted, "Before, we [used] kind of offensive words, near abusive, like 'horrible regime'. Due to the reform process, and the level of reform, transparency and accountability, our media need to take the responsibility to set our tone because we cannot accuse blind[ly]."[6]

Third, by every objective measure, criticism of the government decreased over the time studied, while anecdotes that placed the government in a positive light increased. Further, by 2015, these critiques were very rarely of a structural nature, by which we mean that the underlying structures of government were no longer the target of criticism. It is difficult to pinpoint whether criticism diminished because there was less to criticize in Myanmar or because *The Irrawaddy*, still institutionally precarious through limited resources and structural obstacles, felt the need to hold back from criticism that ran too deep or hit too hard.

Both are possible: on the one hand, a search for commentary about Myanmar related to the 2015 floods in other media, including those that were outside Myanmar, yielded very little in terms of structural critical coverage, suggesting that, at least in the arena of natural disasters, decreased criticism of the government was merited. On the other hand, Brooten (2016) has noted that a neoliberal agenda shapes Myanmar's political context today, as the definition of "democratization" has been conflated with open trade policies and privatization, de-emphasizing transparency, representation and democratic institutions. In this context, journalists inside Myanmar are caught in a bind: at the same time that the international community perceives ever-increasing freedoms in the country and expects coverage that reflects such freedom, *The Irrawaddy* must still consider the risks of its reporting, to its journalists and to their sources. In early 2017, for example, two Kachin pastors were arrested after assisting journalists (Lawi Weng and Rik Glauert 2017). A few months later, one of the journalists covering the Kachin story, Lawi Weng (who has also authored a chapter in this volume), and two journalists from the DVB Multimedia Group were arrested for meeting with ethnic armed organizations in northern Shan State. The three were later released, but the threat remains. The military's enduring presence provides another example: at the same time that *The Irrawaddy* is committed to checking the accuracy of every fact they print about the military, the sources that might corroborate those facts may still be too nervous to speak to the media, particularly in ethnic areas. "We know that [reporting on the military] is a very delicate thing", admits Yeni.[7]

The delicacy of such reporting is not limited to journalists from *The Irrawaddy*, and even affects journalists hired by external media organizations. In a recent high-profile case, in December 2018, two Myanmar journalists who work for Reuters, Wa Lone and Kyaw Soe Oo, were convicted, after a year in jail, for implicating the military in the mass deaths of Rohingyas. The imprisonment and conviction of these two journalists covering an issue of grave importance explains why they were part of a cohort awarded *Time* magazine's 2018 Person of the Year for their role as "Guardians" of the truth. The award notwithstanding, they remain in prison at the time of this writing.

Conclusion

In December 2016, a panel of journalists in Myanmar evaluated media reform in the country. Soberingly, they concluded that the 2015 elections, which ushered in new leadership, had done little to improve media freedom. If anything, they noted, the former opposition party, the National League for Democracy, had become unapproachable since taking office (*The Irrawaddy* 2016). And although one panellist said he did not believe he would be jailed for what he reported, only six months later Lawi Weng was arrested. Immediately after, *The Irrawaddy*'s editor-in-chief Aung Zaw wrote that "Once a reporter in exile like many of us, Lawi Weng took a considerable risk in going back to his homeland.... The return of a climate of fear is very disturbing.... I can't help but recall Lawi's optimism on Election Day in Yangon. No, he was not thinking that he would eventually be locked up under this government" (Aung Zaw 2017). Despite improved access to government sources, Irrawaddy employees continue to note a challenging environment: "No one knows for sure to what extent press freedom is allowed. There is no official guidance from the government, so we continue to expand our work to test our limits. At the same time, we at Irrawaddy understand the potential risks of coverage on sensitive issues and we are preparing for the worst situation by hiring standby lawyers for our organisation."[8]

It is thus too early to declare that reforms in Myanmar have lessened individual or institutional precarity for media in Myanmar;

risk remains a significant and sobering part of the reporting equation, as the Reuters case exemplifies. Future research that examines coverage of non-neutral events (such as ethnic minority issues) would usefully expand these findings, as would research on coverage of high-profile natural disasters after the 2015 elections. What we do know at present is that media organizations in Myanmar still need to make calculated decisions. Under such conditions, it is critical that media organizations working as members of a growing civil society are given the space — through opportunity structures and mobilized resources — to continue operating, even if risks are present.

Appendix

Collecting relevant articles from *The Irrawaddy* required different search techniques across time and language due to a new (and more difficult to search) website for more recent articles after March 2012. For articles from 2008 and 2011, we searched the titles of the archived English and Burmese editions of *The Irrawaddy* in the tabs "Burma", "Feature", "Interview" and "Magazine" in the four to five months during and after the natural disaster. We determined the relevance of the articles based on their titles, contextually deriving disaster-related articles from prior knowledge rather than keywords. For example, rather than simply searching for article titles with the word "cyclone" or "disaster", we singled out for further analysis any articles that we thought might be related, such as "The Show Must Go On", which we assumed (correctly) was an article commenting on the push forward to hold a country-wide referendum despite the devastation of Cyclone Nargis. The "Burma" tab in English in 2008 yielded 341 articles; we pulled out one of every ten for this time period and tab alone in order to keep manageable the number of articles analysed.

The post–March 2012 *Irrawaddy* website does not easily permit searching by title or topic. Therefore, for 2015, Factiva provided us with the easiest means to search for English-language articles. (Factiva was not available for articles from 2008 and 2011.) Using the search term "floods" in *The Irrawaddy*, all articles (not just titles) were searched between July and October 2015, inclusive. In the Burmese edition, we searched in the "Environment" section and used the following five search words, scrolling backwards through all articles from the present to 2014. Article titles were then chosen if relevant to the floods:

1. ရေကြီးရေလျှံ,
2. ရေကြီးနှစ်မြုပ်,
3. ရေကြီး,
4. သဘာဝဘေး,
5. flood

For each instance, we then discarded articles that either (i) only had a tangential reference to the disaster — which we defined as only mentioning the disaster in one sentence of the article — or (ii) were written by another news source (such as the AP) but were licensed by *The Irrawaddy*.

Our searches yielded the following numbers of reviewed articles:

Event	Period of Analysis	# English Articles Reviewed	# Burmese Articles Reviewed
Cyclone Nargis	May–September 2008	65	25
Earthquake in Shan State	March–June 2011	12	8
Widespread floods	July–October 2015	48	70

Notes

1. *The Irrawaddy*, "About Us", https://www.irrawaddy.com/about (accessed 15 July 2017).
2. *The Irrawaddy* former staff member [TN34], interview, 13 December 2005, Chiang Mai.
3. *The Irrawaddy* former staff member [CM12], interview, 15 December 2005, Chiang Mai.
4. Yeni, interview via Skype, 22 January 2017.
5. Ibid.
6. Ibid.
7. Ibid.
8. Yeni, interview in Yangon, 4 May 2018.

References

Andrews, K.T., and M. Biggs. 2006. "The Dynamics of Protest Diffusion: Movement Organizations, Social Networks, and News Media in the 1960 Sit-ins". *American Sociological Review* 71 (5): 752–77.

Atkinson, P., and A. Coffey. 2004. "Analysing Documentary Realities". In *Qualitative Research*, 2nd ed., edited by D. Silverman, pp. 56–75. London: Sage.

Aung Zaw. 2001. "Journalists Beware". *The Irrawaddy* (August).

———. 2008. "Operation Delta". *The Irrawaddy* (June). http://www2.irrawaddy.com/article.php?art_id=12595&page=1.

———. 2017. "Defending Lawi Weng", *The Irrawaddy*, 28 June 2017. https://www.irrawaddy.com/opinion/commentary/defending-lawi-weng.html.

Banki, S. 2013a. "Precarity of Place: A Complement to the Growing Precariat Literature". *Global Discourse* 3 (3–4): 450–63. https://doi.org/10.1080/23269995.2014.881139.

———. 2013b. "Urbanity, Precarity, and Homeland Activism: Burmese Migrants in Global Cities". *Moussons* 22 (2): 35–56.
BBC. 2011. "Burma Earthquake: At Least 75 People Killed". BBC News, 25 March 2011. http://www.bbc.com/news/world-asia-pacific-12852237.
———. 2015. "Myanmar Flooding Affects One Million". BBC News, 10 August 2015. http://www.bbc.com/news/world-asia-33844076.
Bob, C. 2001. "Marketing Rebellion: Insurgent Groups, International Media, and NGO Support". *International Politics* 38 (3): 311–34.
Brooten, L. 2006. "Political Violence and Journalism in a Multiethnic State: A Case Study of Burma (Myanmar)". *Journal of Communication Inquiry* 30 (4): 354–73.
———. 2013. "The Problem with Human Rights Discourse and 'Freedom' Indicators: The Case of Burma/Myanmar Media". *International Journal of Communication* 7:681–700.
———. 2016. "Burmese Media in Transition". *International Journal of Communication* 10 (18): 182–99.
Buck, L. 2007. "Media and Protests in the Myanmar Crisis". *Südostasien aktuell: journal of current Southeast Asian affairs* 26 (6): 50–66.
Carroll, W.K., and R.A. Hackett. 2006. "Democratic Media Activism through the Lens of Social Movement Theory". *Media, Culture & Society* 28 (1): 83–104.
Cho, V. 2011. "Rearranging Beads on a Necklace: Reflections on Burmese Karen Media in Exile". *Inter-Asia Cultural Studies* 12 (3): 465–72.
Edwards, B., and P.F. Gillham. 2013. "Resource Mobilization Theory". *The Wiley-Blackwell Encyclopedia of Social and Political Movements*.
Gleason, B. 2013. "# Occupy Wall Street: Exploring Informal Learning About a Social Movement on Twitter". *American Behavioral Scientist* 57 (7): 966–82.
Htet Aung. 2011. "Death Toll Rising from Earthquake in Shan State". *The Irrawaddy*, 25 March 2011. http://www2.irrawaddy.com/article.php?art_id=21008.
The Irrawaddy. 2000a. "မန်မာပြည်သစ် တည်ဆောက်ရေးအတွက်သာ ပြင်ဆင်ကြပါစို့" [Let's prepare to build a new Myanmar]. 10 May 2008. http://bur.irrawaddy.com/index.php/editorial/2008-10-06-11-24-23/274-2008-10-21-08-34-04.
———. 2000b. "Don't Depoliticize Burma's Cry for Help". (June). http://www2.irrawaddy.com/article.php?art_id=12581&page=1.
———. 2000c. "Hollywood Stars Donate for Burma Relief". (June). http://www2.irrawaddy.com/article.php?art_id=12597.
———. 2000d. "Surviving the Storm". (June). http://www2.irrawaddy.com/article.php?art_id=12594&page=1.

———. 2000e. "ချင်းမိုင်ရုက္ခစိုးနှင့် တွေ့ရာလေးပါး (အပိုင်း - ၂၁၆)" [Chit Chat with a Chiang Mai Tree Spirit, Part 216]. 9 July 2008. http://bur.irrawaddy.com/index.php/ching-mai-nat/6-ching-mai-nat/316-2008-10-22-07-36-17.

———. 2011a. "ရှမ်းပြည်အရှေ့ပိုင်းငလျင် သေဆုံးသူ ၁၅၀ အထိ မြင့်တက်နိုင်" [Earthquake Death Toll Rising to 150 in Eastern Shan State]. 26 March 2011. http://bur.irrawaddy.com/index.php/news/6057-2011-03-26-11-33-26. Death Toll Rising to 150 in Eastern Shan State]. 26 March 2011. http://bur.irrawaddy.com/index.php/news/6057-2011-03-26-11-33-26.

———. 2011b. "ငလျင်ကြောင့် တပ်တွင်း သေပျောက် သတင်း အမှောင်ချ" [Military conceals earthquake death toll in its ranks]. 29 March 2011. http://bur.irrawaddy.com/index.php/news/6073-2011-03-29-09-42-58.

———. 2012. "Burma's Exiled Media Calls for United Front". 20 March 2012. http://www2.irrawaddy.com/article.php?art_id=23244.

———. 2015. "Dateline Irrawaddy: 'I Couldn't Stand Back and Watch People Suffering'". 29 August 2015. https://www.irrawaddy.com/in-person/interview/dateline-irrawaddy-i-couldnt-stand-back-and-watch-people-suffering.html.

———. 2016. "Dateline Irrawaddy: 'It Is Fair to Say the New Govt Is Not Media Friendly'". 24 December 2016. http://www.irrawaddy.com/dateline/dateline-irrawaddy-it-is-fair-to-say-the-new-govt-is-not-media-friendly.html.

Kyaw Zwa Moe. 2008. "Putting Compassion into Action". *The Irrawaddy* (July). http://www2.irrawaddy.com/article.php?art_id=13185&page=1.

Kyi Wai. 2008. "Hunger Pains". *The Irrawaddy* (July). http://www2.irrawaddy.com/article.php?art_id=13186&page=1.

Lawi Weng. 2015. "In Flood-Hit Magwe, Prioritizing Lives with Livestock in Mind". *The Irrawaddy*, 7 August 2015. https://www.irrawaddy.com/news/burma/in-flood-hit-magwe-prioritizing-lives-with-livestock-in-mind.html.

Lawi Weng and Rik Glauert. 2017. "Missing Kachin Pastors Confirmed Detained by the Burma Army". *The Irrawaddy*, 20 January 2017. https://www.irrawaddy.com/news/burma/missing-kachin-pastors-confirmed-detained-by-burma-army.html.

Lawrence, N. 2008. "The Show Must Go On". *The Irrawaddy* (June). http://www2.irrawaddy.com/article.php?art_id=12591&page=1.

Lewis, H., P. Dwyer, S. Hodkinson, and L. Waite. 2015. *Precarious Lives: Forced Labour, Exploitation and Asylum*: Policy Press.

McAdam, D., J.D. McCarthy, and M.N. Zald. 1996. "Introduction: Opportunities, Mobilizing Structures, and Framing Processes – Toward a Synthetic, Comparative Perspective on Social Movements". In *Comparative Perspectives on Social Movements: Political Opportunities, Mobilizing Structures, and Cultural*

Framings, edited by D. McAdam, J.D. McCarthy, and M.N. Zald, pp. 1–20. Cambridge: Cambridge University Press.

McCargo, D. 2003. *Media and Politics in Pacific Asia*. London: Routledge.

Mizzima. 2015. မိုးလေဝသ ပညာရှင် ဒေါက်တာ ဦးထွန်းလွင် NLD အစိုးရကို ဘာဖြစ်စေချင်သလဲ [What does meteorologist Dr U Tun Lwin want from the NLD?]. *Mizzima*, 27 November 2015. http://www.mizzimaburmese.com/article/7929.

Neilson, B., and N. Rossiter. 2008. "Precarity as a Political Concept, or, Fordism as Exception". *Theory, Culture & Society* 25 (7–8): 51–72.

Nobel Zaw. 2015. "Fresh Storm Fears in Flood-Hit Burma". *The Irrawaddy*, 12 August 2015. https://www.irrawaddy.com/news/burma/fresh-storm-fears-in-flood-hit-burma.html.

Nyein Nyein. 2015. "Letpadaung Villagers Briefly Detained after Flood Confrontation". *The Irrawaddy*, 4 August 2015. https://www.irrawaddy.com/news/burma/letpadaung-villagers-briefly-detained-after-flood-confrontation.html.

Pidduck, J. 2012. "Exile Media, Global News Flows and Democratization: The Role of Democratic Voice of Burma in Burma's 2010 elections". *Media, Culture & Society* 34 (5): 537–53.

Ross, A. 2008. "The New Geography of Work Power to the Precarious?" *Theory, Culture & Society* 25 (7–8): 31–49.

Salai Thant Zin. 2015. "Over 10,000 Villagers Washed Out in Irrawaddy Division". *The Irrawaddy*, 3 August 2015. https://www.irrawaddy.com/news/burma/over-10000-villagers-washed-out-in-irrawaddy-division.html.

Saw Yan Naing. 2011a. "Junta Possibly Concealing Earthquake Casualties". *The Irrawaddy*, 28 March 2011. http://www2.irrawaddy.com/article.php?art_id=21023.

———. 2011b. "Mae Sai, Tachilek Residents Still Shaky after Quake". *The Irrawaddy*. http://www2.irrawaddy.com/article.php?art_id=21009.

———. 2011c. "Misery Continues for Earthquate [sic] Victims". *The Irrawaddy*, 29 March 2011. http://www2.irrawaddy.com/article.php?art_id=21033.

———. 2011d. "Over 3,000 Homeless after Shan State Earthquake". *The Irrawaddy*, 31 March 2011. http://www2.irrawaddy.com/article.php?art_id=21051.

———. 2011e. "Quake Victims Fill Tachilek Hospital". *The Irrawaddy*, 26 March 2011. http://www2.irrawaddy.com/article.php?art_id=21016.

Sawer, M., and A. Groves. 1994. " 'The Women's Lobby': Networks, Coalition Building and the Women of Middle Australia". *Australian Journal of Political Science* 29 (3): 43–59.

Shwe Yoe. 2008. "Kissing the Generals". *The Irrawaddy*, 8 September 2008. http://www2.irrawaddy.com/article.php?art_id=14208.

Smith, J. 2007. *Social Movements for Global Democracy*. Baltimore: Johns Hopkins University Press.
Solomon, F. 2015. "Burma Govt 'Hampers' Mandate of UN Rights Envoy". *The Irrawaddy*, 7 August 2015. https://www.irrawaddy.com/news/burma/govt-hampers-mandate-of-yanghee-lee.html.
Standing, G. 2011. *The Precariat: The New Dangerous Class*. London: Bloomsbury Academic.
Stothard, D. 2008. "Altsean Suggests Compromise over International Aid". *The Irrawaddy*, 21 May 2008. http://www2.irrawaddy.com/article.php?art_id=12171&page=2.
Tilly, C. 1978. *From Mobilization to Revolution*. Reading, MA: Addison-Wesley.
Tilly, C., and S. Tarrow. 2007. *Contentious Politics*. Boulder: Paradigm.
Turnell, S. 2008. "A Shattered Rice Bowl". *The Irrawaddy*, 19 May 2008. http://www2.irrawaddy.com/article.php?art_id=12110&page=2.
UN-OCHA. 2008. "Myanmar: Cyclone Nargis OCHA Situation Report No. 54". New York: UN Office for the Coordination of Humanitarian Affairs.
Wai Moe. 2011. "Earthquake Death Toll Rising to 150". *The Irrawaddy*, 26 March 2011. http://www2.irrawaddy.com/article.php?art_id=21017.
Walgrave, S., and P. Van Aelst. 2006. "The Contingency of the Mass Media's Political Agenda Setting Power: Toward a Preliminary Theory". *Journal of Communication* 56 (1): 88–109.
Weeks, W. 1996. "Democratic Leadership Practices in Australian Feminist Women's Services: The Pursuit of Collectivity and Social Citizenship?" *International Review of Women and Leadership* 2 (1): 19–33.
Wolfsfeld, G., E. Segev, and T. Sheafer. 2013. "Social Media and the Arab Spring: Politics Comes First". *International Journal of Press/Politics* 18 (2): 115–37.
Yan Pai. 2011. "In the Wake of the Quake". *The Irrawaddy*, 29 March 2011. http://www2.irrawaddy.com/article.php?art_id=21034.
Yen Saning and Kyaw Hsu Mon. 2015. "Irrawaddy Delta Braces for Upstream Floodwaters' Arrival". *The Irrawaddy*, 6 August 2015. http://www.irrawaddy.com/news/burma/irrawaddy-delta-braces-for-upstream-floodwaters-arrival.html.
Yeni. 2008. "No Happy Endings". *The Irrawaddy* (June). http://www2.irrawaddy.com/article.php?art_id=12593&page=1.
Zarganar. 2008. "Zarganar's Relief Role". *The Irrawaddy*, 2 June 2008. http://www2.irrawaddy.com/article.php?art_id=12448&page=1.
Zarni. 2008. "Pulling No Punches". *The Irrawaddy*, 22 May 2008. http://www2.irrawaddy.com/opinion_story.php?art_id=12190&page=1.

Zarni Mann. 2015. "7 Rescuers Die as Floods Sweep Central Burma". *The Irrawaddy*, 20 July 2015. https://www.irrawaddy.com/news/burma/7-rescuers-die-as-floods-sweep-central-burma.html.

ခင်ဦးသာ (Khin Oo Tha). 2015. "ရခိုင်ဒေသ ရေကြီးမှုကြောင့် ပျက်စီးဆုံးရှုံးမှုဒဏ် ဒေသခံများ ရင်ဆိုင်နေရဆဲဖြစ်" [Locals still suffer detrimental impact of Rakhine state floods]. *The Irrawaddy*, 3 July 2015. https://burma.irrawaddy.com/news/2015/07/03/77423.html.

8

Educating a New Generation of Watchdogs: Interview with Ye Naing Moe, Director of the Yangon and Mandalay Journalism Schools

Interviewed by Nai Nai and Jane Madlyn McElhone

At Myanmar's first national media development conference in early 2012, keynote speaker Ye Naing Moe talked about meeting his wife's family. When asked about his job, he responded: "I'm a journalist." And it was this answer that inspired a follow-up question from his future father-in-law: "I know you're a journalist, but what's your job?"

Ye Naing Moe is a veteran journalist, columnist, mentor and trainer. He started training Myanmar journalists underground in 2000, and then founded the Yangon Journalism School in 2009, followed by the Mandalay Journalism School in 2015. The schools have since trained more than eight hundred journalists and editors. In 2016 the Yangon Journalism School published Myanmar's first editors' manual. To encourage local journalists to do investigative reporting, it is also helping to initiate the Myanmar Centre for Investigative Journalists.

Nai Nai and *Myanmar Media in Transition* contributing editor Jane Madlyn McElhone conducted a series of interviews with Ye Naing Moe between 2016 and 2018.

Q: You've trained and mentored hundreds of editors and journalists. What were the first big changes you noticed post-2010?

YNM: There were actually tectonic changes for the media industry before 2010. We need to start there. Although we had heavy censorship at that time, in 2007 the local media tried to cover the Saffron Revolution. But it was painful for journalists. They knew they couldn't publish their stories in their media outlets, but they still did the coverage. And if they wanted to try to publish their stories, first they had to give them to the government officers. But photographers still went out on the streets and they got the pictures. So did videographers and reporters. Youths across the nation were inspired by these local watchdogs. So it was a tectonic change. It was a revolution. And then there was Cyclone Nargis in early 2008. It shocked the whole nation. Once again, even though they knew they couldn't publish in-depth stories about the cyclone, the journalists went to the Delta region and tried to cover it. When their stories couldn't be published inside the country, they sent them to exiled media. So, even before 2010, there was a lot of tension between local media — editors and reporters — and government officials from the Ministry of Information. Even before the censorship board was abolished in 2012, local media were pushing the limits of journalism.

At the beginning of the political transition you were working as a journalist, as well as doing training. Can you tell us about a moment — or a story — that stands out for you?

In 2012 I decided to go to Laiza (in northern Kachin State) with four other journalists from *7Day News*, *The Modern* and *Venus News*. That's where the Kachin ethnic armed groups had their headquarters and troops. War broke out there in 2009, a year before the political transition began. Yet we rarely covered it because we couldn't get information, and we didn't have access to the government offices. Besides, we knew that we would face serious problems if we tried to publish those kinds of stories. But then, in 2012, before the censorship board was abolished, we tried again. We knew there would be heavy censorship and that we could be charged for communicating with the ethnic armed organizations. But we went out there for almost two weeks, and when we came back we took the risk of writing and sending our stories to the censorship board. And, of course, it was the censorship board's duty to reject our stories. It wasn't my duty. I was the writer.

To protest the orders from the censors, all four reporters decided to run the stories. But afterwards their editors had to sign a letter promising the censors that they wouldn't do it again. So the big difference after 2010 is that local media started filing stories on conflict, war, ethnic issues and human rights. The post-opening abolition of press censorship also coincided with two major conflicts in the country. One was the conflict in Rakhine State and the other in Kachin State. Yet local media weren't skilful in reporting conflicts, so, though they covered them, at first they failed to meet professional standards.

Have reporting standards improved since then?

Yes, I've seen the quality of local journalism improve, especially over the past couple of years. Better story ideas, news-gathering, the use of different formats, timelines and infographics. And media like *7Day*, *Frontier* and *Myanmar Now* are experimenting with different forms of storytelling. Some are even trying to touch sensitive issues. For example, *Myanmar Now*'s story about sexual harassment of children by religious persons. That would have been almost impossible to cover in the past.

But it doesn't mean I'm satisfied. We have to keep improving. Quality heavily depends on the options we have and the rights we achieve. Before the abolition of censorship, for example, quality depended on the censors. After they cut our stories we couldn't do anything. Now we have different challenges. We're trying to cover many different issues we've never covered before. Many government officers are reluctant to talk to the media. They see them as problem makers. And local reporters have to improve their in-depth reporting. It's still difficult because that kind of reporting needs time, money and other resources. Also, many editors in local newsrooms are in their late 20s and early 30s, so they have a lot to learn. That means we still have a great deal to do.

Do you use stories published by local news outlets for your teaching? Which ones serve as examples of good journalism?

Four days after censorship was abolished on 20 August 2012, the monthly magazine *Maw Kun* (The Chronicle) came out. They were digging deeper and trying to focus on issues which other media didn't tackle. That is one good example. Many journalists also started covering issues like copper mining in Monywa, Sagaing Region. That coverage raised the standard of reporting and promoted the status of journalists among the public. Another example was when local media covered the student demonstration against the education bill in November 2014. Many local media sent their journalists to cover that story. Journalists followed the students' march from central Myanmar until they reached the outskirts of Yangon. Their coverage shocked the government. So, during these years, many young reporters and editors thoroughly covered various issues that were important for society.

These days I often reference *7Day*, *Frontier* and *Myanmar Now* as examples of good journalism. But in terms of quality, we shouldn't only focus on how Burmese media cover stories. Another concern is how they select their stories, and what issues they cover the following day. I truly admire young journalists' courage and energy. But they still have to improve the quality of their writing as a craft. And I have to say that most front pages and homepages are dominated by politics. They report what politicians have said and they report on scandals. So readers and audiences have become obsessed with those kinds of stories. At a 21st Century Panglong peace conference reporting workshop held in June 2018, I told the political reporters that they are giving their readers boring stories filled with acronyms. This has got to stop.

And many issues are still off our radar, such as business and the economy, transportation, natural resources, and public health. When reporting on public health, journalists only cover what the World Health Organization (WHO) announced or what the Ministry of Health said. Many fail to dig deeper. Many editors say these stories are not sexy enough to invest time and money. So there are many stories out there that we have yet to report.

What are news organizations doing to ensure their staff have the skills they need to do good journalism — or is that even a priority?

It's a big challenge for newsrooms. Media don't invest much time on in-house training for their reporters and editors. This is especially true for print newspapers because they are struggling financially and have limited human resources. So they don't have time to brush up on their journalism skills. It's a bottleneck situation because they should focus on on-the-job coaching, but they fail to do this. They send their reporters to training programmes. But there is one important question: are those training sessions useful enough? We have to check the quality of the curricula and trainers. Communication and coaching between editors and reporters also need to improve. That's why my school works with editors. One important component of editor training is coaching their reporters.

Are media giving citizens what they want and need?

Local media are providing stories that readers like to read. But they are failing to provide the kind of in-depth stories that they really need. It's all about the survival of newspapers. It's only when they publish sexy stories for their readers that they can become financially sound in the market. This is what has happened with Rakhine. Whenever the international community criticizes abuses in Rakhine, many local media only highlight the government reaction. This reporting — that the government is right and the international community is wrong — has shaped the way local people see the conflict.

My big concern is that financial problems will make it more difficult for media outlets to produce quality in-depth stories in the future. In addition, local media are covering too many issues in a very short period of time, with insufficient skills and too few human and financial resources. We have seven states and regions to cover. We need to develop both quantity and quality. And local journalists from outside of Yangon are really struggling. Though they cover stories for Yangon-based media, many of them do not receive sustainable salaries. Their fees cannot even pay for their own gasoline. It's very difficult for them to survive and sustain themselves. And this triggers ethical issues in the long run.

Are some stories and issues still no-go zones for journalists? How are they dealing with the restrictions?

Maybe you can say that there are "almost no-go" zones. For issues with the army, for example, journalists have to be very careful. In mid 2016, *7Day News*, one of the biggest local newsrooms, published a tiny story about something the former chairman of the Union Parliament had said at a public event. It was a single-source story. The army filed a serious case against *7Day News* and the paper subsequently published an apology. That incident made many journalists unhappy and anxious. Religious issues are another "almost no-go zone", although it has been easier to cover such issues in the wake of the 2015 general elections. Covering the extractive industries is also difficult because we don't have a law on access to information. Even our press law is not being put into practice by government officials and most ministries. But the big no-go zone these days is Rakhine, especially if you have a big audience, because your coverage will be closely monitored. When some local journalists tried to report from Maungdaw they also faced grave danger from local Rakhine mobs.

What about the issue of national security?

The Tatmadaw [the army] will say "national security" means the Tatmadaw, and being safe from foreign and rebel troops at home. Yet, there are many issues related to security, like clean water and food. But this society has been controlled by the Tatmadaw for more than five decades, so it makes sense that the government can only view security through the lens of the armed troops. They use it as an excuse — it's national security so you don't deserve to know. But sometimes that collides with people's right to know and the right of media to ask. The military and the government need to find a balance between national security and the peoples' and taxpayers' right to know.

Does this lead to self-censorship?

Yes. It is in our brain. Whenever I write my Sunday op-ed column (for *7Day Daily*), I have to judge whether I should limit my writing or not. Even for satire we self-censor. Whenever the Tatmadaw or other government ministries file cases against journalists or newsrooms, there is a chilling effect on all of us.

How do newsrooms deal with covering ethnic conflict?

It has always been very difficult for newsrooms based in Yangon. In 2012, nobody liked to travel to the areas controlled by ethnic armed organizations because they could face serious charges. In May 2012, after our group of five journalists returned from Laiza and wrote our stories, this encouraged journalists to push the limit. But, of course, they need to make sure they have the skills. Many journalists went out to those areas but didn't understand the context. Before they reached Laiza, for example, many of them didn't understand the difference between the Kachin Independence Organisation (KIO) and the Kachin Independence Army (KIA). That was not actually their fault, because the situation in the past made them naïve about issues in their own country. We didn't travel enough. So now they are struggling with background issues such as covering the Rohingya [referred to as Bengali Muslims by the government and many media] issue in Rakhine State, near the Bangladesh border. The Rakhine crisis has tested the professionalism and ethics of journalists and editors.

Have journalists become more nationalistic in their coverage?

No. Nationalism hasn't taken over journalism. But ultra-nationalism is threatening it. I often tell people that journalism has nothing to do with nationalism, but some think it does — that our duty is to protect our sovereignty, our country, instead of acting like watchdogs. That is the struggle in our journalism sector since a popular government took office. People still don't understand that watchdogs need to be part of the checks and balances, even when their government is in power. Rakhine is a good example. Many stories about the conflict in Rakhine in local newspapers have amplified the voice of the NLD-led government. But after the two Reuters journalists got arrested, the stories became more critical.

Are journalists sufficiently aware of safety issues in the field?

The 2017 arrests of the two Reuters journalists, Wa Lone and Kyaw Soe Oo, have had a chilling effect for local journalists. I think these two journalists are very brave. But reporting on conflicts, and even writing about them, is very dangerous right now — more than ever before, especially after the civilian government took power. The message is you have to be careful and control your pen, especially if you are writing in Burmese for media outlets that have a high circulation. It is those papers that are in the hands of people in the neighbourhoods. They are the people the government and the military care about. And no one will protect you if the military comes after you. I was a witness for Wa Lone and Kyaw Soe Oo. They are my alumni. You can't be silent.

My concern is that journalists lack both experience and support from their own newsrooms. We understand that local newsrooms are poor, but they have to make at least some arrangements for their journalists before they go out to conflict areas. For example, when conflict broke out in the Kokang area (in northern Shan State) in February 2015, many young journalists — most of them photojournalists — went there without bulletproof vests or helmets, and they never received any safety training. The few journalists who received safety training outside the country are now editors. While covering the Kokang conflict, some of the journalists got injured, but luckily there were no fatalities. And then there is the Rakhine crisis. So local newsrooms have to think seriously about journalists' safety, especially for those who do conflict reporting. With support from some regional or international media organizations, safety training should be provided. And journalists need equipment such as bulletproof vests and helmets.

What kind of support does the news industry need?

One serious problem is distribution. State-owned media have their own printing presses and distribution channels. That is the major issue killing papers. But I do not have a solution. People need to sit down together and think about it. Another thing is radio. It will play an important role. So, international and regional media education organizations should focus on providing capacity building. And other programmes are needed for editors and reporters to diversify their reporting away from "only politics", to education, public health, business and economics. Every time I ask students what kind of news beat they would like to take on, many choose politics. Only a few choose business and the economy. I think that is a failure. Journalists need to realize what is important for the people. Another big issue is that our young editors and reporters need scholarships for really good universities and colleges abroad. Right now, some are studying, but it's not enough. If we get local journalists with master's degrees from prestigious universities, it will mean a lot for us. If we get ten per cent, we can change the media landscape. If twenty per cent, it will be a heyday for Myanmar media.

What would you like to say to international and regional organizations working in media development in Myanmar?
I would like to urge organizations working on media education to conduct a training needs assessment. It's tricky to know what kind of training is suitable for which media, whether in the ethnic states or in the capital. It differs from one area to another, and our assumptions might be wrong. Actually, all media development organizations working in Myanmar should come up with a master plan: who will do what and how. And this really needs the cooperation of editors. Editors need to understand and accept that we should improve the quality of our reporting.

What are the greatest threats to journalism today in Myanmar?
The most important is the lack of an independent judiciary. This affects the entire sector. The second is the rise of ultra nationalism — the ultra-nationalists can sue you at any time and you are not protected. The third is that the current government does not understand media freedom and free expression. Things have been worse since the present government took office. The lines are no longer clear. You no longer know where people stand.

Editors' note: On 10 February 2019, at the Yangon Journalism School's annual Feature Writing Awards, Ye Naing Moe told the well-known story of miners carrying caged canaries into coal mines; if the birds got sick and died, it meant the miners had to get out. Today if you say someone is a "canary in a coal mine", it means he or she is facing threats and danger, and this, Ye Naing Moe said, is the reality for Myanmar journalists and editors. Yet, he added, the canary is still alive.

9

The Metamorphosis of Media in Myanmar's Ethnic States

Jane Madlyn McElhone

In September 2017, editors from the ethnic media network Burma News International (BNI) gathered for a closed-door meeting in Hpa-An, Kayin State to discuss the fresh outbreak of violence in northern Rakhine and the impact on its network. Its Rakhine Buddhist member Narinjara News[1] attended the meeting. Its Rohingya Muslim member Kaladan Press[2] did not. One year later, in September 2018, there are no stories by Kaladan Press on BNI's website.[3] In the current environment, being the only network in Myanmar with a Rohingya member is challenging and contentious.

The Rakhine crisis presents one of the most complex dilemmas BNI has faced during its fifteen-year history.[4] Tensions surfaced with the first wave of anti-Muslim violence in June 2012, in the early days of the political transition. BNI's editor-in-charge,[5] a Buddhist from Rakhine State, decided to stop posting stories from Kaladan Press on the network's news site. This unilateral move silenced the voice of the Rohingya member at a vital time and ensured that only the Rakhine member was heard. This was an abrupt wake-up call for the BNI leadership, already struggling to comprehend the political changes unfolding inside the country. To mitigate a potentially volatile internal crisis — and to create breathing space to evaluate the network's coverage of the anti-Muslim violence — a moratorium was placed on stories from both members.

The tensions did not stop there. In 2016, at BNI's annual ethnic media conference — held for the very first time in Rakhine State, in the historic town of Mrauk Oo[6] — the Rohingya camps and the conflict were the elephant in the room, absent from the conference agenda. Kaladan Press was also absent. A group of Rakhine media outlets had made it clear that they would boycott the conference if BNI's Rohingya member attended, and there were concerns that the Rohingya editor would not be safe if he tried to cross the border from Bangladesh.[7] One of the local Rakhine outlets, Root Investigative Agency — known for its coverage of the Rohingya plight — was also absent.

In August 2017, when violence again flared in northern Rakhine, BNI was once more confronted by its internal membership struggles. Once again, the leadership placed a moratorium on stories from its Rakhine and Rohingya members and endeavoured to calm tensions.

Moving from the borderlands to establish official operations inside Myanmar, while continuing to provide a forum for the ethnic nationalities that constitute an estimated thirty to forty per cent of the country's population, has in itself been a challenging transition.[8] The metamorphosis is made more complex, and at times chilling, given the fragile and contentious ceasefire agreements and peace process, increased armed conflict, Rakhine crisis, and the September 2018 United Nations report detailing serious human rights violations and abuses in Kachin, Rakhine and Shan States, as well as genocide against the Rohingya by the Myanmar military (UN 2018).

In this chapter I explore the challenging move from the borderlands and the growth of the media sector inside the ethnic states. The outlets launched inside now outnumber those that have moved inside. BNI's members — now totalling fourteen — are also in the minority. Yet in many ways it is BNI and its members that have put ethnic media on the map inside Myanmar, and their struggles say much about the sector.

Rakhine State and the Rohingya

Now operating inside the country, the BNI network is facing new dilemmas linked to Rakhine State and the Rohingya. Should they adapt to the status quo as a means of survival, and accept the official line as to who is an ethnic group and who is not? Or should they resist and provoke change, knowing that such efforts could come at great cost? Karen Information Center (KIC) director Nan Paw Gay suggests there is a middle ground. KIC is a BNI member, and as BNI's head of policy, Nan Paw Gay is the network's public voice. "We don't have a solution and we can't make the tensions disappear, but we can be practical", she says. BNI's Rohingya and Rakhine members helped to found the network in the borderlands in 2003, at a very different time in the network's history. "But now we're inside and we stand for news production", she explains. "We aren't here to debate nationalities. We expect our members to do journalism, and if they do, they can stay in the network."[9]

Yet Nan Paw Gay admits that the challenges are enormous. BNI members come from different ethnic states and have varying perspectives and values, including with regard to Rakhine State and the Rohingya. "What we can do on a very practical level is closely monitor all of the stories the members send us before we publish them, especially when it comes to explosive issues like Rakhine", she says. "The problem, though, is that we don't have enough people to do that." Inadequate resources can mean, unfortunately, a lack of due diligence when it comes to monitoring content; namely, ensuring BNI's stories are journalistically sound, and blocking information that both unintentionally and intentionally misleads and inflames. This is one of the reasons BNI has chosen not to post certain members' content during times of crisis — a pragmatic solution, if not a desirable one, particularly as it raises important questions about free expression and censorship.

Nan Paw Gay says her own media outlet, KIC, struggles when it comes to covering Rakhine. "We are Karen and we understand identity struggles. We use the word Rohingya and we covered the UN report released in September. But only in English."[10] It would be dangerous, she says, if KIC covered these same stories, using the same terms, in Myanmar language. These struggles are reflective of the myriad challenges facing ethnic media in the current media landscape.

The Ethnic Media Players

BNI's fourteen members come from Myanmar's seven ethnic states: Kachin, Kayah (Karenni), Kayin (Karen), Chin, Mon, Rakhine (Arakan) and Shan.¹¹ During the decades of military rule, when ethnic media were banned, they operated in the ethnic nationality controlled borderlands of Thailand, India and Bangladesh, as well as overseas in countries such as Canada and the United States. The military junta forbade the publication of ethnic language publications and outlets that were seen to be challenging its Barmanization policy that targeted ethnic minorities. This contravened Article 16 of the UN's Declaration on the Rights of Indigenous Peoples, which states that indigenous peoples have the right to create their own media in their own languages, and that states should encourage media to reflect indigenous cultural diversity (UN 2007, p. 7).

Seven years into the political transition, however, the sector has undergone a metamorphosis, however fragile. Although legislation does not specifically sanction ethnic language publications or media outlets, ethnic media editors say that state authorities and the Ministry of Information have given their tacit approval. In August 2012, for example, the Nationalities Brotherhood Forum (NBF), an alliance of Chin, Mon, Shan, Rakhine (Arakan), Kayin (Karen) and Kayah (Karenni) political parties, released a statement in support of ethnic language publications.¹² This facilitated applications, and now, with very few exceptions, all of the ethnic media are licensed (FEM 2017).¹³

Many of the longstanding outlets — among them BNI members — were born out of the armed political struggle. Yet today these ethnic media pioneers are in the minority. There are now an estimated forty-five to fifty local media operating openly and officially in Myanmar's seven ethnic states, as well as in some of the country's seven regions, and in Mandalay and Yangon. These include a growing number of start-ups and a comparatively large, and constantly shifting, number of small outlets in Chin State and in Kalay, along the Chin-Sagaing border.

That not all of the start-ups identify as ethnic media indicates a shift, albeit nascent, in identity politics.¹⁴ *Myitkyina News Journal* in Kachin State, Root Investigative Agency in Rakhine State, and Hinthar Media in Mon State are three examples. *Myitkyina News Journal*'s founding CEO Brang Mai explains: "We're a news media organization that happens to be located in the ethnic states. That's an important distinction. And that's why we're named after the capital city, not the state."¹⁵ Brang Mai collaborates with ethnic media editors from other states and attends ethnic media conferences, but says it is vital to guard his media's independence from all things political and nationalistic.

Ethnic media outlets also operate in areas controlled by ethnic armed groups. Laiza FM Radio is owned by the Kachin Independence Organisation and broadcasts to Kachin State and northern Shan State from a zone along the Myanmar-China border controlled by its military wing, the Kachin Independence Army (VOA 2016). Some ethnic media are also based across the border in Thailand. Since telecommunications and infrastructure, including roads, are still generally better and cheaper in neighbouring countries, and it is easier and safer to report on taboo issues from outside the country, six of BNI's formerly border-based ethnic media members maintain cross-border operations.[16] Unable to operate openly or safely in Myanmar, the stateless Rohingya media in diaspora — including BNI member Kaladan Press, based in Chittagong, Bangladesh — remain fully exiled, with stringers operating underground inside Rakhine State. Yet following the military operations and violence in 2017, and the mass exodus of Rohingya across the border to Bangladesh, the number of stringers has fallen sharply, and their safety and, in some cases, whereabouts, are uncertain.[17]

The Politics of Language and Ethnicity

Media outlets operating in the ethnic states have made strategic choices about language use, and their choices have clear consequences. Myanmar is by far the most popular language for print and online publications, and adopting it enables outlets to attract larger audiences, to reach those in power, and to find experienced staff. Some of the outlets that use it are adamant that they do not want to be associated with nationalism or ethnic struggles, or to attract nationalistic audiences. They thus deliberately choose not to publish in ethnic languages. Yet this does not shield them from criticism for complying with old restrictions, or from accusations of being pro-government as a result of not actively associating themselves with ethnic nationalism and cultural preservation.

Conversely, a small number of media in Chin, Shan, Kachin and Mon States have elected to publish solely in their local ethnic languages, a choice not without its own set of challenges. While ethnic people's first spoken language is often their ethnic language, being able to read in that language is another matter entirely, and often depends on whether they were taught in mother tongue based ethnic armed organization schools or in central government schools.[18] If the latter, they often cannot read in their own language, and so prefer Myanmar. Ethnic language media also target older rural populations that may not speak Myanmar, and those living in refugee camps along the Thai-Myanmar border.

Given that they often attract smaller, niche audiences, usually in more rural areas, it can be harder for local language media to survive financially and to attract funding and private advertising. The broadcasting experience of the Shan Herald Agency for News, however, belies this assertion. Clips from their Shan Online Radio (formerly Radio Panglong) are downloaded to smartphones and via Facebook as many as ten million times a month. Their Shan-language television programme is also popular.[19] Local language radio and video thus offer great scope for ethnic language use and preservation, as well as audience expansion.

Radio has been particularly identified as having significant influence in ethnic and conflict-affected areas in Myanmar, as has television, although the latter more in urban areas (Dolan and Gray 2014). Yet, since the Broadcasting Law is not yet operational, media are not permitted to set up new terrestrial stations, and the sector remains fully in the hands of the government, military and their business partners (FEM 2018).[20] *Myitkyina News Journal* chief editor Seng Mai cautions that the eventual development of the sector could bring with it the risk that cronies of the military regime will quickly buy and establish new TV or radio stations, especially in the ethnic states, posing a challenge for smaller ethnic media outlets.[21] In the meantime, online experimentation has led to the launching of two pioneer online radio in ethnic languages: Shan Online Radio and Radio Karen. There are also fledgling community radio projects under way in Chin State.

Writer Pascal Khoo Thwe, from Burma's Padaung minority in Kayah State, believes that media are an important vehicle for preserving ethnic culture, as are other forms of expression, such as creative writing, poetry and filmmaking.[22] It is encouraging, therefore, to see them being championed in the ethnic states in an effort to preserve and invigorate local languages and expression. Khon Soe Moe Aung, a young filmmaker based in Demoso, Kayah State, was trained at the Yangon Film School and then produced the award-winning short film *My Leg*, about a group of war veterans who craft artificial legs for their fellow veterans from all sides of the conflict. He currently works for the Kayah Earthrights

Action Network and mentors community activists in filmmaking. His advice to budding journalists, filmmakers, videographers and photographers: "If you want to stay in the ethnic states, you have to create your own opportunities for self expression."[23] In 2015 the British Council and PEN Myanmar collaborated on an anthology of original short stories by ethnic writers in ethnic languages called *Hidden Words Hidden Worlds*. Writer and former political prisoner Letyar Tun mentored participants in Chin State and encouraged them to write about their own experiences. He notes, however, that people are still fearful and don't seem to really know what freedom of expression means: "It'll take a long time to get real freedom and to understand that we can create what we want and innovate in our own personal styles" (Karlekar and McElhone 2015, p. 25).

Fear and Safety

Nan Paw Gay notes that ethnic communities are starting to trust local journalists more than they did in the past, and are thus more willing to speak to them, particularly if they have started to understand the role of media.[24] This is good news. Yet the culture of fear and insecurity is entrenched, and journalists say they need to be careful when tackling taboo yet vital issues for their communities: conflict, peace, ceasefires; child soldiers; the military; refugees, returnees and internally displaced peoples; human rights abuses; forced labour; land grabbing; human trafficking; development; resource extraction; drugs; and corruption. Ethnic journalists also say their interviews with authorities are hampered by their cultural upbringing, particularly the belief that it is impolite to ask tough questions, especially to officials and elders, an issue that can be even more challenging for women.

Ethnic media outlets also widely lack the capacity and resources to carry out in-depth investigations, and thus tend to confine their coverage to publicly visible developments such as news conferences and protests. Many also place their most contentious stories online, where they attract less attention than in their printed journals and, in some cases, hand them over to national media partners in order to limit their own exposure to legal and physical risk. Yet this strategy has been thwarted by the increased use of Section 66(d) of the 2013 Telecommunications

Law as a tool to threaten and imprison those who practise free expression online. In 2015 the mining company Delco Ltd filed, and won, a lawsuit for criminal defamation (under Article 500 of Myanmar's Penal Code) against the activist writer Aung Lwin for a sardonic essay that he published in *Tanintharyi Weekly*. The essay was written from the point of view of a fish mourning the destruction of a local creek. The case is the focus of the chapter by Jennifer Leehey in this volume. In February 2019 *Tanintharyi Weekly* chief editor Myo Aung was found guilty of defamation (under Article 25[b] of the Media Law) for publishing a satirical column called *A Smile for an Election Campaign*, which the Tanintharyi regional government said maligned the chief minister and the regional government.

There are currently no other cases under way in the ethnic states and regions targeting media outlets, writers, journalists or editors. Yet the two cases in Tanintharyi Region have had a strong chilling effect, as they clearly illustrate that it is difficult, if not impossible, to win. Journalists and editors also worry that once they start tackling more controversial topics and conducting more in-depth investigations, lawsuits will escalate. In the meantime, many say they protect themselves through self-censorship.[25]

Restricted physical access to conflict zones also limits coverage of taboo issues; for example, armed conflict with the Kokang group in northern Kachin State on the border with China and conflict in northern Rakhine and Shan States (Lawi Weng 2017). Nai Kasauh Mon, chief editor of Mon News Agency and BNI's former executive-director, says if ethnic journalists are not allowed to report in conflict zones "then the people in all of Burma will not know what is going on, and the peace process will have no hope of progressing".[26] Access to information linked to conflict and security is also restricted, and it is difficult to speak to sources on all sides. Even in states where there is no conflict, access to information is a problem. In Chin State, journalists are not allowed to cover the state assembly; they say their access has deteriorated under the NLD.[27] The Shan State government maintains that it does not have the authority to invite ethnic media into the assembly; as a result, it only allows access to state media.[28] Journalists in Kayin State also say they do not have access.[29] The fact that the state assemblies do not use ethnic languages also creates a structural barrier between the government and the people. And it is not only a matter of covering conflict. If ethnic media do not have access to information, then there is a lack of accountability on the part of those in power, and a greater risk of corruption, both of which affect the development of ethnic states and the peace process.

Journalists in the ethnic states acknowledge that they have more freedom to report, yet in the current transitional landscape the rules have changed. It is not always clear who is in charge and how far you can push the boundaries. Ethnic armed groups have historically considered local media and civil society organizations to be their platforms. Now that there are ceasefires, however fragile, media and civil society worry the government will try to pressure the ethnic armed groups to control them.

Peace and Conflict

Ethnic armed groups control certain areas in the ethnic states, while the Union government and military (Tatmadaw) control others. This adds uncertainty and insecurity to media production, including the practice of journalism. The peace talks, ceasefires and eased restrictions on some ethnic armed organizations have helped to improve free expression, yet journalists covering conflict struggle to balance the tone and content of their reporting.[30] Several bilateral ceasefire agreements signed by the government and ethnic armed groups contain media and free expression provisions, yet the National Ceasefire Agreement — which ten ethnic armed groups have signed since it was created in 2015 — does not.[31]

Ethnic media outlets' historical relationships with nationalist movements and armed groups can also raise questions about their independence. As they tackle issues that tend to be unfamiliar and contentious for the majority population — such as federalism and power sharing — mainstream media and authorities sometimes accuse them of bias.

According to Sai Lek, an ethnic Shan from Kachin State and a researcher on peace and conflict, people in Myanmar are slowly learning about the ethnic states, ethnic nationalities and peace — in other words, about their country's history — yet a culture of taboo topics, misinformation and disinformation still prevails (McElhone

2017, p. 10). Sai Lek notes that local media often have privileged access to stories, including in the conflict zones, yet he laments that there has been little in-depth or investigative coverage of the peace process, either by local media or national outlets, and that both sides in the conflicts try to use media to their own advantage. Covering the peace negotiations in the capital Naypyidaw, or in Yangon and Chiang Mai, Thailand, also demands financial resources which smaller ethnic media often do not have.[32]

In 2012, when the Thein Sein administration began negotiating with ethnic armed organizations, journalists from the ethnic states and Yangon started accessing the conflict zones more easily, speaking to a wide variety of people involved in the conflicts and affected by them, including ethnic armed group leaders, civil society groups, local residents, internally displaced peoples, and refugees. Then, on 3 May 2015, World Press Freedom Day, the military announced that anyone who published or broadcast statements by the Myanmar National Democratic Alliance Army (MNDAA), an ethnic armed organization in the Kokang Region in Shan State that was blacklisted, would be prosecuted. These kinds of threats created a climate of fear and self-censorship early on in the transition, which intensified with the arrests of three journalists by the military in northern Shan State in June 2017 (RFA 2017). Sai Lek notes, however, that while almost all mainstream media obeyed the military's order, ethnic media continued reporting.

The Shan State arrests took place while the fifth annual ethnic-media conference was under way to the south, in Loikaw, Kayah State. The news sent a chill through the conference hall. Ethnic media representatives had planned to kick off the day with a discussion about access to information. They viewed the arrests as an attempt to block independent news about ethnic conflict zones, and as an example of the risks journalists face when they work in the ethnic states where the military and ethnic armed groups continue to fight, and where they can get caught between the two. Nai Kasauh Mon, chief editor of Mon News Agency and then BNI executive director, spoke on behalf of his ethnic media colleagues: "Representatives from the media groups gathered here demand the release of the detained journalists, and the abolition of laws oppressing media freedom."[33]

The arrests brought back bitter memories of the 2014 killing of Mon freelance journalist Aung Kyaw Naing (Par Gyi) while in military custody in Mon State.[34] Members of the Southern Myanmar Journalists Network say the killing has made them more hesitant to report in conflict zones, especially since a colonial era law can be used to prosecute them for engaging with so-called unlawful organizations.[35] Conflicts in Myanmar's ethnic states are often covered by freelance journalists like Par Gyi. According to a countrywide survey in 2015, women face twice the risk as men when covering conflict (Article 19 2015). That the Reuters journalists Wa Lone and Kyaw Soe Oo were found guilty in 2018 of contravening Myanmar's Official Secrets Act has also had a chilling, and silencing, effect.

Looking Forward

That the media sector in the ethnic states has undergone a metamorphosis since late 2011 is indisputable. At the beginning of Myanmar's political transition, ethnic media in the borderlands were barely acknowledged, and their journalism dismissed as biased and weak by much of the Yangon media elite and the government. Since then, BNI has helped put ethnic media on the map. Its accomplishments — and the accomplishments of all of the media in the ethnic states — must be recognized. Yet the sector remains fragile and, as BNI knows from long experience, the issues of identity, ethnicity and belonging have been rendered far more complex by the Rakhine and Rohingya crisis. That the data on ethnicity from the 2014 Myanmar Population and Housing Census has yet to be released is a clear indication of how contentious this issue is (San Yamin Aung 2018). Peace and justice also remain out of reach, especially in Kachin, Shan and Rakhine States, rendering the future of ethnic media there all the more uncertain.

The economic struggles of local media operating in the ethnic states — from market domination by the state media to a broadcasting law that is not yet operational — were starkly laid out by ethnic media representatives at the sixth annual ethnic media conference in Hpa-An in April 2018. They were also echoed in a Media Development Investment Fund (MDIF) report, which states that "Myanmar's local media outlets exist in a perfect storm of undermining forces, which together create an almost impossible environment for achieving commercial sustainability" (Settles 2018).

Protecting and strengthening their independence, professionalism, ethics and sustainability, and resisting co-optation by authorities and special interest groups, are among the biggest challenges ethnic media face. The younger generation are also key; yet, with so few opportunities in the ethnic states, it is hard to convince them to stay put. There is also a concern that younger people are not as interested in, or committed to, journalism or the future of ethnic communities, including the preservation of local cultures and languages. For the moment, in any case, a good number of the ethnic-media outlets continue to be run by their founders. Shan Herald Agency for News — where a 66-year-old turned over leadership to a pair of younger editors — is a rare exception. Managing editor Sai Aw, who co-founded SHAN's pioneering digital radio project, Shan Online Radio, concurs that the younger generation may not have the same political agenda as their elders: "But we want to do good journalism, and we want to experiment with new technology and platforms."[36]

Yet doing good journalism in the ethnic states is not always easy. According to Nan Paw Gay, "Our challenges are bigger than mainstream media because we know the context well, and we have to think about our own security and the security of our communities. If we write everything we know, it can impact on the peace process, but if we don't write everything, the public won't know what is going on. We try to practise media ethics but we cannot always disclose everything."[37]

Given their privileged knowledge, understanding and access to local people and stories, ethnic media are in a unique position. And in some ways this makes them a sought-after commodity. As a platform for ethnic nationalities, their existence is crucial for the achievement of a sustainable peace. Without them, how can anyone really know what is going on in the ethnic states? Yet they are also in a tough position, struggling to practise journalism and promote freedom of expression for ethnic peoples, and negotiating risk-filled relationships with the Union and state governments, the military and ethnic armed groups. Seeking and preparing for a future federal union, where state governments will have real power and where local media will need to hold them accountable, also makes them forerunners of a system that is yet to be established and for which they cannot, therefore, fully prepare.

Appendix
Private Local Media in Myanmar's Ethnic States and Regions

Ethnic States						
Chin State	**Kachin State**	**Kayah (Karenni) State**	**Kayin (Karen) State**	**Mon State**	**Rakhine State**	**Shan State**
Chinland Herald, *The Chinland Post*, *Hakha Post*, *Matupi Times*, *Tedim Times*, *Zingzol*, *Zolengthe*	Kachin News Group, *The Kachin Times*, Kachin Waves, *Myitkyina News Journal*	*Kantarawaddy Times*	Karen Information Center (*The Karen News*, Radio Karen)	*Amartdein Journal*, Hinthar Media Corporation (*Hinthar News Journal*), Mon News Agency, (*Guiding Star*), *Thanlwin Times*	Development Media Group, Narinjara News, Root Investigative Agency	Asia Heart News, Golden Triangle Regional News, The People's Voice – Khamsarngor (Pa'O), Kanbawza Tai News Journal, *The Marnagar Journal* (Ta'ang Palaung), Shan Herald Agency for News (*The Shan Magazine*, Shan Online Radio), Golden Gong – Shwe Moung, Tachileik News Agency, Thanlwin Thwe Chin

The Metamorphosis of Media in Myanmar's Ethnic States

Regions (where ethnic media are also based)			
Mandalay Region The Voice of Shanni	**Sagaing Region** (all Chin) The Chin Voice, Chin World, Chinlung Today, Khonumthung News, Lairawn Post, Zomi Post, Zomi Times	**Tanintharyi Region** Dawei Watch Media (*Tanintharyi Weekly*)	**Yangon Region** Asia Heart News (Shan), *Hsenpai News Journal* (Shan), Khumi Media Group (Chin), Narinjara News (Rakhine - second office), Thazin Pan Khine News (Rakhine)

Note: The author conducted a mapping of media in Myanmar's ethnic states and regions from April to August 2018 for the Media Development Investment Fund's report *An Unfavorable Business: Running Local Media in Myanmar's Ethnic States and Regions*, in collaboration with Ei Phyu Zin Wint (Poe). The outlets listed in this table provide a picture of the media sector in the ethnic states but may not be exhaustive or up to date, as the sector is constantly shifting. Jane McElhone conducted a previous mapping of ethnic media in 2015 for the Open Society Foundations in Myanmar. The Rohingya outlet *Kaladan Press* is based in exile in Bangladesh.

Notes

1. http://narinjara.com/.
2. http://www.kaladanpress.org/.
3. https://www.bnionline.net/en.
4. Kaladan Press and Narinjara News are both founding members of BNI, along with Khonumthung News and *Mizzima*. Based in the western borderlands of Burma, India and Bangladesh, the four organizations founded the network in 2003 in Delhi, India, with a mission to promote peace, tolerance, cooperation and journalistic excellence. For many years, BNI continued working in the borderlands, gradually expanding to include other media outlets based along the Thai-Burmese border. Taking advantage of the political opening, in 2013 the network opened an outreach office in Yangon. During the same period, its members began setting up official operations inside their own ethnic states. As of September 2018, the network's members include (in alphabetical order): *Chin World*, Development Media Group, Hinthar Media, Kachin News Group, *Kaladan Press*, *Kantarawaddy Times*, Karen Information Center, *Khonumthung News*, *Mizzima News*, Mon News Agency, *Narinjara News*, Network Media Group, Shan Herald Agency for News, and *Than Lwin Times*.
5. BNI posts its members' stories on a common website. In 2012 the network had a rotating editorship shared by all member groups. When the anti-Muslim violence erupted, the editor-in-charge was from the Rakhine member, Narinjara News.
6. Annual conferences were also held in Hpa-An, Kayin State (2018); Loikaw, Kayah State (2017); Hakha, Chin State (2015); Taunggyi, Shan State (2014); and Mawlamyaing, Mon State (2013).
7. As Rohingya media cannot operate in safety inside Rakhine State, Kaladan Press is based in Chittagong, Bangladesh, with stringers working underground inside the country.
8. Soe Lynn Htwe (2017), the author of *The Role of Ethnic Media in New Myanmar*, defines ethnic media as "publications, broadcasts or websites that are associated with ethnic minority peoples and that focus on ethnic minority concerns, regardless of whether they use Burmese or an ethnic minority language", as well as "state-based" and "locally-based" periodicals, distributed in ethnic minority areas in Myanmar, that take up ethnic-minority concerns (p. 9).
9. Interview with Nan Paw Gay on 26 September 2018 in Yangon.
10. Ibid.
11. There are also six self-administered areas named after minorities: Naga, Danu, Pa-O, Palaung, Kokang and Wa. There is a Pa'O-language outlet in Taunggyi, Shan State called People's Voice, and an outlet operating

in Ta'ang Palaung in Lashio, in northern Shan State called Marnagar. As detailed in Chapter 1 of this volume, according to the former military junta, and the two governments that have since been in power, there are 135 different indigenous ethnic groups, grouped under eight so-called major races. However, this figure is widely contested; some say there are 135 languages and dialects spoken, not ethnic groups; others say the figure is propaganda as the military was never able to produce any reliable data or list of the "135 national races of Burma" (Smith 1994, p. 18; see also Cheesman 2017; Lintner 2017). The Myanmar government has yet to release the 2014 census data on ethnicity.

12. Interview with Nan Paw Gay in Loikaw, Kayah State on 27 June 2017.
13. If you want to run a print or broadcast media outlet in Myanmar, you are obliged to obtain a special licence.
14. Ethnic media are defined as outlets that function primarily to serve the information needs of a particular ethnic nationality. See also McElhone 2018.
15. Interview with *Myitkyina News Journal* CEO Brang Mai on 7 November 2016 in Yangon during the fifth conference on media development in Myanmar.
16. The cross-border media groups include Khonumthung, *Kantarawaddy Times*, Mon News Agency, Karen Information Center, Shan Herald Agency for News, and Kachin News Group.
17. Rohingya media cannot operate openly inside the country, since they are not recognized as an ethnic group. The most well-known outlets are based in Bangladesh, Malaysia, Saudi Arabia and Europe.
18. For example, for many years now students have attended Karen-language schools affiliated with the Karen National Union (KNU) and schools run by the New Mon State Party (NMSP).
19. Personal email correspondence with Shan Herald Agency for News managing editor Sai Aw on 31 August 2017.
20. The exception is a community radio project called Khayae FM, in Yangon's Htan Tabin township, that was launched in early 2018 as a joint venture with the Ministry of Information (DW 2018).
21. *Myanmar Media in Transition* contributing editor Gayathry Venkiteswaran conducted an interview with Seng Mai in Mrauk Oo, Rakhine State on 16 February 2016.
22. Interview with Pascal Khoo Thwe in Loikaw, Kayah State on 5 December 2015. See also Karlekar and McElhone 2015.
23. Interview with Khon Soe Moe Aung in Demaso Township, Kayah State on 3 February 2017 as part of an evaluation for Search for Common Ground Myanmar.

24. Interviews with Nan Paw Gay on 7 November 2016 in Yangon during the fifth conference on media development in Myanmar and on 6 November 2015.
25. Personal email correspondence with Myanmar Press Council member Myint Kyaw on 26 September 2018 and 19 January 2019.
26. Interview with Nai Kasauh Mon at the BNI editors' meeting in Loikaw, Kayah State on 27 September 2017.
27. Statements made by the Chin State Media Network during the fifth annual ethnic media conference in Loikaw, Kayah state in June 2017.
28. Personal email correspondence with Sai Lek, an ethnic Shan from Kachin State and a researcher on peace and conflict, on 31 August 2017.
29. Personal email correspondence with Nan Paw Gay, Karen Information Center director, on 31 August 2017.
30. Interview with Sai Lek, an ethnic Shan from Kachin State who has conducted extensive research on peace and conflict in the ethnic states, including with BNI's Myanmar Peace Monitor project, on 15 November 2015. See also McElhone 2017.
31. Personal email correspondence with Sai Lek on 8 October 2017. According to Sai Lek, the bilateral ceasefire agreements include the following: the All Burma Students Democratic Front (ABSDF) and the government have agreed that ABSDF can freely talk to media groups; the Chin National Front (CNF) and the government have agreed to freedom of writing and printing; the Karen National Union (KNU) and the government have agreed that national media outlets can participate in peace processes; the Pa'O National Liberation Army (PNLO) has requested the establishment of a free media group; and the Restoration Council of Shan State (RCSS) and the government have agreed that the RCSS can officially register its own outlet called the "Tai Freedom News Agency".
32. Interview with Sai Lek on 4 October 2015.
33. Nai Kasauh Mon addressing the fifth annual ethnic media conference in Loikaw, Kayah State on 27 June 2017. He stepped down from his role as executive director of BNI in September 2018. See also McElhone 2017.
34. Aung Kyaw Naing (Par Gyi) was arrested while covering conflict along the Thai-Burma border in Mon State. Two soldiers were acquitted by the military court and the family's petition to the Supreme Court for an investigation into the murder was rejected, raising suspicion about the military's influence over the judiciary.
35. In 2015 the eight ethnic armed groups that signed the Nationwide Ceasefire Agreement (NCA) with the former quasi-civilian administration were removed from the list of Unlawful Associations. Seven other groups declined to sign. Some bilateral ceasefire agreements, albeit fragile, were

also signed. In February 2018 two more groups signed the NCA. Yet peace remains elusive and the ceasefire agreements are not respected by all of the signatories.
36. Interview with Sai Aw in Loikaw, Kayah State on 28 September 2015. See also Karlekar and McElhone 2015.
37. Public comment made by Nan Paw Gay during the fifth annual ethnic media conference in Loikaw, Kayah State on 27 June 2017. See also McElhone 2017.

References

Article 19. 2015. *Country Report: Censored Gender in Myanmar*. https://www.article19.org/resources.php/resource/38032/en/country-report:-censored-gender.

BNI Multimedia Group. 2018. "Statement of the 6th Ethnic Media Conference". https://www.bnionline.net/en/news/statement-sixth-ethnic-media-conference.

Cheesman, N. 2017. "How in Myanmar 'National Races' Came to Surpass Citizenship and Exclude Rohingya". *Journal of Contemporary Asia* 47 (3): 461–83. https://doi.org/10.1080/00472336.2017.1297476.

Dolan, T., and S. Gray. 2014. *Media and Conflict in Myanmar: Opportunities for Media to Advance Peace*. United States Institute of Peace. https://www.usip.org/sites/default/files/PW92.pdf.

Free Expression Myanmar. 2017. *Printing and Publishing Law*. http://freeexpressionmyanmar.org/printing-and-publishing-law/.

———. 2018. *New Bylaws Are Opportunity to Fix Broadcasting Law Flaws*. http://freeexpressionmyanmar.org/new-bylaws-are-opportunity-to-fix-broadcasting-law-flaws/.

James, K. 2018. *On Air: A Rural Revolution in Myanmar*. Deutsche Welle Akademie. https://www.dw.com/en/on-air-a-rural-revolutionin-myanmar/a-43824644.

Karlekar, K., and J. McElhone. 2015. *Unfinished Freedom: A Blueprint for the Future of Free Expression in Myanmar*. PEN America. https://pen.org/unfinished-freedom-a-blueprint-for-the-future-of-free-expression-in-myanmar.

Lawi Weng. 2016. "Burma Army Obstructs Media Access in Northern Rakhine State". *The Irrawaddy*, 21 October 2016. https://www.irrawaddy.com/news/burma-army-obstructs-media-access-in-northern-arakan-state.html.

Lintner, B. 2017. "Book Review: Myanmar's Enemy Within: Buddhist Violence and the Making of the Muslim 'Other'". *The Irrawaddy*, 4 September 2017. https://www.irrawaddy.com/culture/books/myanmars-enemy-within-buddhist-violence-making-muslim.html.

McElhone, J. 2015. "A Mapping of Media in Burma/Myanmar's Ethnic States". Unpublished. Open Society Foundations, Burma.

———. 2017. "The Role of Media in Peacebuilding in Myanmar: A Multi-stakeholder Reflection. Bangkok, UNESCO. https://bangkok.unesco.org/sites/default/files/assets/article/UNESCO%20Myanmar/publications/FINAL%20UNESCO%20MEDIA%20%26%20PEACEBUILDING%20REPORT.pdf.

———. 2018. "Local Media Research Data". In *An Unfavorable Business: Running Local Media in Myanmar's Ethnic States and Regions*. Media Development Investment Fund. Available at https://www.mdif.org.

RFA. 2017. "Myanmar Journalists Charged under Unlawful Association Act in Northeastern Shan State". 28 June 2017. http://www.rfa.org/english/news/myanmar/myanmar-journalists-charged-under-unlawful-association-act-in-northeastern-shan-state-06282017154844.html.

San Yamin Aung. 2018. "Still No Date for Release of Census Findings on Ethnic Populations". *The Irrawaddy*, 21 February 2018. https://www.irrawaddy.com/news/burma/still-no-date-release-census-findings-ethnic-populations.html.

Settles, R. 2018. "The Media Market: Obstacles to Local Media Sustainability". In *An Unfavorable Business: Running Local Media in Myanmar's Ethnic States and Regions*. Media Development Investment Fund. Available at https://www.mdif.org.

Smith, M. 1994. *Ethnic Groups in Burma: Development, Democracy and Human Rights*. ASI Human Rights Series no. 8. London: Anti-Slavery International.

Soe Lynn Htwe. 2017. "The Role of Ethnic Media in the 'New Myanmar'". Understanding Myanmar's Development Research Report no. 6. Chiang Mai: Regional Center for Social Science and Sustainable Development (RCSD), Chiang Mai University.

UN (United Nations). 2007. *United Nations Declaration on the Rights of Indigenous Peoples*. http://www.un.org/esa/socdev/unpfii/documents/DRIPS_en.pdf.

———. 2018. "Myanmar: UN Fact-Finding Mission Releases Its Full Account of Massive Violations by Military in Rakhine, Kachin and Shan States. https://www.ohchr.org/EN/NewsEvents/Pages/DisplayNews.aspx?NewsID=23575&LangID=E.

VOA. 2016. "On Myanmar-China Border, 'Rebel Radio' Extends Reach of Kachin". https://www.voanews.com/a/on-myanmar-china-border-rebel-radio-extends-reach-of-kachin/3608177.html.

World Directory of Minorities and Indigenous Peoples. n.d. "Muslims and Rohingya". http://minorityrights.org/minorities/muslims-and-rohingya/.

10

Covering Rakhine: Journalism, Conflict and Identity

Eaint Thiri Thu

In December 2016, I made my twenty-fifth reporting trip to Rakhine State in western Myanmar. More than any other state, and any other conflict, Rakhine has changed me and my understanding of my country.

Even though my family is a mix of four ethnicities, I grew up as a Burman Buddhist. That gave me a double majority status and privilege, both religious and ethnic. Living in the capital Yangon, my life was coloured by propaganda from the military government. In our school history books we could only read about the Great Burmese empire. The histories of the minorities were left out. From the state-controlled newspapers we learned that the ethnic armed struggle was an insurgent, rebel movement created by people who wanted to destabilize the country. No one mentioned that the Burman-led military had unjustly taken control of the ethnic lands. All I knew about minority ethnic groups was their traditional costumes and dances. I did not know why they were fighting, or how their lives were affected by conflict. I grew up in ignorance.

In this chapter I explore the challenge of gaining access, and remaining independent, in an ethnic state where you are expected to be on one side of the conflict or on the other. For decades the military junta restricted access to information and wielded a powerful propaganda strategy. This has had a long-lasting impact. There is a massive communication gap between the Burman lowlands and the ethnic states, characterized by historic misunderstandings and misinformation, especially now that social media platforms are the primary way to share information. This has both caused and perpetuated intercommunal conflict between Rakhine Buddhists and Rohingya Muslims. Information is a power and a weapon, with all sides distorting and exaggerating it. It is hard to trust what people say and to do accurate media coverage. Even the words you use to describe northern Rakhine and the Rohingya are highly sensitive. The fact that the military has closed off a large area in the north of the state where the Rohingya historically lived makes access and understanding all the more difficult. In this chapter I use my own experiences doing fieldwork, conducting interviews and building trust to explore identity and language politics in Rakhine State and to explain the challenges of getting to the truth.

When I First Started Seeing

A few days after the 2015 parliamentary elections that brought Aung San Suu Kyi and her party to power, fighting broke out in the north of the country between the military and the Kachin Independence Army (KIA). I travelled to Kachin State so I could observe the conflict and document civilian human rights violations for Human Rights Watch. It was my first assignment in a war zone.

My heart was pumping as I walked up a hill close to the front line in the small town of Moe Nyin. It took only forty-five minutes to get to the top, but knowing there might be landmines made it seem much longer. That is when I started to think deeply about how people in conflict zones live their daily lives. How do they adapt to conflict and survive? Where do they get their information? What is their future? I had only a glimpse of their plight, but I could already feel the bitterness of their lives spent falling asleep to the sounds of bullets and explosions.

Myanmar has long been home to war and an oppressive military regime, so human rights violations are an inevitable part of our daily lives. The pattern and seriousness of violations vary from place to place, one ethnic group to another, one religion to another, and one individual to another, especially between the Burman lowlands and the minority ethnic areas. We all share an education system that has been systematically destroyed, poverty and, on a deeper level, fear, mistrust and ignorance. For a long time, information was blocked and the only media we could easily access were state-controlled newspapers and the BBC, VOA and RFA. Someone from the ethnic states could not understand the difficult life of a Burman in the cities, while a Burman had no clue as to what was going on in the ethnic states. We were many worlds within the same country.

In 2008, when I was eighteen years old, I discovered documentaries and books through the American Center library in Yangon. I realized that people needed information in order to understand. I became an activist. Yet I still could not see the world of people living in the ethnic zones. It was only when I became a fixer[1] assisting foreign journalists, and a researcher, that my eyes were opened about the other parts of my country. My friends in Yangon could not believe my stories. For example, I uncovered one very shocking truth during a trip to northern Shan State. As there are numerous armed groups and increasing conflict in that state, villagers created a voluntary rotation system of porters for the armed forces. Rather than letting soldiers grab people randomly from farms and jungles, they hoped this would increase their chances of returning home safely. When I asked a man in an internally displaced persons camp if he knew that the military was violating his human rights, he answered me with a smile: "How can we care about our human rights or legal protection when we are trying so hard not to die?"

How Our History Laid the Groundwork for Today's Conflict

My country was a British colony from 1886 to 1948. Before that, there was occasional warring between Burmans and the Shan, and Burmans and the Rakhine, but for the most part the different ethnic groups lived separately in their own lands. It was only under the British that they were combined and ruled as part of India. The majority Burmans lived in the lowlands, and the minority ethnic groups lived in the hill areas. During the independence movement in the 1940s, the young educated Burmese man General Aung San, the father of Aung San Suu Kyi, tried to convince the ethnic people in the hill areas to form the Union in order to gain independence for the whole country. After many meetings and a powerful speech by Aung San in parliament that promised that the majority Burmans would never trick the minorities or take over their lands, the historic Panglong Agreement was signed by Burmans and three other major ethnic groups on 12 February 1947. The agreement outlined the federal union that would follow independence, based on principles of self-autonomy and equality among states.

Unfortunately, though, events did not unfold as planned. Aung San was assassinated later that year. And when the country became independent in 1948, the new rulers failed to implement the federal union plan. Instead, their attempt to demolish the long-standing traditional ruling systems in the ethnic states created tense conflicts between the military and the ethnic armed groups. To gain control, the military stepped into politics and ruled the country from 1958 to 1960. Then the power-hungry General Ne Win led a coup in March 1962. The totalitarian military government stayed in power for more than five decades, followed by a quasi-civilian government in 2011, and an almost-civilian government in 2016. None of them has figured out how to deal with ethnic conflict.

Covering Rakhine

I went to Rakhine State for the very first time in late 2012, six months after violence broke out between Rohingya Muslims and Rakhine Buddhists in the north. I learned about the violence from government newspapers. They said ten Muslims had been killed by a mob in the town of Taunggok, and used the derogatory word *Kalar* to describe them. According to oral history, *Kalar* originally meant foreigners or migrants from India. Now, however, it is most often used to describe Muslims and Hindus.

State media claimed that the violence had started after a Buddhist girl was raped and murdered by Muslims. It was surprising to see this kind of news in government papers. For my entire life they had tried to hide the truth, especially about atrocities. So I found it hard to believe what they were saying now. Given the NLD's election victory in the 2012 by-election, I wondered whether those previously in power were simply trying to fuel the conflict.

During the 2012 violence, many people lost their homes and lives. Most of these people were Rohingya. The government segregated the two communities — claiming that this would prevent the violence from escalating — moving Rohingya Muslims outside of the state capital Sittwe into camps, with no freedom of movement and restricted access to healthcare and education, and the Rakhine Buddhists into the centre of the city. Railway tracks divided them. Traditional Rohingya villages had existed outside of Sittwe for a long time. The Rohingya neighbourhoods inside the city were all destroyed and burnt down by the violence, with one exception: Aung Mingalar. This rich neighbourhood somehow survived, but it has remained heavily guarded ever since. Some of the newly homeless Rohingya were sent there as internally displaced persons. For the next two years the two communities had restricted access to each other, including limited trade at the Rakhine-Rohingya border railway intersection. When I last visited the area in December 2016, Rakhine could go into the Rohingya area freely, whereas the Rohingya could not leave their own areas without permission.

Journalists who want to visit the areas where Rohingya live have to ask the government for permission, and that is never easy. The rules and regulations for access to Rohingya camps frequently change, and the officials seem to drag things out as long as they can. In order to avoid long delays, some journalists attempt to sneak into the camps to do their reporting.

It is equally difficult to get the two communities to talk to journalists. When I am interviewing people, I try to establish a relationship of trust and respect. When I am interpreting for foreign journalists, my job is not simply to translate the words people say, but to create a space where they can tell their stories openly and comfortably in their own words. This is when I need to use my identity to gain access.

I will always remember December 2012. I was sitting in the house of a Rohingya Muslim man in Aung Mingalar. I was supposed to interpret for a foreign journalist, but suddenly I was asked to leave the room. Both the house owner, who could speak a little bit of English, and his guests seemed to be uncomfortable at the thought of speaking openly with a Buddhist Burman — me — in the room. I understood that the trust between Muslims and Buddhists had been badly broken, so I left without a fuss for the sake of the interview. When they were done they asked me to come back inside and to tell them where I lived in Yangon. Lan Kyal, I replied, a famous Muslim majority neighbourhood. I had lived there for twenty years and my late Buddhist grandfather had been the headman for thirty years. It was that information that changed the dynamics. They suddenly seemed to accept me. If they had known where I had lived, they said, they would not have asked me to leave the room. They started calling people in the camps, introducing me as a moderate Burmese journalist. This was how the door to the Rohingya community was first opened to me.

It was a different story for the Rakhine Buddhist community. I am myself a Buddhist, so I thought it would be easier. Yet my part-Burman identity risked creating a different kind of barrier. Very few ethnic minorities trust the Burman majority. We have a reputation for dominating them through military action, so that is understandable. In fact, it is said that Rakhine people hate Burmans almost as much as they hate the Rohingya. Yet once again I was able to use my identity to gain access. My family is from Dawei and it is widely believed that the Rakhine and Dawei are relatives. So I use my Dawei-Buddhist identity to gain access. Dawei and Rakhine languages also have some similarities, so the fact that I speak Dawei at home with my family helps me understand the Rakhine language. That means I do not have the same language barrier that I have with the Rohingya. But the Rakhine do not like that I bring foreign journalists with me to meet the Rohingya. One aggressive Rakhine man told me that my parents should have taught me how to protect my nation.

In most situations my identity as a Dawei Buddhist growing up side-by-side with my Muslim neighbours makes it easier to open doors. Yet sometimes I face a dilemma about whether or not to use my identity in my profession. I am well aware that this strategy can backfire, so I have to be careful. People from both sides want me to stand with them against the other side. What they do not understand is that, while I am using my identity to gain access, as an individual I do not truly belong to any particular group or identity. I simply want to report. I do not — and I should not — say one group is right and one group is wrong. Yet if I tell them this, I risk losing their trust.

Getting to the Truth: Identity, Language and Rumours

It is not an easy job to access credible information in Rakhine State. You need to triple-check everything, especially information from the Rohingya community. They are suffering from extreme human rights violations. Their freedom of movement and citizenship have long been denied. They have limited access to education and healthcare. Their job opportunities are restricted. Their human dignity has been ignored. They have been living in extreme poverty, which has led to human trafficking and smuggling to neighbouring countries. Given these dire circumstances, they want their suffering to be heard and cared about, especially by the international community. As a result, there is a tendency to exaggerate and twist information. People do it themselves and so do their translators. The language barrier is thus exacerbated by translation, especially for foreign media that face a double barrier: Rohingya to Burmese,[2] and then Burmese to English. I always try to explain to translators that exaggerating information has a huge impact on its credibility. The Rohingya people suffer many abuses, yet if their information is manipulated they will suffer even more, and the perpetrators of crimes against them will then more easily slip away without being held accountable.

Identity also influences news and information flows among and within communities in Rakhine State. In 2016 I conducted fieldwork on the ways Rakhine Buddhists, Rohingya Muslims and Kaman Muslims (a Muslim community living in southern Rakhine State) access and share information, and the role that news and information, social media and rumours play in creating and solving conflict.[3] Because they place little trust in people outside of their communities, or in traditional media outlets, and have limited media literacy, all three groups tend to place the greatest trust in informal information flows, including community sources and networks. None of them trust state-controlled media, and often refer to it as propaganda.

Over the past six years almost all of the messages in my inbox have been about reporting trips to Rakhine State, and most have been from foreign journalists. Because they have more resources, experience, interest — and sympathy — foreign journalists tend to spend more time in the field covering Rohingya issues than local journalists. This means they have gained the trust of that community in ways local and national media cannot.

Working with foreign journalists has taught me a lot about the way they build a story, conduct research, find sources, identify quotes, and fact-check. I find their stories strong and credible. Yet I have noticed that sometimes they oversimplify the context and dynamics of the conflict and the political situation of the country. Because too much time is wasted waiting for official permission, only a few journalists actually go to the camps. The others report the story of Maungdaw from Sittwe, even though the dynamics of the conflict are different in the two places. And there is a tendency to always paint the same stark picture: Rohingya as victims and Rakhine as aggressors. Many Rakhine Buddhists I have talked to distrust foreign journalists because they feel their own opinions and challenges are being ignored. They themselves have been oppressed by the government, and suffered from poverty and restricted access to services.

Both Rakhine media and national media outlets tend to become nationalistic whenever the Rohingya issue is raised. I have never even seen them use the name *Rohingya* in their Burmese-language editions. Instead, they use *Bengali*, intimating that the Rohingya are illegal immigrants from neighbouring Bangladesh. It is only when they publish in English that they may, in a few rare cases, use *Rohingya*. This could be called identity journalism — changing the language you use for different audiences. Many Rohingya have told me that they do not trust Rakhine or national media because they are biased and do not know or understand the situation on the ground. Local media's ability to cover these stories is further hindered due to limited financial and technical support.

The fact that the government and the military restrict journalists' access to northern Rakhine State makes it even more difficult for citizens to gain access to credible and reliable information sources.

They thus tend to rely on informal information flows. Tea shops, betel nut shops, beer stations and markets are places where information is shared. Both Rohingya Muslim and Rakhine Buddhist communities say they believe information and rumours as long as they come from their own people and are verified by their respected community leaders or reporters who live in their communities. Women tend to get information from their husbands and other male adults. Young people mainly get information from Facebook, which they then usually check with their elders. The dominance of social media — especially Facebook — helps unverified information spread more widely and quickly.

Here is a good example. In late 2016, a rumour spread on the Sittwe university campus. It started off as a joke, but then a subsequent power cut almost led to clashes. According to witnesses, a group of young Rakhine were playing guitars near the university late in the evening when some of their friends passed by on a motorbike and shouted "Kalar are coming", as a joke. A group of ten Rohingya workers were coincidentally on campus, renovating a hostel for university teachers. The campus suddenly lost its electricity supply, so the workers took a break. At this point the teachers who had heard the shouts — "Kalar are coming" — concluded that the Rohingya were trying to attack them, and started shouting for help. The rumour quickly spread that Rohingya were planning to attack Rakhine Buddhists. In response, a Rakhine Buddhist crowd gathered to fight them. Tensions grew until a Rakhine military officer convinced the crowd that it was an unfounded rumour. The crowd was only willing to believe one of their own trusted community members.

The attempt by the government to solve the conflict between the Rakhine Buddhist and Muslim Rohingya communities by separating them and restricting media access is wrong. As people cannot access reliable information, an identity-based information system has emerged which brings with it a high risk of rumour-mongering. The role of identity in information sharing is, in my opinion, extremely unhealthy.

As a result of the previous military junta's policy of blocking access to media and information, my generation has become accustomed to mutual distrust and conflict. If we want to create sustainable peace and understanding among the different ethnic groups in our country, it is vital that the current government allows open access to conflict areas and enables opportunities for peaceful and tolerant dialogue and civil discourse between people of different backgrounds.

Notes

1. A fixer is a local person helping journalists with research, interpretation and logistic arrangements.
2. AFP, "Language of the Rohingya to be Digitised: 'It Legitimises the Struggle'", *The Guardian*, 17 December 2017, https://www.theguardian.com/world/2017/dec/19/language-rohingya-digitised-legitimises-struggle-emails.
3. This research was carried out in December 2016 for Internews in Myanmar, in collaboration with contributing editor Jane Madlyn McElhone.

11

Media in Myanmar: Laws, Military and the Public[1]

Lawi Weng

There are two views in our country on how to develop the media. One is that we need to prioritize proper media legislation. The other is that we need to change our mindsets.

In Myanmar there are times when the military respects the law, and there are other times when it uses the law to protect itself. Take, for instance, my arrest on 26 June 2017 in northern Shan State while I was doing my job — reporting on the war.

Before this incident I had often travelled to northern Shan State for the same purpose — to cover armed conflict — but I had never before faced arrest. In November 2016 there were clashes between the Northern Alliance of ethnic armed groups and the military. This happened in the northern Shan State townships of Mong Ko, Muse and Kutkai. When I travelled to Muse there were several army checkpoints between Kutkai and Namkham. At each checkpoint, soldiers checked my phone and my wallet. On my phone they looked to see whether I had taken photos with the rebels. In my wallet they checked if I had contact information for the rebels. If I had had those things, I would have been detained. But each time they let me go, because I did not have anything incriminating. At one checkpoint an army officer asked me whether I was a conflict reporter. I told him that I was and he said that I could accompany his troops to the front line. But once he understood that I would take him up on the offer, he told me that it would be a long process to inform the top officials and to get permission. It did not happen.

According to the law, I have the right to travel to the conflict areas. But when I was arrested in 2017 the army accused me of not having permission to be there. We have laws, but these laws are not always respected. Those who focus on improving media legislation in Myanmar need to remember that laws are not always followed here. Laws should not favour one side. They should protect everyone in the country, and be applied equally. My idea is, that for change to happen, the army needs to change its mindset, and to see laws as statutes to be respected, instead of as mechanisms to protect itself.

The Myanmar Press Council was involved in creating laws to protect journalists in the country. Those laws have already been approved by parliament. But in reality they have not sufficiently protected journalists detained by the army. Beyond writing laws, the Myanmar Press Council should also work more practically on the ground. When we are arrested, their representatives should come to the court and talk to the judge about the official laws that exist to protect journalists. At least one person from the Myanmar Press Council should stand as a witness for reporters who are detained. In the future this should serve as a method of protecting journalists. If institutions like the Myanmar Press Council do not follow up their legislation with action, it is difficult to imagine how the media in this country will be able to develop. No one will dare go to the front line anymore, as they will always be worried about being arrested.

Another significant struggle for Myanmar's press has been striking a balance between adhering to ethical standards and giving audiences what they want in order to increase their circulation and popularity. The recent violence in Arakan State[2] broke out in late August 2017. The military and the government issued a statement telling media to describe those who attacked the security forces as *terrorists*. The government even threatened to take action against media deemed to be "supportive" of the so-called terrorists. Many members of the Myanmar media changed their tone and acted in the way the government instructed them. Only a few outlets stood their ground, using the more neutral word *attackers* instead of the loaded term *terrorists*. Only a few also used the term *Rohingya* to describe the Muslim community that most others refer to as *Bengali*.

Many Myanmar journalists blame the international media for the divide, accusing them of not understanding the context. The international view was that State Counsellor Daw Aung San Suu Kyi showed poor management in addressing the crisis and the military's actions in Rakhine State. If we look at reports from the Myanmar media, we see many articles about Daw Aung San Suu Kyi's government trying to restore peace and stability in the region. We also see the Rohingya portrayed as guests in the country — guests who attacked their hosts. These reports imply that the army was not wrong in taking up its offensive in northern Rakhine State against the Rohingya.

We have a strong media force in our country from our past struggle against the long-time military regime. The media and political parties like the National League for Democracy (NLD) once stood as one to fight for democracy. But when Daw Aung San Suu Kyi and the NLD became the government, the media did not change its stance, and largely continued to support them, even though they are in power. At times the press has turned a blind eye to mistakes by this administration. If someone else criticizes Daw Suu or her party, there are members of the press who will lash out at them. In this environment, some have even ceased to criticize the military.

The editorial stance we take is largely related to the role our audience plays in our coverage. Myanmar is home to many ethnic nationalities that have long rebelled against domination by the Burmese military and the Bamar[3] majority. Many of these armed struggles and the political struggles continue today. When people read news about the ethnic rebels, many perceive them as criminals, insurgents and drug lords, and do not see their struggles as having any sort of greater purpose.

To illustrate this, I want to tell you about an encounter I had with a taxi driver in Yangon. We were discussing the Kachin Independence Organization. He said that if they wanted to make peace they needed to sign the Nationwide Ceasefire Agreement and join the rest of Myanmar society. We spoke about how he had become informed about politics in our country. He said he liked to read opinion pieces by well-known

Myanmar political commentators. I told him that he should listen to the painful experiences of the ethnic Kachin, related directly by them instead of relying on what others say. He agreed but added that he had never been to Kachin State. The articles people read influence how they see the different political groups in our country, particularly in ethnic states, which many in central Myanmar know little about.

Many journalists in Yangon have a very general understanding of the ethnic struggles, and therefore write about them superficially. This is then transferred to the reader, who fails to grasp the complexity of the issues. We need to invest in changing this view held by our audience, to portray both rebels and ethnic populations less simplistically. I have started to talk to my fellow Mon people about the Rohingya in Arakan State. There is a lot of misunderstanding. I tell them about the situation on the ground in Arakan State, that many Rohingya have had to stay in camps since the violence broke out in 2012. These places are very hot, with no trees. They cannot support themselves there, cannot make a living. They often ask when they can return home, but no one can give them an answer. The conditions in Arakan have left people with no hope.

For those who write about the groups in Arakan State, it is best to get an understanding on the ground, to talk to the people affected. Stories that do not portray this situation carefully can serve to foster hate among readers, which we unfortunately have seen happen.

We need to change the views of our people instead of always trying to earn their support. If we fail to do this, the press will become a propaganda machine, telling everyone what they want to hear — everything except the truth.

Notes

1. The author used this essay as the basis of his talk at the 2017 Conference on Media Development in Myanmar and then posted it on his personal Facebook page. The text was originally edited by Sally Kantar and then subsequently edited by the volume's contributing editors.
2. Arakan was renamed Rakhine by the military junta in 1989.
3. The term "Bamar" refers to the dominant ethnic group in Myanmar, while "Burmese" is used as an adjective for the language and the broader culture.

12

Cracking the Glass Ceiling in Myanmar Media

Thin Lei Win

I remember vividly why a veteran Myanmar reporter said he had not hired women journalists. This was in 2008–9, when the junta was in a foul mood. There was sharp criticism of its slow response to the devastation caused by Cyclone Nargis in 2008 and its brutal crackdown of a popular protest led by monks in 2007. Local journalists were hunted down and jailed for informing both the public and the outside world of the situation inside the country.

The reporter could have used any number of excuses related to safety and security to justify having no women in his team. But no, he said he would not hire them because they "won't be able to climb up the steep stairs to the office". Besides, the office was full of "boys", so the presence of a woman could prove awkward for everyone. A decade on, despite tremendous changes taking place in the country, this perception persists, as does the view that women journalists are somehow less competent and/or better at covering less important topics.

Pre-publication censorship has been abolished, private journals and papers abound (although the issue of consolidation caused by financial strains is another matter) and, depending on your calculations, there are between 2,000 and 5,000 accredited journalists in Myanmar, at least half of whom are women. Yet you could count on one hand the number of women in leadership positions in the local media landscape.[1]

Studies by Sweden's FOJO Media Institute (2015, 2016) and the free-speech advocacy group ARTICLE 19 (2015) provide insight into this problem: while more than fifty per cent of the staff in newsrooms are women, they tend to cover "soft" sections, they are "protected" rather than empowered, there are few, if any, mechanisms for complaints or redress if women feel they have been discriminated against, and their careers end with marriage or childbirth. Even though Myanmar had a history of strong women's voices in literature in the 1960s and 70s, today there are very few women commentators and columnists. And despite the proliferation of journalist networks and unions, they tend to focus on political challenges such as threats, arrests and assaults on journalists, rather than policy and issues concerning gender.

In November 2017, a study of 2,500 radio, TV, online and print news stories found that female representation in Myanmar media is one of the lowest in Asia (Breaking Gender Stereotypes 2017). On average, only 16 per cent of voices are female. There were slight variations between different media platforms, but even on TV, found to be the most gender-balanced in this case, fewer than one in four voices were female.

In the words of Nai Nai, a former journalist who worked first for the Southeast Asian Press Alliance and now FOJO (and conducted the interview with Ye Naing Moe in this volume), "The hardest challenge of all is the attitude from male senior staff who do not want to accept and respect the effort and capacity of women. The top-down communication and 'don't talk back' culture is a huge issue to tackle." Women journalists, instead of being respected, are seen as "incapable, burdensome, emotional and unable to reason", added Nai Nai. Her family of journalistic talent also includes a younger sister who left her job as a producer with a television station to give birth, becoming yet another statistic of female journalists whose careers were cut short after choosing to start a family.

The lack of understanding of what constitutes harassment, even among the media industry, raises another red flag. During the first phase of its research, FOJO conducted a workshop with journalists where the topic of sexual harassment was discussed. "Most people believed sexual harassment equalled rape, so there's so much work to be done to broaden the understanding of what harassment is", Agneta Soderbergh Jacobson, coordinator of the report, told me.

This gender gap in the media is a reflection — and an extension — of women's role in Myanmar society as a whole. Aung San Suu Kyi may be widely admired in the country, with her presence alone winning millions of votes for the National League for Democracy in the 2015 elections, but at home and at work, men are still kings, embodied by the oft-repeated saying, "Treat your son as your master and your husband as God". In this deeply conservative and patriarchal culture, there is little institutional support for women, either at home or in the workplace, and female journalists going out and reporting face multiple hurdles.

Seng Mai Maran, editor-in-chief of *Myitkyina News Journal* in the capital of Kachin State in Myanmar's north, vividly remembers an incident in 2012 when Daw Suu made a trip to the city prior to her by-election win. "As you know, there is always such a big crowd at her talks. We wanted to take our own pictures to accompany the stories, and they built a big stage for the press to take photos. When we went up, [the organizers] shouted through the speakers that only men could come up because there were monks on the ground. So we had to leave. We lost the opportunity to take that picture because we were women." One of the most frustrating things for Seng Mai is that despite living in an area where ongoing conflict between the military and the Kachin Independence Army (KIA) is part of the daily news agenda, women cannot cover these issues "because there's no law to protect us and there's no guarantee for our safety". "The situation has become worse in recent years. Currently, only male reporters usually go to the frontline", she laments.

The discrimination and stereotyping stemming from the lack of prominent women's voices in newsrooms feed into a negative feedback loop in the way women are portrayed, especially on broadcast media. According to the report by ARTICLE 19, "Young women are sometimes presented ... as innocent to the point of gullibility, implying that they are open prey to sexual assault. Mothers whose husbands have died are generally represented facing many difficulties, or as being unable to manage their own lives and families", while "pregnancy and single motherhood [in Myanmar, being pregnant out of wedlock and/or a single mother is considered extremely shameful] are presented as a punishment for 'modern' women who are seen to be controlling their own bodies in their relationships with men".

In addition, whereas current affairs programmes targeted at men cover a wide range of issues — technology, fashion and politics — "similar programmes for women such as *Khit Thit Pyo May* (Young Lady of Modern Times) cover only gender-related subjects such as beauty, fashion, health or personal hygiene". The situation has been exacerbated over the last couple of years with the rise of nationalist movements, which have led to simplistic narratives of women as either damsels needing protection or irreligious and promiscuous. Four laws promoted by these groups which seek to restrict women's behaviour were swiftly passed, even though a law specifically designed to address real violence against women continues to languish (*Myanmar Now* 2016).

In early 2016, I assigned a junior reporter from *Myanmar Now* to do a long feature looking at access to justice for female victims of sexual violence. For weeks she searched in vain to find a victim who would be willing to have her experience written about anonymously. Each and every person she approached spoke to her, but ultimately decided that turning "one shame into two" would be unbearable to their lives and the reputation of their families, even though we promised complete anonymity and assured them that they should not be the ones feeling ashamed.

A March 2018 op-ed in the state-run *The Global New Light of Myanmar* rehashed some of these views while denying Myanmar women face discrimination: "Women are treated not as weaker sex but only as fairer gender. Fairer gender by own virtues has feminine modesty and feminine privilege to be respected and protected by men. Therefore certain jobs, works and places are regarded as not suitable for fairer gender. So these are marked only for men not because of discrimination but out of resped [sic] and regard for fairer gender" (Khin Maung Nyunt 2018).

This gap is not just anecdotal. The 2014 census shows males as generally possessing higher literacy levels than females in all states and regions (Department of Population 2015). The difference is greater in ethnic areas. Men also have significantly higher labour-force participation, at 85.2 per cent compared to 50.5 per cent for women. With hard data notoriously difficult to come by in Myanmar, the most concrete estimates of pay inequality between men and women are more than ten years old; they showed that women were concentrated in lower ranks and lower-skilled jobs and, despite legal provisions for equal pay, that men earned an estimated income of US$1,043 in 2007, while women earned only US$640.48 for similar types of jobs (UN Women, n.d.).

And what about politics? Well, in parliament women hold 67 of a total of 654 seats (Inter-Parliamentary Union 2018; Shwe Shwe Sein Latt et al. 2017). While this is more than double the number of women MPs in the 2010 parliament, Myanmar continues to have one of the lowest female representations in Southeast Asia. Also, currently there are only two women, including Daw Suu, in the cabinet (Republic of the Union of Myanmar, n.d.). Women's participation in the country's vital peace negotiations is glaringly absent too (AGIPP 2017; San Yamin Aung 2017). In short, the marginalization of female journalists in the media industry contributes to the marginalization of women in all fields in the country, and vice versa. This is a vicious cycle that needs to be broken, and broken soon.

The lack of women at the upper echelons of media businesses is, of course, a global problem. Numerous studies have shown that across the world women are under-represented, paid less than men, promoted less often and get fewer bylines. Also widespread is the perception that women are good only for covering soft topics. I remember a Western reporter who was frankly incredulous to discover that I regularly go to disaster and conflict zones as part of my job. His words were to the effect of, "Oh but you always look so feminine", as if my sartorial choices in London were any indication of my professionalism in the field.

Recent global political events have also shown us why we always need to be vigilant when it comes to upholding women's rights. There is always someone in a position of authority and power who cannot wait to undo the gains that have been made so far.

None of the above absolves Myanmar from its snail-like response to women's issues — both in terms of the significant gender gap in the media landscape and in ensuring women's rights are respected in general. In fact these issues are even more important for a country like Myanmar, which is at a crossroads. I believe that Myanmar's future development and much-needed peace are intricately linked to the number of women in decision-making roles in the media industry and the way women are portrayed by the media.

Nai Nai points to Myanmar society's unfortunate familiarity with "authoritative behaviour", and to its

> top-down communication, whether in the family, school or workplaces. The best way to tackle [that] is to have more inclusive newsroom discussions where senior managers encourage everyone, especially women, to voice their ideas, and to counter ideas with healthy criticism. And, [we] have to create a culture of commenting on senior managers' ideas and planning. We need to remove the barriers between men and women, seniors and juniors.

As it brings different perspectives that can improve coverage, for *Myitkyina Journal*'s Seng Mai Maran, who has worked under male chief editors, having a plurality of voices is just good editorial sense.

Much needs to be done. Small steps are being taken, and those taking them need all the support they can get. The establishment of the Myanmar Women Journalists Society (MWJS) — the first ever journalist network focusing on women — is a step in the right direction in tackling this problem. Set up online in January 2014 and officially launched in February 2016 by a group of experienced women journalists, it has been working with like-minded groups to organize training and discussions to highlight the discrimination faced by women journalists and to fight for change. Its first workshop in August 2016, designed to build a network of women journalists, attracted a hundred women reporters, said Eaint Khine Oo, one of the founders. It organized its first general assembly in May 2017, electing fifteen executive committee members from across the country.

"There have already been three organizations in the Myanmar media landscape — the Myanmar Journalists Network, Myanmar Journalists Association, and Myanmar Journalists Union — that work for the social welfare, opportunities and press freedom rights of fellow journalists. But we have found that there is very little activity targeted at women journalists, although the numbers of women journalists are increasing", she said. Among other goals, the Myanmar Women Journalists Society plans to provide training, endorse women journalists who want to study at international universities, and publish analytical papers on the difficulties women journalists face in the workplace, Eaint Khine Oo added. MWJS has launched a dedicated website (https://genderinmyanmarnews.org/en) together with IMS-FOJO, covering everything from policy and research to tips for gender-balanced reporting and lists of female experts to interview.

Of course, it is also of the utmost importance to get men to understand that it is not a zero-sum game and that they too would benefit from having strong, capable women colleagues. As FOJO's Jacobson said, "For anyone who wants to change gender inequality, you have to include men and to try to communicate what they can gain from gender equality."

I fondly remember travelling to London in May 2015 as part of an election-reporting training course. I was a mentor/trainer to four senior political correspondents from Myanmar, all of whom were women. I was delighted when I found out about this, although none of my co-trainers in London batted an eyelid. They knew it was because these women were the most qualified. I am happy to report that at least three of them have continued their upward trajectory, and are themselves becoming role models for young female reporters.

So yes, compared to almost a decade ago when I heard the veteran male reporter use the office's "steep flight of stairs" as a reason not to hire women reporters, there is progress. Since then, at least one woman journalist has climbed the (metaphorical) stairs at that organization, and hopefully more will follow. All we can do is take one step at a time and we must not let up. Our country's future depends upon it.

Note

1. Calculated based on the number of editors-in-chief or publishers who are women. Most became chief editors/publishers as a result of taking over the family business or setting up the media outlets themselves. It is still very rare to have women editors-in-chief who are unrelated to the founders and who came up through the ranks of reporters.

References

AGIPP (Alliance for Gender Inclusion in the Peace Process). http://www.agipp.org/en/infographics.

ARTICLE 19. 2015. "Censored Gender: Women's Rights to Freedom of Expression and Information in Myanmar". https://www.article19.org/data/files/medialibrary/38032/gender-report-v1-3-full.pdf.

Breaking Gender Stereotypes. 2017. "Women's Voices Underrepresented in News Coverage". 27 November 2017. https://genderinmyanmarnews.org/en/news/womens-voices-underrepresented-news-coverage.

Department of Population. 2015. "The 2014 Myanmar Population and Housing Census. Highlights of the Main Results (Census Report Volume 2 - A)". Ministry of Immigration and Population, Republic of the Union of Myanmar. http://myanmar.unfpa.org/en/node/15104.

FOJO Media Institute. 2015. "Gender in the Myanmar Media Landscape. First Study: Yangon and Beyond". http://fojo.se/images/documents/Gender-Myanmar-Fojo.pdf.

———. 2016. "Gender in the Myanmar Media Landscape: Yangon, Kayin, Saggaing, Shan and across Myanmar". https://www.mediasupport.org/wp-content/uploads/2017/07/Eng_GENDER_16_web.pdf.

Inter-Parliamentary Union. 2018. "Women in National Parliaments". http://archive.ipu.org/wmn-e/classif.htm.

Khin Maung Nyunt. 2018. "The Status of Myanmar Women in Myanmar History and Culture". 26 March 2018. http://www.globalnewlightofmyanmar.com/status-myanmar-women-myanmar-history-culture/.

Myanmar Now. 2016. "Abused at Home, Myanmar Women Failed by Law and Traditions. 8 August 2016. http://www.myanmar-now.org/news/i/?id=8cf2bacc-e043-4304-9a01-27ae8222a0e5.

Republic of the Union of Myanmar. n.d. "List of the Union Minister and Deputy Minister". http://www.president-office.gov.mm/en/?q=cabinet/ministries.

San Yamin Aung. 2017. "New Law to Protect Women, Girls against Violence". *The Irrawaddy*, 17 October 2017. https://www.irrawaddy.com/news/burma/new-law-protect-women-girls-violence.html.

Shwe Shwe Sein Latt, Kim N.B. Ninh, Mi Ki Kyaw Mint, and Susan Lee. 2017. *Women's Political Participation in Myanmar: Experiences of Women Parliamentarians 2011–2016*. Asia Foundation and Phan Tee Eain. https://asiafoundation.org/wp-content/uploads/2017/05/Womens-Political-Participation-in-Myanmar-MP-Experiences_report-1.pdf.

UN Women. n.d. "Myanmar". http://asiapacific.unwomen.org/en/focus-areas/cedaw-human-rights/myanmar.

13

Media and the 2015 General Elections

Carine Jaquet

In this chapter, I explore the challenges and opportunities that the 8 November 2015 national parliamentary elections presented for the Myanmar media, and their difficult relations with the Union Election Commission (UEC). A critical benchmark for the country's democratic transition, the elections marked the first time in more than half a century that a Myanmar government had been democratically elected and was able to take office. The quasi-civilian government headed by President Thein Sein acknowledged the defeat of the army-backed party, the Union Solidarity and Development Party (USDP), and the civilian party led by Aung San Suu Kyi, the National League for Democracy (NLD), assumed power.

The findings in this chapter stem from field observations, interviews and print sources in Myanmar and English languages collected between 2014 and 2016. I observed these processes from within the UEC, where I worked as a senior technical advisor for international organizations supporting the electoral processes. I was personally involved in negotiations related to media access and journalists' accreditation.

The first section of the chapter provides a brief overview of the legal framework that defines the concept of media space, with a specific focus on election day. Regulations included constraints on journalists' ability to cover the elections, which affected their access to polling stations. The second section presents two very different — and often diametrically opposed — views held by the UEC leadership and private media representatives. The root causes of the deeply entrenched mistrust that I observed will be placed in the context of recent private media expansion in the country following the lifting of pre-publication censorship. This includes very different institutional cultures, fundamental disagreements about the role of private media, and diverging political preferences. As a result of the mistrust, there were numerous missed opportunities that could have improved communication among key stakeholders and, in turn, increased awareness about the voting process among the general public. That being said, on election day, media played a fundamental role in legitimizing the vote and enabling a wider acceptance of the results.

Media During the Pre-election Period

The people in Myanmar had previously witnessed their electoral choices being ignored by the military government (after the 1990 elections) or affected by systematic fraud (during the 2008 referendum and 2010 elections). This political history triggered a number of challenges for media covering the 2015 elections. Given that the country's education system had deteriorated for decades under the military junta, the vast majority of voters did not have basic civic knowledge. On the one hand, the UEC, whose chairman and senior members were appointed by the president, could not reasonably be considered a neutral entity. On the other hand, the media sector had been systematically controlled and prevented from growing and performing its functions. Only a few journalists had courageously succeeded in reporting on political developments under the junta from inside the country. As a consequence, most Myanmar journalists who covered the elections in 2015 did not possess the formal training and professional experience needed to perform quality coverage.

The asymmetrical power relations between those who had the electoral knowledge — mainly the UEC — and those who were looking for electoral information and had the capacity to spread it to a large audience of voters — the media — lay at the core of the tensions. Their thorny relationship was punctuated by numerous episodes of miscommunication and an omnipresent mistrust. A legacy of the junta that had tightly controlled the media, the UEC was led by former high-ranking military officers who were considered biased and supportive of the USDP. That prior elections in Myanmar had been characterized by institutionalized fraud perpetuated a negative image of the UEC. Prior to 2015 there had been no formal provisions to allow journalists to cover elections, and it was widely assumed that the legal void favoured the pro-military UEC and enabled electoral fraud. As a result, in 2015 journalists were often reluctant to approach the UEC for updates. And, despite the desire by the UEC leadership to reform their image and their acknowledgement that voters needed to be informed, initially it was nearly impossible to convince them to respond to media interviews. However, their attitude evolved over time, and on election day and for results sharing, the UEC increased their engagement with the media.

An Ambiguous Legal Framework

The UEC was created in March 2010, just before the quasi-civilian government took control. Its role is defined in five main laws: the Union Election Commission Law, the Political Representation Law, and the three Election Laws, as well as four by-laws (UEC 2014, p. 8). The UEC played a vital role during the 2015 elections ensuring that the elections would be held in a free and fair manner. In February 2011, Tin Aye was appointed as chairman of the UEC. He was a former member of the junta and chairman of the Union of Myanmar Economic Holdings (UMEHL), a conglomerate owned by the Myanmar military. His appointment indicated the strategic importance that the Thein Sein administration gave to this institution.

The UEC recognized in theory the importance of engaging with various stakeholders, including the media, in its 2014 to 2018 strategic plan (UEC 2014). The media were mentioned in the UEC strategy under two specific objectives: "7.2. Cooperate with Government departments ... and the media to maximize resources and avoid gaps or duplications and ensure effective dissemination of information" and "8.4. Use various mass and social media for broader outreach to inform the public on the electoral process" (pp. 20–21). In an internal briefing to UEC members and advisors on 9 July 2014, UEC chairman Tin Aye said the country lacked experience in conducting elections (only five were conducted; in 1952, 1956, 1990, 2010 and 2012), and voters did not know how to elect their representatives. He identified the electoral officials and staff, civil society organizations, political parties and media as important institutions to carry out voter education.[1] While acknowledging on paper the strategic importance of collaborating with media outlets, in reality the interactions between the UEC and the media were far from straightforward. One of the expressed fears of the UEC was "false reporting in the media" (UEC 2014, p. 7).

In many instances the wording of Myanmar laws is unclear, and it is difficult to enforce them systematically due to discrepancies and contradictions adopted in different historical contexts that have never been harmonized. A number of pivotal pieces of the Myanmar legal framework were reviewed in the pre-election period, including the News Media Law. That law entitles media professionals to access information (within the public domain), with the exception of statements, photographs and records "whose security is rated as per law or directive of a certain authority" (Article 6[a]). Yet, as the definition of security is left exclusively to military or former military decision-makers (as most of the influential leaders under the Thein Sein administration were military or former military officials), this clause does not improve protection for media freedom.

The legal void and non-specific provisions around media and elections tended to lead to interdictions in practice. For example, in the elections by-laws[2] and the UEC Guidelines for the Polling Station Officers,[3] journalists were not included in the list of persons authorized to enter polling stations. Many media and election professionals thus feared they would be denied access on election day. Another example lies in the Electoral Laws[4] and Polling Station Officers Guidelines,[5] which states:

Whoever is found guilty of causing disturbance to the voters or the polling booth officer and members of the polling booth team on duty by using loudspeakers or by such equipment which amplify the voice or by other indisciplined [sic] acts, inside the polling booth or within 500 yards radius from the polling booth shall, on conviction be punishable with imprisonment for a term not exceeding one year or with fine not exceeding one hundred thousand kyats or with both. (State Peace and Development Council 2010, p. 25)

The definitions of "disturbance" or "undisciplined acts" were not provided and were left to the interpretation of polling officers. Given the limited media space to which journalists were accustomed, and the repeated crackdowns of the past, these clauses posed potential risks to media professionals who were interested in covering the elections.

Restrictions on media access to polling stations in order to protect the secrecy of votes are, however, not uncommon. A number of countries with varied electoral histories, such as Australia and Cambodia, have imposed legal limitations on media access to voting processes. Yet, because laws were often used in Myanmar to crack down on media and the political opposition, unclear legal provisions in 2015 were considered particularly problematic. Journalists interpreted them as risks, fearing they would be intentionally blocked from entering polling booths, potentially to prevent widespread independent coverage. Representatives of media outlets interviewed before the elections expressed concerns about the lack of legal guarantees. But as the elections grew closer, the media accreditation process and code of conduct[6] that were endorsed by most private media outlets provided a more pragmatic framework for media coverage than had previously existed.

As a first step, the UEC announced that media professionals from registered media outlets would receive accreditation to observe the elections, and it put in place a fairly straightforward application process. Requirements included filling out a form detailing the identity and assignment of each journalist, as well as providing a photograph, recommendation letter from the media institution in question, and a signed copy of the Code of Conduct for each journalist. For the UEC, the accreditation process provided a means to oversee media activities and to ensure journalists would not create disturbances. In other countries, such regulation could be seen as a hindrance to the media. However, in the context of Myanmar, where private media had formerly been systematically blocked from accessing polling stations, this regulation created a space for engagement. While far from ideal, this accreditation process was perceived by many journalists as a form of authorization — or a guarantee — that they could access the electoral processes.[7] However, some were worried about their media licences, which could still be revoked very easily, and their journalists, who could be charged for doing their jobs.

Whether or not the accreditation would facilitate journalists' access to polling stations was unclear. As far as the UEC was concerned, the existing legal framework superseded all other arrangements — formal or informal — and it had to be respected. Whereas a number of international observers were concerned that media accreditation did not adequately address the issue of access, Myanmar media outlets generally considered it a limited, yet significant example of progress, and largely opted to abide by it. Although accreditation did not provide actual legal protection, journalists widely considered it the only way forward. Inside the country, the deceptive 2008 and 2010 elections had been covered exclusively by state-run media, as other types of media were muzzled. Private and exiled media reported on these elections at their own risk. In 2015, however, journalists from private media applied in large numbers and, with few exceptions, received their accreditation cards. As polling agents were left with unclear instructions with regards to media access, they allowed journalists to cover the vote from inside and around polling stations. This positive turn of events contributed to the general assessment that the elections were free and fair.

In a second step, to avoid political bias in coverage and to promote respect for a common set of minimum standards, the interim Myanmar Press Council produced a code of conduct that did not specifically focus on voting day but which instead emphasized the importance of covering diverse political opinions. Although not a game-changer, this code of conduct was widely distributed, raising journalists' awareness and demonstrating to the government that the media were acting out of goodwill. This was a symbolic step towards transparency in what was otherwise a climate of opacity and deeply rooted mistrust and in which the legal framework remained unclear and did not provide guarantees for safe media access to the voting processes.

Irreconcilable Perspectives?

In addition to the ambiguous legal framework, the media and the UEC's mutually unfriendly relations presented a second obvious challenge.

The UEC Perspective

Prior to the 2015 election, UEC members did not interact with domestic private media. On the contrary, the communications of the commission were limited to sending legal documents to state-run newspapers and "instructing" them to publish them in full. This resulted in countless pages of laws, by-laws and guidelines in formal Myanmar language that voters were not interested in. This was typical junta communications style, based exclusively on legal content, with no attempt to encourage voting or to simplify basic electoral concepts. But the political transition and the lifting of pre-publication censorship enabled an increasing number of private media outlets to report more freely. In this new context, the UEC was called upon to play a more proactive role vis-à-vis the private media operations that were gaining increasing influence in the post-junta society. Given their military background and the fact that they were used to operating with a "securitization mindset" inherited from their military experiences, many of the UEC members were genuinely worried that the vote could be disrupted. They thus saw in journalists a potential for disturbance.

The transition to a quasi-civilian government in 2011, and the appointment of Tin Aye as the head of the UEC, did not represent a paradigm change. Although the UEC leadership continued voicing its intention to organize free and fair elections, its institutional culture did not change overnight. Given the mindset of civil servants who were uncomfortable and insecure about the new ways of working, the narratives emanating from the reformist members of the Thein Sein government did not translate into immediate change. The UEC appointed a media relations focal point; to mitigate what they regarded as risks, other senior members endeavoured to avoid unnecessary interactions with journalists. They did not initially consider responding to media queries to be part of their duties, and they feared making statements that would be incorrect or that would be misinterpreted, as either could trigger internal backlashes and reprimands from senior leaders. But the UEC officers from various administrative levels — down to ward and village tracts — often found themselves obliged to face local journalists, whose queries were entertained — or rejected — on a case-by-case basis, without a clearly defined strategy.

After numerous informal complaints and mounting pressure with the election deadline looming, the UEC gradually came to understand that media may actually be part of the picture in the new era. Some UEC members and staff tried to implement an organizational strategy in which media outlets could play a role in raising voters' awareness. They also realized that media would report on the election, with or without their input. But the modalities of these interactions — especially the private media outlets — often remained problematic. Some of the election commissioners agreed to meet journalists at the national and regional levels, with mixed results. In some cases they refused to be quoted or interviewed, making it frustrating for the journalists. In other cases the commissioners appeared to answer questions rudely that they considered too controversial.

The UEC leadership was largely convinced that journalists from private media were not capable of explaining electoral processes due to their lack of legal knowledge, or that they would not cover the elections independently because of their bias towards the main opposition party, the NLD (a personal choice that many journalists did not hide). As such, the UEC feared it would once more be depicted in the worst possible light and that voters would be ill-informed about the vote and be critical of decisions taken by the UEC.

The Viewpoint of Journalists

Not surprisingly, many journalists had a diametrically opposed view, as they considered the UEC to be a conservative organization that was helping the USDP, the army-backed party, to secure a significant number of seats in parliament in yet another electoral fraud in the making. It could also be argued that journalists in private media outlets tended to idealize democracy and the NLD leader, Aung San Suu Kyi. That they occasionally shared these views during their encounters with UEC representatives was probably not helpful in building trust.

Given the former restraints placed on journalists inside the country, and the mushrooming of the private media sector since the political opening, the majority of journalists did indeed lack basic training, especially with regard to legal matters. Some of them were keen to learn, but the UEC, which had almost monopolistic access to this knowledge, barely provided them with the opportunity to do so. Journalists often complained about their limited access to electoral processes, citing a lack of political will on the part of the UEC and the USDP. They still vividly remembered the junta's appalling treatment of journalists, the fraudulent and cancelled elections in 1990, and the 2010 elections — which were primarily covered by brave journalists, clandestinely or in exile, who risked being imprisoned by Special Branch or Military Intelligence. Veteran journalists who were previously forced to manoeuvre carefully within the confines of the military regime's restrictions inside, or who were based in exile, remembered the numerous risks associated with practising journalism under the junta. To them, these risks were embodied by the UEC.

Moreover, non-political factors should also be taken into account in the challenging interactions between the UEC and journalists prior to the 2015 elections. There was a generation gap and a radical difference in mindsets between the UEC and most journalists. Whereas UEC members, especially at the central level, were at least sixty-five years old, the journalists represented a much younger segment of the population. In the eyes of these younger journalists, the UEC represented the former system that they hoped would end.

During interviews, the UEC members dressed in traditional green civil servants' uniforms and conducted themselves very formally. Journalists, on the other hand, tended to have an informal approach, some arriving late to meetings, and without necessarily having prepared for their interviews. This attitude was easily interpreted by more conservative minds as "carelessness". Journalists more often than not dressed informally, at times even showing tattoos, wearing caps or colourful hairstyles, and t-shirts with fancy large messages in English. While fashion was not the focus of these meetings, it is true to say that these details — which may appear minor — revealed a clash of generations and systems (i.e., military vs. civilian). They often reinforced existing stereotypes and demonstrated to each party that they stood on two sides of a deep socio-political and generational divide.

Many journalists did not trust the UEC, viewing the institution as a junta legacy because of its formal and military-like methods, as well as the selection of the chairman and commissioners. Journalists felt that the UEC's formal, legalistic and security-minded approach was evidence of its conservatism. They were also put off by the fact that many of their interview requests remained unanswered, or that they were shouted at and lectured to when their questions were deemed inappropriate. As a consequence, many assumed until 2015 that the UEC was simply part of the same charade witnessed in earlier elections.

Lessons Learned

From the perspective of international observers, the European Union Election Observation Mission's media monitoring during the campaign period concluded that "Only some media offered a diverse and comprehensive coverage to help voters to make an informed choice. While the campaign was visible on a national level, most of the local media offered only low-key coverage, mainly due to their underdeveloped and limited capacity" (EU-OM 2015, p. 26). The mission also noted the polarization between public and private media outlets:

> State-funded media, including MRTV, Myanma Radio, newspapers *Kyaymon* and *Myanma Ahlin*, still the most important source for a significant part of [the] population, largely failed to cover the political campaign. Instead, they adopted a formal and process-oriented approach, with a focus almost entirely on activities of the UEC and ruling authorities, in particular the President.... In stark contrast to the state media, DVB, a satellite TV channel, foreign radio services, online media and several newspapers presented a wide range of contestants, including from the ethnic states, [providing] for more comprehensive coverage. Nevertheless, a number of monitored media focused on NLD and USDP, with a visible preference for the NLD, both in space and tone. (EU-OM 2015, pp. 26–27)

A study by the Myanmar Institute for Democracy (2015) on pre-election coverage found a widespread lack of in-depth or analytical reporting that would have helped voters make more informed choices. So while the election was less restricted and controlled than the one in 2010, most media were split along party lines, demonstrating open support for either the state or the opposition party, while only a few offered more balanced coverage.

Hence, the 2015 elections coverage cannot be regarded as an example of political neutrality — either by the media or the UEC. However, it was the first time that the UEC played such a visible and prominent role, and the very first test run for an institution managed by a former senior military leader. Government officials in charge of organizing these elections and who agreed to conduct interactions with the private media for the first time passed this electoral test. However, they missed a number of opportunities. While the journalists had to be convinced of the UEC's intentions to organize free and fair elections, the commissioners often became confrontational when asked sensitive questions. On many instances the UEC patronized journalists, refused interviews and did not provide them with timely information that would not only have built up trust but which would also have paved the way for journalists to report accurately on electoral preparations.

In the post-election period, according to international observers, access for media opened up as "a significant transparency measure" (EU-OM 2015, p. 37). For the first time in its history, the UEC chairman and commissioners held daily press conferences to release results by locations and take questions directly from the media.

In summary, during and soon after the election, the UEC and the media found themselves enmeshed in a new and unfamiliar relationship, stemming from a deep mistrust linked to past experiences, politically irreconcilable views, negative perceptions and a generation gap. The UEC perceived media practitioners as unprofessional and politically biased towards the NLD, with a limited understanding of the voting framework and technicalities. Journalists, on the other hand, viewed the UEC as an institution inherited from the era of military rule that resisted transparent information sharing. The election preparations were a unique exercise for both sides in their efforts to reach common ground, each finding itself in a new situation where collaboration was necessary.

Conclusion

Media played a fundamental role in the 2015 general elections, informing voters and improving transparency, hence lending legitimacy to the results. The active engagement of Myanmar journalists ultimately contributed to the legitimization of the elections, indirectly supporting the UEC to achieve its aim (Carter Center 2015). The relationship between the UEC and the media in the pre-election period was symptomatic of the key moments of a political transition. Both sides embodied ideals and rationales that belonged to the older and to the newer socio-political orders, respectively, and that often appeared to be irreconcilable. And yet, in spite of the mistrust and a number of missed opportunities, this was arguably the closest and most interactive relationship yet between the UEC and the media. This contentious relationship led to what was historically the most comprehensive coverage of an election in the country and, potentially, to new approaches towards improved relations should the new administration wish to build on these lessons learnt.

Many uncertainties remain, as this perhaps unique situation may not be replicable given the changes in the UEC leadership. The new chairman, Hla Thein, and his members are strong supporters of the NLD. This mirrors the strategy of the USDP that created this institution to secure its own interests, rather than to ensure a neutral arbitration of the electoral process. However, Hla Thein does not enjoy influence in the NLD nor confidence within the UEC. Two years into his assignment, numerous directors, deputy directors and clerks have resigned from the UEC, reportedly due to internal disagreements and frustration related to decision-making. As the public does not expect the NLD to cheat in order to stay in power, it is unlikely that the UEC will undergo the same level of scrutiny in the coming elections as it did in 2015.

To date, none of the recommendations made by international and domestic election observers with regard to amending the restrictive media framework in the general elections (and beyond) have been implemented by the NLD government. The electoral legal framework still does not guarantee sufficient space and access for the private media, and overall, the strategy of government officials remains avoidance. As for the freedom of the media to cover the next general elections, it could actually turn out to be as difficult, or even more so, than in 2015, based on the recent restrictions placed on journalists who have tried to report independently and critically about the decisions of the government and the military.

Notes

1. Author's note from attending the briefing.
2. Pyithu Hluttaw Election By-Law, Article 48(b); Amyotha Hluttaw Election By-Law, Article 48(b) and State and Region Hluttaw Election By-Law, Article 48(b).
3. UEC Working Guidelines for Presiding Officer, Assistant Presiding Officer and Member of Polling Station Team (2014), Section 5(17).
4. Pyithu Hluttaw Election Law (2010), Article 62; Amyotha Hluttaw Election Law (2010), Article 62 and Region and State Hluttaw Election Law (2010), Article 62.
5. UEC Working Guidelines, Section 5(23).
6. The emergence of several documents called "Code of Conduct" created confusion with regards to which one the media were expected to follow. There was one code issued by the UEC for those "observing" the elections, but also two documents issued by the Myanmar Press Council, an institution backed by the government: the Code of Conduct for Myanmar Journalists (not focusing on elections) and the Guidelines for Media During Elections.
7. This is based on several interviews conducted with media representatives in Nay Pyi Taw between November 2014 and June 2015.

References

Carter Center. 2015. *Observing Myanmar's 2015 General Elections*. Atlanta: The Carter Center. https://www.cartercenter.org/resources/pdfs/news/peace_publications/election_reports/myanmar-2015-final.pdf.

EU-OM (European Union Observation Mission). 2015. *EU Election Observation Mission to Myanmar in 2015*. https://eeas.europa.eu/headquarters/headquarters-homepage/23795/eu-election-observation-mission-myanmar-2015_en.

Myanmar Institute for Democracy. 2015. "Third Preliminary Report on Media Coverage of Contestants during the Election Campaign Period". 6 November 2015. http://www.yangonyoungguns.com/docs/3rdreport_MID.pdf.

State Peace and Development Council. 2010. *The Pyithu Hluttaw Election Law*. Available at http://aceproject.org/ero-en/regions/asia/MM/burma-myanmar-pyithu-hluttaw-election-law-2010.

UEC (Union Election Commission). 2014. *Union Election Commission Myanmar Strategic Plan 2014–2018*. http://uecmyanmar.org/download.php?download_link=/upload_document/pdf/laws/484.pdf.

Part III
Creative Expression

14

Myanmar's Pop Music Industry in Transition

Heather MacLachlan

In the wake of the November 2010 elections, one important signal of the Burmese government's commitment to change was the cessation of the censorship of music recordings in October 2012.[1] Prior to that, the country's Press Scrutiny Board conducted rather rigorous censoring of so-called stereo series (albums), in cassette and later in compact disc formats. Producers wishing to sell their series in retail shops were required to submit a copy of the recording and ten copies of the song lyrics to the censors at the Press Scrutiny Board (MacLachlan 2011, p. 148). Although the censoring was supposed to be provided for free — as a government service to recording artists — producers in fact incurred regular and sometimes hefty costs in the form of "fees" and "fines" (MacLachlan 2011, p. 149). Ending the censorship requirement, then, represented the lifting of a financial burden borne by musicians and producers. Even more importantly, it was a powerful symbol of the transition government's commitment to freedom of artistic expression.

I began conducting fieldwork in Myanmar in 2007, researching the country's popular music industry. I subsequently published a book

(Maclachlan 2011) that describes the norms that prevailed in the music industry during the era of military dictatorship. In one section of that book I examined how musicians and censors interacted, contesting the assertion found in other scholarly accounts that, at that time, censorship of music was total and that the military government controlled all artistic expression in Burma. In fact, musicians and censors engaged in a complex negotiation of power, and musicians exercised a considerable degree of agency in the creation and dissemination of their recordings. Nevertheless, I acknowledged that censorship was an important, although not defining, element of professional pop musicians' lives under military rule. In retrospect, I characterize that research as an analysis of the pre-transition popular music scene. This chapter constitutes the next step in a now decade-long inquiry into the Burmese popular music industry, and describes the situation during the current transition period. My findings are based on fieldwork conducted in Yangon, the centre of the popular music industry, in May and June 2013, and in April and May 2018.

I begin this chapter with a review of the scholarly literature on music scenes during and after political transitions. Next, I report on how Myanmar's popular music scene developed in the immediate wake of the cancellation of censorship. I argue that the popular music scene is being significantly affected by the democratic transition, and that just months after the censorship of recordings ceased, the scene was already marked by important changes. I describe four important changes that were evident less than one year after government censorship ended: the involvement of Anglo foreigners, the democratization of the Myanmar Musicians Association, an increased range of artistic expression, and a shift in how musicians earned (or anticipated earning) income. This chapter concludes by speculating about possible further changes in the Myanmar popular music scene.

Contextualizing the Myanmar Case: Literature on Music Scenes in Transition

A review of the English-language literature on political transitions during the twentieth century reveals varied outcomes for popular music and musicians subsequent to national political transitions of various kinds. Together, the books and articles cited below suggest two conclusions: First, understanding national context — including, especially, the historical forces that led to the transitional events — is crucial to understanding subsequent changes in the music scene(s) in that nation. Second, the fates of musical genres are often tied to national political changes.

Outcomes for music industries and particular genres of music vary widely, because the national contexts in which musics and musicians originate, and then confront change, are so widely different. For example, Wai-Chung Ho (2000) describes a sharp increase in the number of popular songs sung in Putonghua (Mandarin Chinese) in Hong Kong since 1997, when Hong Kong was officially handed over to the People's Republic of China. Ho explains that Hong Kong pop musicians sing in Putonghua in order to promote the idea of a now-unified Chinese community, existing both on the mainland and in Hong Kong. Further, these Hong Kong musicians increasingly engage in self-censorship — avoiding lyrics that mention freedom and democracy — in a "deliberate and calculated act to avoid offending China" (Ho 2000, pp. 348–49). In another example, Donna Buchanan analyses the lives of Bulgarian folk musicians who belonged to government-funded national folk song and dance ensembles during the Communist era. After the transition to parliamentary democracy in Bulgaria in 1989, Buchanan found that these musicians have faced "a more stressful existence in which they and their art have become steadily dislocated from and devalued within the public mainstream" (2006, p. 7, also p. 460), in no small part because the new democratic government dramatically decreased its funding of folk music ensembles (p. 459).

Other studies of post-Soviet contexts — which have been of special interest to scholars interested in the links between music making and political transitions — show that in the immediate aftermath of the collapse of Communism, national governments and fan bases have had a conflicted relationship with Western popular music. Shortly after Vaclev Havel assumed power in Czechoslovakia, he sponsored concerts in Prague by the Rolling Stones and Lou Reed, for which local fans of rock music were deeply grateful (Mitchell 1992, p. 191). Recordings of Western rock and rap became available in Czechoslovakia in 1990, albeit priced very expensively. Similarly, "Polish rock ... was almost completely replaced in the media by Western products" due to "large local demand" (Pekacz 1992, pp. 206–7). However, during this same period, post-Soviet democratic governments failed to clamp down on piracy; that is, the illegal copying and selling of recordings (Buchanan 2006, p. 453). Jolanta Pekacz explains that "Piracy became possible thanks to a chaotic situation ... in which both moral and legal distinctions between 'entrepreneurship' and crime [became] hazy" (1992, p. 207). Ultimately, Western pop super-groups including U2 and Dire Straits refused to perform in Poland due to their concerns about unrestrained piracy.

Scholars have shown particular interest in the question of whether popular music-making is a factor in aiding political transitions; specifically, whether popular music itself can be credited for promoting democracy. Their varied answers to this question underline, once again, the importance of accounting for specific contexts in analysing specific outcomes. Ingrid Byerly (1998) argues that popular musicians used a number of strategies, including collaborations between musicians of different racial heritages, to effectively contest the ideology of the apartheid regime in South Africa, ultimately "prophesying" the downfall of the National Party government. Jeremy Wallach asserts that underground rock music in Indonesia — which both expressed and modelled dissent — became "the soundtrack for an activist youth movement that helped topple an entrenched thirty-two year military dictatorship and start Indonesia on a successful road to democracy" (2005, p. 17). By contrast, Francis Nyamnjoh and Jude Fokwang found that lyrics from most of the popular songs created in Cameroon during the repressive rule of President Ahmadou Ahidjo — from 1960 to 1982 — expressed "pro-establishment" messages and that "lyrics openly critical of politicians or politics were rare" (2005, p. 264). "Critical songs" and "questioning songs", which have since become an important part of the repertoire of Cameroonian popular music, emerged only after Ahidjo was removed from power (2005, p. 266). Craig Lockard found that in Thailand, "overtly political [popular] music" was created after massive student demonstrations in 1973 that led to "the installation of a democratic system" (1996, p. 172). However, popular songs with critical lyrics were repressed when military rule was re-established, leading Lockard to write that "Political music has frequently flourished in Thailand, as long as conditions permit, but it is hard to judge how much actual influence it has enjoyed.... Certainly it was not powerful enough to help prevent the triumph of right wing forces in 1976" (1996, p. 175).

In some cases we observe that the relative popularity of a musical genre and/or the extra-musical ideas with which the genre is associated are directly linked to changes in the surrounding political context. For example, an Indonesian popular music genre called *kroncong*, which centres on two ukulele-like instruments called *cak* and *cuk*, was widely appreciated during the Indonesian Revolution of 1945–49, when the Indonesians successfully fought for independence from the Dutch. During this era, "kroncong was transformed from a despised lower class popular music to a nationalist emblem" (Lockard 1996, p. 160). During the latter half of the twentieth century, however, *kroncong* declined in popularity, as successive generations of young people connected the music with an earlier generation. In Cameroon, two popular music genres emerged during the 1940s: *makossa*, which is associated with the Sawa ethnic group, and *bikutsi*, associated with the Beti ethnic group (Nyamnjoh and Fokwang 2005, p. 254). During the Ahidjo era (discussed above), *makossa* flourished. However, after 1982, when a Beti president assumed power, the national government chose to promote *bikutski*, showing a "noted insensitivity ... towards the music of other ethnic areas in Cameroon" (p. 259). *Makossa* then became the genre of opposition protest.

In post-Soviet Czechoslovakia, Czech folk singers who had been banned by the Communist government were allowed to return to the country and sing freely, and punk music became an officially accepted musical genre (Mitchell 1992, pp. 192, 200). In other post-Soviet countries, the nationalism of the 1990s gave rise to a renewed emphasis on national sounds and symbols in popular music. In the Ukraine, for example, popular music bands began underlining their commitment to their Ukrainian identity and simultaneously symbolically distancing themselves from Russia. They transformed their genre by singing in Ukrainian, using traditional musical forms from Ukrainian folk music, and by showing images associated with Ukrainian tradition in their music videos (such as well-known landmarks, rural settings, clothing, food and musical instruments) (Wickstrom 2008, pp. 66–73). In Hungary, an entirely new genre emerged in the 1990s. "National rock" or "patriotic rock" differs from mainstream rock in that it is openly wedded to the Rock Against Communism ideology (Kürti 2012). The lyrics of the songs in this genre celebrate freedom from communism and evoke a mythic past during which Hungary was a unified and mono-ethnic Christian country. The most extreme examples of such lyrics, sung by "hard-core" nationalist punk and death metal bands, espouse Hungarism (Hungary for the Hungarians), Nazism, racism, homophobia and hatred of Jews and Roma (Kürti 2012, p. 113).

In what follows, I describe Myanmar's popular music during the transition period. Following the scholarship cited above, and the other chapters in this volume, I seek to pay particular attention to the national context in which these changes occurred. Importantly, I acknowledge the reality implicit in the case studies described above (and explicitly stated in Buchanan 2006, p. 25), which is that a political transition is not usually a single event but rather a process lasting years or even decades. Therefore I emphasize again that my statements about the Myanmar popular music scene are temporally bound, referring to a time rather early in the transition process. More research will surely be needed, and I anticipate that further changes, linked in various ways to the evolving political climate, will occur.[2]

Increasing Involvement of Foreigners in the Myanmar Popular Music Scene

One change I noticed immediately when I returned to Yangon in 2013 was that Anglo foreigners (meaning citizens of English-speaking countries) were becoming increasingly involved in the Burmese pop music industry. Just a few years earlier there had been no foreign nationals working in the Yangon music scene in any capacity, and so the presence of Anglo foreigners in a previously mono-national industry was striking. All of the foreigners I met had moved to Myanmar recently, without the intention of devoting themselves to popular music; that is, they came to work in other industries but, after becoming fans of and developing sympathies with local musicians, became their advocates. Their presence in Yangon was linked to the quasi-civilian government's efforts to end the country's isolation and allow foreign immigration.

The small group of Anglo foreigners who were involved in Burmese popular music in 2013 had a shared agenda: they were actively working to promote "originality" in what they believed was a derivative and artistically worthless mainstream industry. The best-known example of this phenomenon is an Australian dance coach named Nikki May who moved to Yangon in 2009. She quickly became involved with a recently formed girls group, then known as the Tiger Girls. Under May's leadership this group changed their name to the Me N Ma Girls and achieved an impressive amount of international success. The Me N Ma Girls became the subject of a documentary film (*Miss Nikki and the Tiger Girls*), performed for Hilary Clinton at a UN summit, and in 2014 moved temporarily to Los Angeles, having received a recording contract from a U.S.-based record label.

In Myanmar, however — as the group members admitted to me — the Me N Ma Girls did not have much of a following. Notably, the group had few links with local industry power brokers. Among the twenty-seven industry members I interviewed in 2013, only one said that he had ever worked with the Me N Ma Girls; the general consensus was that this group was not well known and "not very talented" (e.g., G Latt, personal communication, 23 May 2013).

The group's relationships with Burmese pop musicians may have been weak because during a number of media interviews they had stated their commitment to "original music" and disparaged the *copy thachin* tradition of their country. To explain: during the roughly fifty years that Burmese musicians have been creating popular music in the international pop-rock style, song composers have utilized two composition techniques, both of which are appreciated by Burmese fans and professional colleagues. The first of these techniques, and the only one widely understood in Western countries, involves using all new sonic elements to construct a song: a new melody accompanied by new harmonies and sung using new words. Such a song is called an *own tune*. When using the second technique, Burmese song composers copy varying amounts of a melody, harmony and accompanying timbres from a previously existing song, almost always a hit song originating in the United States or the United Kingdom. In such a song, called *copy thachin*, the only completely new element is the Burmese-language words, which are not a translation of the original English words. Both *own tunes* and *copy thachin* are widely performed by professional pop musicians in Myanmar, although *copy thachin* are frequently derided by outsiders as nothing more than plagiarism (MacLachlan 2016).

The Me N Ma Girls' articulation of their position on *copy thachin* — indeed, the very position that earned them admiring press reports in venues like the *New York Times*, the *Wall Street Journal*, the *Straits Times* and *Newsweek* magazine — may be attributed in part to the influence of their Anglo manager, Nikki May. After all — as group members acknowledged to me — when they were the Tiger Girls, the group performed *copy thachin* (personal communication, 3 June 2013). The Anglo foreigners who became involved in Burmese popular music in the early years of the political transition shared the conviction, widespread in English-language majority countries, that "originality" is the *sine qua non* of artistic endeavours. Their influence was evident in other cases.

The punk band Side Effect, for example, had a Canadian manager named Daniel Gelfer. Due to Gelfer's connections with the Anglo expatriate community in Yangon, Side Effect gained an important following among foreigners. I attended a Side Effect concert at a restaurant in Yangon in May 2013 and was fascinated to be part of an audience that included more Anglos than Burmese. Side Effect toured Germany in 2014, and their lead singer claimed that they have more fans in Europe than they do in Myanmar (Roberts 2014). Darko C, the lead singer, told me that he "hates" *copy thachin*, although Side Effect has covered an English-language song. Darko insisted that covering a song is different than copying it, because covering is a way of paying tribute to a song one loves (Darko C, personal communication, 15 May 2013).

By 2018, both the Me N Ma Girls and Side Effect had disbanded, and both Nikki May and Daniel Gelfer had left the country. However, the trend I first identified in 2013 continued. It was most clearly demonstrated during a "Mixtape" concert, held on 7 April 2018 at the rooftop bar of Yangon's Alfa Hotel. "Mixtape" featured three- and four-song sets presented by seven Yangon-based ensembles, none of which had, as yet, achieved any mainstream recognition. The event was organized by one Anglo foreigner and hosted by another. Roughly fifty per cent of the audience members looked to be of European descent, and all of the band members introduced themselves and their songs in English. Over and over, the musicians emphasized that they were about to present their "own tunes", or "original songs"; audience members around me responded by celebrating the "originality" and "creativity" they were hearing. Indeed, the host commented at one point, "Isn't this great! Five years ago you were hard pressed to find any original music in Yangon." This claim is patently false: one can hear original music at virtually any popular music concert presented by Burmese stars, and original songs have been part of the most successful artists' repertoires since the 1970s. The comment, and the "Mixtape" event at which I heard it, represent the continuation of Anglo foreigners' determination to involve themselves in Myanmar's popular music scene, and to support Burmese pop musicians who — as the foreigners understand or misunderstand it — exemplify the Western commitment to artistic originality.

The Myanmar Musicians Association and the Advent of the Royalty Payment System

The Myanmar Musicians Association, or the Myanmar Gita Asiayon, is an umbrella group that aims to represent the interests of recording artists in Myanmar. I have written elsewhere at length about the work of the MMA, and musicians' responses to it (MacLachlan 2011). Pre-transition, the members of the MMA were appointed by the military government, and therefore the organization was distrusted and dismissed by most musicians, although MMA board members whom I met insisted they were pursuing initiatives that would redound to the benefit of musicians. In September 2012 the MMA had its first-ever fully democratic election, meaning that members were able to vote freely for a board of leaders who make decisions that affect musicians' livelihoods. In 2013 the elected general secretary was Phyu Phyu Kyaw Thein, a highly successful singer, who described the MMA's evolution by saying that the group had become "a real NGO" (personal communication, 18 May 2013). One of the first changes the MMA made was to post the minutes of their monthly meetings on Facebook in an effort to show their commitment to transparent and democratic governance.

Musicians I interviewed in 2013 were generally happy about this development, although they were sanguine about the new leadership, pointing out that while the new leaders meant well, they were inexperienced (e.g., Min Oo, personal communication, 29 May 2013). For their part, the elected leaders seemed sincerely committed to protecting the interests of their members. However, the MMA and its members dealt with a number of controversial issues and, during interviews with me, dissent was evident. In 2013, early in the transition era, the MMA's relationship with its members reflected the messiness of democracy, a messiness which can be disappointing to people who have idealized expectations about freedom and progress.

The most controversial issue the MMA took on was the payment of royalties. The MMA is the body to which radio stations and movie producers are supposed to pay royalty fees each time they broadcast a recording. The MMA is then supposed to disburse these royalty fees to the artists involved in the creation of the recording. As of 2009, virtually no one in the Burmese popular music industry used or even understood the concept of royalties. When I explained this notion to musicians during interviews (conducted pre-transition), they were somewhat puzzled. They told me over and over that "the Burmese way" was for producers — that is, the financial backers of recorded albums — to pay flat fees to songwriters, singers and other performers at the time they purchased their services. Any profits from the sale of recordings were returned to producers. And the only radio station in Myanmar that played a lot of popular music, and which welcomed caller requests for airplay, did not compensate artists or producers for broadcasting their works. The principal way in which musicians made money under this system was by earning flat fees working in recording studios or performing live concerts.

Since 2010 the number of privately owned radio stations in Myanmar has grown exponentially. In 2012 the newly elected MMA board decided to aggressively pursue radio station owners for royalty payments. The MMA decided to charge 750 kyat (slightly less than US$1 by current exchange rates) for each broadcast of any given song. They committed to disbursing the royalty fee as follows: 150 kyat (or 20 per cent) to the MMA, 150 kyat to the lead singer, 150 kyat to the songwriter, 150 kyat to the producer, 90 kyat to be divided among the instrument players, and 60 kyat to the recording studio (Phyu Phyu Kyaw Thein, personal communication, 7 June 2013). The amounts that different industry members earn under this scheme is a direct reflection of their relative amounts of power in the industry. Lead singers, for example, often spend less time in the studio than do instrument players. However, because they are literally front and centre during concerts and in music videos, their faces and names are well known to fans. They are *nammeh-kyi deh*, or big names, and they can therefore command a larger portion of the royalty payment than, for example, guitar players who may have contributed more time and effort to the making of the recording. Note that back-up singers — or "harmony" as they are called in Myanmar — get nothing under this scheme.

As of 2013, the MMA had not paid out many royalty fees — for a few different reasons. Musicians were still, to some degree, uneducated about royalties and therefore did not file the necessary paperwork in order to collect them. (Some musicians told me that they heard the paperwork was so confusing that they did not even bother trying [Ah Moon, Htike Htike and Kimi, personal communication, 3 June 2013]). The MMA also had difficulty extracting royalty monies from radio station managers, many of whom are well-known musicians in their own right, like Zaw Win Htut. These musicians/managers have their own opinions about what kinds of payments are appropriate and what role the MMA ought to play in the newly emerging music economy. And, unfortunately, the MMA hired a corrupt office manager who embezzled 500,000 kyat worth of royalty payments in 2012 (Myint Moe Aung, personal communication, 24 May 2013). The MMA pursued this case in court, but in the meantime the situation of the unpaid fees undermined the trust they asked musicians to place in the organization. The challenges the MMA faced resembled those that scholars have documented elsewhere; in brief, when small-scale music industries in developing countries create organizations to oversee royalty payments, these organizations are often unsuccessful at funnelling the money owed to the artists (Wallis and Malm 1984).

In 2013 I met a number of prominent musicians who told me that they had left, or refused to join, the new MMA (e.g., personal communications with Shwe Gyaw Gyaw, 25 May 2013; G Latt, 23 May 2013; Lin Lin, 24 May 2013; Ayo, 31 May 2013), and in 2018 I met still more (e.g., Ko Tha Htwe, 7 April 2018). These musicians wanted to manage their own careers, and they rejected the control (or "protection") offered by an organization that was, for decades, a patsy of the military regime. These musicians hired, or told me that they planned to hire, lawyers to help them pursue the royalties to which they felt entitled. They pointed out that while lawyers do charge fees, their fees are generally lower than the 20 per cent the MMA reserves for itself. A number of these musicians stated that they felt the MMA's division of royalty monies was inequitable; for example, why should a studio owner who has already profited by renting out his studio to recording artists be further compensated when the recording is broadcast? Songwriters mounted a campaign to advocate for royalties each time singers perform songs live in concert — a campaign that failed, largely because tremendously influential singers like Lay Phyu refused to cooperate. Musicians who disdained the MMA argued further that by dealing directly with radio station managers — who in some cases were their industry colleagues — they could negotiate different royalty fees for their work. A number of them said they would like to offer their latest albums to radio stations for free, in hopes that the radio stations would broadcast them frequently and thereby build a fan following. In other cases they would like to charge far higher royalty fees than the standard amounts set by the MMA. They were particularly angered by the fact that the new and supposedly improved MMA declined to reopen a deal reached with mobile phone companies in which the companies pay 300 kyat for twenty years of use of a recording as a ringtone (G Latt, personal communication, 23 May 2013). Given that the mobile market was exploding in Myanmar, these artists pointed out that they could have negotiated for much more money.

By 2018, Legacy Music, a content aggregator, was a tremendously successful Yangon-based business. Its founder, Dr Ko Ko Lwin, a former general secretary of the MMA, saw the need to address many new platforms created by internet technology and social media. Despite a slow start — the chief operating officer of Legacy Music said that Lwin struggled at first to convince musicians to trust this new business model — the company has succeeded in signing virtually "one hundred per cent of the tier one" Burmese musicians, helping them to distribute their music on Youtube, Facebook, Spotify and other online channels (Steph Koko, personal communication, 17 May 2018). Zaw Htoo Aung, the 2018 general secretary of the MMA, characterized Legacy Music as a "private" analogue to the MMA (personal communication, 24 April

2018), and the similarities are clear: Legacy also negotiates financial partnerships with musicians, and it too takes a percentage of the profits eventually paid to the musicians. Given that advancing technology is being eagerly embraced by Burmese music fans, the future of recorded music in Myanmar may rest with visionary private entrepreneurs like Ko Ko Lwin, rather than with the still radio-centric MMA.

Artistic Freedom and its Discontents

Another thorny issue that the MMA was attempting to arbitrate at the very time I was interviewing musicians in Yangon was that of rating, or somehow otherwise commenting on, recordings. To put this dispute in context, just months after the government ceased censoring music recordings, not one person among the twenty-seven I interviewed in 2013 thought the country should return to the old system of government censorship. Musicians were uniformly relieved that they no longer had to endure the inconvenience of submitting their recordings for approval, and that they no longer had to pay bribes to the staff members at the Press Scrutiny Board. Also, musicians were generally very glad that in the newly free market they were now able to produce "political songs". In truth, few of these "political songs" were available as of May 2013, but a number of my interlocutors pointed me to a recording produced by the National League for Democracy (Aung San Suu Kyi's political party). The CD was titled "Freedom Songs"; this very title would have been disallowed by censors pre-transition. However, in 2013 I found it for sale in the very first retail shop I entered, where a clerk sold it to me without any noticeable reaction. In less than one year, then, forbidden music had become commonplace. Such "political music" is also now performed in public; on 4 April 2018 I heard a concert presented by the PYL band in front of an NLD office in a middle-class Yangon neighbourhood. PYL sang about General Aung San, his daughter, and democracy. U Nyi Nyi Lwin, one of PYL's singers, said that another welcome change ushered in by the transition is that it is now easier to obtain permits to present concerts on city streets (personal communication, 5 April 2018). However, some recording artists are still cautious, pointing out that the federal government had promised a democratic government for decades, and had even allowed general freedom of expression for short periods — only to later punish opponents of the regime. These musicians said that, whatever progressive agenda the government was now proclaiming, they were unwilling to record songs which expressed open and targeted dissent. "I'm pretty sure you can't sing, "Fuck you, Mr President", even now", said Darko C (personal communication, 15 May 2013). As film director Ko Myint pointed out, "They can put you in jail *any* time" (personal communication, 21 May 2013).

Although most of the musicians I talked with were openly glad about the new freedoms they enjoyed, they evinced a range of opinions about how that freedom should be deployed. The leaders of the MMA and many rank and file musicians were concerned about the influence of uncensored songs on the general public. A number of my informants used the English phrases "rude words" or "bad words" to describe lyrics that could now be written, and which they had heard in recent recordings. These "bad words" generally fell into two categories. The first is lyrics or visual representations in music videos that refer to sexual acts. One example mentioned to me in multiple interviews was a hit song called "In Love with You", recorded by a young singer called Eain Eain. Although the words in this song are innocuous, the accompanying video shows a young couple cuddling on a bed, with repeated references to more sexually suggestive visuals (for example, the woman licks her lips and lifts her skirt, and eventually they engage in a very close embrace while beginning to remove each other's clothes).[3] It is important to point out here that musicians objected to this not because they were reactionary conservatives or especially prudish about sex. Rather, they feared that sexual content in music could lead to family breakdown. As Nay Win Htun, a well-known music teacher, said, "We can't listen to this music between mothers and sons, or between brothers and sisters" (personal communication, 16 May 2013). And this is a legitimate concern: while the government elected in 2015 may be more democratic, it is not yet supplying a reliable social safety net to vulnerable citizens. As Burmese people age, they must be able to depend on their children and other relatives to support them financially. Therefore, strong relationships between parents and children are of utmost importance.

The second type of "bad words" which worried my interlocutors in 2013 are those that evoke racist attitudes. Here, again, my respondents were unable to identify many examples of such words, although they were sincerely concerned. One song referenced in interviews (e.g., Myint Moe Aung, personal communication, 24 May 2013) was the "Song to Whip Up Religious Blood", which encourages listeners to "buy Buddhist". This song was not recorded by professionals, but the recording is attractive enough that it is frequently played at Buddhist religious events (Marshall 2013). Musicians feared that more such songs could be recorded and that they could enflame the deadly conflict between Buddhists and Muslims that was then spreading around Myanmar, and which subsequently flared up in Malaysia.

By 2018 the concerns expressed five years earlier seemed prophetic. In May 2018, for example, a song titled (in English) "I Don't Fucking Care" rose to prominence. The song features a "rude word" in the title — which is repeated throughout the song — and the accompanying video shows overt sexual behaviour, including kissing, between two women. In other words, the song celebrates the violating of two Burmese taboos: homosexual behaviour and disrespect for authority. But this is something of a new normal in Myanmar. Indeed, Zaw Htoo Aung claimed, "If you want your album to be a hit [now], you must include at least one eighteen-plus song" (personal communication, 24 April 2018). In addition, five songs extolling Buddhist nationalism were available on YouTube, all in popular music style. The lyrics of these songs call on Buddhists to unite, exhort Buddhist women not to marry Muslims, and praise U Wirathu, the monk best known for preaching hatred against Myanmar Muslims.[4] To be fair, none of the songs were written or recorded by mainstream artists, and none of them were particularly popular. However, their existence was evidence that fears about songs like this coming to the fore were not overblown.

The MMA responded to the concerns about "bad words" in now-uncensored songs. The association's position was articulated by one of their elected board members, Myint Moe Aung: "There has to be some rules, otherwise there will be destruction" (personal communication, 24 May 2013). Late in 2012 the MMA proposed a plan to rate musical recordings. The plan was to assign a classification letter to each song: A, meaning appropriate for all ages; B, meaning something like parental guidance, appropriate for those aged sixteen and over; or C, appropriate for adults only. I asked most of my respondents for their opinions about this plan. Twelve of them said they supported the idea. Interestingly, four of them said that they supported the notion of rating songs specifically because they understand that recordings are rated for content in other countries. (When I asked what they meant by other countries, all said the United States.)

However, I did hear some strongly dissenting voices during my interviews. Several prominent musicians objected to having their music evaluated, in any way, by anybody — but especially by the MMA, which until recently had been controlled by the military government. As they pointed out, it was entirely unclear who would decide what kinds of songs were appropriate for what ages, on what basis these decisions would be made, and how the ratings might affect airplay and, therefore, royalty payments. On 31 May 2013, the MMA announced that they would not pursue a rating system. The general secretary, Phyu Phyu Kyaw Thein, told me that the decision was taken because so many MMA members were "allergic" to the idea (personal communication, 7 June 2013). Instead, she said, going forward the MMA intended to listen to all newly recorded songs and make "comments" on songs that have "dangerous categories for the community". These dangerous categories are (i) lyrics that might promote ethnic or religious conflict and (ii) lyrics that promote drug use, smoking or prostitution. The MMA will forward the comments to radio and television broadcasters. The programme managers will then have to decide whether or not to broadcast these potentially dangerous songs.

By 2018 the MMA had abandoned any notion of formally "commenting" on recordings. Other forms of social control existed, such as the increasingly powerful Legacy Music company's policy of refusing to promote songs that contain either expletives or words encouraging racial discrimination (personal communication, Steph Koko, 17 May 2018). Musicians responded in various ways to the less-censorious environment of the transition era. Sai Sai Kham Leng, Myanmar's premiere hip-hop star, for example, released two versions of his 2018 "Sai Sai is Sai Sai" series — one radio-friendly and another containing swear words.

Future Possibilities

What does the future hold for Myanmar's popular music scene and for the musicians who make their living in it? As the literature review above demonstrated, musical genres and approaches to music making are often profoundly affected by national political changes. In the Myanmar case, it seems possible that, if foreign (Anglo) influences on popular music increase, *copy thachin* will decrease in output and popularity. If Yangon-based musicians collaborate more frequently with foreigners who believe that *copy thachin* creation is nothing more than plagiarism, they may decline to record such songs. Indeed, in 2013 some of my informants claimed that writing *own tunes* — that is, the creation of original songs — was already becoming the preferred composition method among their colleagues (e.g., Minn Chit Thu, personal communication, 19 May 2013).

It seems likely that the majority of Myanmar's professional musicians will embrace the idea that royalties ought to be paid to them by the MMA. Although in 2013 musicians expressed confusion about and even distrust of the MMA's royalty payment plan, just two years later royalties were being paid by the MMA. The payment of royalties is, in effect, its own convincing argument. A sound engineer told me that he was happy to receive approximately US$3,000 in royalty monies in 2015 (Aung Doo, personal communication, 12 September 2016). For him this was a bonus, an addition to the money he earned in the traditional way (that is, being paid a one-time fee at the time tracks are recorded). By 2016, other musicians had come to understand royalties as rightfully belonging to them, and the MMA as responsible for disbursing those royalties. In September of that year, composer Jet Mya Thaung held a press conference to announce that he planned to sue both the MMA and five FM radio stations for unpaid royalties (Su Myat Mon 2016).

Perhaps the greatest concern for the Myanmar music industry in the future is the ongoing tension between the desire for freedom of expression and the perceived need for control of that expression. As composer Shwe Gyaw Gyaw told me in 2013, freedom can be abused in a myriad of ways. He saw this notion being abused by the pirates who make illegal copies of Burmese recordings and sell them for their own profit: "Freedom is good, but they [fellow Burmese] think piracy is freedom. Government does not help to educate them. If you tell someone, 'Don't [illegally] copy this disc or this file, they say, 'Hey! This is democracy!'" (personal communication, 25 May 2013). Piracy undermines the economic security of musicians; and the freedom to sing "bad words" can endanger society at large. The recent history of White Power music in the United States reminds us that music can be a powerful tool in the service of hatred and violence. As both Mark Hamm (2002) and Jonathan Pieslak (2015) have demonstrated, sales of White Power recordings are a major source of funding for vicious racist groups, White Power concerts have sparked violence on numerous occasions, and the musicians in this movement have become attractive role models for disaffected young people. Hamm concludes that "chronic and persistent exposure to [such music] provided American skinheads with the vitality, the emotions and the excitement necessary for committing violence against their perceived enemies" (2002, p. 89). When Buddhist mobs are being encouraged to destroy Muslim schools, businesses, mosques and even people, Burmese people rightly fear any move by musicians to make violence seem glamorous or cool. At the same time, one of the greatest promises of Myanmar's democratic transition and the election of 2015 was that the country's citizens could speak, write and sing without being limited by government censorship. Musicians will continue to expect to see this promise fulfilled.

Notes

1. In October 2012 the Myanmar government announced that it would no longer censor audio recordings. However, at the time of writing this chapter in 2016, the government continued to censor video recordings such as films and music videos.
2. Here I am mindful of László Kürti, who bravely and humbly revised his earlier conclusions about Hungarian popular music when he analysed the scene "twenty years after" (2012, p. 127).
3. See https://www.youtube.com/watch?v=gFBTPQ385tU.
4. See https://www.youtube.com/watch?v=n3bzk9mImYE; https://www.youtube.com/watch?v=RsSpS8oEKHE; https://www.youtube.com/watch?v=dyRNSwY5Dkw; https://www.youtube.com/watch?v=vzvotssVgUU; https://www.youtube.com/watch?v=sru69Ui8-Yg.

References

Buchanan, D.A. 2006. *Performing Democracy: Bulgarian Music and Musicians in Transition.* Chicago, IL: University of Chicago Press.

Byerly, I.B. 1998. "Mirror, Mediator and Prophet: The Music Indaba of Late-Apartheid South Africa". *Ethnomusicology* 42 (1): 1–44.

Friedman, J.C. 2013. "Introduction: What is Social Protest Music? One Historian's Perspective". In *The Routledge History of Social Protest in Popular Music*, edited by Jonathan C. Friedman, pp. xiv–xvii. New York: Routledge.

Gunther, R., and A. Mughan, eds. 2000. *Democracy and the Media: A Comparative Perspective.* Cambridge: Cambridge University Press.

Hamm, M.S. 2002. *In Bad Company: America's Terrorist Underground.* Boston, MA: Northeastern University Press.

Ho, W.-C. 2000. "The Political Meaning of Hong Kong Popular Music: A Review of Sociopolitical Relations between Hong Kong and the People's Republic of China since the 1980s". *Popular Music* 19 (3): 341–53.

Kürti, L. 2012. "Twenty Years After: Rock Music and National Rock in Hungary". *Region* 1 (1): 93–129.

Lockard, C.A. 1996. "Popular Music and Politics in Modern Southeast Asia: A Comparative Analysis". *Asian Music* 27 (2): 146–99.

MacLachlan, H. 2011. *Burma's Pop Music Industry: Creators, Distributors, Censors.* Rochester, NY: University of Rochester Press.

———. 2016. "(Mis)representation of Burmese Metal Music in the Western Media". *Metal Music Studies* 2 (3): 395–404.

Marshall, A.C. 2013. "Ingraining the 969 Ideology". *The Irrawaddy*, 27 June 2013. http://www.irrawaddy.com/news/burma/ingraining-the-969-ideology.html.

Mitchell, T. 1992. "Mixing Pop and Politics: Rock Music in Czechoslovakia before and after the Velvet Revolution". *Popular Music* 11 (2): 187–203.

Nyamnjoh, F.B. and J. Fokwang. 2005. "Entertaining Repression: Music and Politics in Postcolonial Cameroon". *African Affairs* 104 (415): 257–74.

Pekacz, J. 1992. "On Some Dilemmas of Polish Post-communist Rock Culture". *Popular Music* 11 (2): 205–8.

Pieslak, J. 2015. *Radicalism and Music: An Introduction to the Music of al-Qa'ida, Racist Skinheads, Christian-Affiliated Radicals, and Eco-Animal Rights Militants.* Middletown, CT: Wesleyan University Press.

Roberts, R. 2014. "SXSW 2014: Side Effect is First Myanmar Band to Play at Festival". *Los Angeles Times*, 18 March 2014. http://www.latimes.com/entertainment/music/posts/la-et-ms-sxsw-14-side-effect-myanmar-band-20140318-story.html.

Su Myat Mon. 2016. "Musician Cries Foul over Missing Royalties". *Frontier Myanmar*, 2 September 2016. http://frontiermyanmar.net/en/news/musician-cries-foul-missing-royalties.
Wallach, J. 2005. "Underground Rock Music: And Democratization in Indonesia". *World Literature Today* 79 (3–4): 16–20.
Wallis, R., and K. Malm. 1984. *Big Sounds from Small Peoples: The Music Industry in Small Countries*. Hillsdale, NY: Pendragon Press.
Wickstrom, D.-E. 2008. "'Drive-Ethno Dance' and 'Hutzul Punk': Ukrainian-Associated Popular Music and (Geo)politics in a Post-Soviet Context". *Yearbook for Traditional Music* 40:60–88.

15

New Video Generation: The Myanmar Motion Picture Industry in 2017

Jane M. Ferguson

> *We need more films about strong topics, such as about violence against women.... If I make a film like that, I will not portray women as victims only. Some women are powerful, brave to speak up. Other women can learn from those women and that can be empowering for them.*
>
> —Hnin Ei Hlaing, independent filmmaker

Local filmmaking has played a crucial role in Burmese society since the first Burmese feature film hit the silver screen in 1920. Even during the decades of supposed economic stagnation and political isolation, Burmese film studios continued to produce feature-length movies that entertained audiences in the hundreds of cinemas throughout the country. Numerous black and white Burmese motion picture classics continue to be shown on Myanmar television, and, from the 1990s, aspiring filmmakers have increasingly made use of digital production and distribution. With changing technologies, the establishment of the Yangon Film School and the momentum of international film festivals, a new generation of filmmakers in Myanmar have been using film to point to formerly taboo topics, and they have been engaging film communities in the international arena with their works.

In a context in which creative expression inside the country was heavily stifled by a stringent government censor board, what happens when international filmmakers and political documentarians are suddenly allowed to mix with local filmmakers? How has the atmosphere changed for the motion picture industry during the political transition of this decade? In her book on political transition and Brazilian women's filmmaking, Leslie Marsh observed that political aperturism in the country coincided with technological advances in film and video, which set the ground for greater alternative video production (Marsh 2013, p. 32). Although Marsh's study coincided with the transition in video production from celluloid to video, we can also consider the ways in which entirely digital video production, and even smartphone video cameras, have affected the ways in which people document social worlds and produce and distribute motion pictures about them.

Following a summary of secondary and primary sources on the subject of film production in Burma, I will present an overview of the history of the Burmese film industry, from the British colonial period, to independence, to the years of the Burmese Socialist Program Party, and then the SLORC/SPDC years of strict censorship. I will then turn to the 2000s, the advent of the Yangon Film School, and finally the blossoming of film festivals in the past decade. With the public presentation of films, which no longer require the same level of approval from the censor board as they did in years past, filmmakers have increasingly been able to openly discuss social issues in the country, though some circumstances will curtail that openness, and controversial topics can still be off-limits. Through recent interviews with contemporary filmmakers, this chapter will discuss the ways in which they see the relationship between film, documentary, and social change in Myanmar. While this study largely focuses on a relatively elite group of motion picture makers (though one of the interviewees grew up stateless in Thailand), they offer an important perspective on the changing constraints of media production; they — or their families — have decades of experience in filmmaking, and can discuss the industry as insiders. While digital technologies have begun to make production and sharing of motion pictures more accessible to the broader public, courses in subjects like video editing — let alone film theory — are limited in the country.

Film scholars and movie buffs new to Myanmar are often astounded by the sheer size of the local industry and the volume of films which have been produced over the industry's veritable century-long history. This history of film output includes the decades of military rule when the country was ostensibly "closed off" to the outside world. In spite of the size and influence of the motion picture industry in Myanmar, international scholarly work on the subject is disproportionally scant. This can partially be chalked up to the closed economy of the BSPP years, but it is also the result of Myanmar's scholarly disciplinary trends towards political science and religious studies analyses of the country instead of analysis of its popular culture scene. In a few English-language scholarly books about Burma, motion pictures and the motion picture scene have been mentioned in passing paragraphs (Charney 2009; Myint 1993; Elliott 2006). Compendia specifically on the subject of Asian film have mentioned films on Burma (Lent 1990; Holmes 1959). The introduction to the edited volume *Films in Southeast Asia: Views from the Region* laments not having been able to recruit a scholar to write a chapter about film in Burma (Hanan 2000). Hamilton (2006) draws upon English-language sources on the internet to include some information about film in Burma in her article on cinema in "socialist Southeast Asia", and there are various histories and articles about film in exile media such as *The Irrawaddy* (Min Zin 2004; Aung Zaw 2004; Yeni 2006). Through my initial ethnographic work on ethnic Shan interpretations of popular culture, I started to take an interest in researching the Burmese film industry, and since then have published short articles on the subject of Burmese cinema and minority spectatorship (Ferguson 2007), minority representation in Burmese film (Ferguson 2012a), as well as an overview of the history of Burmese film in an edited volume on Southeast Asian cinema (Ferguson 2012b). There is a recent doctoral dissertation on the subject of "Developing Film Cultures in Bhutan, Mongolia and Myanmar" (Grøn 2016).

In contrast to English-language scholarly work, Burmese-language material on the film industry, unsurprisingly, is much more voluminous and extensive. Locally produced magazines and journals dedicated to motion pictures have existed in the country since the early days of Burmese cinema itself. Titles include *Yôkshin Thit* (New Film), *Yôkshin Padetha* (Film World), *Yôkshin Magazin* (Film Magazine) and the more recent *Yôkshin Te Kabya Magazin* (Film, Music and Poetry Magazine), among dozens of other titles over the decades. A number of motion picture studios also published magazines, often in conjunction with the release of new films. These included *A1*, *Shumuwa* and *Nyunt Myanmar*. There are extensive published biographies of Burmese filmmakers, as well as of cinema stars. For example, *Ya Pyi* magazine recently published a 460+ page compendium of articles about revered director U Thuka (ရာပြည့်မဂ္ဂဇင်း 2010). Arguably, the most complete single volume about the industry as a whole is the *Myanmar Yôkbshin Sein Yatu Thabin* (Myanmar Film Diamond Anniversary) compendium published in 1996, coming out of a festival to commemorate the industry's seventy-fifth anniversary (မြန်မာ့ရုပ်ရှင်စိန်ရတုသဘင် 1996), and there is a thorough history of the first twenty-five years of Burmese film production in the volume *Myanmar Yôkshin Thamaing Sin*. Unlike previous volumes, the latter is useful in that it contains an index (မြန်မာ့နိုင်ငံ ရုပ်ရှင်အစည်းအရုံး 2004). Finally, Takatho Khin Maung Zaw's slim 2012 volume *Myanmar Kantawin Yôkshin Anupinya Shin 20* (20 Myanmar Classic Film Artists) offers a concise and useful overview of the history of the industry in relation to political and economic circumstances. Because all of these publications from Myanmar would have acquired approval by the Press Scrutiny Board, these books and magazines tend to focus on plot, presentation and biography rather than on social issues, let alone critique of the government. On the other hand, film scholars publishing during the socialist years would write articles about the ideological goals of the Burmese Way to Socialism, and how this would be portrayed by films, offering useful insight to understanding and analysing Burmese cinematic language during these years.

International news articles and op-eds on film in Myanmar have tended to denigrate the state of the industry, claiming that censorship has left the country with vapid, formulaic love-triangle romance plots. One observer notes that the film industry could not keep up with international films because of its "out-dated technology, government censorship, hackneyed screenwriting and mediocre acting" (Min Zin 2004). Although some might lament that technological and economic setbacks prevented the films from gaining prominence on the international scene, there is still an important critique to be made about disciplinary trends and scholarship about the country precluding film studies interest in this vast, dynamic, influential industry.

Going to the movies in Myanmar, however, offers another side to that story, from understanding the films themselves and the ways in which audiences engage with them. In the numerous film screenings that I have attended in Yangon, Taunggyi and Mandalay since the early 2000s, I have found local audiences to be anything but passive. On-screen victories would be met with enthusiastic cheering, slapstick comedy would be rewarded with cathartic applause and guffaws, all the while accompanied by the crackle of sunflower seeds being shelled by engrossed viewers. Indeed, at the end of the screening, one must wade through a sea of sunflower seed husks to exit the hall. At magazine rental kiosks, popular film magazines would have dozens of dates scribbled in their cardboard covers, indicating high levels of circulation. Although evidence of local films' popularity within the country is ubiquitous, filmmakers also regret that there has been little space for Myanmar's films internationally. "We would like for our films to become more known in the mainstream. We get Hollywood films, we get Indian films, we get Thai films. But if we can be more involved we can have a greater context for knowledge exchange", pointed out contemporary filmmaker Saw Reagan.[1]

"When I was in Germany, I think 80 per cent of the people I talked with didn't even know where Myanmar is", recalled Hnin Ei Hlaing, evidence of filmmakers' awareness that their country, let alone its media, is scarcely known outside of Southeast Asia.

In previous work, I had periodized the history of the Burmese cinema into four eras:

1. The years under British Colonial rule;
2. The independence years following the Second World War;
3. The years of the Ne Win regime and the Burmese Socialist Program Party;

4. Post 1988–89 and the opening of the economy to international investments, or the SLORC/SPDCD years. (Ferguson 2012a, p. 27)

As such, I would like to add another period to Myanmar's motion picture history: 2011 to present, where the Thein Sein regime relaxed censorship laws and the country saw the blossoming of international film festivals, coupled with increased access to the internet and social media. How the establishment of the first elected government in more than fifty years changes the motion picture industry remains to be seen. This chapter examines how Myanmar's cultural politics, coupled with emergent digital technologies, have changed the ways in which the public looks to film for entertainment and for social meaning.

Out of the Past: A Historical Overview of Burma's Film Industry

The early history of cinema in Burma is inextricably bound to the country's colonial situation, and specifically the country's relationship with British India. It was under Section 7(2) of the Cinematograph Act of 1918 that early Burmese films were given permission for public screening (မောင်မောင် 1970, p. 19). Some early Burmese films were shot in Bombay. At the turn of the twentieth century, Yangon (Colonial Rangoon) was one of the most cosmopolitan cities in the world. Following tent showman demonstrations of motion pictures, the shirt-vendor-turned-sound-recording-dealer *Myanmar Aswe* re-branded itself as A1 Film Company and established studios in Mayangone Township in 1932 (Yadana Htun 2012). A1 studios is a family operation, and it is still often thought of as the Hollywood of Burma. By 1939, in varying degrees of collaboration with Indian studios, a total of 640 Burmese films had been produced (ထွန်းလှိုင် 2000, p. 187).

The earliest Burmese films were largely documentary shorts. The first feature film, *Metta Hnint Thura* (Love and Liquor), was made by members of the religious group Young Men's Buddhist Association. The film, released in 1920, features a protagonist whose life is gradually destroyed because of his proclivity for alcohol and gambling. Other early features included biographies, fairy tales, love dramas and

Buddhist-themed stories. Some Burmese nationalist film enthusiasts resented the role of India in film production, and the best-known and most prolific director of nationalist-themed films was "Parrot" U Sunny. Some of his films from the 1930s include a production about traditional Burmese gambling, *36 Kaung* (36 Animals), and *Do Daung Lan* (Our Peacock Flag), encouraging Burmese to pay respect to their flag rather than the British one (ဝစ်ကိုင်းလှရွှေ 1981, p. 47).

During the years of independence there was a tremendous flourishing of Burmese film production. No longer under the thumb of the British colonial political apparatus, film could now be more overtly nationalistic and used for the political interests of Southeast Asian practitioners. Aung San himself was in attendance at the 1945 celebrations to commemorate the twenty-fifth anniversary of Burmese film, and the post-independence government pledged to support the nation's film industry with a grant of 50,000 kyat (ခင်မောင်နု 1980, pp. 17, 19). During the post-war period to 1962, four Burmese films were exported and screened internationally: *Chit Pan Thazin*, *Bawa Thanthaya* (Life's Samsara), *Nga Ba* and *Mone Thint Hma Mone*. The film *Nga Ba*, produced by British Burma Film Company based on the novel of the same name by Maung Htin, was exported to China and the Soviet Union because of their interest in the film's socialist theme (တက္ကသိုလ်နေဝင် 1973, p 36). And whereas silent films were adapted with foreign language titles into their frames, the post-war "talkies" were dubbed into Chinese.

Studio film production in Burma had reached its apex in 1962, with ninety-two new feature films being shown across the 442 cinemas, not including outdoor screenings. But the subsequent decades soon saw a downturn in production (ထွန်းလှိုင် 2000, p. 188). The military coup of General Ne Win in March 1962 and the later installation of the Burmese Socialist Program Party would transform the motion picture industry — economically as well as ideologically. While all broadcast media had been under state control since the early days of colonial independence (Than 2002, p. 146), the post-1962 clampdown was decidedly more severe. Four months after Ne Win's March 1962 coup, the government banned any film — local or foreign — which was deemed to impinge on national unity, character, or the morale of the population (Charney 2009, p. 114).

The Ne Win government also took control of economic aspects of film production and distribution. Cinema magazines published announcements to readers when specific theatres were nationalized. This was a directive of the Ministry of Information, ordinance 3(ဆ) or number 306 (တတည်း 1969, p. 2). In many cases cinemas had been privately owned by foreign business interests, either Indian or Chinese, and with the increasingly xenophobic citizenship and residence laws, many cinema hall owners left the country. During the 1960s, as cinema halls were nationalized, their foreign names were replaced with Burmese ones; Palladium became Ba Ba Win, Excelsior became Waziya, and Galton became Yuzana, to name just a few (တက္ကသိုလ်ခင်မောင်ဇော် 2012, p. 32).

In 1963 the government established the Union of Burma Cinematograph Law, which stipulated government control over every aspect of the industry, from economic, to form, to content. The new law established the film Censor Board as a branch within the Ministry of Information. Depictions of the supernatural, *nats* (lingering ghosts of people who die violent deaths), ghosts and witchcraft were banned (တက္ကသိုလ်ခင်မောင်ဇော် 2012, p. 21). The justification for these ideological changes was that prior to the Revolutionary Council, for-profit films were made for sheer entertainment, but were not "true" entertainment but instead were poison for the masses. Since the installation of the new regime, one film magazine editorial — of course heavily censored itself — argues that since the installation of the Motion Picture Council, the old social, political, educational and cultural systems are gone, and instead the Council strives for the production of "Films for the People".[2] Such films include those that focus on rural and village life, news and documentary films — film artists make films to improve the level of art and knowledge. The purpose of filmmaking, as part of the march to socialism, is to stimulate change and educate, and as such the editorial argues that now ideas about social reality, politics and education are taking root and flourishing because of the new government (ရုပ်ရှင်မဂ္ဂဇင်း 1972, p. 2).

Because of the drastic changes in both the economy and the government scrutiny of all films produced in the country, producers found that a particular genre, the *thone pwint saing* ("love triangle"), would most easily acquire censor board approval. Historical topics, science fiction or anything remotely political would be likely to attract greater scrutiny, and thus less likely to make it to the cinema screens. Although the film industry continued to produce films throughout the Ne Win years, one can observe a distinct shift towards these "love triangle" films.

The political isolation of the country for all intents and purposes completely shut off the country to international film crews. The difficulty of obtaining visas to visit, let alone film a feature-length motion picture, precluded international crews from filming in the country. One exception is documentary filmmaker Adrian Cowell, who, working over a period of three decades, filmed *The Heroin Wars*, a nuanced three-part documentary about the relationship between the ongoing conflict in the Shan State and the United States Drugs Enforcement Administration's approaches to the global narcotics issue.

With the dissolution of the Burmese Socialist Program Party and the coup of the State Law and Order Restoration Council (SLORC) in 1988–89 came some changes to the structure of the film industry. The ideological dictum that the cinema should represent the "Burmese Way to Socialism" fell by the wayside. At the same time, the use of video, and later the VCD, meant that filmmakers could produce features in a fraction of the production time (and expense) that was required in earlier years. Although the censorship board was still in place, the government relaxed some of its strict controls over the economy, and changed immigration laws so that tourists could get longer visas to visit the country.

In the early 1990s, filmmaker Lindsey Merrison, with a background in Film Studies and English from the University of Kent, went to Myanmar to make a documentary about her own family's heritage in Burma. Deeply personal, the eventual 1996 film, *Our Burmese Days*, as Merrison described it, is "all about my mother's denial of her past and my Uncle Bill's embracing of it. The contrast was a real gift to the film."[3]

The experience encouraged Merrison to return to Myanmar a few years later, and she shot a documentary about spirit mediums, *Friends in High Places*, which came out in 2001. As she related to me in a 2016 interview,

Doing the filming was unwieldy. When we went to Mount Popa, kids would come up, curious about our Super 16 mm camera. It was also not easy to get the undeveloped film cans out of Burma. But, seeing the interest in the filming, that's when I realized it was time to give something back.

Merrison organized a film workshop to teach filmmaking to any interested student in Yangon. It took a year to obtain permission from the government to hold the workshop, but the momentum that the endeavour gained led to the establishment of the Yangon Film School in 2005. Since its opening, the Yangon Film School has held numerous workshops and longer courses, and has had more than two hundred students learn various aspects of filmmaking, from screenwriting to shooting, to editing, to animation. As Merrison reflects, "When we began the training, we had no idea it would blossom into this institution. It was the right thing at the right time, and they're in the position to make the films, to tell the stories they want to tell."

The operation of the school has not been without its struggles, often connected to the political climate and the desire to make socially engaged films. Following Cyclone Nargis in 2008, some Yangon Film School filmmakers took a great personal risk in trying to document some of the impact of the disaster. On the other hand, for the students who had never experienced such poverty and strife first hand, the act of working to make documentaries about the events was politicizing. In 2009, two Yangon Film School students were arrested for illegal filming; the police still had the ability to detain anyone filming in public without a permit. But this would change.

The Dawning of a New Era? Floodlights on Myanmar's Cinema

For many of the nation's cinema halls, the 2010 political transition came in like a wrecking ball. With changing technologies and skyrocketing land values in urban Myanmar, the movie theatres of old were purchased by developers, only to be destroyed to make way for new construction projects. Most conspicuously, the southern side of Bogyoke Aung San Road between Sule Pagoda Road and Pansodan Road, formerly the location of six theatres (or "Cinema Row"), now has only two cinemas left standing: Thwin and Waziya (formerly Excelsior). The Yangon Heritage Trust has sought to preserve the city's colonial architecture, and according to its website there are plans to renovate Waziya and update its technology, the projection booth and sound equipment. Waziya has also been used as the site for screenings associated with recent international film festivals, drawing international interest in maintaining the building for its historic value. New multiplex-style theatres have gone up in places like Yangon's Junction Square, but the concession stands sell popcorn, much to the chagrin and frustration of the sunflower seed crowd.

In terms of production, though, one immediately tangible result of the relaxing of media laws has been the launching of independent film festivals in the country. Wathann Film Festival, established in 2011, was the first, and it has consistently been held every rainy season in Yangon. Soon to follow was the Human Rights Human Dignity Film Festival (HRHDFF), held annually from 2013 to 2017, discussed in greater detail by Mon Mon Myat in this volume.

Hnin Ei Hlaing, a documentary filmmaker, was one of Merrison's first students at the Yangon Film School in 2005. She has been active in documentary productions of her own, including the 2013 documentary *Puppets beyond Borders* about puppet cultures in Cambodia, France, Indonesia and Thailand. Her 2011 documentary *Burmese Butterfly*, about Myanmar's gay community, has garnered international acclaim and has been featured in more than eighteen international screenings and festivals, including in Paris, Anchorage, Hanoi and Helsinki.

In response to how filmmaking has changed over the past ten years, Hnin Ei Hlaing immediately pointed out, "Nowadays it is possible to film openly in the streets, something that would never have happened ten years ago. In previous years, police would have questioned someone using a video camera."[4] Like Adrian Cowell, often filmmakers and videographers would document issues in ethnic minority areas protected by different armed groups, such as the Karen National Union or the Shan State Army. Indeed, there were exile media organizations based on producing media about this struggle.

Jai Jai, a young filmmaker from Tachileik, Shan State, is an example of someone who learned the art of documentary filmmaking in this milieu. He has since found his spot among the new generation of filmmakers in Myanmar. Growing up in Chiang Mai, Thailand as a teen, Jai Jai got a job working with the Shan Radio broadcast. Because the recording studio was based in the office of the now defunct media production NGO Images Asia in Chiang Mai, Thailand, he started to take a greater interest in video as a more exciting medium.

> When I was kid growing up in the Shan State, I never saw any documentaries about Burma. This was new to me. When I saw P'Sam (Sitthipong 'Sam' Kalayanee) doing work about social issues, such as the documentary about child soldiers in Burma, I started to really like it. P'Sam inspired me, but also I learned on my own, finding information about making documentaries, watching others make documentaries.

His documentary *An Old Man's Homesickness* was selected to be shown as part of the 2013 Wathann Film Festival. Having spent most of his adult life exiled in Thailand, Jai Jai was initially nervous about going to Yangon for the screening. "When I sent it for consideration, I was not sure if it would make it", recalled Jai Jai.

> I didn't know the situation for what might be censored. In the documentary, there are sensitive issues such as forced relocation and forced porters [for the Tatmadaw] but the documentary doesn't deal with those issues directly or explicitly. It is the old man talking about them. I was worried about what might happen if the police came to watch the film. I was excited and nervous about the film being shown in Yangon, whether I might get caught for that, but here I am back in Chiang Mai, so no problem after all.

Jai Jai also commented on the importance of independent documentary filmmakers, in that they can access topics and information largely ignored by the mainstream media. He used the example of his own documentary *Drowning a Thousand Islands* to illustrate this point. The twenty-minute documentary, freely available on YouTube, is an empathic portrayal of local villagers in Shan State who are confronted with the very real possibility that their homes will soon be destroyed by the construction of a proposed mega-dam project.

Because of the ongoing conflict in Shan State and government regulations on tourism and public access, the proposed site of the Mong Ton Dam has been off-limits to foreigners, including journalists and filmmakers. This proposed mega-dam in Shan State would create a reservoir the size of Singapore, and the Myanmar government would profit through the sale of electricity across the border to Thailand. Jai Jai's socially engaged documentary gives voice to local villagers that otherwise would be inaccessible to more mainstream journalists or filmmakers.

Other current generation filmmakers are eager to discuss the possibilities of making more documentaries on issues close to their hearts, and what it has been like getting the support to do so. Hnin Ei Hlaing commented, "So this year, I tried to make a film on the subject [of violence against women], *Dangerous Mute*. When I pitched the idea to a group, I got support from most of the women, but very few of the men."

Saw Reagan, noting the lack of educational access for children in ethnic minority languages, would like to use documentaries to draw attention and support to the issue.

> The ethnic nationality languages have not been supported by the government. I speak Pwo [in addition to Burmese] and can understand a bit of Sgaw. I would like to make a documentary to encourage more of these languages to be taught and for kids to take pride in these languages.

"For international film interest, now is a very good time for everyone. Before, hardly anyone ever contacted Myanmar, but with more international channels, we have to show what we have learned, we can demonstrate our talent", commented Hnin Ei Hlaing. Other filmmakers echoed this sentiment; Saw Reagan also observed that more people are working together to support the industry than ever before. But others were critical of the national entertainment industry, of the quality of mass entertainment currently screened in the country's cinemas.

Another current generation filmmaker, Thu Thu Swe Thein, sees the international attention and advent of international film festivals as a chance to force the Myanmar creative industries to innovate more than they have in the past. "As if it weren't enough that we have *copy thachin*[5] but in Myanmar there are also 'copy movies'. They take a script from before, make another movie, and they can find a market even with people reading the name alone."[6] This practice of "re-using" film plots is common throughout the industry; Hollywood is no stranger to the film remake, after all. These are referred to as *nam nao* in Thailand, where many television soap dramas constitute examples of the practice. Although the tension between mainstream entertainment "lowbrow" film and socially engaged/high art cinema is certainly not unique to the film scene in Myanmar either, the structural challenges of the years of censorship and lack of economic development make it all the more pronounced, or exacerbate the feelings among some audiences that the popular entertainment in the country is derivative, or easily sold out.

The film festivals have offered an important new venue for the public screening of films and documentaries that touch upon sensitive social issues, especially regarding topics that would have been blocked by the censorship board in years past. The success of the film festival has not been without its challenges. These have included threats of violence. I was on one of the prize juries for the 2014 Human Rights Human Dignity Film Festival when one of the principal organizers received a threat via an anonymous message on social media: if the film festival publicly showed the documentary *The Open Sky*, they would set off a bomb in Junction Square cinema during the screening. Shortly after receiving the message, Ko Min, eyes wide and mouth open in disbelief and concern, handed me his iPhone so I could read the message myself. My first thought was that it was an empty threat. But, feelings of fear and self-doubt enveloped me immediately. I quickly realized I had no way of knowing whether these people would follow through with such a sinister plan. After discussing the threat with the other organizers, they decided to remove the film from the schedule. I was not involved in the decision to pull the film from screening, but vividly remember the fear and concern that the threat engendered.

News of the organizers' decision spread and, arguably, the controversy allowed *The Open Sky* to get even more press than it might have otherwise received. During the awards ceremony, several of the speakers commented on the documentary, about how it was a message of peace and cooperation. The decision to capitulate to the terrorist threat was also met with controversy, some second-guessing the decision, saying that the festival organizers should not have given in to fear.

The twenty-minute documentary itself, by Kyal Yie Lin Six, Lynn Satt New and Phyo Zayar Kyaw, presents the story of the aunt of a young woman whose house has been burned down as a result of anti-Muslim hate. The film provides the aunt's view of the issue but also depicts the warmth of a Buddhist friend who helps her and their views about the conflict as well as their feelings towards each other. Ultimately, the film's message is one of humanity and friendship. During the awards ceremony it was observed that the fear-mongers should see the film.

The mainstream studios continue to play a fundamental role in the country's entertainment, though with the destruction of the old cinemas, audiences have migrated to the multiplexes sprouting up in air-conditioned shopping centres, where sunflower seeds have been traded for buttered popcorn as the movie snack of choice. Just a decade ago, mobile phones were prohibitively expensive for most people in Myanmar and, on top of that, service was spotty. With the increased networks of the government service, MPT, plus the advent of the private providers Ooredoo and Telenor, combined with the veritable flood of inexpensive smartphones from Thailand and China, social media has become the media platform of choice for many. This extends to film and video consumption as well, a point worth considering since solitary consumption changes the social experience of media. Web discussions create a different venue for sharing ideas about films as well, a point that I will not elaborate on here, though it certainly merits further analysis.

By being contemporary, films in Myanmar are not necessarily progressive. The 2016 film *Ot Cha Myak Pauk* ("Vagabond") presents a complicated case in point. A literal translation of the title is "grasses that sprout between bricks", though it is a figure of speech for rootless or vagabond; it could also describe someone who is a non-entity, homeless, jobless, or of poor moral character. *OCMP* (as Myanmar netizens have abbreviated it) was directed by Nyunt Nyi Nyi

Aung, who has more than four decades' experience in the Myanmar film industry. With the company Nyunt Myanmar, he has directed hundreds of films over the years. Upon the film's release in May 2016, it drew controversy and was accused of being Islamophobic, xenophobic and of using hate speech. The controversy re-ignited in March 2017 when *OCMP* received three Myanmar Academy Awards: Best Director (Nyunt Nyi Nyi Aung), Best Cinematography (Shwe Zin Oo) and Best Actor (Tun Tun). The recognition of the film provoked significant debate on social media. At the time of writing, this does not appear to have been resolved, but audiences have moved on to other controversies to debate.

Ot Cha Myak Pauk is an action movie that deals with issues of sex slavery and human trafficking. The perpetrators are evil foreign (Chinese and Thai) mafia, though there is one scene in particular that has attracted the most controversy. In the scene, the protagonist (played by hip-hop star Tun Tun) returns to his mother's home after his release from prison. He enters the house to find two Muslim children apparently reading the Qur'an. After he asks the children the whereabouts of his mother, the children's father enters and tells him that the house is his and that Tun Tun's mother sold it to him. As the story went, Tun Tun's mother had given the Muslim man shelter when he was homeless, but because Tun Tun was away and in prison the mother could not afford to keep the home, and thus sold it. The Muslim man said he would have let her stay on the property but she left to live in a nunnery instead. The scene is consistent with a Myanmar nationalist stereotype that Muslims are not grateful guests and that rather than live in harmony they eject their Buddhist hosts.[7]

Stereotyping and negative depictions of minorities and perceived enemies of the state are nothing new to Myanmar cinema (or popular media anywhere, after all). Incidents and controversies such as *The Open Sky* attracting bomb threats to film festivals or the themes and interpretations present in *Ot Cha Myak Pauk* show that the motion picture industry offers an incomplete reflection of existing social tensions and political change, and its mimetic power creates a site for repression as well as resistance.

Conclusions

The current atmosphere for film production in Myanmar is characterized by both an infectious enthusiasm for the medium as well as continued frustration and anxiety about the role of local filmmakers in the future. Filmmakers are all too familiar with the problems of start-up costs — as local filmmakers get to know more filmmakers internationally, they see that independent filmmakers elsewhere are also struggling. The increased international interest in the film festivals is encouraging, though some filmmakers wonder what will happen when Myanmar is no longer the trendy place that it currently is for the international artistic/development set. Many among the new generation of filmmakers have an ongoing personal commitment to documenting and creating artistic, educational films about social issues. Taking stock of the accomplishments of these young filmmakers in Myanmar, Lindsey Merrison notes how "They are committed in very different ways, and whatever happens to the wave, they will still have these skills; they have learned different ways of telling stories."

Furthermore, film festivals and schools such as the Wathann Film Festival, Human Rights Human Dignity International Film Festival, Yangon Film School and the Human Dignity Film Institute have allowed greater numbers of young people to get involved in filmmaking. Most notably, the graduates of the film school have included an increasing number of women and non-Burman ethnic filmmakers. Though there is much to be excited about in terms of developments in film production and the advent of international film festivals in the country, much work remains to be done. As Jai Jai explains,

> For film production, it is still not really free. If you critique the soldiers, you can still get in trouble. Even though they have a new government, they still can use some old media laws. For the Shan it is still difficult to tell the truth about some issues, they [the Myanmar government] can't accept it. For example: they couldn't show the film *Twilight over Burma* at Naypyitaw Cinema in Yangon because it was critical of the army.

Myanmar's film industry will celebrate its centennial in 2020. Whether the celebration will be just a fluff gala to commemorate the mimetic illusion, or whether it will touch on some of the ways film has challenged the status quo, one thing is certain: the level of critical engagement will be high.

Notes

1. Saw Reagan, personal interview, 2 December 2016.
2. In Burmese: ရုပ်ရှင်သည်ပြည်သူ့အတွက်
3. Lindsey Merrison, personal interview, 14 December 2016.
4. Personal interview, 2 December 2016.
5. A genre of popular music in Myanmar that is a Burmese-language adaptation of an international popular song, akin to a cover song, but in the Burmese language and performed by Burmese popular artists.
6. Personal interview, 4 December 2016.
7. Scene summary courtesy of Nyi Nyi Kyaw, personal communication, 24 March 2017.

English References

Aung Zaw. 2004. "Celluloid Disillusions". *The Irrawaddy* 12, no. 3 (March).
Charney, M.W. 2009. "A History of Modern Burma". Cambridge: Cambridge University Press.
Elliott, P.W. 2006. *The White Umbrella: A Woman's Struggle for Freedom in Burma*, 2nd ed. Bangkok: Friends.
Ferguson, J.M. 2007. "Watching the Military's War Movies: (De)Constructing the Enemy of the State in a Contemporary Burmese Soldier Drama". *Asian Cinema* 18 (2): 79–95.
———. 2012a. "From Contested Histories to Ethnic Tourism: Cinematic Representations of Shans and Shanland on the Burmese Silver Screen". In *Film in Contemporary Southeast Asia*, edited by D. Lim and H. Yamamoto, pp. 23–40. London: Routledge.
———. 2012b. "Le Grand Ecran en Terre Dorée: Histoire du Cinéma Birman" [The silver screen in the golden land: A history of Burmese cinema]. In *Le Cinema d'Asie du Sud-Est*, edited by J.P. Gimenez, pp. 25–37. Lyon: Asiexpo Association.
Grøn, N. 2016. *World Cinema beyond the Periphery: Developing Film Cultures in Bhutan, Mongolia, and Myanmar*. PhD Dissertation, Lingnan University.

Hamilton, A. 2006. "Cultures Crossing: Past and Future of Cinema in Socialist Southeast Asia". *Southeast Asia Research* 14 (2): 219–45.

Hanan, D., ed. 2000. *Films in Southeast Asia: Views from the Region.* Hanoi: SEAPAVAA.

Holmes, W. 1959. *Orient: A Survey of Films Produced in Countries of Arab and Asian Culture.* London: British Film Institute.

Lent, J. 1990. *The Asian Film Industry.* London: Helm.

Marsh, L.L. 2013. *Brazilian Women's Filmmaking: From Dictatorship to Democracy.* Chicago: University of Illinois Press.

Min Zin. 2004. "Digital Killed the Celluloid Star". *The Irrawaddy* 12, no. 3 (March). http://www2.irrawaddy.com/article.php?art_id=930 (accessed 11 December 2016).

Nandar Aung and Zon Pann Pwint. 2015. "A Flick Back to Myanmar's Golden Age". *Myanmar Times,* 22 May 2015. http://www.mmtimes.com/index.php/lifestyle/14633-a-flick-back-to-myanmar-s-golden-age.html (accessed 11 December 2016).

Yadana Htun. 2012. "Director 'Born' with Movie Industry Still Has Passion for Film". *Myanmar Times* 31, no. 615 (February): 20–26.

Burmese References

ခင်မောင်နီ 1980. ဗိုလ်ချုပ်အောင်ဆန်းနှင့်မြန်မာရုပ်ရှင်အစည်းအရုံးငွေရတုသဘင် [General Aung San and the silver anniversary of Myanmar film]. ရုပ်ရှင်မဂ္ဂဇင်း 1, no. 1 (September): 17–19.

စစ်ကိုင်းလှရွှေ 1981. ခေတ်ဟောင်းရုပ်ရှင်တေးအဖွင့် [A glimpse of films from the old era]. ရုပ်ရှင်မဂ္ဂဇင်း 2, no. 8 (November): 45–51.

တက္ကသိုလ်ခင်မောင်ဇော် 2012. မြန်မာ့ဂန္ထဝင်ရုပ်ရှင်အနုပညာရှင် (၂၀) [20 Classic Myanmar film artists]. ရန်ကုန် ရွှေစာပေတိုက်

တက္ကသိုလ်နေဝင်း 1975. နိုင်ငံခြားသို့မြန်မာရုပ်ရှင်တင်သွင်းရေးပြဿနာကိုစေတနနရှိသူတိုင်းစိတ်ဝင်စားကြသည်း [In the interest of international export of Myanmar films]. ရုပ်ရှင်မဂ္ဂဇင်း (February): 14–16.

စာတည်း 1969. ရုပ်ရှင်ရုံများပြည်သူပိုင်ပြုလုပ်ချင် [The process of public ownership of cinema halls]. ရုပ်ရှင်ပဒေသာ S1 (January): 1–4.

ထွန်းလှိုင် 2000. ရုပ်ရှင်ရိုက်သူများ [Filmmakers]. ရန်ကုန် ဝင်းမြင့်အောင်စာပေ

မောင်မောင် 1970. နှစ် ၅၀ မြန်မာ့ရုပ်ရှင်ခရီး [The fifty-year journey of Myanmar films]. ရုပ်ရှင်မဂ္ဂဇင်း 7 March 1970, pp 18–22.

မြန်မာ့နိုင်ငံ ရုပ်ရှင်အစည်းအရုံး 2004 မြန်မာ့သမိုင်း ၁၉၂၀ ပြည့်မှ ၁၉၄၅ ခုနှစ် [Myanmar National Film Organization, Myanmar film history, 1920 to 1945]. ရန်ကုန် မြန်မာ့နိုင်ငံ ရုပ်ရှင်အစည်းအရုံး မြန်မာ့ရုပ်ရှင်စိန်ရတုသဘင်ကျင်းပရေးသုတေသန 1996. ရုပ်ရှင်စာတမ်းငယ်တစ်ဆယ် [Myanmar film diamond anniversary commemorative history]. ရန်ကုန် မြန်မာ့ရုပ်ရှင်စိန်ရတုသဘင်ကျင်းပရေးသုတေသန ရာပြည့်မဂ္ဂဇင်း 2010. စွယ်စုံအနုပညာရှင်ဦးသုခ [Encyclopedia of the artist U Thukha]. ရန်ကုန် ကာလဘုံ

16

Films for Dignity

Mon Mon Myat

The moon is shining, some villagers are laughing out loud, and others weeping while they sit together in a village compound watching human rights films. A young girl stands up and reads Article 26, "the right to education", from a printed handout of the thirty articles of the Universal Declaration of Human Rights. If this were pre-2010, it would have been a dream. In 2004 a group of young men in Yangon were arrested because they handed out human rights flyers in commemoration of human rights day (VOA 2004). For almost five decades while the country was under military rule, even the words "human rights" were forbidden in public spaces. The dream has come true today, but it did not come effortlessly.

In 2013 I became the co-organizer of the Human Rights, Human Dignity Film Festival in Yangon. We organized the festival for a simple reason — we were very suspicious of the political reform process initiated by the Thein Sein administration, the transformed military government. Like many of our fellow citizens, we wanted to push the boundaries of the so-called quasi-civilian rule, by using the human rights film festival as a tool. That's how Myanmar's first international human rights film festival came to be. The landmark human rights event was held in Yangon for five years. A mobile film festival that brought human rights films to audiences across Myanmar also grew in scope.

The abolition of pre-publication censorship in Myanmar resulted in a certain level of media freedom for the print media, but not for the film industry. In 2014 the film censorship board was recreated as the "Film Classification Board" under the Ministry of Information. In order to screen human rights films in downtown cinemas, authorization was required from the Film Classification Board. Without that official piece of paper, none of the commercial entertainment companies would allow us to host the human rights film festival in their theatres.

Therefore, in order to keep the festival running, we did not select overly sensitive films. That might be called self-censorship; yet, in 2013, the first year of the festival, all films submitted to the Film Classification Board — including a documentary film about human rights violations in Myanmar prisons based on the story of a political prisoner — got the go-ahead to be publicly screened. A personal testimony of the human rights violations endured by political prisoners, *Survival in Prison*, gave the audience a platform to discuss the human rights abuses perpetrated by the former military government. San Zaw Htwe, the main subject of the documentary, who spent twelve years in prison, told the audience that his story was personal, and insisted that he did not speak for the many other political prisoners who had suffered more than he had or who had died in custody.

Human Rights, Human Dignity Film Festival in a Win-Win Situation

The first film festival was held during the honeymoon period of President Thein Sein and the newly elected MP Aung San Suu Kyi, a longstanding opposition leader. We were asked to send invitations to high-ranking government officials, including President Thein Sein, the chairmen of the parliament, and members of parliament. The patron of the festival, Aung San Suu Kyi, attended the awards ceremony and delivered a speech. Human rights is an eye-catching phrase for the international community. Allowing the festival to go ahead indicated that the Thein Sein government was supportive of human rights during the so-called period of political reform. We used the festival to highlight the important role of human rights defenders in the country's struggle for democracy (Mon Mon Myat 2013).

The first film festival was dedicated to Aung San Suu Kyi in recognition of her integral role promoting human rights in Myanmar. In her honour the awards ceremony was held on her birthday, 19 June, 2003. Aung San Suu Kyi and Min Ko Naing — the former prisoner of conscience, poet and legendary student leader who spent more than seventeen years in jail for his leadership of the student movement in 1988 — were the patrons.

The festival offered awards in four categories: Best Documentary Film (Hantharwady U Win Tin Award), Best Short Film (Min Ko Naing Award), Best Animation Film (March 13 Award), and Best National Film (Aung San Suu Kyi Award). As it is the date when the 1988 student uprising began, 13 March is widely recognized as Human Rights Day in Myanmar. The late Hantharwady U Win Tin was a human rights defender as well as a prominent veteran journalist.

In the early days of the political reform process, the film festival encouraged the audience members to stand up and speak for their rights. We tried to use the political space allowed by the quasi-civilian government as broadly as possible. Nevertheless, we were very much aware that the change was on the surface and not at the roots. An important barrier was lifted, however, when we began organizing travelling film festivals across the country.

Pushing the Boundaries

When we launched the travelling film festival in 2013 the greatest difficulty we faced was convincing local authorities to allow the festival to take place. Local military intelligence kept their eyes on the movements of the festival team. Although we knew we were breaking the law, over the first year we organized mobile film festivals in more than ten places without permission. In collaboration with university student unions, starting in 2014 we also tried to organize mobile film festivals in universities. But in order to avoid students gathering and organizing a movement in their universities, only a few school authorities granted us permission.

To encourage and support the production of local documentary films that address the key challenges of Myanmar's transition, we also organized human rights filmmaking workshops for young filmmakers. We trained a total of thirty-six students — twelve per year. As a result of running these workshops for three years, we produced more than twenty human rights focused films.

In the second year, 2014, the festival touched on a very sensitive area. As a society, we were a closed one, and the military controlled us by sowing fear and distrust. That is how Islamophobia become deeply rooted in our majority Buddhist country. The conflicts between Buddhist and Muslim communities worsened, especially in Rakhine State, where more than 700,000 people have been displaced since the start of communal violence in 2012.

Although the Film Classification Board had given its permission, a film produced by our students could not be publicly screened because of the objections raised by extreme Buddhist monks and a group of religious fundamentalists. Touching on the religious conflict between Buddhists and Muslims in central Myanmar, *The Open Sky* portrays friendship and loving kindness between a Muslim and a Buddhist woman. We held a press screening and an in-house screening, but the film was banned in theatres.

As a result of that controversy, nationalist monks and their followers disturbed a few of the mobile film festivals, and local authorities banned the festival in two locations due to the potential for religious conflict. These monks, who are members of the notorious religious organization Ma Ba Tha, which has a network across the country, sent letters of objection to the local authority in the town where we had planned to hold the festival. The letter mentioned *The Open Sky* film and warned that it would provoke religious conflict if the local authority allowed the screenings. Based on this concern the local authority denied us permission to hold the travelling film festival in those areas. Using the film festival as a lens, two kinds of censorship — state censorship through the Film Classification Board and community censorship in the name of religion — became clearer.

The third year of the festival coincided with the historic 2015 elections. Prior to the election, security was tightened around the country. Permission for mobile film festivals was denied in many places because of so-called national security concerns.

Social Change in Progress

Based on my experience running the festival during its first four years, media freedom and freedom of expression can be seen as improving and as a work in progress. There are a few indicators to measure the level of progress. It is getting easier to organize human rights film festivals in public areas, not only in large and small cities but also in villages. During public discussions after the screenings, audiences can practise freedom of expression and opinion, and they can participate in the festival without any political concerns. Thousands of audience members received flyers of the Universal Declaration of Human Rights and freely read them out loud in the festival sites and other public areas. Before 2010, under the military government, such activities were considered unlawful and threatening to national security.

Local filmmakers can touch on different human rights issues across the country, with the exception of some sensitive topics. Ethnic language films can tell the stories of human rights violations in remote areas. Rights of women and children are highlighted in the films, too. An award-winning short film, *The Buffalo Boy*, is a Ta'ang Palang ethnic language film that highlights the huge drug problem in ethnic areas and the threat it poses to women and children. With the support of the local civil society group Paung Ku, we also produced a feature-length documentary film, *Across*, in 2015. The film portrays the impact of the Shwe Gas Pipeline Project on local ethnic people living along the pipeline route. The film tackles the stories of people from Rakhine State, Shan State, the central part of Myanmar and the Ta'ang Palang area. In the film, protagonists speak their own local ethnic languages.

Thousands of people attended the screenings in more than ninety locations across the country. Twenty-one human rights films that we produced reached a national audience of seven million through regular television programming. In a short period we established the festival's key role in the culture of human rights in Myanmar.

Situation under the New Government

Myanmar's former president Htin Kyaw was a big fan of the festival. One of our student films, *Wellgyi*, shown in 2015, won an award at the festival. The film portrays the plight of nineteen farmers and their families from Wellgyi village who were sentenced to long prison terms because of their demand for land rights. Htin Kyaw joined the screening of *Wellgyi* in 2015 (before he became president) and offered financial support to a young girl, one of the protagonists in the film, whose parents were in prison. *Wellgyi* had a great impact. All nineteen farmers were released in an amnesty programme soon after Htin Kyaw took office.

The fourth year of the festival, in 2016, coincided with the hundred-day honeymoon period of the new NLD-led government. With huge expectations of the new government, we chose to screen a feature film, *Twilight over Burma*, as the opening film of the festival. The film tells the story of a detained Shan leader and his Austrian wife under the military coup in 1962. Yet unfortunately it was banned because of concerns that it presented a bad image of the military. In reality, banning the film presented a bad image of the new government.

In an interview related to the banned film, the former minister of information, Ye Htut, told the media that only the minister could make a decision to ban a particular film. In this case we learned that Pe Myint, the new minister of information, did not interfere in the decision. An ex-military official in a key position in the Information Ministry, who was notorious for heavy censorship practices and influential with the Film Classification Board, later told us that the board had made the decision. He admitted that although the film classification board is supposed to be an independent body, it is under the ministry's control. This also indicates that decision-making mechanisms in government institutions are largely militarized. Using the film festival as a lens, another sensitive area becomes crystal clear when the festival touches upon issues related to the military.

Six months after the new government took office in 2016, we were able to produce a programme, *Let's Make Film*, and broadcast human rights films in collaboration with the state-run TV station, MRTV. In addition, we implemented the *30 Films, 30 Rights* project, making short films about thirty articles of the Universal Declaration of Human Rights, with the support of MRTV and USAID. In 2016 we also organized more travelling film festivals in universities, together with student unions. During that time we did not experience any resistance to the festival activities in the universities, and university authorities offered support for the festivals.

The 2017 festival was the final one. As we had run the festival for five years during the political transition period, we believe we had raised awareness of human rights. Even without the festival we can continue raising awareness of human rights through other platforms, including submitting films to the *Let's Make Film* programme on the state channel MRTV. We cannot be certain the films will be accepted, but it is worth trying. There are also several film festivals in Myanmar now that not only focus on human rights but also on different contemporary issues. Those festivals can be alternate choices for audiences.

We place the highest value on the dignity of every individual. People have dignity when their rights are known, respected and exercised. Given the power of film and audio-visual communication, we have personally seen that films can set the public agenda, raise the voices of ethnic peoples whose rights are violated, and generate greater understanding among different groups. Because the ultimate goal of our organization was to achieve "a society of dignity" in Myanmar, films like these shown in the festival will continue to have an influence building a better society in our country.

References

Mon Mon Myat. 2013. "Democracy in Motion". *Bangkok Post*, 13 October 2013. http://www.bangkokpost.com/print/374418/.

VOA (Voice of America). 2004. "Distribution of UN Human Rights Leaflets in Burma - 2004-06-20". 20 June 2004. https://burmese.voanews.com/a/a-27-a-2004-06-20-7-1-93480614/1227815.html.

17

A "Fierce" Fear: Literature and Loathing after the Junta[1]

Ma Thida

In the surrounding darkness, bright lights focus on the speaker on the stage, a famous writer. The noise of an electric generator competes with his voice. He uses vivid metaphors to illustrate the wrongdoings of those in parliament and the government. The audience responds with a roar of cheers and applause: "Yes, they are idiots! Curse them some more!"

The speaker needs to wait a while for the people to calm down. But soon enough, words from his speech hit a nerve once again, and the audience goes wild.

This is a typical scene at literary talks in Myanmar. Historically, such talks were a traditional affair that became popular during Myanmar's colonial days, but they were unofficially banned by the military junta during its rule. Though they have once again become popular since the relaxation of restrictions in 2010, most attendees have never before experienced such events. In fact, the audience, especially those from rural areas, has had no exposure to literature at all, given the overwhelming censorship during the junta years.

Even among users of social media — who are likely to be urban, well off and with greater exposure to literature — it is clear that awareness of different literary forms is low. So much so that posts on online forums such as Facebook often include the disclaimer, "The following is a satire. Please don't take it seriously before you make (terrible) comments."

A History of Repression

This lack of awareness is a reflection of how the dictatorship crippled literature, the arts and media. From 1962 until 2000, all major print and broadcast media were owned by the state. The small-scale private media covered uncontroversial topics such as music, celebrity news, entertainment and sports. As a result, many citizens — including some writers — think the media are merely a tool to be used as a weapon for shaming or for propaganda. People also underestimate their own right to information, and the role of the media in ensuring this right. State media were used for government propaganda, and the media in exile turned into activist media determined to counter heavy censorship and the severe forms of control that stymied access to stories. In taking on the role of promoting democracy, the media in exile often lapsed into anti-government propaganda. As a result, instead of seeing independent media as a source of balanced coverage, people still think it is all pro- or anti-government. This is why some writers try to dictate their own opinions at literary talks rather than providing a holistic perspective with different opinions on the topics they talk about.

During the years of censorship, with a draconian censor board in charge, a writer could not write anything that might be seen as remotely anti-government or anti-establishment. Ordinary citizens learned what was going on inside the country either through "fiction" magazines or foreign-based radio stations. To get past the censorship process, writers needed to be careful about the way they wrote, compelling them to find creative solutions.

Metaphor, for example, was used not just as an aesthetic tool but also as a way to get past the eyes of the censor. One example is a story by the famous writer and journalist Hanthawaddy U Win Tin. In late 1988 Tin wrote a story about a crab. The crab, being hard-shelled, was well protected and could not be harmed. However, the mosquito, despite being a far smaller animal, could bite the eyes of the crab, leading to the crab's eventual death. The message to readers was to look for tiny weaknesses, even among the strong and well-protected people in power. Readers drew the conclusion that the socialist government of Ne Win was the crab that could be destabilized if a weakness could be found. Though there was heavy censorship at the time, the censors allowed this story to be published. After this, other writers frequently used "crab's eyes" as a metaphor for dissent. Changing names, genders, dates and other important facts to disguise the true story behind the "fiction" was another common practice for generations of fiction writers.

Oppression by a dictatorship — five decades in the case of Myanmar — not only affects people for the duration of the rule but also has a long-term impact on their way of thinking. These changes in mindset are hard to reverse — fear prohibits curiosity and learning, even after restrictions are relaxed. This repressed fear has already had a huge impact on people's awareness levels and interests. Today, for instance, the only common area of interest and knowledge shared by writers, speakers and their audience is the country's current situation; topics that deal with the current scenario are loosely grouped and categorized as "politics". Given the lack of exposure to literature, and because news was earlier disguised as "fiction", many see literature as a form of media. "Political issues" are at the heart of all communication between writers and their audience. Even poets write poems based on topics of current affairs, such as land confiscation by the military or government cronies, or student strikes for the reform of education laws.

Since reality was heavily fictionalized to evade censorship, readers found it hard to separate hard facts from fictionalized elements. Ordinary citizens could not openly talk about the ground realities. A heavy surveillance system operated under the Special Branch during the socialist days and the Military Intelligence Service during the time of the military junta. Self-censorship became a common practice for all citizens, not just writers, because of the fear of losing one's job, being banned from writing altogether, or worse, being imprisoned or tortured. Even reading certain books that were banned or blacklisted came with the fear of reprisals. Since no press entity could operate without a licence, the Press Scrutiny Board (operating from 1962 until 2012) would instruct licence holders to dismiss targeted staff members from their publication.

In Myanmar, because there is a small pool of "formal" names to choose from, people use nicknames to distinguish themselves from their namesakes. Readers only know a writer's nickname, not his or her "formal" one, with the exception of really famous writers. After writers became blacklisted by the military junta, their nicknames could not appear anywhere in print media, broadcasting media, or even in the obituaries section of state-owned newspapers, effectively blacking out any public presence or engagement.

After the famous writer Thar Du died, the names of his sons appeared in his obituary alongside their pen names — with the exception of the youngest, writer Min Lu, in prison for writing satirical poems. Only Min Lu's formal name was mentioned: Nyan Paw. However, the practice of blacklisting nicknames could also be helpful on occasion. The famous poet known as Tin Moe would have been denied a passport, as he was blacklisted by the authorities. However, he used his formal name, Ba Gyan, to apply for a passport, and got it easily, since his formal name was not commonly known and had not been blacklisted, thus enabling him to leave the country.

State violence towards activists has also had a huge impact on peer groups. Segregation and social discrimination towards family members of political activists were common practice during the junta. Even at school, children of imprisoned writers, editors and activists were discriminated against, both by teachers and other students. After activist Dr Zaw Myint Maung — now the chief minister of the Mandalay division — was imprisoned by the junta in 1990, his children were treated badly by their teachers and peers. People thought they might be seen as an enemy of the state if they showed any signs of supporting the family. During a prison visit to meet his father, Maung's eldest son once told him that though he was a hero among dissidents, he was not one in his own family.

Restricted Access

Militarization, centralization and "Barmanization" (Myanmar's majority ethnic group is Bamar) were effective tools used by the dictatorship to consolidate its hold on power, and everything — including art — was affected. Due to the decades of Barmanization, when only the Barman identity was promoted as a tenet of nation-building, most art forms did not reflect or include minorities. Yangon remains the only hub of art in Myanmar, and other demographically, ethnically and socially marginalized populations cannot easily access art or even the means to create it. The substandard education in schools and colleges — in addition to the censorship and propaganda deployed by the dictatorship — made citizens not only fearful of but also ignorant about basic things like human rights.

In addition, since many people were not allowed to know what was happening in the world, including in neighbouring countries, they were only able to compare their current situation to their own past experiences. This is why ordinary people often say that the 2008 constitution (implemented in 2010) is better than no constitution under the military junta — even though it is not democratic. Awareness about civic issues is low. During the era of the dictatorship, the education system demanded that students memorize texts, while prohibiting discussion and argument. Fear has also destroyed the normal process of thinking; there is a saying in the Burmese language: *"Tway ma lar, thay ma lar so yin, thaymae"* (Given a choice between thinking and dying, people choose to die).

Becoming "Fierce"

Passivity in the general populace is one impact of repression. It has also brought out the most basic instincts of self-preservation. Such attitudes cause people to become selfish in that they think of their own security before others and ignore the possible impact or consequences of their actions on others. I believe this phenomenon — to become "fierce" about one's own well-being — is a reaction to living under an oppressive regime. "Fierce" individuals do not seek to exact revenge on those who caused them harm; instead, they target weak individuals or minority populations — those who cannot retaliate. These acts of revenge are fuelled by a continued fear of dictators and brutal governance. It is my observation that writers and media personnel cannot always escape this cycle of behaviour, since brutality and state censorship were used to control them for decades. Fear not only makes people fierce in terms of their behaviour but also in how they express those thoughts.

The surveillance system made writers and even ordinary citizens distrust each other. The surveillance may not have been overtly carried out by the visible apparatus of the state, but by informers. This caused a great deal of insecurity and distrust of anyone other than one's immediate family members. Though hatred towards the authoritarian rulers may be an overarching emotion that is widespread among the population, it remains hidden within families because people are afraid to talk to non-family members about their miseries.

Since people were forced to suppress their own opinions, the lifting of restrictions led to the venting of repressed feelings of despair, anger and hatred, and, ultimately, violence. Most people still have no space to speak out; they attend literary talks as a form of catharsis. While most of them are still wary, they feel happy when their thoughts are expressed in the bold and vivid speeches of writer-speakers. But the "lecture format" of these events prevents ordinary citizens from participating and exercising their right to express their opinions freely. While people cannot hide their desire to seek revenge, they stop short of exacting it against those who harmed them — their previous fear of the authorities keeps them silent. Instead, they find scapegoats who cannot harm them but who may share freak similarities with their oppressors. The narration of a story at a literary event gives an idea of how this works:

There was a clerk called "A". He was seen as a very polite and quiet person at his workplace. His manager, "B", was a very arrogant and aggressive person and staff members only had bad things to say about him. The clerk, however, never showed any feelings and refused to gossip about B. Every day, the clerk was treated badly by the manager, but he still kept silent. At the end of each day, however, as soon as he left work, he went to a street massage shop. Since he was a regular customer, the owner always called for the person who usually took care of the clerk. This shop gave not only foot massages but also pedicures (in Myanmar, touching someone's feet is still seen as a servile act by many people). After being pampered by his masseuse, the clerk paid the fee and poked the masseuse's shoulder and said "goodbye B".

The trick to the story is that the name of the manager and the name of the masseuse are the same. Both the speaker and listeners enjoyed this story, as it was a blow against "managers" and other executive officials. They liked the way the end of the story had B bowing down to touch A's feet. This was seen as an enjoyable ending. They applauded wildly.

For me, this story and the reaction of the listeners reveal the thought disorder affecting Myanmar's people. Employee A hated Manager B but he could not, or dared not, argue with him. Instead, he held on to his anger and couldn't swallow his desire for revenge. He found someone whose name was also B, only a bit younger, poorer and with a low social status. He enjoys treating Masseuse B as his servant, even though he couldn't change his situation at work where he was the servant of Manager B.

This truly reflects Myanmar's deep and rotten societal wound that breeds intolerance, a desire for revenge, and the diversion of punishment from the powerful guilty to the powerless innocent. The relentless and forceful assault on people's resilience leads to this lack of tolerance. Some forms of hate speech in Myanmar have been very effective in igniting mob violence because people have been holding on to their anger, and now there is a desire to seek revenge against whoever they can target with impunity for their past sufferings. The naïveté of people — even in literary hubs — about what is going on in other parts of the country has encouraged some forms of ethnic and religious tension.

The long dictatorship has taught Myanmar's people that problems are solved only through violent reprisals and social discrimination. Since the dictatorship used existing laws to punish citizens, people think that the law is there to protect the government and allow it to take action against its own people. The culture of a dictatorship is truly infectious; most people just want to become dictators themselves when they have the chance. The blame-game becomes ubiquitous, since most people have no other way of contributing to the shaping of the politics in the country, nor do they dare to do so.

The Path Ahead

Media and literature in Myanmar cannot be successful without having sensational or sentimental elements. Most people are looking for their bitterness and pain to be represented, and they wait for opportunities to wreak their revenge. While ordinary citizens want to read or listen to people blaming the parliament or the government, they see these practices as performances that belong firmly in the media domain or literary sphere. Most do not care that their right to know has been violated by the lack of pluralism in spaces devoted to media or literature.

Even with the relaxation of censorship and improvement in press freedom, people still do not know how to protect their right to freedom of expression. They do not know how to be independent, since they have always depended on either fear of, or favour from, successive repressive governments. Even now, under the new government, people still cannot escape from fear and its consequence — the rabid fierceness. In such a scenario, the empowerment of citizens is critical. Civil and political space for the average citizen is still limited, and, while the number of civil society organizations has increased, most of them are still needs-based ones.

One recent entrant on to Myanmar's literary scene, PEN Myanmar, is hoping to change things. One of its regular activities is called Literature for Everyone (*Yahta Asone Asan*). This activity is participatory and is not like most literary talks. There have been more than a hundred such events in fifty towns. The ground rules for this new kind of "participatory talk" session are that all the participants sit on the same floor, in a circle. Everyone has an equal opportunity to speak, recite literature or make arguments. The lines between the writers and audience blur, and there is no unproductive naming and shaming. Many new members in the audience usually shed tears of excitement, overwhelmed at the opportunity to participate actively. Though most are initially reluctant to speak up, soon enough this inhibition disappears altogether and there is enthusiastic participation in writing and speaking activities. Some write their first original compositions during such events, and most of their work lays bare the realities of their lives and their thoughts about their situation.

Granting social security, encouraging social cohesion and transparency, in addition to encouraging people-to-people exchanges across social, cultural and political divides, would be helpful in treating the scars left on the collective psyche of Myanmar's people. Freedom of expression should be granted constitutionally, legally, institutionally and individually by amending the "Right to Information" and the "Freedom of Information" Bills. Minority-language rights and educational reform to deliver equal education opportunities for every citizen are also necessary, given the level of distrust and xenophobia among the populace. People who express opinions that do not constitute hate speech or incite violence should be protected. Public consultations on law-making processes should also be held systematically across the country. Fear — and its companion, fierceness — can only be vanquished by enacting such measures.

Postscript

I wrote A *"Fierce" Fear — Literature and Loathing after the Junta* in 2015 — just before the NLD took power. Since then, our feelings about the military have not changed. They have changed, however, about the NLD. We feel confused. What does the NLD think about free expression? What does Aung San Suu Kyi think? Someone should research this.

I have one question for Aung San Suu Kyi — is she still free from fear? She wrote a book called *Freedom from Fear*. Is she still free? Fear might be different now than what she described in her book. Fear is very fierce.

A lot of people don't even understand what freedom from fear is, even when they are fighting for free expression. They think they are free now, but it isn't real.

Note

1. This text has been minimally edited and is republished with permission from *Himal Southasian*.

Part IV
Society and Media

18

The Tea Shop Meets the 8 O'clock News: Facebook, Convergence and Online Public Spaces

Yan Naung Oak and Lisa Brooten

> "If the people get the right information about the army they will understand us.... They'll see the military is defending the interests of the people and implementing the interests of the people and defending against threats to the country."
> —Senior General Min Aung Hlaing[1]

> "We can say that we are free. But the problem is that we are not safe."
> —Blogger and activist turned politician Nay Phone Latt[2]

> "I attracted people to express their opinions and attitudes on my Facebook wall. Sometimes I feel upset and disappointed about the profane language used in writing on my wall. But, since the benefits outweigh the disadvantages, I shall continue to maintain this page."
> —Former Information Minister Ye Htut[3]

The opening of online spaces and the rapid dissemination of mobile phones since the beginning of the political transition have made possible a forum for discussion unlike any before in Myanmar's history. Yet shocking examples of online hate speech have dominated international media headlines. Facebook, especially, has been identified as a significant forum for inciting the brutalities perpetrated against the Rohingya Muslims in Rakhine state. In March 2018, the chairman of the UN Independent International Fact-Finding Mission on Myanmar, Marzuki Darusman, told reporters that Facebook had played a "determining role" in the conflict. In April, Facebook's CEO Mark Zuckerberg testified in front of the U.S. Congress about his company's response to these accusations. And in August, a UN-mandated fact-finding mission released its report calling for Myanmar's top military leaders to be investigated and prosecuted on charges of genocide, crimes against humanity and war crimes, and highlighting Facebook's role as a tool for those intending to spread hate. The release of this report sparked Facebook's decision the following day to remove eighteen Facebook accounts, one Instagram account and fifty-two Facebook pages affiliated with the military, including the official pages of Senior General Min Aung Hlaing, commander-in-chief of the armed forces, and the military's Myawaddy television network (Facebook 2018b).

Facebook's role in hate speech and the resultant waves of violence have dominated discussions and are detailed in the introductory chapter and the chapter by Sarah Oh in this volume. Yet the ways in which social media are bringing more hopeful new or hybrid forms of communication and expression are also important to highlight. In this chapter we discuss the rise of Facebook in Myanmar and examine in more depth the Facebook pages and profiles of ten public figures, including Senior General Min Aung Hlaing, to assess how they were using the networking platform during three one-month periods in 2012, 2014 and 2016. These periods allow us to observe as much as possible "everyday" usage of Facebook during times when there was no major election campaigning, outbreak of communal violence or other especially newsworthy event. As a result, Myanmar was also not a special focus of international media coverage during these periods.

During unusual events and everyday life alike, the tea shop has historically been Myanmar's quintessential public gathering space, a place to learn what was happening in the neighbourhood and the country — in essence, to learn what the 8 o'clock news was *not* discussing. In the days when the only available television channels were state-run, they would all air the same news broadcast at 8 p.m. The news was read in a stodgy, uptight manner, and mostly summarized the ritualized activities of the top generals that day: who went where, who opened what school or bridge, who donated or received donations on behalf of the public, who received which foreign dignitary.[4] The tea shop, on the other hand, is an intimate setting where people generally meet in discrete, small groups, but also where neighbours break into the conversation, debates emerge and arguments break out.

The tea shop and the 8 o'clock news now meet, metaphorically, online. This is especially the case on Facebook, by far the country's most popular social networking site, where military leaders and activists share the same virtual space, and where there is no direct way for state authorities to control or censor dissenting voices. In many ways, Facebook conversations mimic the tea shop in their comparative informality as public spaces, very different from the formality of government and officialdom, which also have a place in this forum.

The opening quotations from three of these public figures exemplify a variety of perspectives on the ways in which the new media environment is shifting the relationship between information, the public and the state. New forms of communication emerge when authoritarian approaches to information find themselves in the company of newer attitudes towards openness in online spaces. Here we examine this phenomenon and assess Facebook's contributions to the development of an invigorated public sphere in Myanmar.

Market Liberalization and the Rise of Facebook

The opening of the telecommunications market over the past few years has rapidly increased access to mobile phones and social media. By February 2018, estimates of mobile phone penetration as measured by active SIM cards had reached as high as 105 per cent (Telenor 2018), although this overestimates the percentage of the population with access, as many people own more than one phone (Aung Kyaw Nyunt, 19 July 2016). The number of unique mobile subscribers was estimated at 50 per cent of the population as of February 2018 (Telenor 2018). The telecommunications sector received more than 47 per cent of total foreign direct investment in the fiscal year 2016/17, eclipsing other sectors of the economy (Samarajiva 2016). Even in villages without electricity or running water, villagers own smartphones, and cell towers provide 3G/4G services connecting them with the internet, where many of them use Facebook. By February 2018, 80 per cent of mobile phone users in Myanmar used a smartphone, and 90 per cent of the population lived within the range of 3G/4G network coverage (Telenor 2018). Approximately 30 million of Myanmar's 54 million population are farmers, and many of them have now turned to Facebook for their news, abandoning the radio sets which at one time were the primary or only way for them to get current information (Mod 2016). It has become almost proverbial that for many in Myanmar, especially in the less tech-savvy rural areas, Facebook and the internet are synonymous.

Myanmar's lack of internet connectivity was the bottleneck for the widespread adoption of Facebook. Before cheap SIM cards, smartphones and 3G/4G mobile internet connections, the only people who could use Facebook had to have access to a laptop or desktop computer and an internet connection, so most people could only access it through an internet cafe, an office computer, or a friend's computer. Internet usage was therefore primarily utilitarian, limited to email services (primarily Gmail and G-Chat), VoIP and online news. Social networking was the domain of more privileged users, such as the early bloggers who had access to their own computers and internet connections.

The rise in popularity of social media coincided with political and media reforms under the Thein Sein government, including the 2012 abolition of pre-publication censorship. Many sites containing political content became accessible, such as websites of exiled news media (Poetranto 2012). Following this, the vast majority of previously blocked content was also made available. Online public discourse increasingly moved to Facebook.

These developments have made it harder for the government to impose direct censorship. Directly blocking traffic to Facebook would be ineffective, as they would have to block the entire social networking platform instead of selectively blocking content they deem sensitive. Instead, the Thein Sein government, the NLD government that succeeded it and the military have relied more on legal measures to repress dissent, especially the infamous Section 66(d) of the Telecommunications Law, as Gayathry Venkiteswaran, Yin Yadanar Thein and Myint Kyaw discuss in their chapter on media law in this volume. As of February 2019, 179 cases have gone to court using Section 66(d), despite civil society calls for 66(d) to be abolished, according to freedom of expression advocacy organization Athan (Athan 2008). The vast majority of these cases (all but seven) were introduced under the NLD-led government. Defamation lawsuits are just one of several strategies employed by governments in Southeast Asia to try to deal with the impact of these technologies. We turn next to what research has taught us about social media use and political change.

Social Media, Politics and Change

Although research on social media and social networking is growing rapidly, the literature on social media use by politicians and other public figures tends to focus on election periods, especially in Europe and North America. This research has noted how politics in the late modern societies of the global north have shifted from a focus on political parties to a more personalized genre of politics that blurs the boundaries between political, public and private spheres (Enli and Skogerbø 2013; Loader et al. 2016). This in turn has led to an increased interest in politicians' use of social media. Facebook and Twitter place the focus on the individual politician rather than the political party, thus expanding the realm of personalized campaigning and offering direct and inexpensive access to voters (Enli and Skogerbø 2013; Steenkamp and Hyde-Clark 2014). Facebook seems the preferred online service and, like other social media, provides a means for politicians and other public figures to get feedback from their constituents and to correct misrepresentations in mainstream media or posted comments (Enli and Skogerbø 2013; Steenkamp and Hyde-Clark 2014). Similarly, social networking sites like Facebook allow individual citizens, especially those who historically have not had access to communication technologies, to participate in online political discussions directly with high-profile people (Steenkamp and Hyde-Clark 2014).

Many studies have found that politicians' use of Facebook and Twitter, although growing, is still ineffectual in creating genuine two-way dialogues with the public, despite good intentions (Kakachia et al. 2014; Larsson and Kalsnes 2014; Macnamara and Kenning 2011; Nielsen 2010; Ross et al. 2015; Sørensen 2016; Steenkamp and Hyde-Clark 2014). Politicians are often more idealistic than realistic in their expectations that social media can contribute to democratic dialogue. This is problematic, since having a voice in democratic politics is valuable only insofar as politicians and others are actually listening, and if mechanisms exist to act on feedback from citizens (Macnamara and Kenning 2011). Social media raise expectations that politicians "communicate across the different political, public and private spheres", engaging in a greater degree of participatory communication and interaction (Loader et al. 2016, p. 417).

Social Media as Public Sphere

Many studies investigate the potential for genuine, public sphere-type engagement using social networking sites. In the online context, the public sphere takes the form of the "internet public ... wherein associations increasingly carve out spaces of networked interaction between remote actors" (Rahimi 2015, p. 269). Yet a single, unified and diverse public sphere has never existed (Habermas 1991); it is more useful to conceptualize the actual situation as comprising multiple public spheres (Fraser 1992), exacerbated in the age of digital media and social networking through increasing fragmentation. The resultant fragmented entities have been called "issue publics" or "issue networks", consisting of a "heterogeneous set of entities (organizations, individuals, documents, slogans, imagery) that have configured into a hyperlink network around a common problematic, summed up in a keyword" (Marres and Rogers 2005, as cited in Langlois et al. 2009, p. 428). Robertson et al.'s (2103) study of Facebook use among U.S. politicians suggests that social networking sites might be best described as "user-generated 'potential public spheres,' information-opportunity contexts that provide options for browsing, navigation and participation ...[that] become 'realized public spheres' only when people take action" (p. 122). Yet other evidence suggests that the very forms of online platforms "define the parameters for assembling issues and publics and circumscribe a horizon of political agency" (Langlois et al. 2009, p. 415). As our news is regularly filtered based on our browsing histories, we are increasingly shown what we want to see, and avoid things that challenge our worldviews (Filer and Fredheim 2016). This is detrimental to the development of engaged, inclusive discussion in an active public sphere, as "the internet public" is split into smaller publics increasingly isolated from each other.

Other researchers offer more hope for the development of online public discussions. Facebook and other social media clearly offer space for the emergence of issues and publics that have been marginalized by mainstream media (Langlois et al. 2009; McCarthy 2018; Subramaniam 2011; Weiss 2013). Breaking from earlier findings is a study by Sørensen (2016), who finds a comparatively high level of engagement in political conversation between Danish citizens and MPs using Facebook. Sørensen's (2016) study focuses on Facebook use outside of election campaign seasons, concluding that these conversations are not merely "echo chambers" but "a very lively debate ...[that] allows participants to engage with people they otherwise would not have exchanged political views with" (p. 681). Echoing other findings, however, Sørensen's (2016) analysis reveals varying degrees of engagement by the Danish MPs.

Compared to the research attention paid to Europe and North America, research on social media in Southeast Asia is sparse.

Social Media in Southeast Asia

Much of the early research on the uses of social networking sites in Southeast Asia focuses on the challenge they pose to authoritarian regimes through their ability to mobilize the populace, and only tangentially on their potential for promoting public discussion or interaction between politicians and citizens. Early Southeast Asian examples of the importance of the internet and mobile phone technologies include the 2001 Edsa II overthrow of Philippine President Estrada, the 1998 *reformasi* movement in Indonesia, in which the small number of those with internet access enlisted their sociocultural linkages to engage the broader population, and the importance of the news portal *Malaysiakini* and political blogging in the Malaysian *reformasi* movement (Abbott 2015; Subramaniam 2011). The use of social networking in Myanmar during the 2007 Saffron Revolution is well documented; although internet penetration in the country was low, activists and local journalists used this technology to network with dissidents and journalists in exile and to galvanize the transnational activist support movement (Abbott 2015; Dale 2011). The importance of social media became clear as analysts argued that the crackdown was ultimately far less severe than it might otherwise have been, and the international outcry against the regime's violence was immediate, including further sanctions from the United States and the European Union (Abbott 2015; Chowdhury 2008).

Because the concept of a public sphere, let alone its practice, is generally unknown or at least severely restricted in environments of strict censorship, it is widely assumed that participation in the development of a public sphere must be encouraged during any transition to a more democratic governing system, and online platforms are obvious tools in these efforts. In Malaysia, Subramaniam (2011) argues that online media circumvent traditional media, creating new forms of interaction outside of the control of power that facilitate the role of civil society, educate Malaysian society on key issues, and provide a platform for bloggers as a new set of "thought leaders" (p. 47). Weiss (2013), focusing on political mobilization in Malaysia, similarly found that new media offer new possibilities "for the articulation and activation of new conceptions of the political 'we'", making it "possible to reconceptualize the Malaysian public" (pp. 608–9). This is especially true, she argues, because online platforms provide discursive space unavailable elsewhere in Malaysian media (Weiss 2013).

A key development in building new forms of public communication and community, especially in highly censored and controlled environments, is the emergence of internet memes, which produce "a visual rupture in hegemonic state media and messaging by using the language of participatory creative media" (Mina 2014, p. 362; Rahimi 2015). In a highly censored state, microblogging and the use of social media offer a challenge to the isolation created by fear, providing "puns and images [that] slip past machine and human censors through coded verbal and visual language" (Mina 2014, p. 364). Memes pass rapidly from one user to the next, often being transformed along the way, so that they generally have multiple, unknown creators (Rahimi 2015). Through such tiny actions as sharing or localizing a meme in environments of highly controlled state messaging, people "break the illusion of unitary opinion that propaganda attempts to generate" (Mina 2014, p. 369). As Mina (2014) notes, "in the case of severely-censored topics … memes make the difference between no mention of [the subject] and hundreds of messages about [it], between fearful silence and raucous laughter … a basic declaration of humanity composed of creative, idiosyncratic media" (Mina 2014, pp. 370, 372).

Research has also begun to demonstrate how Southeast Asian political elites have moved their divide-and-rule strategies online, "exploiting deep-seated ethnic, religious and racial cleavages" in a regional version of the broader, worldwide trend of declining internet freedoms (Sinpeng 2017, ¶4; Weiss 2014). Leong (2017) traces how Myanmar mobile phone users adopt apps, arguing that a "two-step access" model of acquisition includes mediators — such as phone shops or social networks — that help common people navigate the complicated process. The internet and mobile devices also "further enhance existing social, economic and knowledge divides", reinforcing this common research finding (Leong 2017, p. 143).

While Facebook is by far the most popular social network across Southeast Asia, studies of its use or importance in the region have only recently begun to emerge. Grömping and Sinpeng (2018) found evidence of a gradual movement towards a more inclusive public sphere in Thailand in their study of differences in communication styles on Facebook by two differently organized social movement organizations. They found evidence of an increasing "actualizing" communication style in the use of crowd-sourced information on the Facebook page of the grass-roots "crowd-enabled" movement's page they examined, compared to the more centrally organized "organizationally brokered" movement's page, although a "dutiful" communication style dominated the pages of both groups (Grömping and Sinpeng 2018). McCarthy (2018) argues that people's access to and use of smartphones and online social media do not immediately change their deeply embedded cultural practices, such as the practice of "swapping rumours and pieces of information in an attempt to construct a narrative of meaning" learned under years of authoritarian rule and censorship (p. 94). Nevertheless, Facebook use in Myanmar has provided a means for people to engage online beyond their kin and friendship networks, "albeit mediated through the Facebook pages of prominent local social and religious actors" who generally reinforce the "echo chamber" effect and in-group and out-group boundaries within their insular networks (McCarthy 2018, p. 94). Yet Facebook is allowing a broader range of actors to become socially and politically engaged online, "inspiring citizen social action, reformulating civil–military relations and playing an essential role in defining parameters of the national political community" (McCarthy 2018, p. 97), including reinforcing existing divisions, such as rural-urban inequalities in access.

The role of Facebook and other online platforms in the communal violence in Rakhine State is now emerging as a topic of academic research. These platforms have provided space for long-suppressed anti-Muslim voices to erupt, and for high-profile Buddhist nationalists such as Ashin Wirathu to spread his sermons — littered with misinformation — and to gain followers (Lee 2016). Schissler (2015) discusses the development of anti-Muslim discourses in Myanmar and asks how the country's long-established communication patterns either align with or are disrupted by new technologies. He points out how Facebook provides the chance to access information with the "plausible deniability of a bystander, one who overhears communication but is not involved and thus not at risk", a deniability that can be furthered by using a fake identity online (p. 218). He also warns us not to focus on these technologies and "assume a kind of false-consciousness for people in Myanmar in which Buddhist-Muslim conflicts are primarily a function of 'untrue' information made newly available and accepted" (p. 231). While the new technologies incorporate traditional communication practices, he argues, they also help in the process of restructuring these practices (Schissler 2015).

This chapter aims to contribute to the ongoing discussion of how social networking sites are being used during periods of political transition and their potential for invigorating public discussion and debate. We address the following questions, which have guided this research:

1. In what ways are key figures in Myanmar using Facebook? How has this changed since the rapid introduction of the internet as a mass medium in Myanmar, beginning in 2012? Which issues have gained the most attention, as indicated by the degree of engagement with posts?
2. To what extent do politicians and other key figures engage in political conversations on Facebook threads in response to posts made by these key figures? Do these conversations suggest that Facebook contributes to political dialogue and a public sphere in Myanmar?

Methodology

We follow the Facebook activity of ten prominent people, examine what kinds of topics they discuss, and assess the degree of engagement in response to these topics. We used a purposive sampling method in which the data analysed were chosen for their relevance in answering the research query (Lindlof and Taylor 2011; Riffe, Lacy and Fico 2014). The public figures analysed here were chosen for their active public profiles and Facebook pages, and to present a cross section of the public Facebook profiles and pages in Myanmar. To assess a heterogeneous sample, we chose public figures who would be recognized by anyone with a basic political awareness of Myanmar, as well as some who are prominent but only familiar to close observers of political news. They are introduced in more detail below. We assessed the degree of interaction in response to their posts using Sørensen's (2016) framework. Merely commenting on a thread did not constitute a conversation in this definition, which requires that the participant re-enter the thread at least one time to reply to a comment on their own post, indicating a willingness to listen and react to others' comments. We coded political posts into Sørensen's (2016) four categories: (1) no conversation; (2) conversation between followers/citizens; (3) conversation between the public figure and followers/citizens; and (4) conversations both between citizens and between citizens and the public figure(s) (p. 667).

The data are drawn from three one-month periods; specifically, September 2012, September 2014, and September 2016. There was no significant election campaigning during theses months. They provide examples of activity during the early days of Facebook use in Myanmar (2012), the year Facebook was most enthusiastically gathering steam (2014), and nearly a year after the 2015 elections (2016). For each of these one-month periods, we analyse:

1. the number of posts and which posts garnered the most reactions for each of the ten active public figures;
2. the degree and kinds of conversations found in these comments (drawing from Sørenson's four categories); and
3. a more in-depth analysis of the topics of these conversations and the general tone of the posts and comments.

There are two primary forms of data available from Facebook: public pages, and private groups and individual profiles. The data from public pages is much more easily accessible through Facebook's Graph API (application programming interface), which allows the contents of posts and comments of public pages to be collected and analysed in bulk. Obtaining data from pages of private groups and profiles requires scraping data from the HTML content of the Facebook pages. In this way, we were able to obtain data about the contents of personal Facebook profiles, such as posts and comments, the number of likes and the number of shares. Both of these methods were used to collect the raw data about each of our key figures' Facebook activities.

Facebook Use in Myanmar

In answering our first research question, which asks how the key figures are using Facebook and how this has changed since 2012, we first sought to quantify the general rise of Facebook usage in Myanmar over the past few years.[5] While newspaper and other reports are often inconsistent, in August 2013 reports indicate an estimated one million monthly active Facebook users (Nyi Lynn Seck 2013), and as of August 2018 this had grown to an estimated eighteen million (Long 2018). As an indication of how Facebook usage has changed since 2012, we plot the Facebook page of *7Day News Journal*, the Myanmar Facebook page with the highest number of fans — 16.8 million when we began this research in July 2017. Figure 18.1

plots the trend in the frequency of posts and the average likes, comments and shares per post, month by month. Although limitations of space permit us only to discuss the trend for *7Day News Journal*, most of the twenty most popular pages in Myanmar follow the same trend.

The number of likes, comments and shares of posts on this Facebook page were almost negligible until 2012, then dramatically increased in the latter half of 2014, corresponding with the liberalization of the telecommunications market. The frequency of posting increased significantly at about the same time. Likes, comments and shares noticeably peaked in mid-2015 and have slowly declined since then. This trend may reflect a change in usage patterns, in that new users of Facebook are more likely to interact with the platform than more experienced users (Armstrong 2017). Another possible reason may be that as more and more public Facebook pages were founded and started posting content, each page's posts would show up less frequently in the user's timeline, resulting in less interaction (Armstrong 2017). Research in various countries also shows that people are increasingly relying on social media for information during election campaign periods, possibly a factor in the increase in Facebook posting and reactions during the months just prior to Myanmar's November 2015 elections (Lang 2016).

The bulk of our analysis focused on the ten public figures, starting with the number of posts, the number of reactions to posts, and the number of comments and shares of posts. We first examined the top twenty posts from the month of September for each of the three years, based on the number of reactions; 19 of the 20 posts were from 2016 (with one outlier from 2012), so we then also examined the top posts from our ten public figures in 2014, resulting in a total of 14 posts (and their comments), as only seven of the ten were posting regularly in 2014.[6] We analysed only original posts and the reactions they elicited, as opposed to posts from other people posted to the public person's timeline. Posts were drawn from the same three months for everyone, although most did not have active Facebook pages or profiles in September 2012, and a few were not then as well known to the public as they are now.

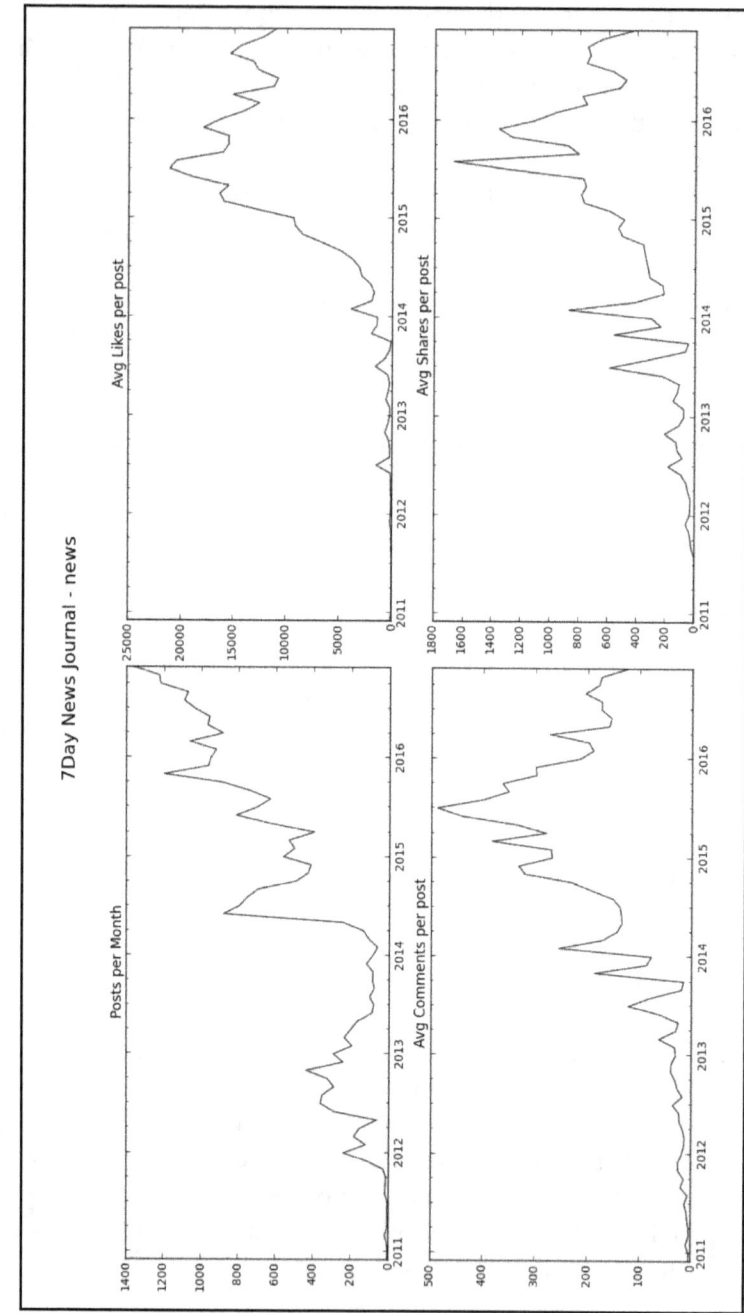

FIGURE 18.1
Facebook posts per month, average likes, comments and shares per post for *7Day News Journal* from the founding of the Facebook page in 2011 to the end of 2016

Ten Public Figures: Profiles

Five of our ten public figures are affiliated with the National League for Democracy (NLD), three with the Union Solidarity and Development Party (USDP) affiliated with the military regime, one with the military, and one with the 88 Generation Students. Two out of the ten are women. Four are serving as members of parliament in the Hluttaw's second session that began after the NLD won its majority in 2015, and five served in the first session from 2010 to 2015. Two served for both sessions. Among the seven who serve as MPs, one serves in a regional parliament (Yangon Region), one in the upper house (Amyotha Hluttaw), and five in the lower house (Pyithu Hluttaw). Five have public Facebook pages, and the other five have publicly accessible but personal Facebook profiles. We introduce them briefly here.

Senior General Min Aung Hlaing, commander-in-chief of the military, had an extremely active Facebook page until it was removed by Facebook in August 2018, to promote the continued role of the military in Myanmar politics. Facebook posts criticizing or mocking the military or Min Aung Hlaing himself often raised his ire, at times resulting in lengthy arguments online as well as several lawsuits and imprisonments (McPherson and Cape Win Diamond 2017).

Former Minister of Information and Presidential Spokesman **Ye Htut** made such active use of Facebook that he was dubbed the "Facebook Minister". Like the accounts of other officials, Ye Htut's Facebook page became a key source of information for citizens and journalists on official government positions, as well as on important issues, such as his post announcing the winning bidders in mid-2013 of the country's two new mobile telecommunications licences. Ye Htut also used Facebook to critique and circumvent media outlets' reporting by addressing the public directly.

Former Myanmar army lieutenant-general and Union Solidarity and Development Party MP **Hla Swe** is so prolific a user that he has published a book of his Facebook posts. He is widely known by the nickname "Bullet Hla Swe", said to originate from his hard-line stance in negotiations with ethnic opposition forces. His conservatism, staunchly pro-military views, and Facebook rants have been controversial, such as his posts calling homosexuals "useless" and "fake people", provoking hundreds of critical comments, which he angrily debated.

Sein Win is an NLD MP from Ayerwaddy region in the Amothya Hluttaw (upper house) and an active user of Facebook, despite maintaining a low profile and a small footprint in English-language media. He was elected in the 2012 by-elections in which the NLD competed. In July 2017 he resigned from the NLD, citing a lack of freedom. He is the only NLD MP elected to the upper house in 2012 who is active on Facebook.[7]

Burmese politician and former political prisoner **Phyo Min Thein** is currently serving as chief minister of Yangon Region and representing the NLD as Yangon Region Hluttaw MP for Hlegu Township. He is an avid Facebook user, informing people about his daily activities and regional government news, generally before the private media post such news.

Min Ko Naing is the former chairman of the All Burma Federation of Student Unions, a leader of the 1988 uprisings, and a long-serving political prisoner who has become one of the most influential leaders in the country. He is a founding member of the 88 Generation Students lobbying for political change in Myanmar.

Thura Shwe Mann is the former Speaker of Myanmar's lower house and a rather late starter on Facebook, establishing his profile in September 2015, around the same time he was ousted from his official position as head of the USDP in a high-profile purge. He had been a protégé of Senior General Than Shwe and was considered the third most powerful man in the State Peace and Development Council. He is known to have built a close relationship with Aung San Suu Kyi and was reportedly expelled from the USDP in April 2017.

Zin Mar Aung is a women's rights and ethnic rights activist, a former political prisoner who spent nine years in solitary confinement, and is currently one of the most active NLD MPs, representing Yangon's Yankin Township. In 2012 she was the recipient of the "International Women of Courage" award presented by then U.S. Secretary of State Hillary Rodham Clinton and then First Lady Michelle Obama.

Hla Hla Soe is a Karen activist of the '88 generation students, a women's rights advocate, and one of only twenty-three women elected as an MP in the upper house of parliament, representing the NLD for the Yangon Region.

Nay Phone Latt is a prominent early blogger who was imprisoned from 2008 to 2012 for his political activism related to the 2007 Saffron Revolution. After his release he formed the Myanmar ICT Development Organisation (MIDO), which promotes digital rights, digital inclusion and digital security in Myanmar. He won a seat in 2015 as an NLD MP for Yangon's Thingangyun Township, and is a founding member of PEN Myanmar.

Baseline Data for the Ten Public Figures

Table 18.1 provides a quantitative overview of the data analysed. It shows the profiles and pages of the public figures sorted in descending order of the median number of reactions to a post, as this was most indicative of the amount of engagement. As can be seen, there is quite a range in terms of frequency of posts and levels of engagement, as measured by comments and reactions. Hla Hla Soe posted on her Facebook profile with the highest frequency, with a total of 584 posts over the three months, whereas Thura Shwe Mann posted with the lowest frequency, with only 8 posts in total over the same three months. This contrasts with the engagement received per post: Thura Shwe Mann's posts received a median number of more than 11,000 reactions and 469 comments, whereas Hla Hla Soe, despite her high frequency of posting, received very few reactions and comments. Not surprisingly, posts from the more high profile of our public figures tended to garner more reactions than those less well-known.

Although our analysis of the top posts in the next section demonstrates public engagement on the Facebook pages and profiles of these public figures, a natural question is whether the same level of engagement is prevalent for all the posts of these public figures, or only for a select few. Table 18.1 shows the highest number of comments and reactions received by the posts within the three months in contrast to the median number of comments and reactions. For example, the highest number of reactions for posts by Phyo Min Thein and Ye Htut have more than 200 times the number of reactions than their median posts. This indicates that the levels of engagement in the top posts that "go viral" are outliers and are not sustained for every post these public figures make. This figure is far smaller for others, such as Zin Mar Aung, suggesting that fewer of her posts go viral.

TABLE 18.1

Posts per month for the Facebook profiles and pages of the ten public figures analysed, along with the median and highest numbers of comments and reactions, sorted in descending order by the median number of reactions to a post

Name	Number of Posts			Median Number of		Highest Number of		Followers as of Aug 2017
	Sep 2012	Sep 2014	Sep 2016	Comments to a Post	Reactions to a Post	Comments to a Post	Reactions to a Post	
Thura Shwe Mann	0	0	8	469	11,501	1,077	19,063	495,135
Min Ko Naing	0	15	8	60	2,290	287	14,768	240,691
Min Aung Hlaing	0	48	63	31	2,167	1,480	29,834	1,236,203
Hla Swe	0	82	119	59	1,273	1,520	15,099	378,445
Nay Phone Latt	5	0	26	9	503	108	3,283	700,429
Ye Htut	67	78	69	37	101	1,629	25,501	Unknown[a]
Zin Mar Aung	0	0	30	0	59	7	389	17,940
Sein Win	0	24	236	2	46	23	301	689
Hla Hla Soe	49	278	257	1	32	103	622	6,407
Phyo Min Thein	0	89	16	0	25	109	5,518	101,679

Note: (a) Ye Htut has set the privacy settings on his Facebook Profile such that the number of followers that he has is not publicly displayed.

Top Posts

To assess what kinds of discussions and topics have generated the greatest response, we examined the top two posts from 2014 and 2016 from the Facebook pages of the ten public figures we feature here, as indicated by the number of comments, reactions and shares. Table 18.2 lists all these posts in descending order of the number of reactions they received. An outlier from 2012 was included because it received the second highest number of reactions out of all of Ye Htut's posts and the third highest number of reactions in our sample.

These posts introduce a wide variety of topics and discussions, including the situation in Rakhine State, news about Aung San Suu Kyi — especially reactions to her September 2016 trip to London — commentary about the arrest of journalist Swe Win, along with posts focused on the military and their activities, on Myanmar identity, and on various local issues. There are also many posts of a personal nature, and others that use parables or present a moral charge to their readers.

Posts by Senior General Min Aung Hlaing, who had the top-ranked post in both September 2014 and 2016, clearly garnered the greatest number of reactions in our sample. The Facebook page of former minister of information Ye Htut came in a close second. The tone of these top-ranking posts is very different, however; Min Aung Hlaing, as well as the former speaker of Myanmar's lower house Thura Shwe Mann, posted more formal posts generally followed by comments of praise and occasional critique, in contrast to the playful, joking feel of some of Ye Htut's posts and the comments that follow, and the informality of former army lieutenant-general and Union Solidarity and Development Party MP Hla Swe's posts. Clearly, not all top leaders feel the need to be formal or serious.

Next we focus on several of the key issues or themes that emerge in our public figures' top posts.

TABLE 18.2
Top two posts of the ten public figures for September 2014 and September 2016 (with an outlier from 2012), ranked in descending ordering according to number of reactions

Rank	Public Figure	URL	Date	Reactions	Comments	Shares
1	Min Aung Hlaing	http://bit.ly/2xExXLG	8 Sep 8 2016	29,598	1,471	11,249
2	Ye Htut	http://bit.ly/2iASa2j	12 Sep 2016	25,394	1,620	2,305
3	Ye Htut	http://bit.ly/2vulA4a	15 Sep 2012	23,888	379	117
4	Thura Shwe Mann	http://bit.ly/2iB4hwz	9 Sep 2016	18,957	771	2,776
5	Thura Shwe Mann	http://bit.ly/2xEE3fh	13 Sep 2016	15,730	1,075	5,680
6	Ye Htut	http://bit.ly/2vu0mDu	26 Sep 2016	15,212	915	2,850
7	Hla Swe	http://bit.ly/2vBl4ke	22 Sep 2016	15,003	1,512	4,031
8	Min Ko Naing	http://bit.ly/2wgB9h6	12 Sep 2016	14,716	285	7,241
9	Min Ko Naing	http://bit.ly/2wKB3l4	18 Sep 2015	13,495	345	3,718
10	Min Aung Hlaing	http://bit.ly/2wTCVaz	24 Sep 2015	11,742	135	815
11	Min Aung Hlaing	http://bit.ly/2xphOL4	16 Sep 2014	10,266	572	424
12	Hla Swe	http://bit.ly/2vtSZfw	12 Sep 2016	6,758	619	2,592
13	Ye Htut	http://bit.ly/2ggwjMX	5 Sep 2014	6,664	386	363
14	Ye Htut	http://bit.ly/2w9PehT	25 Sep 2014	6,016	644	161
15	Phyo Min Thein	http://bit.ly/2izPMc8	4 Sep 2016	5,497	114	0
16	Min Aung Hlaing	http://bit.ly/2ghE05J	20 Sep 2014	4,661	247	255

17	Nay Phone Latt	http://bit.ly/2vB4yAz	3 Sep 2016	3,247	71	243
18	Min Ko Naing	http://bit.ly/2ghXtD7	12 Sep 2014	2,631	52	692
19	Hla Swe	http://bit.ly/2vjcl5n	29 Sep 2014	2,620	314	290
20	Min Ko Naing	http://bit.ly/2xoRVL2	22 Sep 2014	2,291	53	622
21	Hla Swe	http://bit.ly/2xp0plo	30 Sep 2014	2,150	176	88
22	Nay Phone Latt	http://bit.ly/2xEx5GY	27 Sep 2016	2,003	107	156
23	Phyo Min Thein	http://bit.ly/2xoRkJs	Sep 29, 2016	1,959	46	0
24	Hla Hla Soe	http://bit.ly/2vACwFC	24 Sep 2016	621	41	0
25	Hla Hla Soe	http://bit.ly/2wB67Dn	18 Sep 2016	545	103	104
26	Zin Mar Aung	http://bit.ly/2xEx45S	3 Sep 2016	389	7	60
27	Sein Win	http://bit.ly/2ggzJ2j	7 Sep 2016	301	6	178
28	Sein Win	http://bit.ly/2w9XbDY	4 Sep 2016	256	23	31
29	Sein Win	http://bit.ly/2ghh3j1	11 Sep 2014	218	9	2
30	Zin Mar Aung	http://bit.ly/2wKop5B	3 Sep 2016	215	2	19
31	Hla Hla Soe	http://bit.ly/2iAtMht	21 Sep 2014	134	7	1
32	Hla Hla Soe	http://bit.ly/2iAtSpl	20 Sep 2014	133	5	2
33	Phyo Min Thein	http://bit.ly/2vtEcRV	10 Sep 2016	130	21	1
34	Phyo Min Thein	http://bit.ly/2gheKMI	27 Sep 2014	75	0	11
35	Sein Win	http://bit.ly/2vu9R5B	10 Sep 2014	16	5	1

Note: Data obtained from Facebook on 27 August 2017.

Rakhine Commission

The top and fourth-ranked posts in our sample focus on the Rakhine Commission, whose work was launched in 2016, including a visit in September by the commission's head, former UN secretary-general Kofi Annan. The largest number of reactions in our sample was to a post on Min Aung Hlaing's Facebook page on 8 September 2016 entitled "Senior General MAH met Kofi Annan, who had just been appointed to head the Rakhine Commission". This post seems to have been written by a staff member, as it discusses Min Aung Hlaing in the third person, uses formal, official language, and is provided in both key Myanmar language encodings — Zawgyi and Unicode. It includes three photographs of a formal meeting room in the capital, Naypyidaw. The fourth-ranked post in our sample is by Thura Shwe Mann from 9 September 2016, featuring a picture of him at his office desk wearing a formal work jacket, with the hashtag "Things to be Mindful About the Rakhine Commission", and a list of bullet points. Both posts use language that evokes national unity, security and sovereignty and that excludes the Rohingya from their constructions of Myanmar identity, with Min Aung Hlaing identifying them as Bengali and Thura Shwe Mann arguing that they are not a national race.

These posts generate a lot of reaction and play into popular nationalist sentiment by rhetorically excluding the Rohingya from citizenship and questioning the presence of foreigners on the commission. The two comments with the most "likes" (more than 290 each) following Min Aung Hlaing's post about meeting with Kofi Annan praise the senior general as the "most trustworthy leader on issues related to race, language and religion", and on his knowledge of history. The third most liked comment (196 likes) contrasts him with Aung San Suu Kyi, saying "for people who keep asking if there is anyone more qualified than Aung San Suu Kyi in Myanmar, here is [an] example of a true leader". Interestingly, this comment gets considerably more replies than any other, with the majority criticizing the commenter for not thinking highly of Aung San Suu Kyi.

The fourth-ranked post, by Thura Shwe Mann, also focused on the Rakhine Commission and drew comments expressing support for the steps taken by the new NLD government on the issue, criticizing the previous regime's handling of it, and emphasizing the need to avoid blindly nationalistic behaviour. The comment with the most likes on this post argues that the previous government politicized the issue along racial and religious lines, and that the commission is a practical step by Aung San Suu Kyi. Another of the top comments asked why the previous government's handling of the issue exacerbated the problem, to which someone replied, "because they only know how to use guns".

These two posts provide evidence of a more personalized form of political discourse emerging alongside online forms of old-style, official military and state discourse, but they also indicate the transfer of clientelistic patterns of behaviour into Facebook discourse. They provoke discussion between NLD supporters and detractors, but there is also evidence that commenters tend to post on the pages of those they support. This is likely to further encourage the formation of separate public spheres that function to segregate the country's many ethnic and political groups into camps of the like-minded and threaten the development of a collective national identity.

Myanmar Nationalism and Identity

Varying constructions of national identity emerge, yet the overall feeling in these posts is that Myanmar identity is under threat, either from outsiders or from destructive tendencies within. Min Aung Hlaing's 2014 posts rhetorically construct Myanmar as moving towards multi-party democracy in a kind of government-military joint venture, remaining vigilant to keep the peace, protecting against terrorist groups, and contributing to the country's development. Thura Swe Mann's post encouraging "Sister Suu" to "bring back pots of gold" constructs Myanmar as a misunderstood country looked down upon by the international community, which, as the post explains, historically enacted sanctions due to circumstances brought about by previous governments. Thura Swe Mann presents this as a misguided effort harmful to the Myanmar people, and positions Aung San Suu Kyi as the saviour who can end these sanctions.

Less-well-known figures, such as Nay Phone Latt and Hla Hla Soe, present less celebratory constructions of Myanmar identity in their posts sampled here. Nay Phone Latt decries the impact of online hate speech as a negative side of Myanmar culture, and Hla Hla Soe critiques the lack of gender equity in the work to build a federal system of governance. Min Ko Naing's posts from 2014 examine problems in the Myanmar education system, the impact of an overload of news, and the need to leave room for thinking amidst all the contemporary media noise. Many of the critiques of Myanmar identity also occur in the comments section of posts, discussed in more detail below.

Aung San Suu Kyi's Travels, Politics and Sanctions

Several of the top posts discuss Aung San Suu Kyi, recognizing her role as a national leader, including posts from former military officials. In the second-ranked post in our sample, on 12 September 2016, for example, Ye Htut chastises those publicly critical of Aung San Suu Kyi and her (then) recent trip to visit her son and grandchildren in London. Headed "Ye Htut was feeling annoyed" and accompanied by an annoyed emoji, the post calls on people not to criticize inappropriately, referring obliquely to criticisms of the trip appearing elsewhere on Facebook. Ye Htut's frank admission of his sympathy towards the state counsellor is somewhat surprising, given that he served as a minister in the USDP government. As of mid-2016, however, he was no longer holding an official government post and had taken up a position as a senior fellow in the Singapore-based ISEAS – Yusof Ishak Institute, possibly contributing to his openness. Aung San Suu Kyi's trip is also discussed in posts by Phyo Min Thein, who refers to the ups and downs of political life she faces, exemplified by the various reactions to her trip, and Thura Shwe Mann, who has the fifth highest ranking post in our sample, from 13 September 2016, mentioned earlier, appealing to Mother/Sister Suu to come home "bearing pots of gold".

Personal and Promotional Posts

Many of the more popular posts are of a personal nature. For example, Min Aung Hlaing had the top post in September 2014 for a post on the 15th entitled "Then and Now", featuring two pictures of him, one taken many years ago, in his uniform in grainy black and white, and another recently, his uniform decorated with a chest full of medals. In the third-ranked post in our sample, Ye Htut posted a photograph that he describes by writing, "These are my books and my plants." Unusual for its early date of 15 September 2012, this post garnered a lot of generally positive reactions and comments. Ye Htut's top posts from 2014 are also personal; one uses photographs he took in a European museum of a knight in armour and his swords, noting that this type of equipment is necessary if one wants to use Facebook in Myanmar, while the other tells the story and includes two photographs of a family he has visited in a rural area near Naypyidaw. This and other personal posts on Facebook often lean towards the self-promotional, such as the two top posts by former army lieutenant-general and USDP MP Hla Swe (both from September 2016). One focuses on his efforts to fight corruption by praising the journalist Swe Win as a hero, and the other challenges the corruption of legacy institutions from Thein Sein's administration like the Human Rights Commission, and describes his attempts to address an unjust court case.

Using Parables, Moral Lessons

The rich appreciation for philosophy and literature in Myanmar comes through in the use of parables or moral tales throughout these Facebook posts. All of 88 Generation Students founding member Min Ko Naing's top posts function as morality tales, such as his top two posts, which rank seventh and eighth in our sample, from 12 and 18 September 2016. The first, a repost of an essay he wrote for *Pyi Thu Ayae* (People's Affairs) entitled "Which school are you going to go to?", takes the form of a dialogue between a schoolgirl and her uncle, who is challenging the girl about her privilege as she complains about having to take the ferry to school. The second post uses the metaphor of a race to bring home the notion that hard work is not glamorous but that integrity is more important than outward appearance. Several of these posts also encourage moral behaviour or moral leadership. For example, Phyo Min Thein posts a multitude of quotations from Chinese sage Lao Tzu, and Min Aung Hlaing, in his second top post from 2014, discusses the important characteristics of a leader. This is also the topic of one of Min Ko Naing's 2014 posts, while his other post from that year argues that despite the inundation of new information via the internet, people need to set aside time for deeper forms of thinking.

Local Issues

Local issues dominate the top posts from Karen activist and NLD MP Hla Hla Soe and women's and ethnic rights activist and NLD MP for Yangon Zin Mar Aung. Hla Hla Soe's top posts, both from 2016, include a photograph of her dormitory room in Naypyidaw, a personal post followed by comments referring to specific local issues people are hoping she will help with, and an angry post about meeting with the local police commissioner who indicated that rape occurs because women dress inappropriately. Hla Hla Soe's 2014 top posts also focus on local issues, specifically a peace march she participated in, and a photograph with Karen woman Naw Ohn Hla, the recipient of a local peace award. Zin Mar Aung had no posts in September 2014, but her 2016 posts include a discussion of her participation in a local book exchange and photographs of her presence at what turned out to be a false alarm of a fire. Few of the other public figures we looked at posted about local issues in this way, although exceptions include NLD upper house MP Sein Win's 2016 post discussing his involvement in a dispute over a funeral service, and Hla Swe's 2016 post discussing his intervention in a court case.

Facebook has clearly become a site for posting about a wide range of topics, but the degree to which this is invigorating Myanmar's public sphere also depends on the level of public engagement on this platform; an issue we turn to next.

Comments

To address our second research question and assess the degree to which politicians and other key figures engage in conversation on Facebook, we examined the comment threads of the top posts in 2014 and 2016. We began by classifying the conversations following the top posts of our ten public figures according to Sørenson's categories of conversation: (1) no conversation (just comments with no reaction); (2) conversation between followers or citizens/commentators; (3) conversation between the public figure and citizens/commentators; and (4) conversations both between citizens/commentators and between citizens/commentators and the public figure.

Table 18.3 presents a summary of the posts for all the public figures organized according to Sørensen's categories. We can see a marked change from 2014 to 2016 in the number of conversations, as the percentage of posts that had no conversations dropped from 57 to 15 per cent. We can also see that in 2014 none of the posts we analysed had conversations between both citizens with each other *and* citizens with the public figures, whereas in 2016 that percentage jumped to 35 per cent. The number of conversations between citizens also increased significantly. It is not possible to generalize to all Facebook use among public figures in Myanmar based on our sample, and it is even questionable whether a "representative sample" of such use could be achieved, since the development of methodology for rigorous statistical sampling is still only in its infancy.[8] Our data nonetheless demonstrate a trend towards a greater number of conversations between politicians and the public on Facebook since 2012.

TABLE 18.3
Posts of the ten public figures in our sample categorized according to Sørenson's classifications of public engagement

	Number of Posts	Conversations between Citizens	Conversations between Citizens and Public Figure	Both Types	None
2014	14	29%	14%	0%	57%
2016	20	40%	10%	35%	15%

Looking more closely at these threads, the popularity of Min Aung Hlaing's posts and the number of positive comments that tend to follow his posts indicate the continuing strong influence of key military figures in the Myanmar public sphere. Yet these posts include very little engagement by Min Aung Hlaing himself, if at all, in the original post (which is likely to have been posted by a staff member) or in the comments section, where he does not respond to comments about his posts.

The willingness of some people to post comments critical of the military or the government is notable, especially given the increase in defamation suits over the past few years. For example, the comments following the two top posts for 2014 and 2016, both by Min Aung Hlaing, are generally positive, praising and thanking the senior general for his service, although there are exceptions. In reaction to the 15 September 2014 post of Min Aung Hlaing's photos, one poster comments, "You have so many medals it looks like you are from North Korea"; eight people "like" this in a thread of 572 comments, the vast majority of which have no or only one "like". In fact only three of the 572 comments had eight likes, and only four had more than eight. Another comment says "you are just protecting your father, [former senior general] Than Shwe", a comment that also received eight likes, while another asks "what do you expect us to do, pray to you?", which received four likes. But others defend Min Aung Hlaing in the face of such criticism, such as one response saying "all the comments I have read are people feeling jealous. Why don't you try to get to where he is?"

In comparison to Min Aung Hlaing, at times Ye Htut does engage with those responding to his posts. For example, he answers questions following his post about his books and plants. When he criticizes those making unkind comments about Aung San Suu Kyi's visit to London, the first comment is from a monk who argues that Aung San Suu Kyi's children don't respect Burmese culture and that people from other countries look down on Myanmar. Ye Htut replies that he sees politics as different from personal issues, and that while he agrees politically, we should refrain from criticizing other people's personal lives. It is significant that 4,100 people "liked" Ye Htut's reply. These posts make clear that Ye Htut does read the comments and engages with those commenting, and that this engagement itself is noted by those commenting. This type of public interaction between government and other high-profile figures and the public is an emerging trend contributing to the construction of Myanmar's transitional political culture, in which resistance is finding new and more public forms.

The Importance of Memes

Many comments take the form of memes, and many of these are adapted from worldwide internet culture. Memes work especially well in the context of social media, where they can be adapted and shared in creative and expressive ways, and it did not take long for Myanmar Facebook users to start adapting memes to the local context.[9] Memes are especially prevalent following posts with a lighter tone or personal story, such as the top posts by Hla Swe and Ye Htut. The frankness with which some of these memes critique influential public figures would have been unimaginable in pre-2010 Burma. Take for example a lengthy 2014 post by Hla Swe recounting his experience at a wedding. A comment following his post features a picture of Will Smith with the caption, "Say it, say it. After you say it, you will feel the burden on your chest lifting. After that, you'll have to take some medicine" (see Figure 18.2). This is a reference to a popular joke in Burmese in which someone is asked to "take some medicine", implying that they are mentally unsound and must be medicated to restore "normal" behaviour.

FIGURE 18.2

Another example follows a 2014 post by Ye Htut, recounting his visit to a rural family, sharing a meal with them and giving them a gift. A comment posted here features a picture of a boxing match between Ye Htut and the editor of the *Eleven* newspaper, Than Htut Aung, with former President Thein Sein as their referee (Figure 18.3). Ye Htut says to Than Htut Aung, "Hey, be gentle, you know what I mean." Than Htut Aung replies, "I know, I'm purposely missing." Thein Sein says in the background, "Keep fighting, my sons, the more the people are distracted, the more I'm satisfied." The inference is clear: the Information Minister and the press were planning to engage in a

FIGURE 18.3

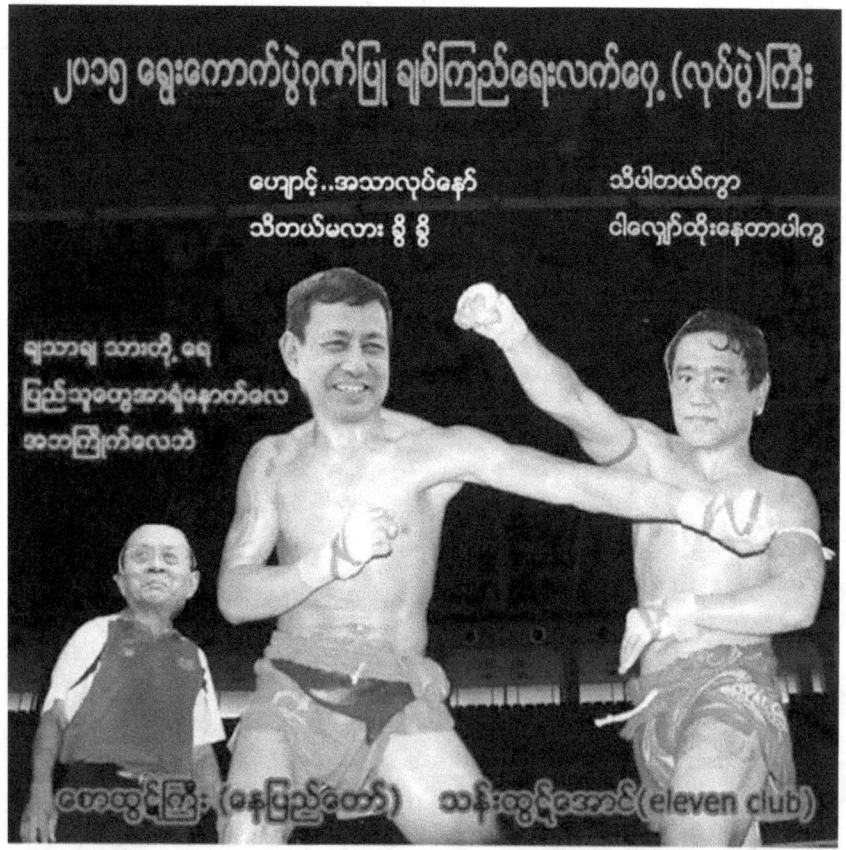

fake fight during the 2015 elections in order to mislead the public, with the president encouraging them, an extraordinarily critical comment in the lead-up to the elections. These memes, while critical of public figures, also suggest that this kind of frankness has become acceptable behaviour within the confines of at least some Facebook pages, despite the risk of defamation lawsuits.

Concluding Thoughts

Facebook has become an increasingly important public communication platform in Myanmar, and over the three one-month periods observed in our sample, the degree of engagement between the public and the prominent figures on the Facebook pages we analysed increased. In almost half of their top posts in 2016, the public figures joined in the conversations in the comments reacting to their posts. Facebook provides a forum for participants, including public figures, to share aspects of their personal lives, debate political issues and find a community of the like-minded.

Public figures share their personal takes on current events, such as the Rakhine Commission or Aung San Suu Kyi's trip to see her family. They also share personal stories about their travels, thoughts and inspirations, allowing the public to see them as personable, or inviting ridicule, but nonetheless as individuals who are more than mere holders of an official title. Facebook allows public figures direct access to the public, but also allows the public the chance to reply. Many of the public figures whose Facebook posts we analysed replied directly to individual commenters, and even for those who did not, such as Senior General Min Aung Hlaing, the public partook in conversations knowing that he could see what they were saying. All of these developments promote more open discussion and stand in stark contrast to the complete lack of direct communication between the public and prominent public figures under the military regime.

There are new narratives developing when a former army lieutenant-general and USDP MP, Hla Swe, publicly praises an investigative journalist, Swe Win, as a hero and sees his own role (or at least his need to project an image) as challenging corruption in government institutions. Or when a commenter posts a public comment that the medals on Min Aung Hlaing's chest make him look like he is from North Korea. Older forms of communication such as the official government line, the morality tale, and the leader's charge to people to behave with integrity and moral leadership have migrated on to social media, where they share space with those posting radically different views. There is evidence that this can at times result in genuine dialogue, but as we have seen in the case of the Rohingya, it can also further entrench a siloing effect, where people can gather with the like-minded and shut out those with differing viewpoints.

The data we analyse here suggest that Myanmar Facebook users in 2012, 2014 and 2016 were beginning to engage primarily with and comment on those posts they tend to agree with, and while there is debate within the comment threads, the tone of these discussions varies. Min Aung Hlaing's posts, for example, are more formal, official messages and garner generally positive comments in response, while Ye Htut's posts are far less formal, often personal and lighthearted in tone, and, in the examples we analysed, provoke more vigorous debate. Min Aung Hlaing's posts, not surprisingly, construct a positive image of the military and seem to primarily attract military supporters, along with a few critics, while Thura Shwe Mann's posts, in contrast, tend to be supportive of Aung San Suu Kyi and attract her supporters. The popularity of some of the higher profile public figures we analysed here indicates the continued importance of clientelistic patterns, along with the development of more personalized forms of political discourse. And while interaction within like-minded groups seems rigorous, the degree to which Facebook supports a strong public sphere will depend on the degree to which these different groups communicate with each other.

The development of a public sphere in Myanmar was long curtailed by the tight lid placed on freedom of expression by successive regimes. A clear boundary demarcated the spaces where expression was tolerated or difficult to police, often confined and localized, as in the tea shops, and the spaces where expression was unidirectional, strictly controlled, but reached out to the whole country, as in the 8 o'clock news. As we have seen, however, information technologies have made this clear boundary increasingly porous.

Transgressing this boundary has always carried risks. Early internet adopters risked imprisonment when their personal blogs took on a more political tone to spread news about the Saffron Revolution in solidarity with activists. Contemporary Facebook users risk defamation suits when they make satirical memes to openly critique high-ranking government officials. The difference is that with Facebook these transgressions are taking place on a platform that is now accessible to an estimated 15 to 20 million people (28 to 38 per cent of the population), and that number continues to grow.[10]

As has become abundantly clear through the horrific events that have taken place since we began this research, Facebook is not a neutral platform. When 15–20 million people rely on this platform as their primary source of information, this is a dangerous reality. In Myanmar, and in many other countries in the global south, information and communication technologies are transforming at a drastic pace how people communicate with each other, and social networking platforms such as Facebook are the main tools for these new modes of communication. However, these social networks are also very lightly regulated and do not have significant incentives to invest in monitoring dangerous content and misuse in countries in the global south, which are not their main target markets. Facebook as a platform is especially vulnerable to manipulation. Civil society groups have for some time argued that Facebook has not invested enough in public safety in Myanmar, lacks transparency and is very slow in responding when notified of abuses on their platform (Phandeeyar 2018). In a 15 August 2018 update on Myanmar, Facebook claims that it has increased the amount of hate speech it has itself "proactively identified", increased its Burmese speaking staff and has plans to hire more, improved its artificial intelligence tools to help in identifying abusive posts, and will be conducting digital literacy training in Myanmar (Facebook 2018a, ¶4). In response, Ei Myat Noe Khin (Khin) of Phandeeyar — a Myanmar tech innovation lab — notes that "it's really too early to talk of progress, but Facebook is showing more willingness to engage with the problem, which is positive" (cited in Solon 2018, ¶23).

The utopian discourse that followed the rapid introduction of mobile phones celebrated the new freedoms that online media were sure to usher forth. This was followed by deep dismay at the role of Facebook and other social media in the horrendous violence in the country. But the situation is far more complex than these simplistic discourses would suggest. Changes are brewing among the 15–20 million users of this platform, a phenomenon far more pervasive yet far less sensational. In the posts we analysed, Facebook brings the intimate atmosphere of the tea shop together with the formality of the 8 o'clock official government line, along with some new, hybrid forms of conversation, debate and critique that have emerged among a broader public than ever before. This new sphere is both intimate, allowing the formation of a multiplicity of public spheres, as well as open for voices of hatred and prejudice alongside those of reconciliation and understanding. As the boundaries between official pronouncements, reliable factual reporting and hearsay rumours blur, the hate speech and propaganda spread by nefarious actors can, with seeming innocuousness, sit side by side with wholesome posts from family and friends within the same stream of information. The internet and social media, especially, function as sites for the struggle over who is shaping the dominant stories of the new Myanmar and the direction of ongoing changes.

Notes

1. Fisher (2015, ¶16-17).
2. Pen International (2013, ¶ 27).
3. Myo Thar Htet (2014, ¶7).
4. Even though choices in television channels have expanded for the public, the main state-run channels under the NLD-led government still continue this practice.
5. Although Facebook is widely considered the most dominant social media platform in Myanmar, it is not the only one with a significant user base. The number of Facebook users is surpassed by the figure for VOIP and messaging service Viber, which reportedly had eighteen million active users as of December 2018, as reported on the Myanmar Ministry of Information webpage <http://www.moi.gov.mm/moi:eng/?q=news/13/11/2018/id-6085>. Viber's functionality is mainly for private chats and therefore does not provide the platform for online public discourse that Facebook does.
6. For public pages, the aforementioned data items were scraped automatically by a Python script that accessed Facebook's Graph API. For the private profiles, the same data items were gathered through a process of first scraping the HTML of the posts and then running a Python script to extract the relevant data items.
7. The other upper house NLD MP in our sample, Hla Hla Soe, was elected in 2015.

8. Lin, Yeh and Li (2013) give a thorough technical overview of the emerging field of sampling and summarization of social network data.
9. The local Facebook group "Myanmar Memes", with over 300,000 members as of August 2017, was one of the first Facebook groups where local meme culture developed (https://www.facebook.com/groups/myanmarmemes/).
10. Obtained from Facebook's Audience Insights Dashboard on 8 September 2018 (https://www.facebook.com/business/news/audience-insights).

References

Abbott, J. 2015. "Hype or Hubris? The Political Impact of the Internet and Social Networking in Southeast Asia". In *Routledge Handbook of Southeast Asian Democratization*, edited by W. Case, pp. 201–22. New York: Routledge.

Armstrong, P. 2017. "Facebook Users Posted a Third Less Content in 2016 than in 2015". *Forbes*. https://www.forbes.com/sites/paularmstrongtech/2017/02/14/facebook-users-posted-a-third-less-content-in-2016-than-in-2015/#60bfe89e776d.

Athan. 2019. Facebook post, 4 February 2019 <https://www.facebook.com/athan.foe.myanmar/photos/a.215675215658218/394114091147662/?type=3&theater.

Aung Kyaw Nyunt. 2016. "Ministry Puts Mobile Penetration at 90 Percent". *Myanmar Times*, 19 July 2016. https://www.mmtimes.com/business/technology/21466-ministry-puts-mobile-penetration-at-90-percent.html.

Chowdhury, M. 2008. "The Role of the Internet in Burma's Saffron Revolution". Berkman Center Research Publication no. 2008-8. http://dx.doi.org/10.2139/ssrn.1537703.

Dale, J.G. 2011. *Free Burma: Transnational Legal Action and Corporate Accountability*. Minneapolis: University of Minnesota Press.

Downing, J.D.H., and L. Brooten. 2007. "ICTs and Political Movements". In *Oxford University Press Handbook on Information and Communication Technologies*, edited by R. Mansell and R. Silverstone, pp. 537–60. Oxford University Press.

Enli, G.S., and E. Skogerbø. 2013. "Personalized Campaigns in Party-Centred Politics". *Information, Communication & Society* 16 (5): 757–74.

Facebook. 2018a. "Update on Myanmar". *Facebook Newsroom*, 15 August 2018. https://newsroom.fb.com/news/2018/08/update-on-myanmar/.

———. 2018b. "Removing Myanmar Military Officials from Facebook". *Facebook Newsroom*, 27 August 2018. https://newsroom.fb.com/news/2018/08/removing-myanmar-officials/.

Filer, T., and R. Fredheim. 2016. "Sparking Debate? Political Deaths and Twitter Discourses in Argentina and Russia". *Information, Communication & Society* 19 (11): 1539–55.

Fisher, J. 2015. "Myanmar's Strongman Gives Rare BBC Interview". *BBC News*, 20 July 2015. http://www.bbc.com/news/world-asia-33587800.

Fraser, N. 1992. "Rethinking the Public Sphere". In *Habermas and the Public Sphere*, edited by C. Calhoun, pp. 109–42. Boston: MIT Press.

Grömping, M., and A. Sinpeng. 2018. "The 'Crowd-Factor' in Connective Action: Comparing Protest Communication Styles of Thai Facebook Pages". *Journal of Information Technology & Politics* 15 (3): 197–214.

Habermas, J. 1991. *The Structural Transformation of the Public Sphere: An Inquiry into a Category of Bourgeois Society*. Boston: MIT Press.

Kakachia, K., T. Pataraia, and M. Cecire. 2014. "Networked Apathy: Georgian Party Politics and the Role of Social Media". *Demokratizatsiya* 22 (2): 255–75.

Klein, E. 2018. "Mark Zuckerberg on Facebook's Hardest Year, and What Comes Next". *The Ezra Klein Show*, 2 April 2018. https://art19.com/shows/the-ezra-klein-show/episodes/0d5f503d-80d0-4e98-aa08-d29599957459.

Kyaw Zwa Moe. 2017. "NLD Govt Must Live Up to Its Manifesto on Press Freedom". *The Irrawaddy*, 3 May 2017. https://www.irrawaddy.com/opinion/commentary/nld-govt-must-live-manifesto-press-freedom.html.

Lang, M. 2015. "Presidential Election Circus: Is Social Media the Cause? *Government Technology*, 5 April 2015. http://www.govtech.com/social/2016-Presidential-Election-Circus-Is-Social-Media-the-Cause.html.

Langlois, G., G. Elmer, F. McKelvey, and Z. Devereaux. 2009. "Networked Publics: The Double Articulation of Code and Politics on Facebook". *Canadian Journal of Communication* 34 (3): 415–34.

Larsson, A.O., and B. Kalsnes. 2014. "'Of Course We Are on Facebook': Use and Non-use of Social Media among Swedish and Norwegian Politicians". *European Journal of Communication* 29 (6): 653–67.

Lee, R. 2016. "The Dark Side of Liberalization: How Myanmar's Political and Media Freedoms Are Being Used to Limit Muslim Rights". *Islamic and Christian-Muslim Relations* 27 (2): 195–211.

Leong, L. 2017. "Mobile Myanmar: The Development of a Mobile App Culture in Yangon". *Mobile Media & Communication* 5 (2): 139–60.

Lin, S.-D., M.-Y. Yeh, and C.-T. Li. 2013. *Sampling and Summarization for Social Networks*. Presented at the SIAM International Conference on Data Mining, Austin, Texas, USA, 2013. https://www.siam.org/meetings/sdm13/social.php.

Lindlof, T.R., and B.C. Taylor. 2011. *Qualitative Communication Research Methods*, 3rd ed. Thousand Oaks, CA: Sage.

Loader, B.D., A. Vromen, and M.A. Xenos. 2016. "Performing for the Young Networked Citizen? Celebrity Politics, Social Networking and the Political Engagement of Young People". *Media, Culture & Society* 38 (3): 400–19.

Long, K. 2018. "Facebook Investigated Myanmar's Military-linked Accounts. It Found a Covert Propaganda Campaign". *Time*, 1 September 2018. http://time.com/5383780/myanmar-facebook-propaganda-rohingya/.

Macnamara, J., and G. Kenning. 2011. "E-electioneering 2010: Trends in Social Media Use in Australian Political Communication". *Media International Australia, Incorporating Culture & Policy*, no. 139 (May): 7–22.

McCarthy, G. 2018. "Cyber-Spaces". In *Routledge Handbook of Contemporary Myanmar*, edited by A. Simpson, N. Farrelly, and I. Holliday, pp. 91–105. New York: Routledge.

McPherson, P., and Cape Win Diamond. 2017. "Free Speech Curtailed in Aung San Suu Kyi's Myanmar as Prosecutions Soar". *The Guardian*, 8 January 2017. https://www.theguardian.com/world/2017/jan/09/free-speech-curtailed-aung-san-suu-kyis-myanmar-prosecutions-soar.

Mina, A.X. 2014. "Batman, Pandaman and the Blind Man: A Case Study in Social Change Memes and Internet Censorship in China". *Journal of Visual Culture* 13 (3): 359–75. https://doi.org/10.1177/1470412914546576.

Mod, C. 2016. "The Facebook-Loving Farmers of Myanmar". *The Atlantic*, 21 January 2016. https://www.theatlantic.com/technology/archive/2016/01/the-facebook-loving-farmers-of-myanmar/424812/.

Myo Thar Htet. 2014. "Interview with the New Information Minister Ye Htut". *Mizzima News*, 7 August 2014. http://archive-3.mizzima.com/opinion/interviews/item/12009-interview-with-the-new-information-minister-ye-htut/12009-interview-with-the-new-information-minister-ye-htut.

Nandar Aung. 2016. "Project Monitors Social Media Hate Speech". *Myanmar Times*, 7 April 2016. https://www.mmtimes.com/lifestyle/19874-project-monitors-social-media-hate-speech.html.

Nielsen, R.K. 2010. "Mundane Internet Tools, Mobilizing Practices, and the Coproduction of Citizenship in Political Campaigns". *New Media & Society* 13 (5): 755–71.

Nyi Lynn Seck. 2013. "Infographic: Myanmar Facebook Users Statistic (August, 2013)". https://www.slideshare.net/lynnseck/infographic-myanmar-facebook-users-statistic.

Pen International. 2013. "Interview with Myanmar PEN's Nay Phone Latt". 1 November 2013. http://www.pen-international.org/newsitems/interview-with-myanmar-pens-nay-phone-latt/.

Phandeeyar, MIDO, et al. 2018. "Myanmar – Open Letter to Mark Zuckerberg". 5 April 2018. Available at https://drive.google.com/file/d/1Rs02G96Y9w5dpX0Vf1LjWp6B9mp32VY-/view.

Poetranto, I. 2012. "Update on Information Controls in Burma". Opennet Initiative, 23 October 2012. https://opennet.net/blog/2012/10/update-information-controls-burma.

Rahimi, B. 2015. "Satirical Cultures of Media Publics in Iran". *International Communication Gazette* 77 (3): 267–81.

Riffe, D., S. Lacy, and F. Fico. 2014. *Analyzing Media Messages*, 3rd ed. New York: Routledge.

Robertson, S.P., S. Douglas, M. Maruyama, and B. Semaan. 2013. "Political Discourse on Social Networking Sites: Sentiment, In-group/Out-group Orientation and Rationality". *Information Polity* 18 (2): 107–26.

Ross, K., S. Fountaine, and M. Comrie. 2015. "Facing up to Facebook: Politicians, Publics and the Social Media(ted) Turn in New Zealand". *Media, Culture & Society* 37 (2): 251–69.

Samarajiva, R. 2016. "Telecom is Biggest Attractor of FDI in Myanmar". *LIRNEasia*, 25 December 2016. http://lirneasia.net/2016/12/telecom-is-biggest-attractor-of-fdi-in-myanmar/.

———. 2017. "Backhaul Networks in Myanmar Gain Additional Financing". *LIRNEasia*, 5 February 2017. http://lirneasia.net/2017/02/backhaul-networks-in-myanmar-gain-additional-financing/.

Schissler, M. 2005. "New Technologies, Established Practices: Developing Narratives of Muslim Threat in Myanmar". *In Islam and the State in Myanmar*, edited by M. Crouch, pp. 211–33. New Delhi: Oxford University Press.

Sinpeng, A. 2017. "Southeast Asian Cyberspace: Politics, Censorship, Polarisation". *New Mandala*, 1 November 2017. http://www.newmandala.org/southeast-asian-cyberspace-politics-censorship-polarisation/.

Solon, O. 2018. "Facebook's Failure in Myanmar is the Work of a Blundering Toddler". *The Guardian*, 16 August 2018. https://www.theguardian.com/technology/2018/aug/16/facebook-myanmar-failure-blundering-toddler.

Sørensen, M.P. 2016. "Political Conversations on Facebook – the Participation of Politicians and Citizens". *Media, Culture & Society* 38 (5): 664–85.

Steenkamp, M., and N. Hyde-Clark. 2014. "The Use of Facebook for Political Commentary in South Africa. *Telematics & Informatics* 31 (1): 91–97.

Subramaniam, S. 2011. "Assessing Political Dynamics in Contemporary Malaysia: Implications for Democratic Change". *ASIANetwork Exchange* 19 (1): 42–52.

Telenor. 2018. "Realising Digital Myanmar". 6 February 2018. https://www.telenor.com/wp-content/uploads/2018/02/Telenor-Realising-Digital-Myanmar-Report-06-February.pdf.

Thiha, A. 2010. "Revolution through Cyberspace: Burmese Blogosphere and Saffron Revolution". Proceedings of the 4th ACM/IEEE International

Conference on Information and Communication Technologies and Development article no. 48.

Trautwein, C. 2016. "Myanmar Mobile Leaps Along". *Myanmar Times*, 1 April 2016. http://www.mmtimes.com/index.php/business/technology/19801-myanmar-mobile-leaps-along.html.

Weiss, M. 2013. "Parsing the Power of 'New Media' in Malaysia". *Journal of Contemporary Asia* 43 (4): 591–612.

19

From Blogging to Digital Rights: Telecommunications Reform in Myanmar

Htaike Htaike Aung and Wai Myo Htut

The story of the Myanmar ICT for Development Organisation (MIDO) is closely related to the rise of blogging, which became popular in the country in the mid 2000s. Despite poor internet connections — which were mainly accessed at cyber cafes — and high levels of state surveillance, blogging offered individuals a platform to own their content and for expression, whether to discuss politics, social development or other personal interests like food and fashion. One of the well-known bloggers was Nay Phone Latt — now an elected member of the Yangon regional parliament for the National League for Democracy (NLD) — who was keen on creative writing as well as political commentary. Together, we formed the Myanmar Bloggers Society in 2007 and conducted basic training and workshops for start-ups and the blogging community.

Our first major public event in August 2007 was themed "We Blog, We Unite", and we were able to attract about three hundred participants and private sponsors. A month later, the Saffron Revolution unfolded, and some of the bloggers and citizen journalists in the country, including Nay Phone Latt, wrote about the political situation and uploaded videos and footage of eyewitness accounts to the internet. These were shared by other media outlets and by individuals with their community members (OpenNet Initiative 2012). Because of this, the bloggers and citizen journalists became targets of the government, and some were eventually arrested. So, in the span of a month, the bloggers went from being popular to being avoided by everyone, as people were afraid and would not talk to us. In January 2008 Nay Phone Latt was arrested and charged under three different laws, including the 2004 Electronic Transactions Law, and sentenced to twenty years imprisonment.[1] We had to stop our public activities because we thought it would be dangerous for us. We channelled our work to quietly supporting activists and journalists to develop their technological capabilities.

In 2011 the quasi-civilian government of President Thein Sein announced the political opening of Myanmar, and in January 2012 Nay Phone Latt was released as part of an amnesty for political prisoners (CPJ 2012). We came together again, but this time we shifted our focus from merely promoting blogs to advocating for wider digital rights. Together, we formed MIDO, and our first activity was in Hpa-An Township in Kayin State, where Nay Phone Latt had been jailed, to conduct basic training over five days on digital literacy. The location was selected because it was a way of showing appreciation to the community that had supported him when he was a political prisoner. The training involved teaching young people, who were mainly affiliated with the NLD, how to operate desktop computers and laptops, and how to use email and Facebook. It was only then we announced the launching of MIDO, and we have been going around the country giving training to communities on various aspects of digital rights ever since. We have provided training for about two thousand people. During this time, MIDO also stepped up its work to advocate for free expression.

Threats to Free Expression

The military regime wielded the 2004 Electronic Transactions Law to put many activists and bloggers — like Nay Phone Latt — behind bars. Others jailed under the law include Sandar Min, also an MP in Yangon, journalists from the Democratic Voice of Burma, pro-democracy activists like Min Ko Naing, and comedian Zarganar (Human Rights Watch 2009). In August 2013, during the transition, the law was amended to reduce penalties for offences related to online expression deemed as threats to national security, peace, national solidarity or the national economy. To us, the amendments meant little, as expression remained criminalized by the law. In October 2013 the Thein Sein government introduced the Telecommunications Law as part of its plan to liberalize the sector (as discussed by Gayathry Venkiteswaran, Yin Yadanar Thein and Myint Kyaw in this volume). The process was led by the World Bank, who, together with the government, called for public feedback. This was the first time our organization became involved in advocacy. As MIDO was the only civil society group with experience on issues related to digital technologies, we felt compelled to speak up. We knew that the proposed law was not right. Like the Electronic Transactions Law, the new law contained provisions to criminalize speech, thus placing the burden on expression (Human Rights Watch 2013). Armed with a research paper prepared by human rights groups, we made our first submission to parliament, but our points were largely ignored.

We have since witnessed the law being used against individuals from different backgrounds over comments made on the social media platform Facebook. In 2015 and 2016, seven Facebook users were arrested and convicted under Section 66(d) of the Telecommunications Law. Since the NLD took office in April 2016, 168 cases have been filed under the law. The provision in question criminalizes "Committing extortion, bullying, illegal obstruction, defamation, harassment, abuse of power, or threat with the use of a telecommunications network". In many cases the Facebook users were charged with posting content that defamed Myanmar military chief Senior General Min Aung Hlaing.

One of those charged under the law was poet Maung Saungkha, who was imprisoned for six months in 2016 for posting a satirical poem on Facebook that was deemed to be insulting to then president Thein Sein (McPherson 2017).[2] Upon his release he reached out to MIDO to help conduct research on the law and its implications. Together with other groups working on issues of free expression, as well as business and human rights (this included PEN Myanmar, the Myanmar Centre for Responsible Business, and Phandeeyar), we formed a coalition in late 2016 — the Telecommunications Law Research Team — to campaign for reform of this controversial law. By mid 2017 the coalition had twenty-two members and was carrying out public awareness activities such as a cartoon exhibition, press conferences and meetings with legislators, politicians, lawyers and other stakeholders. It was one of the first locally driven free expression coalitions to emerge during the transition period, prompted by the arrests.

Past experiences with the legislative process have motivated civil society to push for meaningful public consultation and to take a broader perspective on the legal framework. For example, the coalition was not only focused on Section 66(d) of the Telecommunications Law but also on other provisions that are just as punitive, like Section 77, which gives the government excessive powers to shut down the internet. There was much resistance to our work from the NLD and its members in government and parliament. They used a range of excuses to justify the Telecommunications Law, and in response the civil society coalition used legal arguments as well as an online campaign using memes to mock the "14 most commonly cited reasons to keep 66(d)".

The absence of meaningful consultation in the drafting of the Telecommunications Law was repeated in the enactment of the privacy law. Parliament passed the privacy law in March 2017, but no one knew about the draft law until it was discussed by the lower house (Pyitthu Hluttaw), which adopted it in September 2016. The upper house (Amyothar Hluttaw) passed the law in March 2017. We are disappointed with the process, which excluded civil society and experts, and with the outcome: an eight-page law that does not provide adequate measures to protect privacy or data. The law does not provide for a strong oversight body or give specifics about lawful interceptions. The government and parliament have disregarded the basic principles of freedom of expression and rights to privacy enshrined in the Universal Declaration for Human Rights and the ASEAN Declaration of Human Rights.

Although the NLD promised to amend some of the laws deemed undemocratic, after two years in office it has done little, if anything, to improve the legislative framework in support of digital rights, including online free expression and the right to privacy.

The Smartphone Nation

Threats to free expression online are particularly worrying because of the phenomenal growth in the ownership and use of smartphones and the internet since the political opening. A survey we conducted with LIRNEasia in December 2016 indicated that 78 per cent of mobile phones in Myanmar were smartphones with access to the internet; in mid-2018 these levels remained largely the same. That level of penetration is similar to the rates in countries like the United States, although Myanmar also has very low digital literacy rates. So, although smartphone ownership is considered high, the number of people who access the internet for information is still limited. Based on the training we have conducted over the last few years, it is clear that there is still a long way to go before people will be using their smartphones to their full potential. What most people in Myanmar believe is that Facebook is the internet; that is where people get most of their information, whether from their friends or news media outlets. In rural areas people even have Facebook pages where they buy and sell livestock. To a large extent this phenomenon was a result of the liberalization of the telecommunications sector.

Development of the Telecommunications Sector

As SIM cards became more affordable following the liberalization of the sector, and cheap smartphones were imported from China and other neighbouring countries, Myanmar's smartphone usage experienced a significant growth, which in turn drove improvements in internet speeds (Cunningham 2016). In 2012 Myanmar had an international bandwidth below 15 gigabytes per second (Gbps), or 0.3 kilobytes per second (kbps) per capita — the lowest data-transfer speed in the region.[3] By 2015, thanks to new submarine and cross-border cables, the bandwidth had increased to 70 Gbps, or 1.3 kbps per capita, increasing video streaming capacity (MMRD 2017).

According to official data, internet usage in Myanmar rose from 2 million users in 2012 to 39 million in 2016, or about 70 per cent of the population, although it is common for many people to own more than one device (Aung Kyaw Nyunt 2016). Most people use the internet to access social networking sites like Facebook. In 2016 there were 9.7 million active accounts — one-third of the total internet users in the country, and two times as many as the year before. The figure for June 2018 was 20 million. Telenor chief executive officer Lars Eric Tellman has been quoted as saying that 70 per cent of the traffic on his company's data plans consists of web browsing, with more than half accessing Facebook. The remaining traffic consists of video streaming, with YouTube being the most popular platform (Gillmore 2016).

Facebook's dominance in the online landscape has attracted news and information content providers, including government institutions and departments, from the President's Office to the Ministry of Information and the parliament (Pyitthu Hluttaw), as detailed by Yan Naung Oak and Lisa Brooten in this volume. Social media, with their interactive features, have largely replaced organizational websites; the latter are now viewed as outdated or static. Another popular service in Myanmar alongside Facebook is Viber, an internet messaging application founded by an Israeli developer and acquired by a Japanese company. It has nearly 20 million users in Myanmar (Kanale 2017). Smartphones have replaced cyber cafes, although there are still uses for such cafes in some states. In MIDO's community training in Chin State, for example, we saw a cyber cafe that provided access to Wi-Fi and power plugs where people could use their own phones. Such Wi-Fi access points may become popular in the future to address the lack of mobile coverage in certain areas.

Mobile Applications for Civic Engagement

Most people in Myanmar access the internet through mobile phone applications (apps) rather than Web browsers. This has increased opportunities for businesses, technology start-ups and other organizations to engage users through mobile apps to complement their Facebook presence. In some cases apps have become a necessary communication tool. In 2015 the Yangon-based innovation hub

Phandeeyar organized a series of hackathons[4] to promote and support civic technology related to electoral monitoring and education. One of the winning apps of the Mae Pay Soh ("Let's Vote") Hack Challenge, *M-Voter*, became one of the most downloaded apps during the November 2015 general elections. In addition to being downloaded 211,000 times to mobile phones before election day, it was used as a training tool during election-related workshops (Oh 2016). MIDO also developed a crowd-sourced election monitoring application called *Kyeet* (www.kyeet.org), which was used by citizen monitors to report electoral fraud and as a timely source of information for journalists. Local tech developers have also developed civic apps to assist women's empowerment, civic education and human rights reporting.

The enthusiasm of young people has been encouraging. Their participation in hackathons to develop technologies for society show they are interested in political engagement. However, there is still a lot of work to be done to raise literacy levels with regard to the use of media platforms. MIDO has collaborated with youth from community-based organizations and charities, and works to protect human rights and the environment. According to one youth participant from Mawlamyaing, "internet platforms like mobile apps and Facebook have showed us how technology could assist in civic engagement if used properly. During the elections, it was very fascinating to see how news got distributed instantly and to see Facebook becoming a good tool to hold government accountable." Young people are generally well informed about current affairs but have little awareness about the relationship between human rights and the internet. They tend to perceive it as a purely tech-driven space, but they also acknowledge that it is instrumental to their community work (particularly Facebook and Viber).

Given the growing popularity of Facebook for individuals and local groups that want to publish their news and information, MIDO used to provide digital literacy and citizen journalism training. But the focus of our training has since shifted to security, privacy and the use of technology to promote peace. We developed a curriculum called *SOS* — Safe Online Space — consisting of news/media literacy, digital security and the use of social media and peace to counter hate speech. In light of the criminal charges brought against those who use digital platforms to express themselves, this work is both timely and relevant.

Weaponizing Facebook

There is no doubt that Facebook has had some positive impact in Myanmar, both as a channel for improved civic engagement and as a platform for the mobilization of civil society. Yet it has also been wielded as a weapon by extremist groups and their supporters, as well as by the military, to spread their ideology and shift public opinion, spread hate, justify violence, instigate conflict, and target critics and opponents. This is the downside of the rise of social media, which has been clearly demonstrated by the ongoing Rakhine crisis.

In April 2018 six Myanmar organizations that monitor social media and promote human rights and peace, including MIDO, sent a letter to Facebook founder and chief executive officer Mark Zuckerberg after he downplayed the company's problems in responding to the violence in Myanmar. The groups said that contrary to claims, the company's internal systems failed to detect the spread of hate speech on the platform and only acted after repeated appeals to Facebook employees. In the letter, they recommended several actions: set up a dedicated country team, including senior staff who speak Burmese and understand the local context; develop a clear and reliable escalation system for content that can cause real world harm; commit to clear and accountable performance benchmarks for the removal of dangerous content; commit to removing users of the platform who repeatedly violate community standards; and publish data on the levels of hate speech detected by Facebook. Our coalition received a response from Mark Zuckerberg, and Facebook has now conducted a third-party human rights assessment (which they have not done in any other country). Yet there is still a need for more sustainable efforts and consultation.

The Digital Future under the NLD

Since the NLD government took office in April 2016 there have been notable changes in the way ministries are organized. Previously under the purview of the Ministry of Communication and Information Technology, the portfolio for ICT and telecommunications has been merged with that of the former Ministry of Transport — the resultant merged ministry was named the Ministry of Transport and Communication. Since both the minister and the deputy minister come from a transport background, the merger raised concerns that the telecom sector would become less of a priority. As part of its reform process, the ministry launched a twelve-point economics policy in July 2016, including the development of a digital government strategy and e-government (State Counsellor Office 2016), but there have been no announcements yet as to how these will be implemented. Another major concern involves the possible renegotiation of operating licences, as private telecommunication companies are hoping to avoid having to provide coverage to all areas of the country, which would limit access to those in areas with ongoing conflicts. By proposing universal coverage based on population instead of geographical areas, the private sector operators are indicating their lack of interest or support for ensuring access to services in all parts of the country. But the main threat during this transition has been the abuse of the Telecommunications Law to arrest critics, whether activists, politicians, journalists or members of the public. The government's insistence on using the law, and its reluctance to engage with civil society, illustrate the challenges we will face in the near future as Myanmar becomes more connected.

Conclusion

The uptake of telecommunications technology in Myanmar has been nothing short of dramatic. After years of restricted access to information and freedom of expression, it has been a remarkable journey for civil society groups like MIDO to witness the growing interest and demand, especially among the youth, to use smartphones to engage politically and socially. Yet the challenges are still there, not only because of the restrictive laws but also because of the threats resulting from hate speech and misleading information that affect people's right to know. There are still missing pieces in terms of privacy and data protection, which will be crucial if the government goes ahead with its plans to introduce e-government systems and digital identification methods. If private telecommunication operators succeed in amending their licensing agreements so they are no longer responsible for offering coverage to all areas of the country, especially those with ongoing conflicts, it will mean that communities or individuals that most need connectivity will not have access through mobile telephones.

It is becoming increasingly important to demand governmental and corporate transparency, as well as meaningful public participation, in the formulation of policies and laws for the telecommunications sector.

Notes

1. Nay Phone Latt was charged under Sections 33(a) and 38 of the Electronic Transactions Law, unlawful distribution of videotapes (Section 32[b] and Section 36 of the Television and Video Law) and making statements causing public mischief (Section 505[b] of the Penal Code).
2. Two of the lines in the poem read, "I have a tattoo of the president's face on my penis / My wife is disgusted."
3. The speeds are 0.4 kbps in Laos, 0.8 in Cambodia and 258 in Singapore.
4. A hackathon (from the combination of *hacking* and *marathon*) is an intensive sprint-like event that brings together computer programmers, developers and designers to collaborate on software projects.

References

Aung Kyaw Nyunt. 2016. "Ministry Puts Mobile Penetration at 90 Percent". *Myanmar Times*, 19 July 2016. http://www.mmtimes.com/index.php/business/technology/21466-ministry-puts-mobile-penetration-at-90-percent.html.

CPJ (Committee to Protect Journalists). 2012. "In Mass Amnesty, Nine Journalists Released in Burma". 13 January 2012. https://cpj.org/2012/01/in-mass-amnesty-nine-journalists-released-in-burma.php.

Cunningham, S. 2016. "Myanmar: 45 millions Mobile Phones and $19 3G Smartphone". *Forbes*, 10 October 2016. http://www.forbes.com/sites/susancunningham/2016/08/10/myanmar-45-million-mobile-phones-and-the-19-3g-smartphone/#38d8c1d02fe8.

Gillmore, S. 2016. "Telenor CEO Talks Data Consumption, Competition and Reinvestment. *Myanmar Times*, 21 November 2016. http://www.mmtimes.com/index.php/business/technology/23804-telenor-ceo-talks-data-consumption-competition-and-reinvestment.html.

Human Rights Watch. 2009. *Burma's Forgotten Prisoners* (September).

———. 2013. "Reforming Telecommunications in Burma: Human Rights and Responsible Investment in Mobile and the Internet". 19 May 2013. https://www.hrw.org/report/2013/05/19/reforming-telecommunications-burma/human-rights-and-responsible-investment-mobile.

Kanale, H. 2017. "Myanmar to Reach 28% Internet Penetration and 15 Million Users". *Internet in Myanmar*, 12 October 2017. https://www.internetinmyanmar.com/internet-penetration-sept-17/.

McPherson, P. 2017. "Free Speech Curtailed in Aung San Suu Kyi's Myanmar as Prosecution Soars". *The Guardian*, 9 January 2017. https://www.theguardian.com/world/2017/jan/09/free-speech-curtailed-aung-san-suu-kyis-myanmar-prosecutions-soar.

MMRD. 2017. "5 Facts about Internet Market in Myanmar". 17 February 2017. http://www.mmrdrs.com/5-facts-about-the-internet-market-in-myanmar/.

Oh, S. 2016. "Tech and 2015 Elections: What We'd Learnt?" Phandeeyar, 2 March 2016. http://phandeeyar.org/tech-and-the-2015-elections-whatd-we-learn/.

OpenNet Initiative. 2012. "Country Profile: Burma (Myanmar)". https://opennet.net/research/profiles/burma#footnoteref39_47ke7nm.

State Counsellor Office. 2016. "Government Launches Economic Policy". The Republic of the Union of Myanmar, 1 August 2016. http://www.statecounsellor.gov.mm/en/node/171.

20

Counter-Narratives: Myanmar's Digital Media Activists

Sarah Oh

Eventually it would help her understand comments on her Facebook feed, like "Kalars should get out of our country" and "Kalars are setting our country on fire". A gift to her from her father when she passed her school matriculation exam, her vintage radio played the BBC, Voice of America, and Radio Free Asia for three hours every morning and night. She listened to it faithfully, earning her the nickname "grandmom". Then, in 2012, when Khin Oo was 28, her radio reported that violence had broken out between Rakhine Buddhists and Rohingya Muslims in Rakhine State.

Khin Oo is Muslim. She has a small frame and speaks in whispers. "I love getting and sharing information", she told me. After the 2012 Rakhine riots, and what she learned from the news, she said, "I knew I needed to work for peace and educate my people and those who hate us." She set her sights on working in Mandalay, a town a few hours away from her home in Shan State, with an organization working to promote peace and education.

Khin Oo finally made it to Mandalay in 2014, where she began working with a peace organization, and also enrolled in law school.

The deadly beating of a young Buddhist man that same year, publicized on Facebook, led to an unexpected beginning. "Muslims are responsible for the beating" and "Muslims should leave the country" someone behind her said when he thought she could not hear. No one would sit near her in class after the beating. One day, in her second year of school, she saw several posts on her Facebook newsfeed about a monk who had fallen in the market. The posts said a woman, said to be Muslim, tripped him. Users threatened revenge against the Muslim responsible, and others weighed in with slurs against the Muslim faith. The next day, mobs burned several shops and homes in retaliation. The truth, she later learned, was that a young Muslim girl had accidentally run into a monk, causing him to fall. A minor incident had escalated into an aggressive act, leading people to blame a religious community, wrongly, and to commit acts of violence for revenge. She saw what could happen when people take action based on incomplete or incorrect information.

During a visit home to Shan State in 2015, her non-Muslim neighbours said things like "Muslims will kill our daughters" and "Muslims will disrupt our peace". When she asked her friends, "where did you get this information?" they unanimously said, "Facebook". Her neighbours and friends spoke about Facebook the same way one would talk about information published by a newspaper or broadcast on the radio. They tapped their phones to scroll down through their feeds to show her status updates, stories and photos to prove the point: they were afraid of Muslims. She saw what fear could drive people to believe. She also felt it personally. After graduation she worked in the courts but she was unable to obtain a lawyer's licence because of her non-citizenship status. At the time, her family faced difficulty paying the fees and getting her a citizenship card because she was Muslim.

Khin Oo admits she once felt the same fear towards Buddhists that her neighbours felt towards Muslims. She had seen pictures on Facebook of monks destroying homes and shops during riots in Mandalay in 2014. These images became imprinted in her consciousness, making her afraid in the presence of monks, even when she rode around Mandalay on her motorbike. "In my eyes", she said, "they are the problem maker that created conflict." It was only later, after she began to learn about communal tensions, that she began to distinguish nationalist monks from other monks and was able to conquer her fear.

She told her neighbours, equipped with their newly purchased smartphones, to find and follow reliable information through verified media sources. "The problem is they do not know what I mean by good information", she says. The people from her home community, who she calls "ordinary grass-roots people", read the hate speech fed into their palms. Even her teachers, who she looks up to and turns to for advice, believe what they see on Facebook and often become filled with fear. "I can't control them", she said.

Taking Action

In the months before Myanmar's national elections in November 2015, Khin Oo says she began to engage directly with Facebook users to dispel rumours and misinformation that, in her view, propagated hate and inflamed intercommunal tensions. She posted "right speech" and "right information" by commenting on other users' comments and posts to correct misunderstandings and challenge errors and misinformation.

Khin Oo is one of several Facebook commenters or social media activists I spoke with in 2015 and 2016 who identified themselves as working to counter hate speech. Some are Muslim, but some are not; in fact some are monks worried about protecting their religion. Many are youths and students, but some are older, in their 30s and 40s. They all, however, collectively feel the weight of the future of their country. They desperately want to take action against online hate speech and the spread of misinformation. These individuals, almost all of whom asked to remain unnamed, describe their work as "sharing" new points of view and "talking about different ideas". A review of some of the posts and comments they have distributed and collected, however, shows they are much more intentional and strategic about their actions.

A significant amount of online hate speech in Myanmar occurs in comment threads on Facebook pages of Myanmar-language news outlets, such as BBC Burmese and *7Day News*, and on Facebook discussion groups organized around various topics, such as politics. In December 2016 a commenter posted a photo of men wearing prayer caps with the comment "Muslims speak like dogs" in a discussion group. One user responded, "Muslims worship five times a day in a timely manner. I found them worshipping quite often on the train." To this comment, another user replied, "They are doing good deeds. We should have empathy ... they pay homage, like to the Buddha." In this case these commenters were trying to tap into the original poster's humanity.

There are also examples of commenters posting real news to counter rumours and misinformation. In September 2015, gruesome photos of a dead monk in Rakhine State, rumoured to have been killed by a Muslim man, went viral on Facebook. In the tense pre-election environment, many worried that the post alone would spark communal violence, as similar posts had in previous years. On the same day the photos were shared, the news outlet *The Irrawaddy* published a story confirming that police investigators believed the monk had most likely committed suicide, countering the rumour that a Muslim man had killed him. Activists and journalists actively shared the article and quashed the rumour. One young woman, a civic activist who posted the article the day it was released, told me, "[users] really appreciate [me] when I explain news events." "I teach people online through Facebook comments", she said.

I reviewed some of Khin Oo's Facebook comments that were more direct. During the Muslim holiday of Eid in 2015, a user posted a photo of a grotesque animal, saying "BREAKING NEWS: This animal is assumed to be Allah which was found on Eid inside a mosque." The following exchange took place:

Khin Oo:	We cannot make Buddhism flourish by insulting other religions. Respecting other religions is the noble act taught by Buddha.
User:	I respect every religion except this one. Thank you.
Khin Oo:	Why? You posted it because you don't like the religion.
User:	Because they are destroyed other religions except their own. If you don't like it, I will take it down.

The user deleted the photo.

It is human nature for people to get confused about information, Khin Oo told me. "Counter messaging with real information means giving [a] second thought to the people", she said.

Htin, another activist, shared another strategy with me. He posted graphics of lotus flowers and quotes from Buddhist scripture under hate speech comments. He hoped they would influence the person who posted hate speech and make others think twice before adding more hateful comments to the thread.

A thread of comments on a BBC Burmese article in September 2015 about a stampede near Mecca that killed more than seven hundred people taking part in the hajj included hate speech. Muslims are violent, many comments read. Underneath the comments, Htin showed me where he had posted an image of a pink lotus flower, a Buddhist symbol that represents purity of speech. There were no more comments after he posted the flower. He believed this would make people think twice about posting additional hate speech.

Khin Oo says people are afraid to express their feelings on their own. When a person has a different opinion on an issue, they will only vocalize it when they see others express their views, she says. "[Countering] will make people see that people are thinking in different ways", Khin Oo reflects. Yet, even if they do agree, in most cases people do not directly reply to her messages. They simply hit the Facebook "Like" button. When she posted "We youth in Mandalay do not like this photo" on a post that included a dehumanizing photo comparing a Muslim man to a dog, her message received thirty likes but no comments.

Ma Ba Tha, the Committee for the Protection of Nationality and Religion, a Buddhist extremist organization, actively and systematically created and curated online hate speech content. The group strategically produced content on online blogs and Facebook pages supporting messages like "Muslims threaten Myanmar's sovereignty", promoting Burmese racial purity, and Buddhist religious sanctity. Some posts developed and shared by Ma Ba Tha supporters received up to sixteen thousand shares within days of posting.

Ma Ba Tha has been difficult to counter, activists have told me. In July 2016, Yangon Chief Minister Phyo Min Thein said in an interview, "We don't need Ma Ba Tha." This was viewed by the public as a rebuke of the organization. Yet, even when greeted by protests in Yangon, he did not take back his comment, which had gone viral on Facebook. Several users shared messages in solidarity with Phyo

Min Thein in the days and weeks after he made his comment. Several hundred people used a Web application made by a young developer to overlay their Facebook profile picture with the message "We Stand with Phyo Min Thein". Ma Ba Tha demanded an apology, threatening the minister with nationwide protests unless his party apologized on his behalf. Later that month the National League for Democracy (NLD) said they had no interest in responding to Ma Ba Tha's demands for an apology or response.

By dismissing Ma Ba Tha, the state authorities allowed others with the same opinion to speak up and reject them. When people saw other users — including their peers and powerful leaders — express a message that resonated with them, this made them more willing to share their beliefs publicly.

Challenges to Countering Hatred

People in Myanmar, like elsewhere, engage more readily with lyrical poems, cartoons, videos, animations, graphics and photos than with plain text on Facebook. Even with plain text, witty or clever online content performs better. In an analysis of anti-extremist content in six countries, Demos — a UK-based think tank and research organization — found that videos and humorous content were likely to engage people more readily, suggesting that the look and feel of counter content has an impact on its effectiveness (Bartlett and Krasodomski-Jones 2015).

The social media activists I have spoken with admit that they need more support to develop skills to create better content. One young man, Ko Gyi, points to the skills gap between himself and nationalist organizations, for example, when it comes to online content. "There are many things that can support their content. There are many websites that write about Islamic terrorists. They can translate it easily. Under their posts, there are strong people who will comment and agree", he says.

The emotional stress that results from engaging with hate speech online for extended periods is significant. Khin Oo is often attacked online. Users have sent her messages through Facebook Messenger asking, "Are you married to a Muslim man?" "Have you been brainwashed?" "Why do you speak like that?" These messages remind her of the harassment that she and her family have experienced since she was a child simply because they are Muslim. Khin Oo says she has often felt like screaming out of rage in reaction to these messages; there are times when she is worried she will not be able to control her anger. Other times she feels confused and frustrated when people do not respond as she expects to her comments and posts.

In October 2016, nationalist hardliners shamed and attacked civic activists and local journalists covering a deadly attack on a Myanmar police station on the Bangladesh-Myanmar border near a town called Maungdaw. At least one local journalist based in Yangon left Myanmar for his safety when he received more than a thousand insulting and threatening Facebook messages and posts. He was criticized for reporting information that diverged from the government's narrative about the attacks. Smear campaigns are frequent, and often the people targeted by these campaigns close their Facebook accounts or pages or go into hiding, shutting down a vital communication outlet.

Countering Fear Itself

Immediately following the October 2016 attack near Maungdaw, "jihadi" videos featuring members of a Muslim insurgent group that claimed responsibility went viral on Facebook. A search for the word *Rakhine* in English and Myanmar language on Facebook uncovered posts with graphic, unverified images of tortured children, people fleeing villages, and dismembered bodies. Photos of mutilated pigs and comments dehumanizing Muslims were posted.

The Myanmar government provided status updates about the attack and forthcoming military clearance operations on Facebook through the official pages of the President's Office and the Ministry of Information, yet little more information than "an investigation is ongoing" was shared. The government restricted access to Rakhine for media and international government leaders.

After these events, the absence not only of information but also of posts countering inaccurate reports was highly noticeable. Frustrated that he could not speak his mind on social media, Myo Win Nyunt, a young political observer, said, "I feel like my freedom is threatened."

The situation made him feel too vulnerable to share views inconsistent with those communicated by the military and supported by the government. Another activist often vocal on Facebook on anti-hate issues, who asked not to be named, said she could not express even her most basic feelings about the attack and the military's response. Posting about the situation in Rakhine State on Facebook "would lead to more anger and fighting and create more problems", she said. Fear was at the heart of both of these responses — fear of law enforcement, but also of the opinion of their peers. There was no countering.

In this environment, organizations focused on hate speech can develop methods to better track hate speech accounts and promote information-literacy programmes to help the public better resist content produced to coerce or inflame tensions. Yet researchers involved with the Myanmar Media and Society project led by researchers from Oxford University and the Myanmar ICT Development Organization (MIDO) have observed that society's fearful responses deserve far more attention than questions about information literacy when studying dangerous speech and conflict. They ask whether our time might not be better spent addressing the justifications people use when they share modified images, rather than the fake pictures themselves. In other words, how might one look beyond the narratives and posts that are designed to stoke that fear, and conquer the fear itself?

Doing What We Can

Facebook has allowed immediate access and connectivity for users in Myanmar, an undeniable fact, whether it is following the elections, swapping opinions on current events or learning about whether there was an earthquake. "Facebook is freedom", Htet Khine, a young BBC Action radio journalist told me, reflecting on how the platform has allowed her to report on complicated issues and to express her opinions on social topics. The scale of this change is significant in a place where young people like Khin Oo previously received credible news from a few foreign radio stations. Khin Oo was a university student when she first opened her Facebook account in 2009. She signed up for the social media platform at a computer class in Mandalay. SIM cards and data were still expensive then, so she went to her neighbourhood internet cafe to use the social media platform to chat with friends about their daily lives. Facebook was "very peaceful" she says, and she does not remember seeing any hate speech.

Khin Oo used to believe that the internet, and by extension Facebook, could be a space for peace, where people could openly express their opinions without fear of attack. She posts counter comments with this conviction and belief in the platform's potential, but she told me it is growing more difficult. She worries now that her friends and family will never truly realize the full potential of the internet, or Facebook, as a vehicle for expression, and her work is "not enough". But she is doing what she can, for now, she says.

Editors' Postscript

This chapter was written in response to the violence that began in 2012, but before later military offensives, especially in 2017, that have driven nearly 700,000 Muslim Rohingya from Myanmar. After the 2012 violence, Facebook was widely recognized as a primary platform for the spread of virulent hate speech, contributing to further violence. In June 2018, Facebook removed the account of the Buddhist organization Ma Ba Tha and the accounts of its leaders. These have since reappeared under different guises.

The author of this chapter, Sarah Oh, is now working for Facebook on a range of issues, including social conflict, hate speech and misinformation.

In December 2016, Khin Oo began working with a social media campaign that supports civil society organizations working for peace, tolerance and intercommunal harmony, especially in relation to Facebook content. She conducts training and coaches civil society groups on these issues. Yet she is concerned that countering hate speech with challenging comments is not effective on its own, especially since those organizations promoting hate speech far outnumber and often threaten the activists challenging their activities. She also finds that Facebook is slow to respond to reports of hate speech and to remove such problematic posts. "In my opinion", she says, "we should raise awareness about digital literacy in our communities." Most people do not understand how to check for fake news or the accuracy of the news or accompanying photographs. "If we don't have a plan to debunk fake news and hate speech, we will face a big problem between majority and minority religious groups during the 2020 elections."

Reference

Bartlett, J., and A. Krasodomski-Jones. 2015. *Counter-Speech: Examining Content that Challenges Extremism Online*. London: Demos. http://www.demos.co.uk/wp-content/uploads/2015/10/Counter-speech.pdf.

Epilogue: Media Studies in Myanmar – Where Do We Go from Here?

Lisa Brooten, Jane Madlyn McElhone and Gayathry Venkiteswaran

Media have immense power to shape the stories we hear and see and, by extension, how we understand the world. Through new technologies we contribute to the ongoing construction of these stories. It is no surprise that media are one of the first targets of authoritarian leaders who seize control, repressing or assimilating them somehow into the power structure. Forms of control in democratic societies are more subtle, and the threats less severe for those who challenge power holders, but media are nonetheless sites of struggle over who defines the public agenda as well as the discourse used to discuss it. Media play multiple, shifting and highly contextual roles, perpetuating the status quo as agents of stability; holding officials and official institutions to account as agents of restraint; and challenging the status quo and holding the powerful to account as agents of change (McCargo 2003). We have seen throughout this volume how a single media outlet can play all of these roles at various times. As media have become more pervasive in our lives, it is vital that we understand as much as possible about the people and organizations that produce the stories we see, what effects these representations are having, and how these phenomena function for or against the interests of the various key stakeholders, especially the public, at local, national and global levels.

The field of media studies in Myanmar is just beginning to develop.[1] This short summary addresses only the research published in English, but we encourage a similar assessment of the research available in Myanmar language. The majority of research in English is comprised of reports written by advocacy organizations or journalists, and is mainly descriptive, although some reports do analyse new or reformed media laws, or assess the changing state of freedom of expression. This body of work is also largely focused on journalism and on events in the major cities of Yangon and Mandalay. While media studies include the study of journalism, the field is much broader in scope, incorporating all types of media platforms and content and moving beyond the "how-to" to focus critical and analytical attention on three primary areas: media texts, media audiences and media industries. In Myanmar, media-related educational opportunities focus on practical journalism skills training, and to some extent filmmaking. The systematic, critical study of media that includes, but is not focused on, journalism has not yet been established in Myanmar's research and educational institutions.

Academic studies of Myanmar media in English are few and far between, although this is starting to change as the country continues to open and a new generation of Myanmar scholars emerges. Many of the studies that do exist fall into common conceptual traps, such as an overemphasis on journalism or the conflation of "media" and "journalism"; the tendency to analyse texts combined with a relative lack of attention to audiences' uses of, trust in, and interpretations of media; a media-centric focus that does not take into account the context in which events occur or pay attention to the political economy of the media or those key structural issues such as the interconnections between ownership, economics and political interests that also influence content. Much of the recent media research is focused on digital media, especially Facebook and its role in the violence that began in 2012 in Rakhine State.

Major gaps in the English language scholarship on Myanmar media, which mirror critiques of media studies generally, are the relative inattention to the study of Myanmar language media, the study of audiences, and research on the political economy of media. Those studies in English that analyse content tend to focus on English-language media in Myanmar. The analyses by the Myanmar Institute for Democracy, in collaboration with Memo 98, of the 2015 election coverage, 2017 Rakhine coverage, and 2018 political and social issues coverage are rare examples of Myanmar-language media content analysis (MID 2015, 2016, 2017, 2018). This volume provides two exceptions to this lacunae: chapters by Jennifer Leehey on the legal case against *Tanintharyi Weekly* in which she analyses the editorial column that triggered the lawsuit, and Susan Banki and Ja Seng Ing's chapter assessing precarity and risk through an analysis of content from *The Irrawaddy* in English and Myanmar language. The exceptions to the dearth of audience studies are the few functional assessments of audiences, such as periodic ratings measurements conducted to assess who is consuming which forms of media, and small surveys or anecdotal accounts of audiences' media use by journalists and media development or advocacy organizations. Assessments of the political economy of Myanmar media are a much-needed contribution to an in-depth analysis of the Myanmar media landscape, and they would ideally include a mapping of media ownership and consolidation, cross-media ownership, and conglomeration of ownership that includes non-media holdings leading to potential conflicts of interest. This is an area that needs immediate attention. These gaps in the literature are reflected in *Myanmar Media in Transition*, as we were unable to find scholars conducting systematic research on the political economy of Myanmar media, on audiences and their interpretations of the media they consume, or in-depth analyses of Myanmar-language news media or state-run media.

This volume endeavours to avoid the common weaknesses in media studies research generally. While journalism is a necessary focus of research, there are many other media that also influence change; we thus take a broader view of media studies by paying attention to culture as a factor in the process of change. We also emphasize the need to take history seriously and to avoid the pitfalls of assuming, for example, that journalism began with the recent changes, that the long period of exile had no influence on the current media landscape, or that journalism studies not focused on Yangon or Mandalay are less relevant. We have heard versions of all of these arguments. Finally, we have chosen to avoid the "media systems" approach to understanding Myanmar media in this period of political, economic and social change and instead to think about *processes* of change and media as agents in this process themselves, or as tools for other agents, as in the case of social media. Helping to highlight the multiple and shifting roles of media, this framework is more nuanced than a "media systems" approach. It allows researchers to explore the three areas of media studies research — media texts, audiences and industries — and points to areas of policy and aid support that need attention.

Media as Active Agents in the Process of Change

The academics, writers, journalists, reform advocates and activists contributing to this volume amply illustrate the multiple roles of media as agents of stability, restraint and change as laid out by McCargo (2003).

Myanmar media are often agents of stability, promoting and maintaining the status quo, unstable as the status quo may be. The state-run media are obvious examples. State control over broadcasting and print production and distribution infrastructure, state media's ability to dominate ad revenue, and the state's structural advantages through economies of scale in print and ink, for example, ensure this stability-promoting role for state-run media. The status quo is also promoted as media succumb to the culture of fear and silence around sensitive topics, as journalists self-censor, and as the legal environment lacks basic protections for journalists and does not yet provide for transparency of information about government practices and processes. These are themes that are amply developed throughout this volume. Thin Lei Win demonstrates the ways in which the media reinforce gender relations and perpetuate patriarchal discourses. Both Eaint Thiri Thu and Ye Naing Moe discuss the need for journalists and editors to carefully consider the words they use, such as the much-maligned and debated use of the name *Rohingya* and how this functions to maintain the status quo and the dominant narrative on citizenship and political participation. Many restrictive laws used to sue journalists also serve as examples of how media are often forced to play stabilizing roles via their reporting, whether or not that is their intention. Those in the creative industries such as filmmaking and music who rely on government distribution and exhibition opportunities and as a result are unable to challenge the status quo offer additional examples of stability-promoting media.

Even before the political opening, both internal and exiled media functioned as agents of restraint in their role as watchdogs, by reporting critically on those in power, reporting on corruption and, especially for the exiled media, critically covering the conflicts in the ethnic states. Yet, for media inside the country, this often led to censorship or arrest, resulting in more subtle forms of promoting restraint, such as critique through "writing between the lines" and the ample use of metaphor and analogy to point out social ills. Journalists and other media makers have slowly been expanding the boundaries by writing, singing, and documenting on film important public interest issues and by holding the authorities accountable, even if this has come at a price. Since the opening, media have increasingly functioned as agents of restraint, pushing the authorities to follow the laws themselves. The high-profile case of the Reuters journalists Wa Lone and Kyaw Soe Oo is a good example, as their investigation focused on the role of Myanmar soldiers in the killing of ten Rohingya men and on the laws broken by those soldiers. Shortly before Reuters published the report, the Myanmar military admitted to having a role in the killings and jailed seven of the soldiers involved. Artists, including writers, poets and cartoonists, used their craft to critique the Thein Sein and NLD governments, as well as the military, as social commentaries on the abuse of power and laws, or as expressed frustrations over broken promises of reforms. These are efforts to pressure the government and other powerful forces to obey existing laws and make use of existing regulatory structures. This function of media has been suppressed for decades, but if the space for free expression expands, we should expect to see more media performing this function.

It is not surprising that Myanmar media have been active participants in many of the country's struggles for political change, and this current period is no exception, as Chapter 1 details. Journalists, writers and media activists have been at the forefront of efforts to push for changes to regressive laws and in protests against the mistreatment of journalists and artists, as discussed in Chapter 2. Media have also been tools for the promotion of change sought by other groups, at times partnering with them on stories. Civil society groups have engaged with media and influenced reporting in the push for legislative changes, notably the challenge to Section 66(d) of the Telecommunications Law, which has become a new tool of repression. Launched by a group of bloggers, Myanmar ICT for Development Organization (MIDO), as described in Chapter 19, is another example of the use of new media as tools for change, including empowering young people and communities to use media to exercise their rights and to operate as a check on the government.

Media promote change when they introduce new narratives, new forms of discussion, and new openness, and when they provide a forum for the production of counter-narratives that challenge dominant perspectives in society. Work done by online activists, for example as highlighted by Sarah Oh in her chapter, is intended to offer critical and nuanced challenges to problems in Myanmar society, such as the hate speech disseminated online and through the news media. This work challenges the dominant social and media narratives used in discussing these issues, such as the Rohingya and the violence perpetrated against them. Other examples highlighted in this volume include the work of the Human Rights, Human Dignity Film Festival, which was able to openly discuss human rights in the country after decades of forced silence around this topic, and to provide a platform for young independent filmmakers to explore social issues previously regarded as taboo. As demonstrated in Chapter 18 on Facebook's use among public figures, despite being used as a forum for hate speech, or in mimicking state-run media, Facebook and other online platforms have also introduced new forms of communication with the state and offered people new opportunities to push for progressive forms of change.

Media's Multiple and Conflicting Roles

Media generally play multiple roles, which are highly contextual. Their function in promoting stability often conflicts with their role as agents of restraint. For example, ethnic media have to perform checks and balances on government and military actions, as well as ethnic armed organizations, but are also unwilling agents of stability because of the self-censorship that this demands, as Chapter 9 details. For example, members of the ethnic media network BNI are caught in limbo; while one of its co-founders was a Rohingya media group located in the borderlands during military rule (suggesting the network's role as an agent of change), now that it has moved inside the country it is grappling with new journalistic and ethical dilemmas, as well as internal tensions, that often advantage the network's Rakhine voices. Other media once in exile and now back in the country have also witnessed a fluidity in roles. The chapter on *The Irrawaddy*'s coverage of three natural disasters in 2008, 2011 and 2015 demonstrates how it has shifted its role to become more of an agent for stability than it was while in exile, toning down its criticism of the quasi-civilian Thein Sein government over the period under study.

These cases illustrate a larger trend during transition periods; namely, gaps in expectations between media and other institutions that contribute to the multiplicity of roles media perform. Despite their longstanding mistrust of the government and expectations of freedom of the press surrounding elections, during the 2015 elections most journalists accepted the realities on the ground, including the regulations and accreditation process set out by the Union Election Commission, as this was the only way to access polling stations and conduct interviews with the authorities. This required their acquiescence to the status quo. In some ways, the military-led commission was legitimized through the media's acceptance of rules promoting stability, but the media also used the historic opportunity to conduct extensive coverage of elections for the very first time inside the country.

The international donors, INGOs and foreigners who have worked with media and activists inside and outside of the country for decades have contributed to the capacities of Myanmar journalists, writers, photographers, researchers, filmmakers, artists and activists to advocate for political change. Arguably, however, international assistance has also helped recipients from the state media become stronger as agents of stability. These contradictions highlight the need for more critical work on the influence of international aid and media reform efforts in the country.

Myanmar media, like all institutions, are active in shaping, as well as being shaped by, the environment in which they operate. For a long time they have been either agents of change, pushing for political reforms and fighting for more space to air diverse viewpoints, including critiques of those in power, or agents of stability, perfunctorily reporting the government line. There has been very little space for media to act as agents of restraint, as watchdogs and commentators on the contemporary scene, provoking conversation and reflection on key issues of the day. This has started to change. Ideally, this change should come from the ground up, from engaged individuals and groups who, for the time being, push media to operate primarily as agents of change, and, if the space for free expression allows, increasingly as agents of restraint. Hopefully, media will eventually function in all three capacities at the same time: to promote the stability of democratic practices and culture; to restrain leaders and others from corruption or misbehaviour and to keep them accountable to the people; and to continue to act as change agents when there is such a need. This would provoke the open discussion and debate for which so many in Myanmar have struggled for so long to achieve.

Note

1. The study of media and their impact on society emerged as an increasingly organized focus of research in the 1940s and 1950s in Europe and North America, with roots largely in literary and early cultural studies in Europe, and in sociology and the social sciences in North America. A long history of research, discussion and debate have broadened the field considerably since then, and research methodologies now range from large-scale surveys and content analyses intended to be representative of audiences and texts, respectively, to smaller scale, more detailed and contextualized studies employing ethnographic methods, in-depth interviews and close analyses of specific texts. Media studies tend to be highly interdisciplinary, drawing on fields as diverse as psychology, sociology, economics, political science, law and ethics. Contemporary media studies scholarship falls into two main camps. Some scholars work on functional or administrative research intended to assist governments, regulators and advocacy organizations to regulate and improve media, while others focus on analysing media's use by various stakeholders in the interests of power. These critical scholars work to redirect or at least minimize the damage caused by the major global trends of ownership consolidation, corporate conglomeration, privatization and deregulation that have so drastically challenged the ability of media around the world to remain independent from the state and the dictates of commercial interests.

Index

Page numbers followed by "n" refer to endnotes

A

ABSDF. *See* All Burma Students Democratic Front (ABSDF)
AGIPP. *See* Alliance for Gender Inclusion in the Peace Process (AGIPP)
Ahidjo, A., 270
Ahr Man, 114
Akyab Commercial News, 16
ALC. *See* Art and Language Center (ALC)
All Burma Students Democratic Front (ABSDF), 226n31
Alliance for Gender Inclusion in the Peace Process (AGIPP), 15
Alliance Française, 26
Allott, A., 25
anti-government protests, 5
anti-mine activists, 188
anti-Muslim violence, 210, 211, 224n5
Ant Khaung Min, 78
Art and Language Center (ALC), 154
Article 8(f) of the privacy law, 70
Article 16 of the UN's Declaration on the Rights of Indigenous Peoples, 213
Article 17(1) of the Unlawful Association Act, 82
Article 18 of the Peaceful Assembly and Peaceful Procession Law, 84
ARTICLE 19 (organization), 106, 244, 245
Article 19 of the Universal Declaration of Human Rights, 61
Article 19(a) of the News Media Law, 67
Article 25(b) of the News Media Law, 73, 78, 82, 175n15, 217
Article 75 of the 2013 Telecommunications Law, 142
Article 354 of the constitution, 67
Article 500 of the Penal Code, 82, 152, 165, 168
Article 505(b) of the Penal Code, 78
Athan, 4, 26, 45n3, 80, 331
Atkinson, P., 184
Aung Htun U, 117
Aung Kyaw Naing, 40, 82, 220, 226n34
Aung Kyi, 67
Aung Lwin, 152, 153, 159, 160, 162–72, 174n9, 217

Aung San, 14, 18, 232, 279, 293
Aung San Suu Kyi, 74, 82, 241, 245, 247, 345, 350
  boycott of elections of 2010, 2
  expectations for her as leader, 3, 323
  house arrest, 22
  and human rights, 309
  as leader of the opposition, 22, 73
  media coverage of, 4, 37, 78, 133–34, 241
  and peace negotiations, 15, 82, 241
  release from house arrest, 39
  social media coverage of, 345, 348–50, 354
  as State Counsellor, 45n4
Aung Than Htut, 185
Aung Thet Mann, 34
Aung Zaw, 178, 192
Ayaun Thit, 21
Aye Aye Zin, 156
Aye Mye Htet, 107

B
Ba Ba Win, 294
Bagan Cyber Tech, 28, 46n16
Ba Gyan, 318
Ba Htoo, 154
Bangkok Post, 154
Ban Tha Song Yang, 24
Barmanization, 213, 319
Ba Thaw, 22
BBS. *See* Burma Broadcasting Service (BBS)
bilateral ceasefire agreement, 218, 226n35
Bi Mon Te Nay Journal, 78
BNI. *See* Burma News International (BNI)
Bo Aung Kyaw, 17
Bob, C., 181

Brang Mai, 116, 213–14
BRC. *See* Burma Relief Centre (BRC)
British Colonial Period, 4, 15–18, 25, 65, 168, 288, 292
Broadcasting Law, 36, 67, 68, 215
Brooten, L., 179, 191
BSPP. *See* Burmese Socialist Program Party (BSPP)
Buchanan, D., 269
Buddhist nationalism, 281
Burma Broadcasting Service (BBS), 25
Burma Herald, 16
Burma News International (BNI), 45n6, 108, 210–14, 220, 392
Burma Press Council, 18
Burma Relief Centre (BRC), 105–7
Burma Socialist Program Party (BSPP), 21, 157
Burma Translation Society, 133
Burmese Socialist Program Party (BSPP), 18, 288, 293, 295
"Burmese Way to Socialism", 19
Byerly, I., 270

C
Ca Mu, 186
Carroll, W.K., 179
Censorship, 3, 13, 21, 22, 35, 202
  creative expression under, 20
  military rule and, 1962–2010, 18–19
  of music, 267–68
  of online content, 80
  Printers and Publishers Registration Law of 1962, 18, 65
  Press Scrutiny Board, 19
  relaxation of, 37–38, 72, 133, 155, 204, 292
  rules, colonial origins of, 16, 168

Index

self-censorship, 40, 81, 206, 219, 269
See also pre-publication censorship
Center for International Media Assistance (CIMA), 98
Centre for Law and Democracy, 102
Cheesman, N., 65, 165
Chen, W., 115
Chiang Mai, 106, 115
CIMA. *See* Center for International Media Assistance (CIMA)
civic engagement, 373
  mobile applications for, 371–72
civil society, 63, 66, 83, 142–43, 154
  actors, 43, 85, 88, 156, 157
  groups, 43, 71, 145, 359, 391
  mobilization, 152
clientelism, 7–8
clientelistic systems, 9
Clinton, H., 273
Code of Conduct, 56, 255, 263n6
Coffey, A., 184
colonial-era laws, 4, 220
commercial media, 10
communal violence, 123, 230–34, 237, 377
communism, 125n5, 269, 272
communist regimes, 10
Comparing Media Systems, 6
Computer Science and Development Law, 27, 142
Conference on Media Development, 59, 84, 85, 95, 120, 121
copy thachin, 273–74, 283, 300
coup
  of 1962, 18, 37, 232, 293, 312
  of 1988, 20, 21, 22, 24, 295
Cowell, A., 295, 297
"cultural activism", 180
Cyclone Nargis, 28–30, 118, 133, 183–85, 202

D
Darusman, M., 328
Dawei Development Association (DDA), 153, 155
Dawei Special Economic Zone (SEZ) megaproject, 153, 157
Dawei Township Court, 175n15
Dawei Watch Media Group, 153
Daw Suu. *See* Aung San Suu Kyi
DDA. *See* Dawei Development Association (DDA)
defamation laws, 168–69
defamation lawsuits, 331
Delco, 158–60, 163, 170, 172, 173
democracy movement, 109, 121, 178
democracy spring, 20–22
Democratic Voice of Burma (DVB), 26, 28, 105, 113
Dhamma Thadinsa, 16
digital free-to-air channels, 68
digital media activists, 377–86
digital media convergence, 61
digital technologies, 61, 288
Ding Ying, 158
"discipline-flourishing democracy", 12
documentary filmmaking, 17, 26
Draft National Land Use Policy, 161
Dunkley, R. 25, 35
DVB. *See* Democratic Voice of Burma (DVB)

E
Eaint Khine Oo, 248, 249
Earthrights International (ERI), 155
"echo chamber" effect, 336
economic liberalization, 10
Ei Ei Moe, 2
EITI. *See* Extractive Industry Transparency Initiative (EITI)
Election Laws, 253

electoral legal framework, 262–63
Electronic Transaction Law, 69, 141, 142, 367, 368
Eleven Media, 35, 72, 76, 80, 132, 135, 137, 155
Emergency Provisions Act, 65, 78
Environmental Conservation Law, 160
Environmental Impact Assessment Procedure Law, 160, 161
ERI. *See* Earthrights International (ERI)
ethnic armed organizations, 15, 214, 218–21, 231–32
ethnic civil society organizations (CSOs), 14
ethnic media, 3, 38, 210–21, 213, 220–23
   challenges, 77, 215, 219, 221
   institutional support, 105, 107, 120
   operating overseas, 213
   relationships with ethnic armed organizations, 106, 214, 218
   training, 108, 112
   See also Burma News International (BNI)
ethnic rights, 41, 352
European Union Election Observation Mission, 260
Extractive Industry Transparency Initiative (EITI), 70

F
Facebook, 1–2, 144, 145, 335, 338–40, 373
FESR. *See* Framework for Economic and Social Reform (FESR)
film industry, 17, 38, 287–304, 308
filmmakers, 13, 38, 287–88, 291, 297–99, 303, 311
   development assistance for, 114
   from overseas, 26, 288, 295, 299
   young filmmakers, 108, 215, 296, 297–98, 310, 392
film studios, 20, 287, 290, 292, 301
financial technology companies, 144
Flew, T., 9
Fokwang, J., 270
Forever Group, 36, 45n15, 67
Framework for Economic and Social Reform (FESR), 141
Free Basics, 144, 145
Freedom of expression, 2, 17, 71, 124, 311, 323
   and Aung San Suu Kyi, 82
   and film industry, 38, 308, 311
   legal framework for, 63–66, 179, 280, 331
   and music industry, 280, 283
   promotion of, 221
   public awareness of, 60, 216, 322, 374
   restrictions on, 10, 39, 66, 71, 358, 369
Free Expression Myanmar, 80
Free Voice Netherlands (FVN), 110
Frontier Media, 35, 203–4
FVN. *See* Free Voice Netherlands (FVN)

G
"Gagging Act", 16
Gelfer, D., 274
gender balanced reporting, 86, 244, 246, 249, 390
gender equality/inequality, 15, 107, 244, 246, 249, 350
   in the peace process, 15
   in the media industry, 86, 244–49
Generation Wave movement, 2, 27
The Global New Light of Myanmar, 34, 68, 246

Index

grass-roots change agents, 11–13
Grömping, M., 335

H
Hackett, R.A., 179
Hallin, D.C., 6, 8
Hamilton, A., 289
Hamm, M., 284
hate speech, 27, 71, 88, 123, 302, 321
 against Rohingya, 42, 328, 385
 laws, 70, 71, 81
 online, 31, 42–43, 140, 328, 349–50, 359–60, 372–74, 379–86
Hinthar Media, 213
Hla Hla Soe, 342–43, 349, 350, 352
Hla Swe, 341, 345, 351, 352, 355, 357
Hla Thein, 262
Hnin Ei Hlaing, 291, 297, 299
Ho, W.-C., 269
Holmertz, D., 108
HRHDFF. *See* Human Rights Human Dignity Film Festival (HRHDFF)
Hsan Moe, 79
Hsa-tu-gaw, 16
Htet Khine, 384
Htin Kyaw, 4
Human Rights Human Dignity Film Festival (HRHDFF), 297, 308–9
human rights violations, 1, 44n1, 82, 190, 211, 231, 235
 documented in films, 308, 311
Human Rights Watch, 106, 230

I
IMMF. *See* Indochina Media Memorial Foundation (IMMF)
Indochina Media Memorial Foundation (IMMF), 105, 106–7
Indonesian Revolution of 1945–49, 271
information and communications technologies (ICTs) sector, 137
 and current regulatory framework, 141–43
 data revolution and explosion of digitally stored data, 139–41
 political transition, 138
 risks and opportunities, 143–45
"instrumentalism", 7
"insurgent press", 17
Interfaith Harmonious Coexistence Law, 71
Interim Press Council (IPC), 66, 67, 85
International Covenant on Civil and Political Rights, 61
International Criminal Court (ICC), 1, 44n1,
International Media Support (IMS), 102
Iosifidis, P., 9
IPC. *See* Interim Press Council (IPC)
The Irrawaddy, 36, 76, 136, 380
 analysis of its natural disaster coverage, 177–79, 184–93
 DDoS attack on, 137
 media development aid, 105, 115, 118
 news coverage of Tanintharyi, 154

J
Jacobson, A.S. 245, 249
Jacquet, C., 39
Jai Jai, 297–99, 303
Ja Seng Ing, 38, 87, 389
Jet Mya Thaung, 283
Jones, L., 157
journalism training, 98, 105, 108, 372
judiciary, 79, 166, 168
 and censorship, 60, 80
 and corruption, 71, 166
 independence of, 65, 82, 86, 167, 209, 226n34
 judicial torture, 80–81, 166

and media reform, 60, 64–66, 72, 82, 87
Judson, A., 16

K
Kachin ethnic armed groups, 202
Kachin Independence Army (KIA), 207, 245
Kachin Independence Organisation (KIO), 207
Kanbauk, mining in, 158–59
Karen Information Center, 108
Karen National Union (KNU), 108
Keane, J., 9
Kean, T., 59
Khin Hla, 185
Khin Maung Hla, 186
Khin Maung Win, 118, 125n9
Khin Nyunt, 23, 35, 46n16
Khin Oo, 377–85
Khin Soe, 160, 162
Khon Soe Moe Aung, 215
KIC, 212
King Mindon, 16
KIO. *See* Kachin Independence Organisation (KIO)
Knaus, J., 110, 111, 113
Kofi Annan, 348
Ko Gyi, 382
Ko Ko, 36
Ko Ko Lwin, 278
Ko Myint, 280
Ko Ni, 4, 45n4, 80
Krishna Sen, 7
kroncong, 271
Kürti, L., 284n2
Kyal Yie Lin Six, 301
Kyaw Hsan, 45n15, 67
Kyaw Min Swe, 125n8
Kyaw San, 38, 134

Kyaw Soe Oo, 2, 41, 77, 85, 192, 207, 208, 220, 391
Kyaw Swa Win, 78
Kyaw Thu Win, 41
Kyaw Win, 45n15
Kyaw Zwa Moe, 115, 118
Kyeet, 372
Kyemon, 34, 68

L
Lall, M., 12
Lan Kyal, 234
Lao Tzu, 351
law and order, 65, 165–68
Lawi Weng, 76, 191, 192
lawmaking process, 62–64, 82–83
Leehey, J., 19
Legacy Music, 278, 282
legal reform, 59–70, 82, 87, 141
Leong, L., 335
Letyar Tun, 216
Li, C.-T., 361n8
Li, L.J., 157, 161
Lin, S.-D., 361n8
literacy campaigns, 19
Lockard, C., 270
Lok-tha Pyei-thu Nei-zin, 21
Lyndal Min, 104, 105
Lynn Satt New, 301

M
Ma Ba Tha, 4, 5, 41, 80, 81, 381, 382, 385
Mae Pay Soh, 372
Mae Sai, 185
Mae Sot, 104, 105
Mai Naing Naing Oo, 116
Mancini, P., 6, 8
Mandela, N., 22
market liberalization, 329–31
Mark, S.S., 174n11

Marsh, L., 288
Ma Thein, 185
The Maulmain Chronicle, 15
Maung Saungkha, 3, 45n3
Maung Thawka, 22
McCargo, D., 7, 179, 190, 390
McCarthy, G., 335
McElhone, J.M., 95, 96, 120, 125n7, 238n3
McLean, S., 107, 108, 112
MCM. *See* Myanmar Consolidated Media (MCM)
media
  activism, 151, 179
  actors as social mobilizers, 179–81
  assistance, 11, 60, 97–98
  during pre-election period, 252–53
  and Rohingya situation, 41–43
media development, 60, 99, 104, 114, 120, 209
  organizations and networks, 100
  and political transitions, 97–104
Media Development Investment Fund (MDIF), 103, 111, 220
media laws, 59–70, 82, 87, 141
  during political opening, 66–69
media mobilization, 98
media policies, 61–63
media reform, 60, 64, 135, 168–69
media studies, 387–90
media systems approach, 389, 390
media transition, 5–8, 62
Mekong Media Fellowship, 115
memes, 355–57
Merrison, L., 26, 295, 296, 303
Milton, A., 10, 63
Mina, A.X., 335
Min Aung Hlaing, 1, 2, 328, 341, 345, 348–51, 353, 354, 357, 358, 368
Mingalar Company Ltd, 37
Mining Law, 160

Min Ko Naing, 342, 350–51, 368
Min Lu, 318
Mizzima, 34, 35, 36, 76, 136, 224n4
media development aid, 105, 118
MMA, 276–78, 280–81
mobile applications for civic engagement, 371–72
mobile services, growth in, 32
Mon Mon Myat, 114, 115, 117, 119
Motion Picture Council, 294
Motion Picture Organization, 23
Moustache Brothers, 30
M-PESA, 144
Myanma Alin, 17, 34, 68
Myanmar Consolidated Media (MCM), 131
Myanmar Core Press Council (MCPC), 67
Myanmar Dana, 132
Myanmar Egress, 29, 108, 109, 118
Myanmar ICT Development Organisation (MIDO), 343, 368, 372
Myanmar Institute for Democracy, 261
Myanmar Journalists Network (MJN), 84
Myanmar media, 30, 239–42, 251, 390, 393
  British Colonial Period, 15–18
  Cyclone Nargis, 28–30
  ethnic states, 210–21
  and free expression, 13–15
  Generation Wave movement, 27
  military rule and censorship, 18–20
  National League for Democracy (NLD), 24, 40–41
  political and legal framework for, 63–71
  political economy of, 32–34
  private media, 35–37

and Rohingya situation, 41–43
state/media relationships, 8–10
state-run broadcasting, 25
Myanmar Media Association, 23
Myanmar Musicians Association, 268
Myanmar National Democratic Alliance Army (MNDAA), 219
Myanmar nationalism and identity, 349–50
Myanmar Now, 80, 118, 203, 204, 246
See also Swe Win
Myanmar Peace Centre, 84
Myanmar Posts and Telecommunications (MPT), 27
Myanmar Press Council, 67, 78, 81, 85, 240, 256
Myanmar Radio, 20, 26
Myanmar Thandawsint, 78
Myanmar Times, 25, 35, 117, 131, 135, 136
Myanmar Women Journalists Society (MWJS), 248–49
Myawaddy Daily, 34
Myint Kyaw, 115, 117, 119, 167–69
Myint Moe Aung, 281
Myitkyina News Journal, 213
Myo Aung, 154–56, 166, 217
Myo Win Nyunt, 383
Myo Yan Naung Thein, 78

N
Nagai, K., 28
Nai Kasauh Mon, 77, 120, 217, 219, 226n33
Nai Nai, 244, 248
Nair, L., 101
nammeh-kyi deh, 277
Nan Paw Gay, 212, 216, 221, 227n37
National Broadcasting Council, 79
National Broadcasting Development Authority, 79, 80
National Ceasefire Agreement, 218
National Endowment for Democracy (NED), 105, 106, 110, 125n5
Nationalities Brotherhood Forum (NBF), 213
National League for Democracy (NLD)
digital future under, 373–74
engagement with civil society, 65, 85
formation of government in 2016, 40–41, 59–60
and free expression, 3, 323, 330–31
general elections of 1990, 24
general elections of 2010, 2
general elections of 2015, 251
and Human Rights, Human Dignity film festival, 312
and Ma Ba Tha, 382
and media law, 3–4, 66, 70, 73–75, 81–82, 87, 122, 368–69
silencing critics, 80, 87, 368
national security, 206, 311
content deemed harmful to, 37, 69, 77, 79
media laws pertaining to, 61, 64, 69, 142, 144, 311, 368
Nationwide Ceasefire Agreement (NCA), 226n35, 241
Nay Phone Latt, 116, 343, 349, 366–67, 375n1
Nay Win Htun, 280
Nay Win Maung, 35, 108
NED. *See* National Endowment for Democracy (NED)
Nelson, M., 100
New Democratic Army-Kachin (NDAK) militia, 158
Ne Win, 16, 18, 21, 65, 133, 232, 293–95, 317
New Light of Myanmar, 34, 134, 246

News Media Law, 65–66, 71, 77, 78, 85, 89n6, 254
Norris, P., 101
Nyamnjoh, F., 270
Nyan Lynn, 117
Nyan Paw, 318
Nyein Nyein Naing, 114

O
O'Brien, K.J., 157, 161
Official Secrets Act, 2, 65, 71, 77
Oo Oo Nyein, 82
Ooredoo, 34, 70, 143, 301
Open Society Foundations (OSF), 105–6, 116
Open Society Foundation's Burma Program, 109
OSF. *See* Open Society Foundations (OSF)
over-the-top (OTT) service, 140

P
Panglong Agreement, 14, 232
Pan, M., 116
Panneerselvan, A.S., 101
"pariah-state" status, 151
Pascal Khoo Thwe, 215
path dependency, 10
Peaceful Assembly and Procession Law, 69, 84, 162
Pekacz, J., 270
Pe Myint, 86, 89n14, 116
Penal Code, 65, 77
PEN Myanmar, 3, 116, 216, 322, 343, 368
personally identifiable information (PII), 141
Phandeeyar, 372
Phyo Min Thein, 342, 343, 350, 351, 381–82
Phyo Zayar Kyaw, 301

Phyu Phyu Kyaw Thein, 275, 282
Pieslak, J., 284
Piper, T. 111, 112
PII. *See* personally identifiable information (PII)
Polarized Pluralist Model, 8
policy inaction, 62
policy silence, 62
political cartooning, 18, 21
"political music", 279
Political Representation Law, 253
political transitions, 5–8, 123, 138, 202–3, 213
  media development and, 97–101
  media legal reforms during, 61–63
politics of language and ethnicity, 214–16
pop music industry in transition
  artistic freedom and its discontents, 279–82
  foreigners in Myanmar popular music scene, 272–75
  literature on music scenes, 268–72
  Myanmar Musicians Association and Advent of the Royalty Payment System, 275–79
post-Communist East Central Europe, 63
post-independence civilian rule, 15–18
Posts and Telecommunications Department (PTD), 139
post-Soviet Czechoslovakia, 271
post-Soviet democratic governments, 270
pre-exhibition censorship, 38
pre-publication censorship, 30, 37, 38, 132, 133, 243
  lifting of, 66, 86, 120, 135, 252, 257, 308

Press Scrutiny Board (PSB), 19, 20
Price, M.E., 11, 98, 100–102
Printing and Publishing Enterprise Bill, 66
Printing and Publishing Enterprise Law (PPEL), 65, 66, 71
private media, 35–37, 135, 256, 259
private newspapers, 18
privatization, 9, 11, 103, 191, 394n1
public service broadcasters, 68, 80, 98, 103, 124
Public Service Media Bill, 68
Publishers Registration Law, 18

R

Rakhine State, 16, 211–12, 229
   Buddhist community, 234, 237
   humanitarian crisis, 122, 210–11, 220, 373
   human rights violations in, 1–2, 211, 231, 235
   identity, language and rumours, 235–38
   media coverage of humanitarian crisis, 40, 41, 123, 207, 210–11, 241
Rakhine Commission, 348–49
Rangoon, 104
Reagan, R., 104
reformasi movement, 334
resource mobilization, 180
Resources Survival group, 160–62, 173
Reuters journalists Wa Lone and Kyaw Soe Oo, 2–3, 41, 76, 77, 85, 122–23, 192–93, 207, 220
Revolutionary Council, 294
Roadmap to Democracy. *See* Seven Step Roadmap to Disciplined Democracy
Robertson, S.P., 331
Rock Against Communism, 271
Rohingya
   citizenship status of, 14, 71, 207, 236, 241, 348
   crisis, 41–42, 44n1, 122, 192, 211, 385
   hate speech against, 42, 328, 385
   ICC evaluation, 44n1
   identity, 235–36, 348
   intercommunal conflict, 230–34, 237, 377
   massacre of, 2
   media, 210–14, 224n7, 225n17
   reporting on, 2, 41–42, 74, 76, 77, 192, 207, 210–14, 230–35, 241–42, 390
Root Investigative Agency, 211, 213
Rotberg, R., 82
Roudakova, N., 6
Rozema, G., 107, 112

S

Safe Online Space (SOS), 372
Saffron Revolution, 28–30, 38, 45n12, 113, 118, 133, 202, 334, 359
Sai Aw, 221
Sai Lek, 218–19, 226n28, 226n30, 226n31
Sai Sai Kham Leng, 282
Sandar Min, 367
Sawa ethnic group, 271
Saw Reagan, 291, 299
Say Yaung Zon, 30
Schissler, M., 336
Section 131 of the Penal Code, 85
Section 66(d) of the Telecommunications Law, 4, 40, 41, 70, 79–83, 172, 216–17, 331, 368, 369, 391–92
Segura, M., 12

Sein Win, 116, 125n8, 342, 352
Sekine, Y., 157
self-censorship, 40, 206–7, 217, 219, 269, 317
self-regulation, 78–80
Seng Mai, 77, 117, 215
Seng Mai Maran, 245, 248
Sen, K., 11
Seven Step Roadmap to Disciplined Democracy, 2, 29, 39, 63–64, 133
SEZ, 154
Sgaw Karen language, 16
Shan Herald Agency for News (SHAN), 107–8
Shwe Gyaw Gyaw, 283
Shwe Mann, 34, 35, 45n14
Shwe Ta Lay, 17
Shwe Taung Group, 37
Shwe Than Lwin, 36, 45n15
Sinpeng, A., 335
SkyNet, 36, 68
A Smile for an Election Campaign, 175n15, 217
Smith, M., 17, 23
social media, 1, 237, 316, 329, 331–37
  platforms, 42, 230
  as public sphere, 332–33
social mobilization, 181
social mobilizers, 179, 180, 190
social movements, 181
social networking, 329
social welfare organizations, 154
Soeharto, 11
Soe Lynn Htwe, 224n8
Soe Moe Tun, 40
Soe Myint, 118
Soe Soe Myar, 117
Soe Yazar Tun, 84
Sonny Swe, 25, 35
Sørensen, M.P., 333, 337, 352
Southeast Asian Press Alliance, 110

SPDC. *See* State Peace and Development Council (SPDC)
stakeholder engagement, 142
state-centrism, 8
state-funded media, 260
State Law and Order Restoration Council (SLORC), 21–23, 158, 295
state media, 4, 233, 316
state/media relationships, 8–10
state-owned entities, 135
state-owned newspapers, 68
State Peace and Development Council (SPDC), 154
state-run broadcasting, 25
Steemer, J., 9
"Stop Killing Press", 84
Subramaniam, S., 334
surveillance, government, 144, 177, 178, 320, 317, 320
  easing of, 155
  of the internet, 28, 138, 142, 144, 366
Swedish labour movement, 109
Swe Win, 5, 41, 80, 81, 87, 117, 351, 357

T
Ta'ang National Liberation Army, 81
Tai Freedom News Agency, 226n31
Takatho Khin Maung Zaw, 290
Tanintharyi, civil society and media in, 153–57
Tatmadaw, 70, 206, 218, 298
telecommunications
  development of, 27, 31–32, 89n9, 329, 370–71, 374
  licensing of, 69, 70, 341
  ownership of, 33
  reform and liberalization of, 37, 329, 339, 366–68, 370
  regulation of, 141–43

Telecommunications Law, 4, 40, 41, 69, 70, 79–83, 216–17, 331, 368, 369, 391–92
Than Htaik Thu, 79
Than Htut Aung, 35, 356
Than Shwe, 59, 187
Than Zaw Aung, 167, 169, 172
Thaung Su Nyein, 35
Thee Lay Thee, 30
Thein Sein, 356
  administration, 37–41, 77–78, 160, 253, 254
  mass amnesty by, 78
  negotiations with ethnic armed organizations, 219
  political transition under, 60, 69, 292
  reform agenda of, 59, 141, 155, 257, 307, 308–9, 330, 351, 367
Thein Swe, 25
Thein Tun, 35
Thiha Saw, 19, 83, 124
  interview with, 131–36
Thingyan water festival, 23
Thura Shwe Mann, 342, 343, 345, 348–50, 358
Thurein Hlaing, 154–56
Thu Thu Swe Thei, 299
Tin Aye, 253, 254, 257
Tin Tin Thet, 169, 171
Toe Naing Mann, 34
Tydeman, L., 109, 111–13, 120

U
U Ba Thaw, 22
UEC. *See* Union Election Commission (UEC)
U Kyaw Winn, 116
UNESCO, 97, 102
UN Human Rights Council, 44n1

Union Election Commission (UEC), 39, 253, 255–58, 261, 262, 393
Union Election Commission Law, 253
Union of Burma Cinematograph Law, 294
Union of Myanmar Economic Holdings (UMEHL), 253
Union Solidarity and Development Party (USDP), 64, 158, 187, 251, 341
United Nations Human Rights Council (UNHRC), 1
unlawful assembly, 73, 89n4
unlawful association, 4, 65, 76, 81, 82, 226n35
Unlawful Association Act 1908, 4, 65, 76, 81, 82
U Nyi Nyi Lwin, 279
USAID, 105, 106, 313
U.S. civil rights movement, 180

V
Van Toll, K., 110, 111
Vernacular Press Act, 16
violence against women, 246, 287, 299
Voice over Internet Protocol (VoIP), 139
Voltmer, K., 63, 82

W
Wade, F., 42
Waisbord, S., 12
Wallach, J., 270
Wa Lone, 2, 41, 77, 85, 192, 207, 208, 220, 391
The Way To Heaven, 16
Waziya, 297
Weiss, M., 334
Win Aung, 35

Win Maw, 45n15
Win Oo, 158, 165, 170, 174n7
Win Tin, 22, 309, 317
Wirathu, 4
women activists, 86
women editors, 86, 249n1
women journalists, 86, 108, 220, 243–49
women's empowerment, 372
women's filmmaking, 288
women's rights, 243–47, 352
Working People's Daily, 21
World Bank, 69, 89n9
World Health Organization (WHO), 204
World Press Freedom Day, 219

Y

Yadanabone Daily, 34
Yae Khe, 84
Yanghee Lee, 189
Yangon, 16, 37, 45n9, 59, 84, 155, 204, 231, 268, 274, 292
  movie industry, 292
  music scene, 272–82
Yangon City FM, 26
Yangon Film School (YFS), 26
Yangon Heritage Trust, 297
Yangon Journalism School, 95, 114, 119, 201
Yangon Press International (YPI), 117
Yangon Times, 36
Yeh, M.-Y., 361n8
Ye Htut, 59, 89n8, 120, 341, 343, 345, 350, 351, 354–56
Ye Naing Moe, 40, 87, 96, 114, 115, 119, 122, 123, 390
  interview with, 201–9
Ye Naing Win, 35, 46n16
Yeni, 185, 186, 191
YPI. *See* Yangon Press International (YPI)

Z

Zakhung Ting Ying, 158
Zargana, 21, 23
Zaw Htoo Aung, 278, 281
Zaw Myint Maung, 318
Zaw Win Htut, 277
Zayar Thaw, 27, 45n12
Zin Mar Aung, 342, 343, 352
Zuckerberg, M., 42, 43, 328, 373

www.ingramcontent.com/pod-product-compliance
Lightning Source LLC
Chambersburg PA
CBHW070007010526
44117CB00011B/1454